# Achieving Accountability in Higher Education

## Balancing Public, Academic, and Market Demands

Joseph C. Burke and Associates

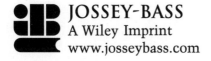

JOSSEY-BASS
A Wiley Imprint
www.josseybass.com

Published by Jossey-Bass
A Wiley Imprint
989 Market Street, San Francisco, CA 94103-1741   www.josseybass.com

Jossey-Bass books and products are available through most bookstores. To contact Jossey-Bass directly
call our Customer Care Department within the U.S. at (800) 956-7739, outside the U.S. at (317) 572-
3986 or fax (317) 572-4002.

Jossey-Bass also publishes its books in a variety of electronic formats. Some content that appears in
print may not be available in electronic books.

**Library of Congress Cataloging-in-Publication Data**

Burke, Joseph C.
　　Achieving accountability in higher education : balancing public, academic, and market demands/
　Joseph C. Burke and associates.— 1st ed.
　　　p. cm.
　　Includes bibliographical references and index.
　　ISBN 0-7879-7242-8 (alk. paper)
　　　1.  Educational accountability—United States. 2.  Education, Higher—United States—
　Evaluation.  I. Title.
　LB2806.22.B87 2004
　379.1'58—dc22                                                                                    2004016954

Printed in the United States of America
FIRST EDITION

*HB Printing*                                                             10 9 8 7 6 5 4 3 2 1

# Contents

# Preface

*Joseph C. Burke*

Over a decade ago, *Reinventing Government* proclaimed, "Words like *accountability, performances,* and *results* have begun to ring through the halls of government" (Osborne and Gaebler, 1992, p. 141). They also began to reverberate in the halls of academe, for the 1990s became known as the decade of accountability for higher education in the United States. Though time has multiplied accountability efforts, their effectiveness remains questionable. Year after year, accountability tops the policy issues listed by state government and higher education associations, yet doubts persist about the accountability, performance, and results of higher education.

In 1994, Stanley Katz, president of the American Council of Learned Societies, asked a question about accountability that, as usual, evoked additional questions (Katz, 1994, p. A56). "Who can be against accountability?" he asked rhetorically. "The answer, of course, is that it all depends upon how accountability is defined, assessed, and enforced."

As Shakespeare says, "Ay, there's the rub" (*Hamlet*, Act III, Scene 1). A decade after Katz's comment, calls for accountability continue in federal and state capitols and business and civic roundtables. Despite the number and range of accountability programs, the concept continues largely undefined, its practices mostly unassessed, and its mandates loosely enforced. The chapters in this book attempt to provide those definitions and assessments and to probe the problems that affect the enforcement of accountability. The authors differ in preferences and points of view, but they share a wealth of experience in examining one or more of the faces and forms of accountability for higher education in the United States.

## Why Another Book on Accountability?

Many books about higher education have *accountability* in their titles, but the term is usually an adjective and seldom the noun—a sideshow next to the main event of affordability and access or quality and standards. These are worthy goals of accountability, but they fail to suggest its full sweep and scope. Other books often jump to the end of the accountability conundrum by proposing a program to solve the problem before defining the concept, determining its dimensions, or developing its goals. None of the current books describe the many faces of accountability and the many forms of its implementation in the United States. Other books do not explore all of the critical questions in accountability: Who is responsible to whom, for what purposes, for whose benefit, by which means, and with what consequences? No other book examines the major approaches to accountability for higher education in the United States and the jurisdictions and governance that affect their implementation. None of the other volumes proposes potential linkages among existing accountability programs or suggests the characteristics of a comprehensive accountability system.

## The Accountability Triangle

Other books also do not conceive of the major challenge of accountability as balancing the response of higher education to *state priorities, academic concerns,* and *market forces*—what this volume calls the Accountability Triangle. Neither do they attempt to assess the success of accountability programs in reaching that balance. This Accountability Triangle borrows from the figure used by Burton Clark of state control, academic oligarchy, and market model to assess the coordination of national systems of higher education around the world (see Chapter One in this book). Our triangle views state priorities, academic concerns, and market forces as the primary imperatives of accountability for higher education in the United States. We argue that colleges and universities, public and private, must respond to all while submitting to none of these imperatives. They must balance public, academic, and market demands.

# Accountability and Autonomy: Champions and Critics

Accountability for higher education has been a topic since the 1970s, but calls for accountability have become more intense in the last decade and a half. Two developments have driven the rising insistence on accountability. First and foremost, the mass movement of postsecondary education from the private privilege of the favored few to the public right of most Americans has made it a public necessity that demands accountability for its actions.

Second, the growing public perception that higher education has become the source of success for states and individuals in a knowledge and information era has reinforced the demand for accountability. Despite its increasing importance, higher education in the United States has trailed—happily in many ways—the trendsetters in public accountability of health care and public schools. Calls for accountability from state and federal officials have received what outsiders view as outright resistance or reluctant responses from colleges and universities, public as well as private. Many academics claim that public accountability to external groups endangers the academic freedom required for the unfettered pursuit of learning and scholarship. Outsiders call this claim self-interested by noting that the interest of academics in accountability rises or falls in direct proportion to the distance from their campuses and departments. The cries for accountability come mostly from external groups such as governors, legislators, and business leaders. The academic community of administrators and professors spawns most of its critics. Outsiders often see accountability as an obvious necessity; insiders usually view it as an external intrusion.

The reluctance of the academy in the United States to look at accountability for itself is shown by the considerable literature abroad on higher education and accountability and the extensive writings of political scientists in this country—most of them professors—about accountability in government and other organizations but not in higher education. Some might say the lack of writing about accountability for higher education arises from the reality that the federal system leaves responsibility for the operations of colleges and universities to the states, with the federal government participating largely in relation to its student loans and research grants. Yet, this same division of responsibility has not prevented a seemingly endless series of books on accountability for elementary and secondary education.

## Questions About Accountability

This book attempts to clarify at least some of the ambiguities of accountability for higher education by searching for answers to the following questions:

What does accountability mean for higher education, and what are its essential requirements?

How has accountability for higher education altered over time?

What are the roles of the states and, to a lesser extent, the federal government in accountability for higher education?

How does the accountability of private colleges and universities differ from their public counterparts?

How does accountability reflect the gap between the "civic," "collegial," and "commercial" cultures on issues such as improvement versus accountability, inputs versus outcomes, reputation versus responsiveness, trust versus evidence, and qualitative versus quantitative evidence?

How do the various governance organizations of higher education in states and within colleges and universities reinforce or retard accountability for higher education?

What are the major approaches to accountability for higher education in the United States?

What are their strengths and weaknesses and their current status and future prospects?

How do these approaches connect with each other, and how could they cooperate in a comprehensive system?

How well does each of these accountability approaches respond to the imperatives of state priorities, academic concerns, and market forces that frame the Accountability Triangle?

What are the major characteristics of an effective accountability system for higher education?

What commitments do these characteristics require from the higher
  education community, federal and state governments, business
  and civic leaders in each state, and individual colleges and universities?

## Undergraduate Focus of Accountability

Accountability approaches in the United States focus almost exclusively on undergraduate education, except for reputational
ratings that are based largely on faculty research prestige and sponsored research and graduate programs in areas that support state
economic development. The reason is that external publics perceive undergraduate education rather than graduate studies or faculty research as a problem. Currently, assessment and academic
audits stress undergraduate issues, although Massy (Chapter Eight)
sees audits expanding to cover graduate studies and research. The
state-by-state report cards do not include research and consider
graduate studies only in terms of total degree attainment. Performance reports slight graduate studies and research, except for an
indicator on sponsored research.

## Contents of the Book

Like Caesar's Gaul, this book has three parts, although Gaul probably proved easier to conquer than accountability. Part one includes the introductory chapter on the many faces and forms of
accountability. Two chapters follow—one on federal and state accountability and private higher education and the other on governance structures and accountability. Part two contains nine
chapters covering each of the major accountability programs. A
concluding chapter constitutes the third part
    The introductory chapter, "The Many Faces of Accountability,"
reflects my fascination with the topic of accountability generated by
over two decades as a campus president and system provost in the
State University of New York. It explores the changing emphases of
accountability in higher education in the last three decades and proposes public agendas for higher education in each state prepared
by business, civic, government, and education leaders. That first

chapter argues that effective accountability programs must balance the legitimate demands of state priorities, academic concerns, and market forces—the three corners of the Accountability Triangle.

Chapter Two, on federal accountability and the impact of state accountability on private higher education, demanded an author of broad interests and experience such as Bill Zumeta, the associate dean and a professor in the Evans School of Public Affairs at the University of Washington. In a range of publications, he has examined higher education and public policy, private colleges and universities, and the rising demands for accountability. His chapter reviews the renewed rumblings in Washington about expanding federal accountability over college tuition and graduation rates and describes the limited impact of state accountability on private colleges and universities. He believes the demands for accountability for private institutions will increase as states strive to develop the sophisticated workforce and applied research equal to the demands of a highly competitive and technological world economy. Zumeta argues instead for accountability based on markets rather than mandates for public, as well as private, colleges and universities.

In Chapter Three, Dick Richardson, a professor of higher education at New York University and an expert on higher education governance, along with Tom Smalling, a doctoral student, lead us through the labyrinth of governance at the state, system, and institutional levels and track their effect on accountability. Their chapter suggests the governance structures that work best for accountability and explains why they have a positive impact. The authors graphically describe the state and federal policies, the system design and funding strategies, and what they call "the rules of the game" that affect the governance of higher education and influence its accountability.

The next nine chapters present the strengths and weaknesses, current coverage, and future prospects of the major approaches to accountability for higher education in the United States. They divide into approaches more internally focused, such as institution and program accreditation, student assessment, academic audit, and student-alumni surveys, and those more externally centered, such as standardized tests, state-by-state report cards, performance reporting, budgeting and funding, reputational ratings, and higher education markets.

In Chapter Four, Ralph Wolff, executive director of the Accrediting Commission for Senior Colleges and Universities of the Western Association of Schools and Colleges (WASC), examines the pressures on accreditors to hold campuses and programs responsible for performance results rather than the more traditional inputs and processes. He recounts the efforts of accrediting bodies to respond to these external concerns while retaining the support of colleges and universities based on candid but largely confidential peer reviews. The question remains whether accreditation can serve the two goals of voluntary peer review and external government accountability.

Assessment covered in Chapter Five, has the perfect author—Peter Ewell of the National Center for Higher Education Management (NCHEM)—one of the most knowledgeable experts on assessment in America. His chapter details the conflicting aims and claims of external accountability and internal improvement and concludes that assessment must focus directly on improvement and can assist accountability only indirectly.

What better author for Chapter Seven on student and alumni surveys than George Kuh, Chancellor's Professor of Higher Education at Indiana University and director of the center that developed the popular National Survey of Student Engagement (NSSE)? Although conceding that such surveys cannot supply all of the information policymakers want to know about higher education performance, Kuh insists that they are essential to answering the inevitable question, how are we doing? by asking the groups most likely to know: their students and alumni.

Bill Massy, president of the Jackson Hole Group, has studied academic audits around the world and helped shape them in such different places as Hong Kong and Missouri, which he uses as case studies for Chapter Eight. He makes a strong case that the newer, mature forms of academic audit are publicizing results and beginning to present some sense of student learning assessments, as well as internal quality processes. Massy argues that academic audits constitute the only accountability program that simultaneously encourages both external accountability and institutional improvement.

The other five chapters examine accountability programs that stem primarily from external concerns. In Chapter Six, Dary Erwin, a professor and associate vice president at James Madison University, describes the reasons for the external demands for standardized tests of student learning and for campus resistance to their use. He examines the weaknesses of the current tests for general education and, to a lesser extent, for academic majors and notes the possibilities opened by computer-based testing. Erwin concludes that the failure to develop appropriate standardized tests arises not so much from a lack of ways as from a lack of will in the academic community and from a lack of resources from the federal and state governments.

Chapter Nine, on state-by-state report cards, goes to the source for its authors. Pat Callan, as president, and Joni Finney, as vice president, lead the National Center for Public Policy and Higher Education, which issued *Measuring Up 2000* and *Measuring Up 2002*—the monumental effort to compile state-by-state comparisons on higher education performance. Their chapter describes the continuing effort to grade the states on critical indicators of educational outcomes and human capital development and to develop credible and comparable methods for assessing student learning. They insist that state policies encouraging human capital development through statewide higher education systems offer better avenues for accountability than those directed at individual institutions.

I return in Chapter Ten to probe the current problems of performance reporting, budgeting, and funding and to propose changes that could help make them more responsive to academic concerns and market forces, as well as state priorities. The authors of the eleventh chapter—Fred Volkwein, from the Center for the Study of Higher Education at Penn State, and Stephen Grunig, a legislative analyst in Arizona—consider the impact of reputational ratings on accountability for higher education and conclude that most of them reflect resource inputs rather than institutional results—prestige more than performance.

Bob Zemsky, president of the Learning Alliance, has long tracked the responsiveness of colleges and universities to public priorities, campus concerns, and market forces. His Chapter Twelve argues that markets neither limit prices nor promote quality in higher education and explains why they fail to respond to these critical goals.

In the concluding chapter, I sum up the possibilities, problems, and prospects of accountability programs in higher education. This chapter claims that higher education must serve all but submit to none of the three corners of the Accountability Triangle: state priorities, academic concerns, and market forces. It presents some characteristics of an effective accountability system and recommends actions on accountability by the higher education community, state and federal governments, and individual colleges and universities.

## An Editor's Final Reflection

As I reread the chapters and reassessed their conclusions, I felt like an old-time accountant confronted with a wealth of numbers that somehow did not add up to an appropriate total. The authors of each of the chapters were national experts on their topics. Indeed, many of them initiated or helped shape the accountability program about which they wrote. Clearly, one could not fault the authors. Moreover, each of the accountability approaches had some, even many, elements to recommend it. The problem, I concluded, as so often occurs in higher education, is that the sum of a number of well-intended—even good—accountability initiatives did not add up to a comprehensive accountability system. All too often, each became a separate and segregated program—an add-on, unlinked to existing accountability efforts. Like the American tariff system in the late nineteenth century, they resemble a patchwork of individual initiatives adopted to address particular problems that competed with one another.

Despite their differences, the champions and critics of accountability (and all of our authors) do concur on two points. First, that higher education is the source of economic success for states and their citizens in a knowledge and information era. And second, largely for this reason that accountability is here to stay. Democracy and accountability go together. Day and Klein declare, "Who says democracy, it is tempting to say, also says accountability" (1987, p. 7). Although the authors in this book differ in their attitudes and approaches to accountability, all agree that higher education has become too important to the success of society and its citizens to leave the academy unaccountable for its responses and results.

They also agree that accountability for higher education is much too important to be left to a single segment of society, whether drawn from government, education, or business.

As with most policies and actions in a democratic society, with all its diversity, obtaining agreement on accountability for higher education will not be easy. Deciding who is responsible to whom, for what purposes, for whose benefits, by which means, and with what consequences is a daunting challenge in higher education.

This book makes many suggestions but offers only one definitive answer to the accountability challenge—that it is a collective challenge, not subject to a solo or segmented solution. It requires consultation and consent from the leaders of the business, civic, government, and education communities in every state. We offer this book to those courageous leaders who take on this challenging task. The stakes are high. The conflict over accountability is eroding what was once a national consensus—that higher education is a public good for all Americans, not just a private benefit for college graduates.

## Giving Credit Where Credit Is Due

Giving credit to those who contributed to this book is almost as challenging as planning an accountability system for higher education. As always, thanks for help in preparing a book must go to many more contributors than can be mentioned in a short paragraph. As editor, my special thanks go to that exceptional group of thirteen experts who put their busy schedules on hold to join me in trying to make some sense of this amorphous thing called accountability in higher education. Although I know that at times they rued the day they committed to this task, I thank them for staying the course.

Many people have bolstered my end of the project. Henrik Minassians, my former associate, participated in the early planning and drafting of the book proposal. John Williams, my current graduate assistant, has done a yeoman's job of reading and helping to review and edit the chapters. Tom Moran, director of the Center for Ethics and Public Life at the State University of New York at Plattsburgh, and Tom McCord, formerly of the New York State Education Department, have slogged for far too long through the multiple drafts of my musings and writings. Jorge Balan and the Ford Foundation for several years have generously supported my struggle to understand accountability, especially performance reporting.

Finally, no words can ever convey the contribution of my wife, Joan, whose belief in me always exceeds my best hope.

JOSEPH C. BURKE
Rockefeller Institute
Albany, New York
September 2004

# The Editor

*Joseph C. Burke* is director of the Higher Education Program and is a Senior Fellow at the Rockefeller Institute of Government and a State University of New York Professor of Higher Education Policy and Management. He combines the experiences of professor, administrator, and researcher. After receiving his Ph.D. in legal history from Indiana University, Burke taught for a dozen years. He then served three years as academic vice president at Loyola of Montreal and negotiated a merger with Sir George Williams, creating Concordia University. Burke served as president of the State University of New York at Plattsburgh, followed by nine years as provost and one year as interim chancellor of the State University of New York system.

Burke has written and lectured on a wide array of topics in higher education, including the role of college and university presidents, system governance, accountability and autonomy in higher education, outcomes assessment, and performance reporting and funding. He has published over forty books, book chapters, monographs, and articles on these subjects. His latest book is *Reporting Higher Education Results: Missing Links in the Performance Chain* (2002). The Henry Luce Foundation, The Pew Charitable Trusts, and the Ford Foundation have awarded him grants for national studies of state performance funding, budgeting, and reporting of public colleges and universities.

# The Contributors

*Patrick M. Callan* is president of the National Center for Public Policy and Higher Education. Established in 1998, the National Center is an independent, nonprofit, and nonpartisan organization that promotes public policies that enhance all Americans' opportunities for a quality higher education. From 1992 through 1997, Callan was executive director of the California Higher Education Policy Center.

Prior to leading the California and the National Centers, Callan was vice president of the Education Commission of the States and served as executive director of the California Postsecondary Education Commission, the Washington State Council for Postsecondary Education, and the Montana Commission on Postsecondary Education.

Callan has been a member of national, regional, and state commissions and has written and spoken extensively on educational opportunity, public accountability, and leadership. He is coeditor of *Public and Private Financing of Higher Education: Shaping Public Policy for the Future* (1997) and coauthor of *Designing State Higher Education Systems for a New Century: A Study of State Organization and Governance of Higher Education* (2001). He collaborated with Gene Maeroff and Michael Usdan on *The Learning Connection: New Partnerships Between Schools and Colleges* (2001).

*T. Dary Erwin* is associate vice president of academic affairs for assessment and program evaluation at the Center for Assessment Research and Studies and professor of psychology at James Madison University. The center houses master's and doctoral programs in assessment and measurement and publishes assessment instruments in student development and general education, many of which are computer based. Erwin has written over fifty articles or chapters about college impact and assessment, including the 1991 Jossey-Bass book titled *Assessing Student Learning and Development: A Guide to the Principles, Goals, and Methods of Determining College Outcomes*—one of the first comprehensive volumes published about assessment. In addition, he has presented over one hundred papers at professional meetings and spoken about assessment at over sixty institutions and agencies. He received his Ph.D. from the University of Iowa and has previously been at the University of Tennessee and Texas A&M University.

*Peter T. Ewell* is a senior associate at the National Center for Higher Education Management Systems (NCHEMS)—a research and development center founded to improve the management effectiveness of colleges and universities. A member of the staff since 1981, Ewell both conducted research and was involved in direct consulting with institutions and state systems on collecting and using assessment information in planning, evaluation, and budgeting. He has authored six books and numerous articles on the topic of improving undergraduate instruction through the assessment of student outcomes. Among his publications are *The Self-Regarding Institution: Information for Excellence* and *Assessing Educational Outcomes*. In addition, he has prepared commissioned papers for many agencies, including the Study Group on the Conditions of Excellence in American Higher Education, the Education Commission of the States, the National Governors' Association, the National Conference of State Legislators, and the National Center for Public Policy in Higher Education. In 1998, he led the design team for the National Survey of Student Engagement (NSSE) and currently chairs its technical advisory panel. A graduate of Haverford College, he received his Ph.D. in political science from Yale University in 1976 and was on the faculty of the University of Chicago.

*Joni E. Finney* is vice president of the National Center for Public Policy and Higher Education. Finney directs the National Center's research and policy studies program. Her interests and publications focus primarily on the finance, governance, and performance of American higher education. Finney directed the National Center's project to develop the nation's first state-by-state report card for higher education—*Measuring Up 2000*. Prior to assuming her position at the National Center, Finney held senior policy positions with the California Higher Education Policy Center and the Education Commission of the States (ECS). She has also served in administrative positions at the Pennsylvania State University and the University of Southern Colorado.

Finney has consulted closely with state policy leaders and speaks frequently to legislative leaders, education associations, and regional and national organizations. She testified to the U.S. House of Representatives' committee on economic and educational opportunities. Finney is also a coeditor and author of *Public and Private Financing of Higher Education: Shaping Public Policy for the Future* and *Designing State Higher Education Systems for a New Century* and has written articles, policy reports, and book chapters on public policy and higher education issues.

*Stephen D. Grunig* is currently an analyst for the Arizona state legislature. He has researched higher education issues under the auspices of the Arizona board of regents and the Arizona state legislature. He holds a B.S. and an M.B.A. from the University of Colorado and a Ph.D. from the University of Arizona. Grunig has published articles on university fundraising and reputational ratings in the *Journal of Higher Education*.

*George D. Kuh* is Chancellor's Professor of Higher Education at Indiana University at Bloomington. He directs the Center for Postsecondary Research, which is home to the National Survey of Student Engagement and the College Student Experiences Questionnaire research program. He received a B.A. from Luther College, an M.S. from the St. Cloud State University, and a Ph.D. from the University of Iowa. At Indiana University, he served as chairperson of the Department of Educational Leadership and Policy Studies, associate dean for academic affairs in the School of Education, and associate dean of the faculties for the Bloomington campus. Kuh has published about 250 works and has been a consultant to about 140 institutions and agencies of higher education. He has received awards for his research contributions from the American College Personnel Association, Association for Institutional Research, Association for the Study of Higher Education (ASHE), Council of Independent Colleges, and the National

Association of Student Personnel Administrators. He is past president of ASHE and serves on several higher education editorial boards.

*William F. Massy* is president of the Jackson Hole Higher Education Group, Inc., and an emeritus professor at Stanford University. He has been active as a professor, consultant, and Stanford vice provost and vice president for more than thirty years. His recent work has been on academic quality assurance and improvement, faculty roles and responsibilities, cost analysis, processes for resource allocation, and mathematical modeling of higher education institutions, including a full-scale computer simulation of university behavior, released under the title, "Virtual U." He served on the Yale University Council during the 1980s and 1990s and from 1991 to 2003 on the University Grants Committee for the Hong Kong government. In 1995, he received the Society for College and University Planning (SCUP) annual career award for outstanding contributions to college and university planning. Massy holds a Ph.D. in economics and M.S. in management from the Massachusetts Institute of Technology, as well as a B.S. from Yale University.

Massy has published eight books and more than one hundred edited volumes, journal articles, and conference papers. His *Planning Models for Colleges and Universities* (with David Hopkins) won the Operations Research Society of America's Lanchester Prize in 1981. His latest book, *Honoring the Trust: Quality and Cost Containment in Higher Education* (Anker), was published in February 2003.

*Richard C. Richardson Jr.* is professor of higher education at NYU and professor emeritus of educational leadership and policy studies at Arizona State University. His recent studies have examined policy and higher education performance, structural design, and systemic change for state higher education systems. He currently directs a research project, funded by the Ford Foundation, that aims to improve understanding of the linkages between federal and state policies and changes in college and university outcomes and behaviors in the United States, Mexico, and Canada and to serve as a vehicle for training a small cadre of younger policy scholars in both nations (http://www.nyu.edu/iesp/aiheps/).

Richardson is the author or coauthor of six books, including *Designing State Higher Education Systems for a New Century* (1999),

*Achieving Quality and Diversity: Universities in a Multicultural Society* (1991), *Fostering Minority Access and Achievement in Higher Education* (1987), *Literacy in the Open Access College* (1983), *Governance for the Two-Year College* (1973), and *The Two-Year College: A Social Synthesis* (1965).

*Thomas R. Smalling* is a doctoral candidate in the Department of Administration, Leadership, and Technology in New York University's Steinhardt School of Education. He holds a B.S. and M.S. from Stony Brook University. Smalling is currently an assistant professor of health sciences at the State University of New York at Stony Brook. He currently serves on the governance committee of the SUNY faculty senate, where he is involved with universitywide and campus governance issues. His research interests include the role of faculty governance in the performance of state multicampus systems and the role of the SUNY faculty senate and its interaction between collective bargaining organizations and system administration.

*J. Fredericks Volkwein* is professor and senior scientist in the Center for the Study of Higher Education at Penn State, having had a forty-year career as a researcher, administrator, and faculty member. He holds a B.A. from Pomona College and a Ph.D. from Cornell University. With interests in policy analysis and organizational effectiveness, he is well known for his studies of accreditation, academic program review, assessment of student learning and growth, institutional research, state regulation, and performance indicators.

Volkwein's scholarly work is related, directly or indirectly, to the topic of organizational effectiveness. He has produced more than one hundred journal articles, research reports, conference papers, and book chapters. He currently is the principal investigator or coprincipal investigator on projects in the areas of accreditation, engineering education, and training institutional researchers. He also serves as editor in chief for the Jossey-Bass series *New Directions for Institutional Research* and is a recent winner of the AIR Suslow Award for Distinguished Scholarship.

*Ralph A. Wolff* was appointed executive director of the Accrediting Commission for Senior Colleges and Universities of the Western Association of Schools and Colleges in 1996, after having served as associate executive director since 1981. He has written and spoken extensively on assessment, diversity, and the redefinition of accreditation to serve the public interest more directly. Prior to joining the commission staff, Wolff was on the law faculty of the University of Dayton Law School. Previously, he was a founder of the Antioch School of Law—the first law school expressly designed to prepare lawyers to serve in public interest or poverty law positions. He also served as associate provost of Antioch College and dean of the Graduate School of Education. He received a bachelor's degree in history from Tufts University and a J.D. degree, with honors, from the National Law Center of George Washington University.

*Robert M. Zemsky* currently serves as the chair and CEO of the Learning Alliance. From 1980 through 2000, Zemsky served as the founding director of the University of Pennsylvania's Institute for Research on Higher Education. He was a postdoctoral Social Science Research Council Fellow in linguistics and was later chair of that council's committee on social science personnel. At the University of Pennsylvania, Zemsky has been the university's chief planning officer and has served as master of Hill College House.

In his research, Zemsky pioneered the use of market analyses for higher education. He is currently a senior scholar with the National Center for Postsecondary Improvement and is directing the University of Pennsylvania/Thomson Corporation's Weatherstation Project, which is mapping the market for e-learning. In 1998, *Change* magazine named him as one of higher education's top forty leaders for his role as an agenda setter.

Zemsky is a former Woodrow Wilson Fellow. In 1998, he received a Doctor of Humane Letters (Hon.) from Towson University. He is currently a trustee of Franklin and Marshall College and a member of the National Advisory Board for the National Survey of Student Engagement (NSSE).

*William M. Zumeta* is professor and associate dean of the Daniel J. Evans School of Public Affairs and professor of educational leadership and policy in the College of Education at the University of Washington. He teaches courses in public policy analysis, public budgeting, and higher education policy and finance. He has previously held faculty appointments at UCLA, the University of British Columbia, and the Claremont Graduate University. He holds a bachelor's degree from Haverford College and a master's and Ph.D. degree from the Goldman School of Public Policy at the University of California-Berkeley.

Zumeta's research and writing have emphasized four areas of higher education and public policy: public policy and private higher education, state finance and budgeting of higher education, accountability policies affecting higher education, and state and federal policies relating to graduate and postdoctoral education.

# Chapter One

# The Many Faces of Accountability

*Joseph C. Burke*

*Accountability* is the most advocated and least analyzed word in higher education. Everyone uses the term but usually with multiple meanings (Western Interstate Commission for Higher Education, 2002). Writers say it faces in every direction—"upward," "downward," "inward," and "outward" (Corbett, 1996; Vidovich and Slee, 2000). It looks, in turn, bureaucratic, participative, political, or market centered. To many beleaguered leaders in colleges and universities, accountability appears two-faced, with sponsors and stakeholders demanding more services while supplying less support. To many outsiders in government and business, higher education seems more interested in autonomy than accountability—in demanding support than supplying services. Falling public funding and rising client demands contribute to the confusion by shifting the focus of accountability from governments to markets and incentives from public subsidies to private purchases. As Day and Klein comment, "[I]f there is a great deal of interest in accountability, there is also a great deal of confusion about what this chameleon word means" (1987, p. 1). Clearing up the confusion is critical, because the conflict over accountability is eroding what was once a national consensus—that higher education is a public good for all Americans and not just a private benefit for college graduates.

## Accountability Definitions

Merriam-Webster defines *accountability* as "an obligation or willingness to accept responsibility or to account for one's actions" (Merriam-Webster, 2003); *answerability* is its closest synonym (Schedler, 1999, p. 14). Accountability imposes six demands on officials or their agents for government or public service organizations, including colleges and universities. First, they must demonstrate that they have used their powers properly. Second, they must show that they are working to achieve the mission or priorities set for their office or organization. Third, they must report on their performance, for "power is opaque, accountability is public" (Schedler, 1999, p. 20). Fourth, the two "E" words of public stewardship—efficiency and effectiveness—require accounting "for the resources they use and the outcomes they create" (Shavelson, 2000, p. 8). Fifth, they must ensure the quality of the programs and services produced. Last, but far from least, they must show that they serve public needs. The last five of these accountability demands represent tall tasks for higher education because of its unique purposes, collegial governance, and diverse constituencies.

## Accountability Questions

The term *accountability* raises several deceptively simple but devilishly difficult questions: *Who* is accountable to *whom,* for *what* purposes, for *whose* benefit, by *which* means, and with *what* consequences? (Lingenfelter, 2003; Behn, 2001; Trow, 1996) The pronouns *who, whom,* and *whose* represent, respectively, the traditional trio of agent, principal, and beneficiary in political and organizational theory. In democracies, elected officers such as governors and legislators are the agents, while the "general public" plays the dual role of both principal (delegating the authority) and beneficiary (receiving the ultimate rewards). Delegation of authority down the chain of government agencies adds to the confusion about *who* is accountable to *whom.* As delegation and decentralization drop deeper in government and public service organizations, agent self-interest rises while the sense of public purpose recedes (Moe, 1984).

Delegation especially affects the academy, with its prized autonomy and collegial governance. At the state level, higher education coordinating or consolidated governing boards are nearly always the agents exercising the authority delegated by governors and legislators as the principals, mostly over public colleges and universities but, to some extent, over private institutions as well (see Chapter Three). The beneficiaries are, ultimately, the general public and, more immediately, students, businesses, governments, and social and civic organizations.

At the campus level, senior administrators become the agents, exercising the delegated authority of their principals and boards of trustees for the immediate benefit of students and external clients and, ultimately, for the public at large. Moving down the campus-delegation ladder, professors, in theory, exercise the authority delegated through deans for the same beneficiaries. It is indeed a long distance from the initial delegation of authority from governors and legislators to state higher education boards to the professors providing the instruction, research, and service that benefit society. Not surprisingly, in such long-distance delegation, both the connection and the communication often become unclear.

## Accountability Concepts

The concepts of upward, downward, inward, and outward accountability represent types of connections between principals and agents in higher education and other public services (Vidovich and Slee, 2000).

- *Upward accountability* represents the traditional relationship of a subordinate to a superior. It covers *procedural, bureaucratic, legal,* or *vertical accountability*.
- *Downward accountability* focuses on a manager being responsible to subordinates in participatory decision making or *collegial accountability* in higher education.
- *Inward accountability* centers on agents acting on professional or ethical standards and often appears in organizations dominated by professionals, such as in colleges and universities, where it becomes *professional accountability*.
- *Outward accountability* means responding to external clients, stakeholders, supporters, and in a democratic society, ultimately, to the public at large. It includes *market* and *political accountability*.

## Accountability Purposes

Accountability for *what*—its purposes or goals—becomes even more confusing and changeable. "You can't have accountability without expectations," says Behn. "If you want to hold people accountable, you have to be able to specify what you expect them to do and not do" (2001, p. 7). But clarity is an uncommon characteristic in elected government and collegial governance. Both often sacrifice clarity for closure, if not consensus. In addition, higher education—the knowledge and information institution in a knowledge and information society—suffers from too many, often conflicting expectations. The purposes or goals of accountability programs for higher education have shifted over time from system *efficiency,* to educational *quality,* to organizational *productivity,* and to external *responsiveness* to public priorities or market demands. As is often the case in public policy, new purposes are always added, but earlier goals are seldom abandoned.

## Higher Education: Accountability with a Difference

Academics always argue that the academy is different, and accountability is no exception. Insiders see the differences between higher education and other public services as arising from the special character of the academic profession and its responsibilities. Outsiders counter that discovering and disseminating knowledge is no more complex and challenging than the problems confronting other professions, such as medicine and law. The presence of professionalism in higher education and other specialized organizations does complicate accountability. "The growth of professionalism and expertise. . ." according to Day and Klein, "has led to the privatization of accountability, in so far as professionals and experts claim only their peers can judge their conduct and performance" (1987, p. 1). Contrary to popular opinion, professors are not the only professionals who make that claim.

The correct claim of academics for special treatment relates not to their profession but to the special role of higher education in society. Robert Berdahl (1990) vividly describes the dual demands of this unique claim. "Universities have generally had ambivalent relations with their surrounding societies: both involved and withdrawn; both serving and criticizing; both needing and being needed" (p. 169). Berdahl and others insist that colleges and universities must stay sufficiently safe from external pressures to safeguard their societal critique yet sufficiently responsive to external needs to sustain societal support. They must simultaneously serve and scrutinize the society that supports them.

These dual roles demand both autonomy and accountability. As is often the case, balance is the key. Too much autonomy encourages colleges and universities, both public and private, to slight society's needs. Too much accountability produces dependent institutions subservient to society's whims (McGuinness, 2002). Somehow, higher education and society's representatives must reach for an agreement that seeks the middle ground of service without subservience.

## The Higher Education Social Compact

Society and the academy once appeared to have such an agreement. After World War II, stimulated by the success of the GI Bill, a social compact seemed to exist between American society and higher education. Although bows to state and regional differences are always in order, this compact clearly covered the country. It rested on a few felt but unwritten principles—on trust, not rules. Americans accepted as an unquestioned act of faith that access to a college education was a public good for society, as well as a private good for students (Knight Higher Education Collaborative, 1999; Selingo, 2003). Access to college opportunities allowed our nation to champion both sides of the American dilemma of how to achieve both equality and quality. Equality meant that society offered the opportunity for college to a growing percentage of the population while leaving the achievement of quality to the talents and efforts of individuals. Americans also acknowledged the need for a surprising degree of academic autonomy from governmental control.

On a more practical plane, the compact obligated state taxpayers to provide adequate operating funding for public colleges and universities, which in turn would keep tuition reasonably low. In addition, states with strong private colleges and universities supported some level of choice for students who wished to attend private or independent institutions. The compact depended on mutual trust that each side would keep its share of the bargain.

The federal policy of supporting basic scientific research in universities added research and service to the social compact of public benefits. People who never went to college or directly benefited from research or service saw higher education as a public good (Zemsky, 2003). They would nod with approval as leaders of colleges and universities claimed, in a paraphrase of GE's slogan: "We bring good things to life."

## Decades of Decline

Like most compacts, the one between American society and higher education became strained when rights and responsibilities moved from vague generalities to specific demands and competed for funding with other public services. Specifics always strain consensus, as do funding constraints. In addition, external complaints about the rampant costs, questionable outcomes, inadequate outputs, and the internal focus of colleges and universities raised successive questions about their economy, quality, productivity, and responsiveness to societal needs (McGuinness, 1997). Not surprisingly, recessions and falling revenues contributed to these complaints. As a result, says Massy, "universities and professors began a long slide from objects of awe to subjects of accountability" (2003a, p. 20).

The social compact that provided the glue between the general public and higher education stuck fairly well through the 1950s to the late 1960s, when student lifestyles and war protests alienated some of the general public and government officials. During these decades, the older public and private colleges and universities expanded, and new campuses emerged to meet the burgeoning demand for college education spurred first by the GI Bill that encouraged returning soldiers to enroll in college and then by the so-called baby boom of their sons and daughters. The following decades brought problems that undermined the consensus of the social compact. Although the problems and programs of accountability never fall neatly into ten-year spans, the decades described next capture the changing trends.

## The 1970s

By the early 1970s, fissures in the social compact opened up, beginning with the falling revenues from a recession and fears of enrollment declines at the end of the baby boom. States adopted more centralized governance through coordinating boards and multicampus systems to control development of new institutions and program duplication (McGuinness, 1994). In response to an anticipated decline in enrollment demand, more centralized governance sought to limit the resources granted to higher education. With economy as the goal, regulation became the lever of accountability and bureaucrats the agents. A pattern developed in this first decade of decline in the social compact. Each partner started holding the other side to more specific and stringent tests. States and society reduced support and demanded more services; colleges and universities requested more funding and started raising tuition, although not nearly to the degree as in the next decade.

## The 1980s

By the 1980s, external concerns moved from economy to quality. Complaints about the lack of student learning in public schools, as voiced in *A Nation at Risk* (National Commission on Excellence in Education, 1983), eventually moved to college campuses. Two-thirds of the states mandated, by legislation, that public colleges and universities adopt plans for assessing student learning. State officials dictated the policy but left the method of determination to campus professionals (see Chapter Five). Assessment shifted the focus of accountability from centralized state regulations to decentralized campus processes for identifying the knowledge and skills that graduates should possess, developing the method for assessing the extent of their achievement, and using the results to improve institutional performance. Although assessment programs focused on campus processes, the real goal was improving quality outcomes in student learning (McGuinness, 1997). This approach tried to combine public accountability with professional autonomy by tying external accountability to institutional improvement (see Chapter Five).

## The 1990s

By the late 1980s and especially the early 1990s, the expanded services provided by federal, state, and local governments shifted the emphasis of public accountability in government and public services from procedural protection to performance production. Osborne and Gaebler (1992) called for "reinventing government," which focused on organizational results and customer services. Governments, in line with businesses, should decentralize authority while holding unit managers responsible for reaching designated results. Reinventing government combined *decentralization* with *direction* by being tight on setting goals and evaluating performance but loose in allowing managers to choose the means for achieving the desired results. Decentralization encouraged "managerial" accountability, while direction on the desired results ensured "political" accountability (Peters and Pierre, 1998, p. 232).

In line with reinventing government, the 1990s continued decentralization for higher education but this time with definite directions. Programs in the 1990s dictated the goals of efficiency and effectiveness through indicators measuring institutional performance but generally left campus managers to determine the means of achieving these ends (see Chapter Ten). Aside from the deregulation movement, several factors forced the change. The first two stemmed from the decline in public funding and from what outsiders perceived as the slow response of higher education to the needs of a knowledge and information society. Burgeoning enrollment demand in the South and West as a result of the "baby boom echo" added to the pressure (King, 2000; Zumeta, 2001; Ewell, Paulson, and Wellman, 1997). State governments and coordinating boards adopted policies of performance reporting, budgeting, and funding (Burke and Associates, 2002; Burke and Minassians, 2002b; Chapter Ten). Whereas assessment policies focused on campus processes, performance programs supposedly centered on outputs and outcomes (McGuinness, 1997). State policymakers replaced campus professionals as the agents of the new accountability (Lively, 1992).

## The Early 2000s

In the first years of the new century, the thrust of accountability seemed to shift again. Reduced state revenues from another recession and competition from rising costs of Medicaid and public schools once more reduced taxpayer funding for colleges and universities. As public support diminished, public demands escalated, confirming that taxpayer support and public demands are seldom in sync.

Increasing student enrollments and exploding state needs in workforce and economic development, as well as in public schools and teacher training, call for increased responsiveness from colleges and universities. Although the rhetoric on a college education as a public good remains in speeches by governors and legislators, students and parents are expected to pay a rising share of the costs through tuition and fees for what is often seen in state capitols as more of a private benefit for graduates. Private markets increasingly drive developments in public as well as private colleges and universities. "[N]ow it's the market, not the commonweal, that calls the shots," says Kirp (2003a, p. 2). States leave more and more of the directions and costs of higher education to private markets, while managing them at times, by intervening to encourage public priorities through program and funding initiatives (McGuinness, 2002).

## Tensions Among Three Cultures

Although recent decades brought changes in accountability concerns, the conflict continues between "civic" and "collegiate" interests and cultures (Bogue and Hall, 2003, p. 229). Recently, a third interest has arisen: the "commercial" or entrepreneurial culture. To outsiders reflecting civic and commercial interests, campus resistance to public accountability in the name of academic autonomy seems a cloak covering self-interest to protect special privileges. To academics immersed in the collegiate culture, external insistence on accountability often appears as an intrusion on the independence required for critical appraisal of society and government and for the nurturing of the arts and humanities. As usual, the motivations on and off campus toward accountability and autonomy are mixed. The civic and collegiate cultures create a series of accountability conflicts or, at least, tensions.

The following contentions between the cultures build on those presented by Bogue and Hall (p. 229). All of them represent variations on the single theme of tensions between institutional autonomy and external accountability—internal interest coming first and the external concern second:

- Institutional improvement versus external accountability
- Peer review versus external regulation
- Inputs and processes versus outputs and outcomes
- Reputation versus responsiveness
- Consultation versus evaluation
- Prestige versus performance
- Trust versus evidence
- Qualitative versus quantitative evidence

These contentions represent not only self-interests but also realistic concerns of the academic community and society's representatives. A beginning in the process of reconciliation of societal interest and academic concern is to recognize the validity of each of these elements. Effective accountability systems should address both sides of these dualisms—a tall task in a land that all too often applies the sportlike scoring of "win" or "lose" to policy decisions.

## Accountability Models

The past and present models of accountability suggest little progress in the process of reconciliation between the collegiate, civic, and commercial cultures. Higher education has featured at least six models of accountability: *bureaucratic, professional, political, managerial, market,* and *managed market* (see Table 1.1).

Each model has its own levers or drivers, agents or actors, and goals or purposes. The goals have shifted over time from efficiency to quality to productivity and, finally, to responsiveness to public priorities and market demands.

The techniques differ by model. Bureaucrats like rules. Professionals demand consultation. Policymakers prefer planning, although government officials still revert to regulation. Managers calculate costs and benefits; entrepreneurs respond to customer satisfaction and anticipate market demand. Each approach seems suited to different conditions. The *bureaucratic* model demands stability, the *professional* requires autonomy, and the *political* necessitates consensus or at least majority consent. The *managerial* model works well in dynamic periods of considerable change. Both *market* models adjust capacity to demand, with government incentives shaping supply and demand to suit public priorities in *managed markets.*

Each model has positive or negative consequences based on performance or results. The bureaucratic rewards compliance with continuation and penalizes deviations with sanctions. Success in the professional model encourages consultation on decisions; failure results in neglect of professional advice. Financial incentives represent the positive and funding losses the negative in the political model, although performance reporting usually has only a positive or negative effect on the reputations of colleges or universities because it lacks a formal connection to funding. The management approach involves either promotion or demotion, or possibly acclaim or disapproval. Markets produce profits or losses, and managed markets add incentives to the positive consequences.

Bureaucratic accountability centralizes governance. All the other models, with the possible exception of the political, demand decentralized decision making, although the political, managerial, and managed markets add varying degrees of policy directions. The political model can lead to intrusive regulations. Some of the accountability models rest on mature theories, but others represent practices outrunning theory. Each accountability model has generated accountability programs that accent the goals of efficiency, quality, productivity, market responsiveness, and public priorities.

Of course, the accountability systems in place are seldom as pure as the above categories may suggest. Each model has advantages and disadvantages, depending on application and timing. Bureaucratic accountability lives on in many states and constantly threatens a comeback in all organizations, public or private. Recent scandals in the stock market remind us that some regulation is required to prevent outrageous behavior. Conversely, uniform regulations do not work well in diverse and complex organizations such as colleges or universities. Professional accountability (or faculty participation) is essential to effective accountability systems in colleges and universities, but it can lead to gridlock in collegial decision making and to diminished responsiveness to public priorities or market needs. Policies and politics, management and

**Table 1.1. Accountability Models**

Accountability Models

| Accountabiliy Features | Bureaucratic | Professional | Political | Managerial | Market | Managed Market |
|---|---|---|---|---|---|---|
| Levers | Rules | Expertise | Policies | Management | Markets | Markets Policies |
| Agents | Bureaucrats | Peers | Policymakers | Managers | Entrepreneurs | Entrepreneurs Policymakers |
| Goals | Efficiency | Quality | Priorities | Productivity | Responsiveness | Responsiveness Priorities |
| Indicators | Inputs Processes | Processes | Outcomes | Inputs Outputs | Outputs | Outputs Outcomes |
| Conditions | Stability | Autonomy | Consensus | Dynamic | Demand Capacity | Demand Capacity Incentives |
| Techniques | Regulation | Consultation | Planning | Cost-benefit analysis | Customer satisfaction | Customer satisfaction Priority planning |

| Consequences | Continuation Sanctions | Participation Neglect | Incentives Losses | Promotion Demotion | Profits Losses | Profits Incentives Losses |
|---|---|---|---|---|---|---|
| *Governance* | Centralized | Collegial | Direction Decentralized | Decentralized | Market forces | Public-private partnerships |
| *Theory* | Scientific management | Collegial governance | Public policy | Reinventing government | Market economics | Market steering |
| *Programs* | Financial Program audits | Assessment Accreditation Academic audits Standardized testing | Report cards Performance reporting Budgeting Funding | Performance reports | Student-alumni satisfaction surveys Reputational ratings | Charter colleges Vouchers Financial aid |

Accountability Features

markets are necessary parts of accountability in state higher education systems and in public and private colleges and universities. Yet each of these levers can divert higher education from its fundamental purposes in favor of momentary fads.

Zemsky, the author of Chapter Twelve, makes the point, at least in part. He calls for triple-threat leaders for higher education who are mission centered, politically savvy, and market smart (Knight Higher Education Collaborative, 1999). He might have added several other talents, such as bureaucratically wily, academically chaste, collegially committed, and managerially keen. Leaders of colleges and universities need not walk on water, but they must know how to wade the waves of accountability.

## From Public Benefits to Private Commodities

Declining state funding, strong market pressures, and growing political involvement in state coordination and campus governance are undermining consensus on the public benefit of postsecondary education. Mark Yudof, the chancellor of the University of Texas System, declared the basic compact between state government and public universities dead or dying. Though he spoke only of public research universities, his claim resonates on baccalaureate campuses, especially those where enrollment demands far exceed available spaces.

"State governments and public research universities developed an extraordinary compact. In return for financial support from taxpayers, universities agreed to keep tuition low and provide access for students from a broad range of economic backgrounds, train graduate and professional students, promote arts and culture, help solve problems in the community, and perform groundbreaking research. Yet over the past 25 years, that agreement has withered, leaving public research institutions in a purgatory of insufficient resources and declining competitiveness" (Yudof, 2002, p. B24).

In response, Yudof (2002) proposed a "hybrid university"—public in some purposes but private in most operations, including the tuition charged, the markets served, and the programs offered. The governor and the Texas legislature approved Yudof's proposal, and policymakers have adopted and are discussing similar initiatives in a number of other states (Couturier, 2003). Stanley Fish (2003,

p. C4) would go all the way. "Give Us Liberty or Give Us Revenue," he cries, in a less heroic but more commercial slogan than Patrick Henry's "liberty" or "death." The governor of South Carolina accepted Fish's challenge and proposed to let some public colleges and universities become private, provided they agree to forgo state funding (Schmidt, 2003). So far the governor has no takers.

Yudof and others laud the attractions of market-driven universities, but Derek Bok sees some inevitable sins in the "entrepreneurial university" that responds mostly to markets. In the struggle for competitive positions and increased revenues, Bok believes a few colleges or universities will succumb to the temptation to enter questionable commercial ventures. In time, he says, "suspect behavior will become accepted practice" (2003a, p. B7). Bok fails to mention the greatest problem with market accountability. If colleges and universities become too accountable to market forces, they diminish their autonomy to criticize the business or popular interests that drive those markets. Moreover, markets led by the ratings from *U.S. News & World Report* really reward prestige, not performance. "Institutional behavior has become increasingly market driven," declares Massy, "but markets generally reward prestige—they don't gauge the true quality of education, and therefore they produce a perverse set of incentives" (2003a, p. 5). In Chapter Twelve, Zemsky claims that this struggle for prestige means that markets neither constrain tuition nor improve quality in the competitive parts of higher education (see also Volkwein and Grunig's Chapter Eleven).

Arthur Levine, president of Columbia Teachers College, cites a more disturbing reason for the weakening of the compact than market pressures or declining funding. He argues that a decline in the appeal of access has undermined the compact. Higher education remained, until the late 1990s, a growth industry driven by the access goal of enrolling an ever-increasing percentage of high school graduates. Levine (1997) believes that governors, legislators, and opinion leaders may have privately abandoned that goal of continued expansion. "More than 60 percent of all high-school graduates now go on to some form of postsecondary education, and many state officials see that rate as sufficient or even too high. I see no enthusiasm among government officials for increasing the college-attendance rate to 70 or 80 percent of high-school graduates" (p. A48).

Perhaps Levine is mistaken when he says that government officials no longer support expanded access. Still, access has clearly declined as a priority in state capitols, in comparison with education from early childhood through high school. Moreover, a recent study for the Education Commission of the States notes that the United States has been falling behind other developed nations in its college participation rates for over a decade (Ruppert, 2003). What the commission and Levine do not mention is the questionable commitment of some segments of higher education to access. Too often, baccalaureate colleges and universities respond to increasing enrollment demands, when they can, by raising admission standards and tuitions rather than expanding access.

Additional anecdotal evidence may support the thesis of a declining real interest in access in relation to highly visible initiatives in economic developments. Governors and legislators do seem more willing these days to fund expensive high-tech research ventures that stimulate economic development than they are to pay fully for rising enrollments (Hebel, 2003). Perhaps this shift suggests the next stage of higher education markets, in which states will purchase what they want from any source rather than provide general funding for public colleges and universities. This shift is relatively recent; governors and legislators in the early 1990s criticized professors for stressing research and neglecting undergraduates. It may also explain the irony that governors and legislators say higher education is a public good in a knowledge and information society but see it as a private benefit when limiting general funding for enrollment growth and approving (or at least allowing) tuition increases. Moreover, outside supporters and critics and increasing numbers of inside champions now agree that access is not enough. The priority has shifted from mere access to degree attainment and even to job placement in critical fields such as nursing, teaching, and the high-tech sciences. Finally, equity and diversity, twin partners to access, apparently have diminished support in state capitols and the national government, despite the recent ruling of the U.S. Supreme Court.

The strongest threat to higher education autonomy these days comes not from government power, whether state or federal, but from market forces. Market accountability leaves the setting of public priorities to market demands. Its supporters doubt the efficacy of collective planning of program initiatives and funding decisions and believe that market forces are more efficient and effective in allocating programs and resources. Others counter that markets reflect private interests of dominant segments of society and not the public interests of society as a whole. A new approach combines public and private interests called *managed market* accountability. It follows the admonition in reinventing government of "steering" rather then "rowing." Instead of owning and substantially funding organizations of service delivery, governments can shape or "manage" markets by purchasing or subsidizing the services they want. This approach allows government to shape higher education's response to market mechanisms to achieve greater efficiency in the use of scarce public resources. (Old examples of managed market approaches are federal financial aid and research funding, which go to students and professors rather than institutions.) Again, balance is the key. Effective accountability systems must include enough market pressure to ensure reaction to external demands and sufficient policy direction to ensure responsiveness to public needs while considering legitimate academic concerns.

## Creating a Public Agenda

The lack of agreement on those public needs—what states and society need most from colleges and universities—agitates the antagonism between academic organizations and external groups. Absent agreements on expectations from higher education, commitments remain open-ended, demands unrestrained, and stakeholders dissatisfied. Governors, legislators, and business leaders continually call for colleges and universities to start new programs and services while constantly castigating them for trying to be all things to all people. In turn, academics complain about being labeled unresponsive, when government and business leaders are unclear about their priority needs or change them with election or market cycles (Knight Higher Education Collaborative, 2002).

Few forums exist that bring academic and civic and business leaders together in ways that produce mutual understanding. The two groups too often see each other at their worst rather than their best. Governors, legislators, and business leaders see administrators and professors mostly at budget times haggling for more money like other special interests rather than at work delivering relevant programs in teaching, research, and service. Academics often complain of shortfalls in state and private funding instead of recognizing the sizeable support that governments and businesses already supply. The widening gap between stakeholders and academics undermines the one characteristic that all the writers see as essential to the balance between accountability and autonomy—*trust* (Lingenfelter, 2003; Massy, 2003a; Trow, 1996; Graham, Lyman, and Trow, 1995). Contrary to the cliché, familiarity is more likely to bring appreciation than breed contempt.

## From 360-Degree Harassment to 360-Degree Accountability

Outsiders criticize the lack of accountability in higher education as an inalienable right but accept no responsibility for creating effective accountability systems. The role of critic without commitment has long been popular in civic circles, no less than on college campuses. Behn, in *Rethinking Democratic Accountability,* talks of moving from "360-degree harassment" of government from all sides of society for failing to satisfy their special interests to "360-degree accountability," where civic and business groups accept responsibility with government officials for setting priorities and ensuring their achievement (2001, p. 199). His approach transforms criticism into commitment. In some states, business, civic, government, and education leaders are beginning to move from 360-degree harassment to 360-degree accountability in higher education.

Roundtables supported by The Pew Charitable Trusts and summit meetings of government, business, civic, and education leaders sponsored by the Association of Governing Boards and other organizations have tried to develop comprehensive public agendas for higher education in several states, including North Dakota and Mississippi (Burke, 2003; North Dakota Roundtable, 2000; Mississippi Steering Committee, 2002). Representatives of government, business, civic organizations, and higher education in commissions, summits, and roundtables have identified, collectively, priorities of what their states need most from their public and private colleges and universities in instruction, research, and service, especially for workforce and economic development and K–16 partnerships.

Such forums can transform complainers into creators with a commitment to ensuring that higher education responds to priority needs and receives the public and private support to address that public agenda. Although these gatherings are still too few and their recommendations too new to assess their ultimate impact, they appear to offer the hope of moving higher education from a debate of 360-degree harassment to at least a discussion of 360-degree accountability.

The North Dakota Roundtable has brought a continuing commitment from state, business, and education leaders to its "accountability with flexibility" program (North Dakota University System, 2002). That roundtable report advocated something close to 360-degree accountability:

> The Roundtable report calls for all parties to the relationship to change their behaviors and methods of doing business in important ways. While the report contains many specific recommendations, the overarching themes call for:

- The [North Dakota University System] to cease thinking of itself as a ward of the state and to take greater responsibility for its own future.

- The legislative and executive branches of government to free up and unleash the potential of the [University System]—to change the budget-building, resource allocation, and audit practices to reflect the new compact between the state and the University System.

- The private sector to meet [the University System] half-way in establishing mutually beneficial partnerships and to provide mentors and learning opportunities for a new generation of North Dakota entrepreneurs.

- All parties to keep alive the spirit of the Roundtable, continuing the dialogue which has already borne fruit and maintaining the momentum that has been achieved through a process of bringing together leaders, many with conflicting views, to deal in an atmosphere of mutual respect with the problems they have found to be their common concern. (North Dakota Roundtable, 2000, p. 3)

Higher education has a long list of participants who must become partners in accountability. They include, internally, students, faculty, staff, and trustees and, externally, leaders of schools, governments, business, labor, civic organizations, and electronic and print media—all of which benefit from higher education programs, activities, and services. Collaborative or 360-degree accountability suggests the truth in the cliché, "If you are not part of the solution, you are part of the problem."

The *Report from the Steering Committee for the Mississippi Leadership Summit on Higher Education* echoed that theme: "The Mississippi Leadership Summit on Higher Education has worked hard to identify what all of higher education—public and private, two-year and four-year institutions—can do to advance the competitiveness of our state and to improve the quality of life of our people. Through this package of priorities and initiatives, our intention is to provide a shared framework for educational, economic, and social progress. . . . It will not be easy to implement that framework. We feel, however, that with concerted and collegial effort, we can make our dream of the future a reality" (Mississippi Steering Committee, 2002, p. 1).

The Joint Committee on the new California Master Plan (2002, p. 78) stressed the importance of such collaborative goal setting: "Too often goals are only casually considered if they are considered at all. . . . The more important objective, however, should be to derive consensus on what is meant by performance. What is it about education that is important to individuals, the State, and society at large? What are our expectations about effectiveness and efficiency? What about breadth of opportunity and depth of achievement? These are the questions that give accountability its deeper meaning, and efforts to collaboratively generate answers to them are what provide the 'buy-in' from stakeholders that ultimately will make or break any accountability system."

Although the recommendations of the Joint Committee on the new California Master Plan fall far short of that state's needs, they call for collaborative goal setting by all the stakeholders as the key to accountability for higher education.

## Sticking, Serving, and Selling

"360-degree accountability" calls for courageous leaders of colleges and universities. Zemsky's trinity of mission-centered, market smart, and politically savvy leaders for higher education suggests the conflicting requirements for preserving autonomy while producing accountability. Colleges and universities must *stick* to their missions, *serve* their society, and *sell* their services. Each of these actions in some ways fights with the others. A college or university, public or private, that sticks with its mission may well miss the next market wave. One that "sells" usually tells customers what they want to hear; one that "serves" often sends a needed but unwelcome message. Indeed, the college or university that serves society best may well be the one that criticizes and resists a slavish devotion to market forces, which are often momentary fads. A single campus cannot do everything that markets demand. It should do what it does best or better than others, which means sticking to its mission while selling to clients who need its services most. Finally, the politically savvy leader in higher education is the one who can distinguish public needs from partisan demands and persuade the general public and hopefully government officials to see the difference.

The current monolithic model of excellence for colleges and universities encourages not "mission centeredness" but "mission creep." The diversity of American higher education is a wonder of the world, with its marvelous mix of community and technical colleges, liberal arts and comprehensive campuses, and doctoral and research universities. But at home, our academic culture and the general public confer the hallmark of quality only on large, graduate, research universities and, to a lesser extent, on small, selective, liberal arts colleges. This narrow notion of quality flourishes in the national ratings of universities and colleges published by *U.S. News & World Report* and a growing number of popular magazines (see Chapters Eleven and Twelve). Effective accountability systems must honor multiple models of academic excellence based on performance not prestige, on results not reputations, on mission centeredness not mission creep.

## The Accountability Triangle

Burton Clark's famous triangle used *state control, academic oligarchy,* and *market model* as the three forces dominating coordination of higher education systems in a comparative international context (Clark, 1983). His governance triangle estimates the influences of these three factors in coordinating national systems of higher education. The following figure substitutes *state priorities, academic concerns,* and *market forces* to create an Accountability Triangle (Figure 1.1) for higher education in the United States. It assesses the responsiveness of accountability programs to the three interests and pressures that most affect higher education in this country: (1) *state priorities* reflect the public needs and desires for higher education programs and services, often as expressed by state officials but also by civic leaders outside government; (2) *academic concerns* involve the issues and interests of the academic community, particularly professors and administrators; (3) *market forces* cover the customer needs and demands of students, parents, and businesses, as well as other clients of colleges and universities. State priorities, academic concerns, and market forces also reflect, respectively, the civic, collegiate, and commercial cultures and interests. State priorities represent political accountability, academic concerns reflect professional accountability, and market forces push market accountability.

Each of the three corners of the Accountability Triangle has a bright and a dark side, reflecting both broad needs and special interests. State priorities can constitute what the citizens of a state need most from higher education, such as better schoolteachers, an educated workforce, and an informed citizenry. It can also replicate the partisan interest of the party in power. Academic concerns can encourage free inquiry and discussion of ideas, beliefs, and institutions infused by openness, scholarship, and objectivity. It can also reflect the resource-reputation model of higher education that views institutional quality as mostly a matter of recruiting the brightest students, hiring the faculty stars, and raising the most resources. Market forces can mean meeting the real needs of citizens and society for programs and services or responding to the dominant economic interest in a state or to commercial schemes or consumer fads.

By and large, state priorities, academic concerns, and market forces present conflicting demands, with some interesting exceptions. At times, the drive for prestige and reputation merges academic concerns, public priorities, and market forces and succumbs to the wiles of the resource-reputation model of excellence for colleges and universities. This odd coupling produces more lawyers and physicians than society needs rather than the nurses and teachers that society requires. At times, the demand for research in an

### Figure 1.1. The Accountability Triangle

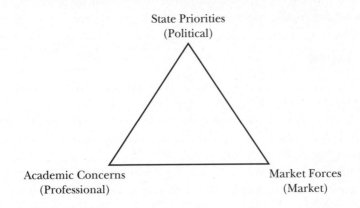

State Priorities
(Political)

Academic Concerns
(Professional)

Market Forces
(Market)

economy driven by innovation unites the interests of state priorities, academic concerns, and market forces. State priorities and market forces have some common interests, but the former calls for public priorities, whereas the latter relies on private preferences. In addition, state priorities should last longer than market forces.

Higher education and its colleges and universities, both public and private, are inevitably accountable to state priorities, academic concerns, and market forces. They should serve all while submitting to none of these imperatives. Being accountable to each of the three corners of the Accountability Triangle means balancing the response to ensure service without subservience to public priorities, academic concerns, and market forces.

Given the importance of state priorities, academic concerns, and market forces as representing political, professional, and market accountability, the center of the Accountability Triangle seems the ideal spot for an effective accountability system and perhaps for some of the accountability programs. The following chapters and the conclusion place the practice of current accountability programs in the appropriate spot on the triangle. Some of the authors also suggest changes that could move their programs more toward the center of the triangle and discuss whether such changes are feasible or even desirable. They may also propose linkages between programs that could contribute to an effective accountability system by combining state priorities, campus concerns, and market forces. Whatever the accountability programs of the past and present, effective efforts in the future must combine each of these angles of the Accountability Triangle.

## Conclusion

Accountability in higher education in the United States has run the gamut from trust and self-regulation, to bureaucratic rules and stipulations, to performance goals and results, to policy initiatives and political intrusions, and, finally, to private markets and government incentives. As often happens, policymakers introduced new initiatives without abandoning earlier efforts. Three higher education leaders complained in perhaps the fullest discussion of accountability: "Higher education does not lack accountability. Rather it lacks enough of the proper kind and is burdened with too much of an unproductive kind" (Graham, Lyman, and Trow, 1995, p. 4). Readers may dispute their prescription for achieving accountability, but few would quarrel with their diagnosis. The key is to clarify the reaches and limits of accountability and to develop effective and integrated systems of accountability. Higher education is too important to society to become either off-limits to external influence or the passive object of external control, whether by state priorities or market forces.

Accountability has assumed many faces and has seen many changes. But its critics, as well as its champions, agree on at least one point: accountability is here to stay. For too long, outsiders have advocated accountability for their special interests in higher education without accepting responsibility for developing realistic accountability systems. All too often, academics have resisted outside scrutiny as an invasion of their academic autonomy and have failed to hold themselves accountable for their results. If higher education is to escape the curse of 360-degree harassment from all sides of society, it must turn complainers into creators of a 360-degree accountability plan designed and defended by all segments of society. If accountability for higher education is here to stay, it is time for all supporters to devise an acceptable way to balance public, academic, and market concerns.

# Chapter Two

# Accountability and the Private Sector: State and Federal Perspectives

*William M. Zumeta*

Chapter One introduces the metaphor of the Accountability Triangle—the notion that accountability approaches and policies can be usefully conceptualized according to where they fit on a hypothetical triangle where the nodes are *academic concerns, market forces,* and *public priorities.* Each of the nodes represents an important dimension relevant to higher education's contributions to the society that supports it.

But how does this conceptual schema apply to the private postsecondary sector? This question will be the overarching concern of this chapter. First, however, we must tackle the more basic issue of whether and how the notion of public accountability is even relevant to private postsecondary education. If the providers are private, what business are they of public policymakers, and in what sense do they need to be accountable? Part of the answer is that, like businesses and nonprofit organizations in other fields, private postsecondary institutions must seek governmental license to operate, similar to a corporate charter. They are accountable to public authorities representing the citizenry for their behavior as

Thanks go to my research assistant Jennifer A. Vasche for unusually diligent research and documentation assistance.

employers, as occupants of land and operators of physical plants that may produce spillover problems for local jurisdictions (for example, pollution, congestion, student misbehavior), and for fiscal probity and the basic integrity and quality of their primary services to students and other clients.

State governments in the United States have thus long overseen the performance of private colleges and other postsecondary institutions in their basic role as corporate entities. Their oversight on matters of quality of performance has traditionally taken a very light hand, however, consisting mainly of some checking at the initial incorporation stage of the apparent integrity of purpose and fiscal stability of the operation and occasional response to financial malfeasance and consumer fraud complaints. Private for-profit and vocational postsecondary institutions are required to provide certain data about the efficacy of their programs to federal authorities and in some states are subject to periodic reviews by state agencies designed to ensure that they provide the programs they advertise in a way that is not patently fraudulent. Private, nonprofit (independent) colleges and universities have traditionally gotten little regulatory attention from state and federal educational authorities, as long as they are accredited by one of the regional accrediting organizations recognized by the federal government (see Chapter Four). Accreditation is thought to ensure at least a floor on educational quality for institutions enrolling students who receive federal and state student aid (that is, nearly all degree-granting institutions) and, along with market forces, to provide some basic accountability that these public funds are used competently for the educational purposes for which they are intended.

Many would argue that this system of limited accountability of postsecondary institutions has served the nation well, particularly as respects private colleges and universities. The "system" of private postsecondary providers is extensive and diverse; the U.S. Department of Education recognizes some 1,800 degree-granting private nonprofit colleges and universities and several hundred degree-granting for-profits, in addition to thousands of nondegree private postsecondary schools (National Center for Education Statistics, 2003a). The independent collegiate sector is the envy of the world for its quality and diversity and is very dynamic (Birnbaum, 1983; Zumeta, 1999). The number of degree-granting for-profits has been growing rapidly, mostly in response to increased demand for job-relevant postsecondary education and the possibilities created by diffusion of personal computers and Internet access (Kirp, 2003c). Excessive governmental regulation could stifle this market-based dynamism. On the other hand, the very growth in this sector in numbers of students enrolled might argue for closer governmental attention to them to make sure citizens are well served and to be cognizant of competitive effects on more traditional private, and even public, institutions that could affect their ability to deliver services. To the extent that these for-profit private institutions and their students are seeking or receiving publicly funded student aid—as they are (Burd, 2003c)—the argument for closer governmental oversight and accountability is stronger.

Although few question the academic quality of most of the collegiate institutions in the private postsecondary sector, the era has produced new interest in ensuring that limited public funds are spent in ways that efficiently achieve public priorities. As will be described more fully later, private colleges and universities receive a variety of forms of public aid, ranging from tax exemptions through various forms of (mostly indirect) financial support to recognition of their concerns in policymaking about public higher education. So some policymakers now feel that both public and private colleges should be more accountable for graduating students in a timely way, proving that students are learning, and doing their utmost to control costs and prices (McKeon, 2003; Boehner and McKeon, 2003). Indeed, many fear that the billions of dollars available annually in federal and state student aid provide little incentive for colleges to avoid raising tuition by hefty percentages each year. Thus, private colleges and other postsecondary institutions are potentially subject to the same types of pressures for increased and more direct accountability that public institutions now face.

This chapter explores further the basis for these new claims for increased accountability: how they mesh with the history of and traditional views regarding the social accountability of private higher education in the United States and how extensively recent movements for greater accountability have so far affected this sector. The chapter also examines the current push at the federal level for increased accountability and what this might mean for the various subsectors of private higher education (for the American private postsecondary sector is exceedingly diverse). Finally, I offer some suggestions as to how the current interest in strengthening the weight of the "public priorities" element in policymaking for higher education might be accommodated without damaging the capacity of our dynamic and generally high-quality private sectors. The conceptual framework provided by the Accountability Triangle and the notions of academic concerns, market forces, and public priorities are used as touchstones throughout the chapter.

## Social Accountability in the Private Sector

To understand contemporary accountability issues as they bear on private higher education in the United States, it is necessary first to cover some background on the American system of higher education, its connections with government, and the ways in which the accountability of higher education has traditionally been conceived. The early colleges in America mixed public and private elements. The colleges held state (and earlier, colonial) charters, often included public officials on their governing boards, generally enjoyed tax-exempt status like other nonprofit organizations serving public purposes, and occasionally received public funds. But they were also largely religious in orientation, were not consistently supported financially by legislatures, and were not generally closely overseen by public authorities (Trow, 1993). Indeed, a key innovation in American higher education, in sharp contrast to its European ancestors where faculty guilds and central church and state authority predominated, was the idea of a governing board of accessible, responsible citizens to ensure a kind of social accountability under the institution's public charter. Eventually, this form of accountability was sufficiently trusted that legislatures no longer felt the need to appoint their members to governing boards of the colleges they chartered. After the Supreme Court's ruling in *Dartmouth College* v. *Woodward* (1819) established the autonomy of state-chartered colleges from their legislatures, such appointments were no longer an option for what we now call private colleges, and the boards evolved into self-perpetuating legal entities. Occasionally, the state authorities might have to intervene to ensure protection of student or donor interests in the face of corporate malfeasance or ineptitude, but in the vast majority of cases, this arms-length accountability mechanism proved satisfactory and able to produce a socially acceptable balance of institutional autonomy—an important consideration in higher education—and basic accountability to society.

## The Federal Role

Notably absent from the discussion to this point is the federal government. In the United States, which is different from the rest of the world in this regard, the national government, for much of the nation's history, played only a minor role in higher education. The U.S. Constitution (by omission) leaves oversight of education to the states. From an early controversy over President Washington's suggestion that Congress establish a national university (which it never did) until 1862, when the Morrill Act provided land grants to the states for the establishment of practical universities, the federal government did virtually nothing in the higher education sphere. Even the land grant act, momentous though it was, essentially "left the money on the stump" for the states, after which the federal government essentially walked away (Trow, 1993, pp. 57–58). In the 1880s, under the Hatch Act, Congress created the agricultural extension service, which was based at the land grant institutions, but then had only minimal dealings with higher education (for example, funding specialized institutions like the military academies and a few others, along with the extension service) until World War II.

At this point two major types of federal involvement emerged that helped shape subsequent policies and debates that inevitably have implications for the evolution of thinking about accountability. One was the emergence of large-scale, federally supported research and development at universities, both public and private. Although in the early postwar years grants were made on a peer-reviewed, competitive basis to university investigators with remarkably few strings attached (Smith, 1990), as the sums and importance of the federally sponsored research enterprise grew, so, inevitably, did the accoutrements of accountability. Grants and contracts were monitored ever more closely, although mostly for compliance with increasingly complex accounting rules rather than for the merits of their scholarly products. Universities suffered some serious public relations damage in the early 1990s over questionable practices in charging overhead costs to federal grants, and the most egregious offenders were private institutions (Trow, 1993). As early as the 1970s, federal policymakers had begun to use the leverage of their extensive grants and contracts with universities to pressure them to adhere more closely to federal policy goals regarding equal employment opportunity and affirmative action in recruiting faculty and students. In the early and mid-1990s, Congress sought to impose substantial regulatory controls over postsecondary institutions, especially private institutions, in an effort to combat high rates of student loan defaults. Also, around the same time, legislators became concerned about a surge in tuition rates and talked about creating strong incentives for controlling prices but ended up settling for a commission to look into the matter. So the extent to which policymakers asserted forms of accountability on universities, including private ones, for certain public priorities has been on the increase for several decades. Nonetheless, the range of issues on which the federal government sought accountability from private colleges and universities remained quite narrow.

Research and development connections with the federal government affected relatively few private (or public) institutions, mainly the research-intensive universities. But also at the end of World War II, the much more pervasive phenomenon of federal aid to postsecondary students emerged. The first manifestation was the GI Bill of 1944, which provided aid for college directly to more than 2.3 million students, as well as another 1.2 million after the Korean conflict (Department of Veterans Affairs, 2003). Other federal student aid programs—National Defense Student Loans— followed the sense of crisis created by the Soviets' success in launching the first *Sputnik* space satellite in 1957. Then came broad programs of grants and loans created in 1965, when the first Higher Education Act (HEA) was enacted, and expanded in 1972 in the act's first reauthorization. Here also the federal government explicitly chose to make use of market forces in allocating to students the benefits of these aid programs rather than choosing to aid institutions directly, although the latter path had strong advocates (Trow, 1993).

Many analysts have concluded that this major strategic choice has played a key role in sustaining the autonomy and diversity of the nation's higher education system, and it has shaped the nature of the accountability discussion. In the system that has evolved to date, the market is the main accountability mechanism for ensuring that private colleges and universities in particular are accountable for achieving results that people want with the mostly indirect public subsidies they receive. If an institution is not providing a socially desirable service or level of quality, presumably students, including those with government aid, will reflect this in their enrollment choices, and the school will adjust what it provides or face financial disaster.

Current discussion at the federal policy level about higher education accountability should be understood in light of this historical background. Indeed, to employ the conceptual categories guiding the analyses in this volume, one might say that federal policy in higher education to date has proceeded largely by harnessing broad *academic concerns* with the advancement of knowledge (through both education and research) via *market forces* in the competitive research grant and student aid systems—that are fully open to private institutions—to pursue *public priorities*. The rub now is that policymakers today see more divergence between the academy's concerns and public priorities than has been true in the past.

## The States' Role

The states still have the primary policy assignment of overseeing higher education. Once we get beyond the basic chartering and public protection functions, the extent of state involvement with private colleges and universities varies considerably. In all fifty states, there exists a public higher education sector, "owned" by the state, that serves the majority of enrolled students (National Center for Education Statistics, 2003a) and occupies most of policymakers' attention.

Before sketching some of the basic features of the variation in state relations with private higher education and considering the implications for accountability, it is necessary to describe the major state policies that can have an impact on private colleges and universities and their outcomes. Perhaps most basic are tax policies. Like most other nonprofit service organizations, colleges and universities are eligible in all fifty states for exemption from state and local property taxes and in the main from corporate income taxes. Also, most states provide for deductibility of donations to nonprofit colleges from individual and corporate taxes, and some have programs that waive sales taxes for certain purchases by these institutions. Like the analogous federal tax policies, these exemptions are based on the notion that such organizations serve a public purpose to be encouraged, which merits the social subsidy represented by the tax revenue foregone. Part of the implicit logic of including private colleges and universities is that, if there were fewer of these institutions in the absence of tax subsidies, the public sector would be pressed to pick up the slack.

In the aggregate, the subsidies provided to private higher education through tax preferences are quite substantial (Thompson and Zumeta, 2001). Potentially, this creates a powerful lever for demanding public accountability from them. Traditionally though, neither states nor the federal government have used this leverage to any significant degree. Their pursuit of accountability has been almost entirely limited to ferreting out institutions that benefit from tax preferences but are not truly nonprofits and to identifying income streams within nonprofits that could be taxed as "business" income (for instance, property rental or bookstore income). This hands-off policy is consistent with the historic American higher education policy approach that has offered general subsidies very substantially through students and allowed them to "vote with their feet" as to where the money ends up rather than fully supporting institutions directly.[1]

Given that their tax exemptions and preferences are assumed to be largely unassailable, the state policies that private college interests see as most important to them generally are student aid policies (Zumeta, 1989, 1996). As indicated, nearly all states provide scholarships and other forms of aid to postsecondary students, including state residents attending accredited independent colleges (National Association of State Student Grant and Aid Programs [NASSGAP], 2003). Some states allow students attending for-profit and even nondegree private institutions to participate. Wide variation exists across the states in the relative size of their student aid programs, ranging from two states that provide no aid at all to Georgia, which provided more than $1,500 per enrolled undergraduate in 2001–2002 (NASSGAP, 2003). The size of these programs and the terms on which private college students can participate—size and number of grants, role of financial need versus academic merit in determining eligibility, how much tuition can be counted in the student's need calculation, and so on—are key issues for many private colleges, particularly those that draw many students from their home state. Empirical research has shown that the funding for these aid programs has significant effects on enrollments of low- and moderate-income students and some minority groups at less selective private colleges and universities (Thompson and Zumeta, 2001). Although substantial state dollars flow to private colleges from these programs through their students, research to date shows little sign that states have used this link to pursue aggressive accountability measures affecting private higher education. If federal accountability measures tied to student aid are successfully pursued, however, states could well follow the federal lead.

More direct fiscal links between states and private colleges and universities exist in some states. Zumeta (1996) identified at least seven states with long-standing programs of direct financial support to private colleges and universities and another eighteen with contracts of some kind with such schools. These programs are most commonly arrangements in which the state pays the private institution on a per-capita basis for enrollment of certain types of state-resident students, often in health professions but in some cases other fields as well. Other instances show the state paying a "bounty" to private colleges for all enrollments of state-resident undergraduates, regardless of field. In studies conducted in the late 1980s and early 1990s, Zumeta found little evidence that states had used these programs as levers for enforcing outcome-based accountability on private institutions (1989, 1996). Burke notes that his surveys reveal just two such cases in recent years (2003). One was an effort in Pennsylvania to link state performance funding for both public and private colleges and universities to their graduation rates. This lasted only one year because of political fallout when only private institutions achieved the target rates. In Ohio, some performance funds for which private colleges and universities are eligible under the Research Challenge program reward institutions in proportion to their external research support. Burke reports that two private universities received some funding from this program in the fiscal years 2000–2003 (Burke and Associates, 2002). It is notable that in both cases these programs offered additional funds as rewards for performance rather than attempting to tie existing funding streams to performance measures.

Among the powers that most states have in the higher education policy realm is the power to review and either veto or refuse to fund new academic programs proposed by public colleges and universities. In a few states, state authorities can also call for the termination of existing academic programs. Private higher education interests may encourage the fairly aggressive use of these program review and approval powers when public institutions seek new programs that private schools feel will encroach on their "turf." Private colleges charge higher tuition, as they operate with much smaller public subsidies. They argue that the higher charge puts them at a competitive disadvantage and may threaten their fiscal health. Publics say that their programs will provide additional low-priced access to students whom the privates cannot afford to serve. Implicit in these debates is the claim that private colleges and universities are serving public purposes in ways that may preclude the need for additional public provision and that public authorities should thus at least pay attention to these institutions' basic interests.

Beyond this, a few states have asserted authority over private colleges and universities directly in program reviews. Most prominently, in the state of New York, higher education agencies have revoked the certification of doctoral programs at private as well as public universities on grounds of inadequate quality or productivity (Roy, 1996). In a few other states, government agencies have occasionally commented unfavorably on the quality of private institutions' doctoral programs and suggested they be pared. Beyond this, states have done little to use legal authority or funding leverage to influence the program configurations of independent colleges and universities.

Another higher education policy issue of interest to private colleges is the pricing policies of public institutions, which are normally influenced or even set by state policymakers. Here private colleges are sometimes concerned that low, or very slow-growing, public tuition prices put them at a competitive disadvantage. Thompson and Zumeta (2001) provide evidence that such competitor pricing can make a difference in private college enrollments. Of course, there is little sign that private sector interests would welcome state involvement in their own price-setting practices as a quid pro quo.

Finally, state agencies play a greater or lesser role in "information policies." Some states have actively sought to work with institutions in all sectors to increase information about the advantages of college and how to pay for it in order to increase participation rates. Such policies can work to the advantage of all institutions. States have a basic responsibility to pay some attention to the representations institutions make to potential students, and as the modern information age has emerged, some have also sought to encourage the quality and comparability of information available about programs, students, costs, and other characteristics of institutions to enhance students' ability to make wise choices. Wide variation exists in how aggressively states pursue these types of policies, particularly with respect to private institutions, but they are likely to be increasingly significant in the future.

## State Policy Postures Toward the Private Sector

Taking this range of policies into account, there is great variation in the states' approaches to their independent higher education sectors. In an earlier empirical analysis, I identified three "policy postures" of states toward this sector that, together with two hybrids, captured fairly well this range of variation. (See Zumeta, 1996, for details about the methodology. A state need not have all the properties of its type but must exhibit several.) In the *laissez-faire posture,* states largely ignore private sector contributions to state policy goals in higher education and devote nearly exclusive attention to public segments. Not surprisingly, most of these states (many of which are less populous ones in the plains or western regions) have proportionally small private sectors.

At the other end of the spectrum are a few states (notably, Florida, Illinois, Maryland, and New Jersey) described as *central planning* states, characterized by efforts to take explicit advantage of the private sector to serve state needs in planned ways. For example, private institutions in such states are explicitly considered in master plans and more or less "assigned" specific shares of growing enrollments or initiatives to meet programmatic needs in specialized fields. They are also typically represented on state higher education policymaking bodies and subject to more-than-average state data collection and programmatic oversight. Concomitantly, independent institutions in such states generally receive (whether directly or indirectly via student aid arrangements) substantial state funds; they are also favored in that tuition levels in public institutions are comparatively high and are subject to considerable state regulation.

Another modest-size group of states were characterized as *market competitive* in their policy posture (for example, Colorado, Georgia, Michigan, and Texas), taking account of the private sector's potential contributions but letting market forces rather than explicit state planning and direction play a key role in such matters as allocating students and state subsidies. A sizeable group of states (fourteen) also showed important elements of both the market-competitive and central planning postures in their policy mix. Prominent examples in this cluster included Indiana, Minnesota, New York, Pennsylvania, and Virginia. (There were also a few laissez-faire–market-competitive hybrids, as well as three states whose policy mix was unclassifiable using this schema.) The market-competitive and market-competitive–central-planning hybrid states tended to show larger private sector enrollment growth, lower overall spending on higher education per capita (but not lower per-student spending in public institutions), and higher overall participation in higher education than other types of states. This would seem an attractive package of outcomes for states with significant private sectors that could help meet current growing demands for higher education in the current era of limited public resources.

This analysis shows that states see, to a greater or lesser extent, private colleges and universities as serving public purposes and as legitimately meeting citizens' educational needs. These institutions receive, at least indirectly, public resources and policy preferences to facilitate pursuit of their social mission. Their presence serves to reduce the demands on government to finance directly the education of all students in the public sector. State governments clearly have a responsibility to ensure some measure of social accountability from these institutions, then, in terms of the quality of their service and stewardship. Despite this responsibility, to date states have rarely gone beyond providing mechanisms for basic assurance that the schools are legitimate educational institutions, competently managed financially, and at least minimally respected as educators within their field (that is, accredited).

This permissive approach may change. As demands for the accountability of public institutions ramp up, we may well see state policymakers considering the forms of implicit and explicit public support that these quasi-public institutions receive and asking why they too should not be called to account for educational and related outcomes. Certainly, this process will be accelerated if the federal government asserts its extensive potential leverage to demand outcome-based accountability from private colleges and universities.

## The Contemporary Accountability Climate for Private Higher Education

It is worth considering at this point why the traditional views and mechanisms in place for responding to society's claims for accountability from higher education institutions, in particular private ones, may no longer be considered sufficient. At the root of the matter, the globalized, rapidly changing, technology-driven economy puts increased competitive pressure on all kinds of organizations, governments, and nonprofits, as well as business firms. Firms must compete directly with low-cost producers all over the world, and these competitors and the technologies they use change rapidly. To an increasing extent, colleges and universities must compete in the same way, especially the less well-known, tuition-dependent private colleges that must constantly struggle to maintain enrollments (Breneman, 1994). Nearly all academic institutions are finding competition particularly stiff and demanding in the fast-moving virtual learning realm. Also, college and university trustees and business-oriented legislators now expect institutions to be quite up-to-date in their programs and technological capabilities, as well as streamlined and efficient. Many of these policymakers have been through painful belt-tightening and reengineering in their own organizations and expect the same of their colleges and universities.

Meanwhile, taxpayers are notoriously resistant to calls for increased public revenue for programs, including those from which private colleges and universities benefit. As a result, pressures rise for efficiency and cost-effectiveness.

On the effectiveness, or performance, side of the equation, changes in expectations have also appeared. Rapid advances in information technology and its powers of dissemination have made it possible to amass, interpret, and present a wealth of data about organizational performance that was unimaginable twenty years ago. Health providers, for example, both public and private, are asked to provide elaborate data about patient characteristics, costs, and outcomes that can be compared over time and across organizations. Elementary and secondary schools are now required to demonstrate and report extensively on student characteristics, academic achievement, and the effectiveness of programs. Why, policymakers ask, can't the same performance measurement be applied to higher education—a sector whose critical contribution to individual and state or regional prosperity is increasingly recognized? Why can't costs per student, student retention and completion rates, postgraduation attainments, and even measures of student learning be devised and compared over time and across institutions to provide information and incentives for improving institutional performance and informing students' choices among schools? The basic idea seems simple and broadly applicable, given the ubiquity of modern information technology. Private colleges and universities, overseen by trustees with experience in business, along with other sectors similarly aided by public policy preferences and (mostly) indirect subsidies, seem unlikely to remain exempt for long from these demands.

Legislators and college and university trustees—and even large donors—are less prone than in the past to defer to academic values, caveats, and traditions that may balk at many proposed new accountability measures. Most of them have been through college and have paid for children to attend, which gives them an inside perspective that sometimes leads to skepticism about how, and especially how efficiently, some things are done in the academy. At the same time, boards of trustees, traditionally seen as the guardians of both academic autonomy and social accountability, are now often viewed by legislators and opinion leaders as too protective of institutional interests and prerogatives at the expense of outsider perspectives on appropriate forms of accountability (see Chapter Three). Although in the past such governance concerns have been leveled mostly at public institutions, there are emerging signs that policymakers, who supply tens of billions in scarce tax dollars each year for student aid, are as skeptical of the need for perennial tuition increases well in excess of inflation in the private sector as in the public (Boehner and McKeon, 2003). Private colleges and universities are also as vulnerable as their public counterparts in their inability to demonstrate unambiguously what skills and knowledge their students gain.

Yet there are important differences between public and private sectors that are pertinent to the accountability debate. Private higher education providers have always been creatures of the market to a much greater extent than public institutions (Trow, 1993). Private colleges and universities must compete for students and for donor support; most are highly dependent on annual tuition and related student revenues, for they have very modest endowments in relation to their annual budgets (Breneman, 1994). Competitive pressures in much of this sector are fierce, and a sizeable number of private colleges end up closing their doors (Birnbaum, 1983; Zumeta, 1999)—a very rare occurrence for their public counterparts. Institutions that have substantial endowments (and usually also surpluses of qualified applicants) are much more insulated from market forces against threats to their survival, but they compete vigorously with peers for top students, faculty, donations, and grants. The sector is quite dynamic overall, in that new private institutions appear on the scene almost as frequently as obsolete ones leave, indicating a notable responsiveness to changing social needs as expressed through student demands for particular forms of higher education. Although more than one hundred institutions ceased to operate, the independent collegiate sector managed to maintain its share of enrollments in relation to the more directly subsidized public academic sector over the period 1980 to 1995—a remarkable accomplishment during a time when demographic and economic factors were generally quite unfavorable (Zumeta, 1999).

This competitive dynamism represents an important form of social accountability on the part of private higher education. Signals in the student, donor, and research grant markets reflect values of importance to American society, so few private colleges can survive or prosper without being responsive and accountable to them. Indeed, the influence of such markets becomes all the more pervasive as states reduce their direct subsidies of public colleges and universities, prices rise in this sector, and student aid plays a greater role in higher education finance (Mortenson, 2002b). Given advances in information technology, accountability policies can be harnessed to these forces to provide market decision makers with more complete information about their choices.

One can imagine an approach to accountability designed to be more "outward" to consumers and clients than "upward" to government policymakers, at least for private institutions. It would be built on valid, comparable information about formerly opaque performance elements such as "value-added" to student learning by an institution from entry to exit, completion rates by student characteristics at entry, and career attainments attributable to the institution's efforts. Public policy's main role in such a regime would be to monitor the quality and comparability of information in the market, to ensure quality floors, to act in those occasional cases when individuals were exploited, and, of course, to set and manage the social subsidies of higher education's costs. Such a regime would not be without its challenges but would mitigate many of the problems of upward accountability systems that can threaten desirable institutional autonomy and produce a narrowness of vision and social responsiveness that is much less likely in a thriving marketlike system. I will return to this set of ideas later.

## The State Accountability Movement and the Private Sector

As already indicated, there is little evidence thus far that states have extended to private colleges and universities their efforts at linking higher education funding with institutional performance. Even states that provide direct funding to private institutions appear to do little more than assure themselves that the buildings they support have been built or the students they pay for have enrolled in the specified programs. These are compliance-accountability procedures rather than performance-accountability measures. New York, in its Bundy Aid program, and Michigan, in its much smaller health professions aid program, offer an interesting twist on the usual capitation-payments-for-specified-enrollments approach. In these states, independent colleges and universities receive payments for certain degrees granted to state-resident students. In New York, state funding under the Bundy Aid program is paid for each bachelor's, master's, or doctoral degree awarded to a New York resident. In Michigan, funding is provided for degrees granted in the health professions by independent institutions (Hebel, 2003b). This is a type of simple performance payment, but it is nothing new. These programs have been in place for several decades. Also, there are no performance standards as to degree cost or length of time enrolled to qualify for the payments. Conceivably, such standards could be added, but the long-standing tradition of simply paying for degrees suggests that there would be considerable inertia to overcome in making changes.

The Ohio and Pennsylvania cases described earlier could be harbingers of things to come in the realm of performance funding, at least in states with a long history of substantial state financial links with independent institutions. (Ohio was classified as a central planning state in the Zumeta [1996] typology and Pennsylvania as a market-competitive–central-planning hybrid.) However, the Pennsylvania program was short-lived, which is indicative of some of the difficulties of comparing private and public institutions' performance directly, and Burke's 2002 and 2003 state survey results suggest that the push toward performance funding in general may be weakening. Many states do impose satisfactory academic progress requirements on students receiving state scholarships, including students attending private colleges (National Association of State Student Grant and Aid Programs, 2003). They generally defer to the school's judgment about satisfactory progress. But an important recent development involves more intrusive conditions: many of the fast-growing state "merit scholarship" programs require students to maintain a specific grade average to retain eligibility, which could place pressures on the academic integrity of schools' grading systems.

As performance funding appears to be waning, Burke documents that more states are turning to performance reporting as a "no-cost" approach to accountability (2003; Chapter Ten). As of 2003, Burke reports that no fewer than forty-six states were using performance reporting. He surveyed twenty-nine states in 2000 for an in-depth study of performance reporting (Burke and Minassians, 2002b) and generously provided access to the data about reporting by private institutions for this analysis.

Several patterns are notable in these data. First, a large majority of the states (twenty-one of the twenty-nine) did not include private institutions at all in their performance reporting schemes. Of the remaining eight, two (Connecticut and Texas) called for only basic enrollment figures for private institutions to be reported, whereas Ohio showed interest in just one specialized measure: sponsored research support. Alabama collected a broader range of enrollment data on private institutions (enrollment by age, gender, race, and part-time versus full-time status) and some similar data on their degrees awarded. These data elements suggest some interest in the effects of the independent higher education sector on state policy goals. The remaining four states—Illinois, Missouri, New Jersey, and Tennessee—showed interest in data elements not limited to enrollments and degrees. In Illinois, the reports on private colleges included student transfers (presumably mainly from community colleges) and faculty workload and compensation. Missouri reported expenditures per student, financial aid received by students, and enrollment of students receiving college credit for courses taken during high school. New Jersey's report indicated financial aid awarded, including merit-based aid, retention-graduation, sponsored research, and faculty-staff diversity. The Tennessee presentation showed the contribution to the state's college participation rate, enrollments of top students, financial aid awarded, retention-graduation, grade average of community college transfers, licensure examination pass rates, and average salaries of teacher education graduates. The reported measures in New Jersey and Tennessee were independent sector aggregates, however, whereas those in the other states were institution-level measures.

Unlike nearly all the states with no performance reporting about private higher education, Alabama, Illinois, New Jersey, and Ohio are among the handful of states that provide direct state aid to private colleges and universities, suggesting that there probably is a linkage between state funding and this form of accountability of private institutions. (Among the states in Burke's sample that provide regular direct state support to private colleges and universities, only Maryland indicates no performance reporting.)[2] As argued in the Zumeta (1996) analysis, a private sector that receives substantial state aid over many years is less likely to resist state efforts to collect such data, which policymakers seek to better understand and oversee the entire "state system" of higher education.

Missouri and Tennessee provide no direct state support to private colleges, but, as is made clear in Chapter Ten, they have been leaders in pursuing outcome-based accountability in higher education. In Tennessee, the data are reported only for the independent sector as a whole, whereas in Missouri the data elements are rather few and fairly narrowly focused. Regardless of these states' policy interest in collecting more performance-oriented data from private colleges and universities, without more direct incentives it may be difficult for state authorities to elicit much more information from them. In summary, no strong trend toward private sector accountability by performance reporting is apparent, except perhaps in a few states with a history of strong direct fiscal linkages.

One potential external influence merits mention. The National Center for Public Policy and Higher Education's series of *Measuring Up* "report cards" for states on higher education (2000 and 2002, with more to follow) purposely encompasses dimensions of private higher education in its series of measures of state performance (see Chapter Nine). These publications and the accompanying publicity campaigns appear to be having some impact on thinking and even policymaking in state capitols (Nodine, 2001). *Measuring Up*'s participation rate, completion rate, and affordability indicators in particular are clearly affected by the relative size and performance of a state's private higher education sector, as well as its public institutions (National Center for Public Policy and Higher Education, 2002). This has led some policymakers to complain that they have little or no control over the private schools within their borders and thus over their scores. Yet this is only partly true. If a state wished to improve its completion rate performance, for instance, it might consider using student aid policies to divert more students to private colleges where completion rates are generally higher than at public institutions. This, in turn, might lead to increased state interest in ensuring that the private schools maintain or improve their completion rate performance.

Similarly, state affordability scores in the *Measuring Up* schema are affected by the ratio of private (as well as public) four-year college prices to typical family incomes, by the amount of need-based student aid provided by the state, and by students' reliance on loans. State policies, if affected by concerns about a state's *Measuring Up* scores, could come to take more interest in private colleges' pricing and financial aid policies, seeking perhaps to influence these by seeing, at minimum, that they were widely reported and publicized. State policymakers could also involve private institutions in aggressive measures to increase overall participation rates in higher education. In all these areas, increased state financial aid for students would likely play a role in pursuing policy goals. State policymakers bent on using all the state's colleges and universities in seeking improved performance might not be willing to exempt the privates from performance reporting (or even mandated performance requirements tied to performance funding). The way in which the impact of the *Measuring Up* report card series plays out in influencing state higher education policymaking will indeed be interesting to watch. It could significantly affect relationships between states and their private colleges and universities, at least in those states where the private sector is large enough to be consequential.

## Implications of Federal Pressures for Increased Accountability

The federal Higher Education Act (HEA), scheduled for reauthorization by Congress in 2004, is the vehicle for the main federal student aid grant and loan programs that provide more than $60 billion annually to college students attending nearly all accredited public and private institutions in the country. During 2003, some Republican congressional leaders made statements and offered proposals asserting federal leverage through the HEA that would be more forceful than has ever been enacted in the past (Burd, 2003b; McKeon, 2003). Representative Howard McKeon (R-CA), chairman of the House subcommittee that will do the primary work on reauthorization, and Representative John Boehner (R-OH), chairman of the full Education and the Workforce Committee, indicated support for linking institutions' eligibility to enroll federally aided students to performance standards in three areas (Scott, 2003): (1) holding annual cost-of-attendance increases to less than twice the general rate of inflation, as measured by the Consumer

Price Index; (2) improving undergraduate student persistence and degree completion rates; and (3) demonstrating what students have learned and are able to do as a result of their college attendance. The Bush administration was reported to be contemplating a similar set of proposals, not only as its position on reauthorization of the HEA but also as a key part of the president's campaign platform for the 2004 election (Burd, 2003a).

These proposals were thought to offer a response to a public aware of the importance of higher education to individual life chances in modern society but frustrated about student fees rising much faster than typical incomes. They also react to a taxpayer and business community skeptical of the efficiency of academic institutions (Boehner and McKeon, 2003). Lurking here too is a conflict in values. Traditional academic concerns with certain kinds of scholarship and emphases in education that are seen by some outsiders as esoteric or even subversive are at odds with claims that public priorities in higher education should focus more on efficiency and skills and knowledge that have clear relevance to jobs and other primary functions of citizens.

## Historical Perspective

Although federal interest in some of these matters is not unprecedented, the recent proposals go beyond anything seriously advanced before in terms of scope and reach. A bit of history provides some perspective. During the Reagan years, the U.S. secretary of education, William Bennett, shocked the higher education world by aggressively criticizing colleges and universities (most prominently private ones) for inefficiency and particularly for tuition increases he thought were excessive. He even argued that generously funded federal student aid programs facilitated the questioned price increases (Cook, 1998). This opening salvo did not lead to serious legislative proposals, but it seems to have paved the way for subsequent forays into previously unexplored waters for federal policymakers (Mumper, 1996).

In the early 1990s, after a round of sharp tuition increases following the economic downturn of that period, influential members of Congress (mostly Republicans led by Representative McKeon) rekindled criticism of what they considered excessive growth in higher education's costs and prices and again noted that federal student aid programs might be fueling it by helping students pay the prices charged. Although stronger regulatory action was discussed, the end result was the creation of a commission to look into the causes of cost and price growth in higher education. Some accused the commission of being captured by higher education interests, particularly those of independent colleges (Cook, 1998). The Cost Commission issued a report in 1997 that carefully described the various factors affecting higher education expenditure trends and called mainly for clearer reporting and explaining by colleges and universities about their finances and why they charge the prices they do (Cook, 1998). There has been a federal effort over the intervening years to get institutions to report these data in forms that would better facilitate comparisons, but progress has been slow. The Cost Commission's report appeared after the period of sharp tuition increases had largely subsided. Tuition hikes moderated further as the economy boomed in the late 1990s; the issue lay largely dormant until the economy sagged in 2001, when college prices again began to soar.

On a slightly different front but also pertinent to the current debate was another, more aggressive, federal foray into the business of higher education in the 1990s. In the late 1980s and early 1990s, the federal student aid programs were plagued by high rates of student dropout and default on federally guaranteed loans (Cook, 1998). Although much of the problem was concentrated in the for-profit trade school sector, which aggressively enrolled students with a high risk of dropout and helped them apply for loans, federal policies enacted as part of the 1992 reauthorization of the HEA cast a broad net. A set of administrative regulations and procedures was developed under the authority of the 1992 HEA for the ostensible purpose of better ensuring the integrity and fiscal probity of *all* postsecondary institutions whose loan default rates and various other markers exceeded relatively low thresholds (Cook, 1998). Offending institutions, whose numbers would have included a significant number of nonprofit colleges, both private and public, were to be audited in depth and then could be subject to sanctions that could include the cutoff of their eligibility to enroll federally aided students. In deference to concerns about excessive federal intrusiveness into institutional oversight, the whole process was to be administered through "state postsecondary review entities," which in many states were to be closely associated with existing state higher education oversight boards. States would almost certainly have followed the federal lead in regard to eligibility criteria for their own student aid programs had this federal policy approach survived.

As is well documented by Cook (1998), the whole initiative was stopped in its tracks by an unusually aggressive campaign of substantive and political opposition waged during the implementation phase by the Washington higher education lobbying establishment, led in this case by the group representing private institutions—the National Association of Independent Colleges and Universities (NAICU). On the one hand, as Cook emphasizes, this shows the potential of the higher education lobby when its tactics are well designed for the situation. But the fact that legislation passed Congress strongly asserting policy concerns about the linkage between federal student aid and completion rates and that included nonprofit colleges and universities in its reach is significant. It is likely that some version of this battle will be replayed in 2004, when the HEA is again up for reauthorization.

## Implications of Recent Proposals

Now let us turn to specific implications of the recent accountability proposals for private colleges and universities. In regard to pricing, although tuition in the public sector has increased at a faster rate in recent years as state support has stagnated (College Board, 2002), private colleges and universities are often the objects of greatest attention because, lacking direct public subsidies, their prices are generally far higher than those of public schools. The average figure for tuition and fees in four-year private colleges and universities in 2002–2003 was $18,273, compared to $4,081 in four-year public schools. Private sector "sticker prices" run as high as $35,000 per academic year (College Board, 2002, p. 5).

Although these tuition figures are imposing, they do not typically cover the full cost of education at private colleges, which is subsidized in greater or lesser degree by gift and endowment income. A high percentage of private college students receive some form of financial aid, and a substantial fraction of this comes from the schools themselves. In the aggregate, tuition revenue at private colleges and universities covers only about 62 percent of the cost of education, with the remainder coming from endowments, annual giving, and the like (National Association of Independent Colleges and Universities, 2003b). These percentages vary greatly in private institutions, depending on the relative importance of endowments and gifts in supporting institutional expenditures. Unlike the much better-known Harvards, Princetons, and Williamses, with endowments in the billions, a large majority of private colleges and universities have minimal or modest endowments and are highly dependent on annual tuition and related student income. They typically spend far less per student than the elite schools (Breneman, 1994). These lesser-known private colleges generally enroll many students from modest personal circumstances and have proportions of ethnic minority students comparable to public four-year institutions (National Association of Independent Colleges and Universities, 2003b). They can hardly contemplate losing access to federally aided students.

Although the elite privates might be able to weather a period of mandatory reduced tuition increases by drawing on their large endowments (though even some of them are showing signs of financial pressure [Pulley, 2002]), the great majority of private colleges would have little alternative but to cut costs in response to pressure on their main income source. The main alternatives for cost cutting lie in personnel (fewer faculty and staff and minimal pay growth), institutionally funded aid to students, equipment purchases such as computers and related infrastructure, and building expenditures, including maintenance. It would be difficult for these hardworking institutions to sustain quality and student diversity in such an environment. Moreover, if they lost ground to competing public institutions as a result, burdens on the public purse would grow.

Federal policies might more productively work to slow cost and price growth in higher education by pursuing more positive approaches than simply punishing institutions for seeking to sustain essential revenue growth. One promising direction lies in making prices in higher education work more effectively, as they normally would in a competitive market, to support price discipline among competitors by making true prices clearer to students and their families. The main issues here involve simplifying the student aid system so that students can better gauge what they will actually pay (stated tuition price minus financial aid) at the different schools in their choice set at an early stage in the decision-making process (Kane, 1999). Another possibly fruitful direction could lie in support of research and development on instructional technologies that might make it possible to teach more students per faculty without sacrificing quality of learning.

The evident federal interest in mandating improved student retention and completion rates is a new wrinkle. In the past, to the extent that federal policy was concerned with this issue, it worked through simply aiding needy students financially so they did not drop out or slow their progress and, in limited ways, by supporting special programs of academic assistance to disadvantaged students. There is evidence that degree completion rates have been on a declining trend in recent years, partly because colleges have enrolled more disadvantaged students. Mortenson reports that the nationwide five-year institutional graduation rate—defined as the proportion of students graduating in this time from the institution at which they initially enrolled—for four-year private colleges and universities fell from 59.5 percent in 1983 to 55.1 percent in 2001, while it dropped from 52.2 percent to 41.9 percent over the same period for four-year publics (Mortenson, 2002a, p. 4). Moreover, there is evidence that private colleges tend to produce higher graduation rates, even when relevant student characteristics are taken into account (National Association of Independent Colleges and Universities, 2003b). Thus, as Frank Newman, head of the Futures Project, pointed out in recent congressional testimony, only about half of four-year college students complete their degrees within five years of entrance, whereas the comparable figure for low-income students is below 20 percent (Burd, 2003a; Newman, 2003). Two-year colleges generally have even lower degree completion rates.

Surely, there is room for improvement here, but it is far from clear that the types of federal mandates currently contemplated will do much good. Indeed, they may well do harm. For one thing, the strong incentives to cut costs built into the contemplated federal legislation would themselves make it harder for institutions to provide the supports known to be necessary to improve retention and graduation rates (see Newman, 2003). Perhaps most important, student retention and graduation rates are powerfully influenced by the characteristics of the students admitted. It is no surprise that elite schools report graduation rates above 90 percent, while colleges enrolling high proportions of less advantaged students tend to have far lower success rates. If a particular institution is under pressure to improve retention and graduation rates (and its applicant pool permits), the surest route to success is to reduce the "risk profile" of the students admitted. Some private institutions with adequate pools of qualified applicants would be able to adjust their admissions in this way, whereas others less blessed with such applicants would not, which would further stratify student bodies socioeconomically across these different types of schools. This is surely a socially undesirable result. At a minimum, one would hope that the federal mandates would be designed, despite the difficulties, to take account of student educational characteristics at entry in setting persistence and graduation standards to mitigate these powerful "creaming" pressures.

Although there is probably no substitute for increased resources, if student educational deficits are to be remedied during the postsecondary years, an approach to the retention-graduation issue that built on market mechanisms would likely be more fruitful than a pure mandate. Policy's key lever here would be to require publication and active distribution to prospective students of schools' graduation rates, compared to peers enrolling students with similar entering characteristics. Market forces should see to it that better-performing schools attract more applicants, and lower performers would be induced to reallocate resources, to the extent possible, in order to improve persistence and graduation. Private institutions would generally fare well in such comparisons, compared to publics, but some would look better than others. The methodological debate on precisely how to match characteristics and institutions would inevitably be complex and politically charged. Still, an approach along these lines might well be where the debate begun by the proposed mandate to improve graduation rates ends up. In this scenario, public priorities thought to be insufficiently attended to by academics on their own would be advanced via careful supplementation of market forces by a policy mandate to collect and distribute consumer-relevant information in a controlled format.

The third area of concern in the federal accountability proposals currently under discussion is that of the objective assessment of student learning. Like improved graduation rates, if properly conceived and executed, improvements in this area are desirable, though not a top priority of academics left to their own devices. (They tend to believe that end-of-course grades provide adequate and customized assessments of student learning.) Considerable research and development activity has occurred in the field of undergraduate learning assessment over the past fifteen years or so, and some promising approaches are beginning to move forward (Reisberg, 2000; Benjamin and Chun, 2003; Chapters Five and Six). Independent colleges and universities have played an important role in these developments (National Association of Independent Colleges and Universities, 2003a). The most promising approaches are still in the early development and testing stages, however, and the whole enterprise is fraught with complexity (Shavelson and Huang, 2003; also Chapter Six).

Reasonable federal help to the "industry" to move these research and development projects forward would be positive, but urgent mandates with tight deadlines could well produce undesirable side effects. These include pressure to use off-the-shelf tests that are not well designed for each institution's curricular and student characteristics and related pressures for premature national standardization of instruments to facilitate interinstitutional comparisons in the name of accountability. Such developments would be particularly unfortunate for private higher education, which in the United States has responded to the needs of a diverse society via a great diversity of institutional forms, curricula, and approaches. The sector's performance under rigorous market conditions, including the demise of some institutions, suggests strongly that the necessary mechanisms are in place for a very considerable measure of social accountability via the market. It seems wise for public policies on assessment to work sensitively with this socially desirable diversity rather than creating powerful pressures to narrow it. Eventually, one might hope that self-regulatory mechanisms such as accreditation could be used to create professional incentives for the various types of institutions to show credible evidence that their students acquire the knowledge, skills, and capacities that their curricula and programs claim to instill (see Chapter Four). Competitive forces can be expected to do much of the rest of the work of ensuring institutional accountability for what students learn.

In summary, the new federal pressures are likely to be a mixed bag in terms of the social desirability of their effects on private colleges and universities. Some pressure on colleges to be more attentive to student learning and completion rates and to costs is not a bad thing. But effective price controls will almost certainly have an impact on educational quality, particularly among institutions that can least afford this, and very likely on student diversity, unless heretofore unknown shifts in the technology and efficiency of teaching and learning somehow occur. Premature, narrowly conceived mandates on student persistence and graduation and learning assessment would likely produce serious and undesirable side effects for diversity, both in the distribution of student characteristics across institutions and in the range of institutional forms themselves. More desirable approaches to all the issues of concern would build on competitive market mechanisms that are already strong in American higher education, increasing the capacity of the market to allocate efficiently by improving the quality and distribution of decision-relevant information. Government policy also has a role to play in supporting industrywide research and development initiatives and best-practices dissemination in areas like student assessment, uses of instructional technology, and student retention strategies.

## Conclusion

The challenge today is to respond to new calls for accountability of private higher education without giving up the social benefits provided by the diversity, market accountability, and relative independence of these institutions. Private colleges and universities add a remarkable diversity of institutional forms and options to the U.S. higher education scene—a diversity not seen in most other nations with largely public systems. In a large, heterogeneous country and one becoming ever more diverse, this has always been seen as a strong, positive feature. Recent evidence shows that new private schools come on the scene about as frequently as old ones die off, suggesting substantial responsiveness to changing societal needs at a rate the public sector could never match. Indeed, private institutions are obliged to respond much more directly to market forces than are their public counterparts, plainly providing an important form of social accountability via responsiveness to student and other clients' desires and priorities.

To be sure, the wealthy, highly selective institutions that most people think of when they contemplate private higher education but that represent only a small percentage of all private colleges and universities and a modest share of the sector's enrollments are considerably more insulated from market forces in the sense of immediate threats to their survival. Yet even they compete vigorously on important dimensions and are not immune to changing societal needs by any means. The relative security of some of the private institutions provides some balance in the system, in terms of the values represented in the Accountability Triangle; these institutions can give greater play to academic concerns than either the other privates that are closer to the market or public institutions that must respond more directly to currently expressed public priorities, as well as increasingly to the market (Duderstadt and Womack, 2003). Having such priorities represented fairly strongly somewhere in the system also has social value; for example, elite private colleges are crucial players in carrying on the liberal arts tradition in undergraduate education (Breneman, 1994), and elite private universities are disproportionately represented among the very best doctoral programs in the humanities. More generally, whether they always use it or not, these institutions have greater latitude than either less advantaged privates or than most public institutions to take risks in exploring new fields and educational approaches that might or might not make it in the market or cause political fallout. These types of values may be difficult to square with aggressive accountability measures if the latter are not very thoughtfully conceived.

The major point here is that public accountability policies will do the most good by working with the market forces that private colleges and universities are naturally responsive to rather than forcing the adoption of narrowly conceived approaches that work against some of the diversity-rewarding tendencies of markets. State and federal policies should focus on researching and promoting adoption of cost-reducing best practices, including in the area of instructional technology, but mostly on merging accountability and market-oriented information policies. This approach would allow well-informed student consumers to select the combination of net price, institutional characteristics, learning goals and achievements, and quality and efficiency as indicated by retention and graduation rates that best suits their individual needs and desires. Such a policy regime would serve public and private colleges and universities, as well as the interests of students and society, in a varied, dynamic, and responsive system of higher education.

### Notes

1.  The federal government provides institutional support to only a few specialized schools. Even state governments, which do support public institutions through direct appropriations, provide more than $5 billion annually to higher education via student aid, the vast majority of which is tenable at accredited private colleges and universities (National Association of State Student Grant and Aid Programs, 2003).

2.  In the Zumeta (1996) typology, the other four states in Burke's sample with regular direct state support for private institutions were all classified as central planning or central planning-market competitive hybrid states (p. 397).

# Chapter Three

# Accountability and Governance

*Richard C. Richardson Jr. and Thomas R. Smalling*

Concerns about accountability are prompting elected and appointed officials in a growing number of states to review higher education governance arrangements and institutional decision making. At the root of such concerns is a growing reluctance to have system performance represent the aggregate of institutional decisions about how best to maximize the professional aspirations of administrative leaders and faculty. Conceptually, accountability requires expectations, roles and responsibilities, performance measures, and regular assessment. Although it is, in theory, possible for a state to adopt accountability legislation without providing guidance on priorities or performance measures (as evidenced by New Mexico legislation scheduled to take effect in 2003, North Dakota's 2001 "flexibility with accountability" legislation, and current Florida legislation requiring that 10 percent of the universities' appropriated dollars be subject to performance-based budgeting measures yet to be determined), this approach leaves the responsibility for accountability to individual institutions or their lobbying organizations—an approach that seems unlikely to satisfy public concerns about the return on public investments in higher education.

More consistent with emerging state trends is the recent action by Governor Taft of Ohio in appointing a Commission on Higher Education and the Economy and directing the commission to answer three key questions (Taft, 2003):

1. What should the state's goals and expectations be for the higher education system based on the needs of students, employers, and the economy?
2. How should Ohio's higher education institutions be structured, organized, governed, and financed so as to best promote the state's goals and expectations?
3. How should the higher education system be held accountable for meeting the state's goals and expectations?

The process through which public investment in higher education is transformed into outcomes and performance is *governance*. We use this term broadly in the sense proposed by Marginson and Considine, who define *governance* as encompassing relationships among academic divisions within the institution, as well as linkages between the internal community and the larger worlds of government, business, and the community. From this perspective, governance defines the environment within which teaching, learning, and service occur. Governance also affects the future direction of the higher education enterprise through decision making, resource allocation, and assignment of missions and goals (Marginson and Considine, 2000).

The governance task of responding to the needs of external stakeholders is complicated by internal structures and processes that create an uneasy balance of power. Executives and governing boards responsible to state government through hierarchical lines of authority must seek responsiveness from tenured faculty who exercise board-delegated authority on academic issues. In many states, faculty members also exercise significant political leverage through collective bargaining and through direct external participation in the political process at state and national levels. The departments and programs in which they reside are the basic building blocks of internal governance. They can also represent the principal stumbling blocks to better and more competitive relationships with external constituents and higher education markets.

The purpose of this chapter is to consider how differing rules of the game influence accountability and performance. We begin by proposing a governance model that links state policy to higher education system performance. We then focus on selected elements of the model, including state and federal priorities, system design, and fiscal policies, to show how rules in varying combinations provide different levers for influencing institutional behaviors in purposive ways. We next consider the issues and opportunities presented by faculty senates and collective bargaining as key elements of internal governance that often have significant presence in the external policy world. We conclude by summarizing the implications of this analysis for designing governance arrangements that support accountability for performance in the attainment of public priorities.

## Policy Decisions, Governance, and Performance

Governance provides the vital link between purposive state policy and responsive institutional leadership. In essence, the priorities that colleges and universities pursue, the leadership they encourage or tolerate, and their response to such system unifiers as communication, collaboration, and accountability are significantly influenced by "rules of the game," that is, by the written and unwritten constraints within which colleges and universities pursue organizational advantage according to their respective values (North, 1990). Governors, legislators, and state administrative agencies establish, alter, or reinforce explicit or implicit priorities and rules of the game through the policy process. These rules represent the principal means that governments use to influence institutional accountability and associated outcomes (Richardson, Bracco, Callan, and Finney, 1999). Rules may emphasize regulation, rely on structured markets, or defer to professional values (Clark, 1983; Williams, 1995). The model depicted in Figure 3.1 provides a way of thinking about how state governance links policy decisions to institutional governance and ultimately to the performance indicators that represent evidence of accountability.

No two states have exactly the same rules. While governments are seeking to influence higher education behavior and performance, the higher education community is working equally hard to influence policy. Professionals within a system adopt the behaviors they believe most likely to further institutional goals under the prevailing rules of the game (Richardson and Martinez, 2002).

• *Policy environments* are made up of elements that are relatively stable in the short term (population demographics, history, geography, political culture). The costs to modify others (state

**Figure 3.1.  The Role of Governance
in Linking Policy to Performance**

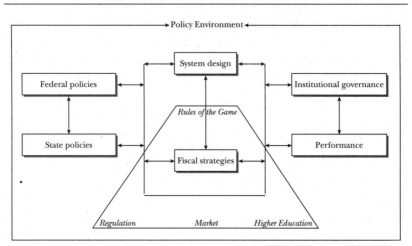

constitutions) are very high. Political culture and traditions determine whether elected officials believe they can or should revise policies aimed at influencing higher education performance. The relative authority of the executive and legislative branches of state government and the constitutional or statutory status of institutions also play an important role.

- *Federal policies* establish priorities and determine the amounts and purposes of fiscal appropriations; they can mandate accountability measures or require collaboration. In addition to their unique impact on system behaviors, they may also enhance or moderate the effect of related state policies, depending on the degree of alignment.

- *State policies* reflect less stable aspects of the policy environment, including economic cycles, changes in political leadership, court mandates, and the impact of popular preferences for a changing mix of available public services. The responses of institutional leaders may not reflect those preferred by elected state officials, who must find ways of encouraging them to seek an appropriate balance between public priorities, consumer needs (the market), and the goals valued by the higher education community.

Responsibility for maintaining this balance is at the heart of accountability concerns.

• *Rules of the game* are the principal means governments use to influence processes and outcomes in higher education. As regulator, the state provides facilities and operating support and tells institutions how to achieve state priorities. When steering by the use of market mechanisms, the state establishes priorities, creates policies to support priorities, and holds institutions accountable but does not tell them how priorities should be pursued. States defer to higher education when they provide resources and trust institutional governance to create the appropriate balance between public priorities and professional values (Richardson, Bracco, Callan, and Finney, 1999).

Rules of the game take two principal forms: (1) system design and (2) fiscal policy:

1. *System design* includes the number and type of service providers and the missions assigned to each; the characteristics and powers of agencies in the interface between government and providers; the information systems that collect, organize, and report data essential to understanding and influencing performance; available technology and its uses; and the role assigned to the private sector.

2. *Fiscal policy* includes the amount of operating support and the regulations that apply to its distribution, institutional autonomy in determining capital needs and in securing funding, the amount and use of incentive funding, types and amounts of student assistance, and tax policy.

• *Institutional governance* reflects the impact of rules of the game on institutional leadership, priorities, communication, collaboration, and accountability. Rules of the game may afford higher education professionals considerable freedom to pursue institutional goals, or they may direct or encourage institutions to pay greater attention to public priorities.

• *Performance* reflects the outcomes produced by aggregated institutional behaviors within a state system of higher education in relation to such goals as access, choice, participation, quality degree completion, preparation, and economic development.

In the discussion that follows, we focus on priorities, system design, fiscal policies, and institutional governance as the principal levers that create state capacity for defining and assessing accountability in relation to higher education performance.

## Federal and State Policies and Priorities

All states share a common federal policy environment characterized by a constitution that is silent on education and a context in which fiscal policies have been the predominant strategy for pursuing national priorities (see Chapter Two). During the past decade, federal priorities have focused in particular on consumer protection, transparency in reporting, accountability, and collaboration. The impact of these priorities in any given state depends on political culture, priorities, fiscal policies, and system design. Currently, the Council for Higher Education Accreditation's (CHEA) Reauthorization Agenda for Accreditation and Accountability Reform and the proposed changes to the Higher Education Reauthorization Act extending principles from the No Child Left Behind Act to higher education institutions suggest a continuing federal agenda involving accountability (see Chapter Four).

In a general sense, most states have priorities for higher education. Officials hope their systems will provide access, quality, equity, and choice, with some reasonable degree of efficiency. They also expect contributions to economic development (Richardson, Bracco, Callan, and Finney, 1999). A growing number of states assess current performance on related outcomes regularly and track changes over time. About half of all states have adopted strategies that link some part of the annual operating appropriation, usually very minor, to institutional success in meeting targets for improvement. At present, this comes very close to "state-of-the-art" accountability.

State governance that supports accountability benefits from a clear understanding of how priorities are established and by whom. The governor, the legislature, or the members of system governing or coordinating boards can define priorities in consultation with their respective constituencies and with each other. Both elected and appointed leaders have a responsibility and a role. The challenge for governance is to coordinate priorities arising from different actors and to resolve inevitable conflicts. Developing priorities is not a onetime task. Ideally, priorities are revisited annually or biannually as part of the resource allocation process.

To achieve effect, priorities once identified must be communicated to higher education providers, to the general public, and to the policy community. Ideally, they are communicated in ways that identify the gaps between present and desired performance and provide incentives for addressing them. Georgia's Special Funding Initiatives and the Illinois Performance-Based Incentive System focused on teaching and learning and provided additional funds "at the margin" to recognize high performance and improvement. Segmental responsibilities for making improvements also need to be clear. Arizona, for example, identifies transfer as a priority. The state's accountability scheme holds community colleges responsible for addressing this priority but leaves public universities, on which effective transfer largely depends, without specified accountability for results.

## Rules of the Game

Through their constitutions or statutes, states create higher education systems and define the arrangements for coordinating and governing them. They invest in infrastructure to provide institutions with the capacity for attracting competitive research grants or to provide training opportunities attractive to the types of employers they hope to attract. States determine who will collect information about higher education systems and whether data systems will have the capacity to track individual students and to integrate information collected by the federal government. They determine responsibility for reporting information and whether the public will have access to institutional outcomes beyond those mandated by Congress.

States determine the role of their independent institutions and whether they will be eligible to receive public funds (see Chapter Two). States determine the amount of funds available for capital and operating purposes and the basis on which funds are distributed. They also determine the amount and type of additional aid available to students and the degree of coordination between state and federal programs. And they award incentive funds for special initiatives such as distance education or distribute all funds incrementally in ways that support "business as usual." All of these actions occur by design or default.

Taken together, these rules of the game contribute in powerful ways either to sustaining institutions as they have evolved over time or to shaping institutional behaviors in ways that respond to new needs and emerging priorities. During much of the past fifty years, the issue of state governance has been framed as a choice between institutional autonomy and state regulation. There is now very clearly a third way. Institutions can be held accountable for contributing to the attainment of state priorities through market practices that foster entrepreneurial activity and competition without telling boards of trustees or their chief executive officers which priorities to address or how to pursue them. Performance funding, public reports on institutional performance, incentive funding, and aid to student consumers can all be strategies that call attention to the outcomes a state identifies as important (see Chapter Ten). The trick is to define rules that are mutually supportive of the priorities a state believes to be important. We return to this point several times in the sections that follow on system design and fiscal policies.

## System Design

All states have higher education systems developed through some combination of planning and historical accident. The components of these systems—community and technical colleges, comprehensive colleges and universities, research universities, and independent institutions—are similar across states, but their responsibilities for providing educational services and the arrangements for coordination and governance vary widely. In seven states (Florida, Illinois, Maryland, Michigan, New Jersey, New York, Pennsylvania), independent sectors have been incorporated in plans for providing higher education services (see Chapter Two). In most of the rest, students attending independent institutions may be eligible for some form of state assistance, but the institutions do not receive funds directly as part of the state design for and response to higher education needs.

States with higher education systems designed to respond to public priorities for access, choice, career training, baccalaureate degrees, graduate education, research, and service perform better on most indicators and are more cost-effective than those that have evolved largely as a result of the aspirations of individual institutions or separate communities. New Mexico is an example of a system that has evolved primarily as a product of institutional initiatives and community choice. The system is composed of a bewildering array of university branch campuses, former technical institutes, two-year and community colleges operating under different legislatively approved statutes, and rurally located regional universities struggling for market share under fiscal policies that reward enrollment growth and equalize student costs across research and comprehensive institutions. The system may have very high costs yet underutilize several of its campuses; there is no coordinated approach to determining access for place-bound students. By contrast, the systems in Illinois and New Jersey involve a much larger element of central planning. Both Illinois and New Jersey receive higher grades on the *Measuring Up* report cards and are more cost-effective (see Chapter Ten).

Students' preparation for college hinges on collaboration between higher and basic education in setting standards, offering transition programs, and preparing teachers. Increasingly, such federal programs as GEAR UP require collaboration across systems as well. States like New York that do well in improving student preparation approach preparation issues from a statewide perspective that fosters collaboration and partnerships across institutions and sectors. States that do less well on this indicator are more likely to have systems in which preparation and transfer initiatives are left to the discretion of individual institutions.

A president of Indiana University successfully blocked the development of a system of comprehensive community colleges in the late 1960s and early 1970s. The state consistently scored low on access and participation measures. A recent design change created collaboration between the state's only comprehensive community college and a statewide system of vocational and technical institutes that has begun to address this problem. West Virginia changed its governance system in 2000 from a system governing board to institutional boards, with a policy board in the interface. Now the governor is threatening to separate community colleges, as was done in Kentucky, if their host institutions do not do a better job of managing them so they meet state priorities.

Most systems need to change in small ways over time to respond to new needs and circumstances. Illinois and New Jersey strengthened the authority of institutional boards to make regional colleges and universities more entrepreneurial and more competitive in a market environment. By doing so, they also changed the environment for their research universities and independent sector. Pennsylvania created a governing board for its comprehensive colleges and universities to remove them from the close regulation of a state bureaucracy. Texas realigned its four-year colleges and universities, partly to provide struggling Hispanic-serving institutions with a closer relationship to the state's flagship universities. Colorado has evolved into a state system made up largely of community colleges in an effort to equalize opportunities and costs in a state characterized by significant geographic barriers and vast resource differentials. One opportunity made possible by this series of small adjustments over time is the Colorado Electronic College—a system innovation that pools resources across state-funded community colleges to better deliver distance education to all residents.

System change, of course, is not an end in itself. And not all system change produces better performance; some changes may even produce unacceptably high political costs. Florida is the prime example of dramatic system redesign in the absence of consensus about need or consequences. California is an example of the opposite extreme. Its 1960 Master Plan, once the envy of the world, has begun to fray around the edges, but the agreements and commitments on which it was based remain largely intact, despite a series of plan reviews and any number of institutionally or legislatively sponsored change initiatives.

## Interface Agencies

A comprehensive system of higher education providers has to be linked to state government through some type of interface. Here the possibilities are almost endless. The task of understanding this element of system design is complicated by the considerable variations found within the planning agency and coordinating board types, as well as the frequent modifications that states make to forms and powers. For purposes of this chapter, we focus on the environment for accountability provided by differing ways of linking institutions to state government without trying to classify states according to the ways they manage such tasks as mission review, program approval, and budget review. Such a classification can be found in the *ECS Sourcebook* (Education Commission of the States, 1997).

Highly regulated systems provide weak environments for accountability to public priorities. In such systems, states tell institutions what they should do and how to do it, so the state bureaucracy is really accountable for performance; all that can be expected from institutions is compliance, as enforced by audits. Most if not all states recognize this fact of life and have placed at the minimum some type of system governing board between state bureaucracy and institutional administration. The most prominent large-state exception to this general rule is Michigan, where all four-year institutions enjoy constitutional status. Presidents and governing boards (three of which are popularly elected) represent institutional interests directly to state government; there is no effective interface agency charged with representing the public interest. In theory, institutional governing boards are supposed to represent the public interest, as well as professional values, but in practice, as many have noted, they do a much better job of the latter than the former. Elected officials in Michigan often refer to higher education as the fourth branch of state government.

Many of the larger states group all institutions under no more than two or three segmental or consolidated governing boards, the members of which are appointed by the governor with some sort of legislative concurrence. Segmental or system governing boards and their chief executives in New York and California regularly interact with their respective governors and legislators. In California, there have been formal arrangements for spelling out the governors' expectations as the quid pro quo for support for funding appropriations. Although the process is not as formalized in New York, it works in very much the same way. In both states, community colleges are primarily accountable to their local sponsors, with statewide oversight provided by a coordinating or governing board with direct links to state government.

States with a single board governing all degree-granting institutions provide the least complex environments for accountability but not necessarily the most powerful. Boards that govern institutions must often choose between their allegiance to the professional values and priorities of higher education administrators and faculty and the broader values and priorities of external stakeholders, including state government. Happily, these are sometimes the same, but there is always the question of what happens when they are not. Most of the states with this type of interface have small systems, as in Utah and Hawaii. Where the system is large and has constitutional status, as in Georgia, additional issues arise. Community colleges may not fare well in the internal competition for resources and remain underutilized. Such systems have as much capacity to resist as to embrace accountability for state priorities. And the regular release of information related to accountability has not been one of the Georgia system's strengths.

Accurate information, consistently available both to policy leaders and to the general public, is essential to the effective use of market mechanisms and to any reasonable definition of accountability. This is one major reason why such states as Illinois, Texas, Ohio, and Washington have placed a coordinating board with the authority and resources to collect and disseminate information in the interface between institutional and system governing boards and state government. The governor, with the advice and consent of the senate, appoints these boards. They typically manage the process of defining goals and priorities, assigning missions, and approving new programs in ways that balance the public interest against institutional and system values. Most important for accountability, they serve as independent and reliable sources of information about higher education performance in relation to statewide goals and priorities.

Coordinating boards and planning agencies with the capacity to collect data and report information can encounter significant challenges in carrying out responsibilities for generating regular performance and accountability reports. Richard Wagner, former executive director of the Illinois Board of Higher Education, was fond of pointing out that coordinating boards had no football teams, students, or alumni and that in every legislature there was, at any given time, a bill sitting that would do away with the board. And the position of state higher education executive officers (SHEEOs) is very demanding. SHEEOs must constantly walk a tightrope between the priorities and concerns of elected state leaders and those of the governing boards and presidents. Success in achieving the correct balance under one governor may quickly evaporate under a successor with different priorities. Difficulty in finding the right balance between advocacy and accountability is at the root of many coordinating board and planning agency problems.

Over the past decade, the role of the interface agency (either governing or coordinating board) has been shifting from one of advocacy to a greater emphasis on oversight and public accountability. Higher education officials are becoming increasingly more sensitive to changing interests of the various stakeholders and to the shifting demands of the market (Association of Governing Boards, 2001). In many settings, this shift has led to confrontations over issues involving the degree of faculty participation and autonomy. Although the actions and intentions of boards may be questioned, in the final analysis the interface agency is primarily accountable to the public purposes a state has defined and to the needs of its various stakeholders. Through exercising its accountability role, the interface agency can serve as a check on mission drift and the pursuit of institution-specific goals that are not aligned with state priorities (National Center for Public Policy and Higher Education, 2003b).

## Fiscal Policy

Although most federal funds continue to be awarded to students on the basis of need, there is now less emphasis on need-based grants and more on subsidized loans. Clearly, low-income and underserved populations remain a federal concern, but the middle class has been the focus of most new initiatives. Federal changes in fiscal policy have been better aligned with the policies of high-aid, high-tuition states than with states that have pursued keeping tuition low as their access strategy. Because of a focus on consumer choice and fiscal incentives, federal initiatives have largely favored the market as the principal accountability mechanism, but market incentives for both research and educational services have increasingly been accompanied by substantial and growing regulation. For much of the past decade, the federal government has at best been unresponsive to the concerns of higher educational professionals and at worst actively hostile.

Performance funding, discussed in detail in Chapter Ten, is the most obvious example of allocating institutional operating support in ways that reflect defined state priorities for performance. Aligning fiscal policies to support accountability must extend beyond the use of performance incentives. Most state dollars are awarded to support operating costs. The institutional maintenance approach, as reflected in formula funding schemes used by such states as Texas, Illinois, and New Mexico, awards dollars on the basis of student enrollments in majors grouped according to estimated credit-hour costs. The incentives in this approach reward institutions for enrolling students in programs in which revenues exceed costs. But paying for enrollments may focus institutional efforts on admissions rather than graduations. It may also encourage mission drift, as institutions add programs perceived as aids to recruiting. Cost-based formula funding and its close cousin, incremental funding, benefit those institutions at the top of the prestige hierarchy most. Formula and incremental funding approaches are not supportive of accountability, whether administered by a coordinating board, dictated by a master plan as in California, or maintained largely as the unexamined consequence of political culture and tradition as in Michigan.

A number of states, including New Jersey, have chosen to divorce operational funding from enrollments, investing heavily in student aid, giving institutions greater autonomy in setting tuitions, and allowing them to retain the tuition they generate. Market approaches benefit from defined goals and information about performance. Under market-oriented rules of the game, institutional accountability is measured first by success in attracting revenues that offset costs and secondarily by the attainment of implicit or explicit performance targets established through the governance process. Market approaches are not a panacea for maintaining accountability. Because higher education leaders are expected to pursue institutional advantage, any set of rules produces unintended, as well as desired, consequences. Access suffers in New Jersey because institutions receive operating appropriations without regard to enrollment changes. To offset that disadvantage, the state has undertaken statewide initiatives aimed at improving college access, community college transfer, and K–12 and higher education collaboration.

States are clearly struggling to find a combination of regulation and market reliance that will produce the results they want.

States capable of fine-tuning their systems through a series of changes of the sort that have been made in Illinois, Indiana, Kentucky, New York, and West Virginia seem advantaged in this effort over states like Florida and California, which seem stuck with major transformation or maintaining systems that no longer seem to offer cost-effective approaches to contemporary issues. The governance diagram presented earlier suggests the complexity of changing a system in which everything is linked to everything else.

States also use infrastructure support and special incentives to promote institutional collaboration and business–higher education partnerships that are aimed at economic development. States like Vermont, South Carolina, New Jersey, and New York offer prospective employers some combination of university research centers, custom workforce training programs, tax incentives, and a statewide coordinating agency that simplifies negotiations and ensures the delivery of promised services and support. States like Colorado and Washington combine incentive grants and infrastructure investment to enhance capabilities for the delivery of distance education that transcends the service boundaries and instructional capabilities of any single institution. Most states want economic competitiveness and the use of technology to deliver educational services to citizens who do not reside within commuting distance of a traditional campus. The attainment of these goals efficiently requires more market-oriented fiscal policies and more collaboration across institutions than is usually present in states where system design emphasizes institutional maintenance.

## Institutional Governance

Institutions are increasingly confronted by fiscal constraints, concerns about mission alignment with state priorities, and pressures to improve performance in a competitive, consumer-driven market. These forces have sparked renewed interest in institutional accountability measures that have consequently and understandably led to greater scrutiny of institutional decision making and escalating calls for a reevaluation and restructuring of internal governance arrangements.

Although under assault from a variety of directions, the idea of shared governance remains an important contextual influence in any discussion of institutional decision making and account-ability. The concept of shared governance assigns specific rights and responsibilities to stakeholders, provides for a separation of powers, and establishes a structure and process for governing boards, administrators, faculty, and students to share responsibility for spe-cific undertakings (Hirsch, 2001). Political structures, partisan pol-itics, the pressures of state government, and the interests of multiple stakeholders have increasingly influenced the practice of shared governance.

## Faculty Participation

Central to any discussion of institutional governance and account-ability is the degree of faculty participation and influence in insti-tutional decision-making processes. The notion that faculty should have a role in institutional decision making is not often questioned. The degree and scope of that influence and the context in which it is exercised is a different matter. During most of the past century, faculty members in established universities governed themselves in academic matters, making key decisions about what should be taught, who should be hired, and how other key academic issues should be resolved. The faculty role in the emerging regional uni-versities and community colleges was much less clear. The suscep-tibility of these latter institutions to collective bargaining was, in large measure, attributable to their lack of acceptable arrange-ments for institutional governance.

Faculty involvement in governance occurs on three levels. The core of faculty governance is at the academic unit—the depart-ment or school. At this level, faculty generally have a significant role in decision making about such issues as curriculum develop-ment, promotion and tenure, the evaluation of teaching and of the quality of academic programs, posttenure review, and undergrad-uate education policy. The mechanisms for faculty governance at the department and school are the use of standing or ad hoc fac-ulty committees. Although the department chair or dean may have considerable authority in decision making, it is the faculty, pri-marily through committee work, who accomplish the majority of governance-related work processes (Duderstadt, 2001).

At the second or institutional level of governance, faculty generally have an advisory role in influencing faculty-related personnel policies, institutional priorities, budget priorities, intellectual property regulations, and the selection and evaluation of top administrators. Faculty participation in these issues occurs primarily through faculty senates or administration-faculty committees; final decisions are typically taken by institutional administration or by the governing board.

Faculty generally have a much more restricted role at the third, or system, level of governance because decisions here often affect multiple institutions. Faculty participation in decision making at this level occurs primarily through systemwide senates or committees, including some combination of system administrators and campus administrators and faculty (Center for Higher Education and Policy Analysis, 2003). Even though the degree of influence is diminished, systemwide senates can make important symbolic gestures, as in the example of the vote of "no confidence" in the State University of New York board of trustees in 1999 after they were accused of unilaterally developing new general-education requirements intended to mandate a traditionalist-style curriculum.

## Collective Bargaining

Collective bargaining, whether at the institution or system level, is often viewed as a means of addressing imbalances in decision-making authority between faculty and administrators. Opponents of faculty unions frequently charge that the confrontational character of collective bargaining inevitably weakens the sense of collegiality necessary for meaningful faculty involvement in academic governance issues. Proponents see unionization not simply as a strategy to improve wages and benefits but as a way of enhancing faculty voice in governance. The ideal requires both union and management to take on issues such as resource allocation, accountability systems, teacher assignment policies, evaluation practices, and pay structures, with an eye to the bottom line of improving institutional and system performance. Clearly, the dice are loaded against collective bargaining as a key contributor to effective accountability, particularly when negotiations are conducted outside normal institutional channels (as in New Jersey and New York, where the governor's office has this responsibility for all or part of public sector bargaining). Nevertheless, collective bargaining can play a role in accountability, as in New Jersey, where the contract required state colleges and universities to develop more rigorous procedures for promotion and tenure.

Apart from their role in institutional or system governance, faculty unions in states like New York and California are powerful actors in local and state political arenas. In Los Angeles, the faculty union for the community college system elects the board members with whom they subsequently negotiate collective bargaining agreements. No chancellor can safely make many decisions that incur their wrath. In New York, the governor and members of the legislature consider with care faculty union priorities and concerns, as does the mayor and council for New York City. On many issues, governing boards, administrators, and faculty unions are natural allies; where they are not, the advantage in states that are heavily organized not infrequently rests with the faculty unions. Because unions and senates often play complementary roles and exchange faculty leaders, governance arenas can be a way of building allies for advocacy of higher education priorities, as well as a way of resolving disputes over personnel deployment and resource allocation.

## Tenure

Tenure, in particular, has been attacked as an impediment to faculty accountability and a constraint on institutional capacity to optimize performance and meet market needs. Such concerns led the Arizona Board of Regents to implement a process of posttenure review in 1995. Since this early effort, posttenure review has emerged in many states as an approach for ensuring faculty responsibility and accountability and a means of getting rid of unproductive workers. Many public institutions now require some sort of performance review of tenured professors; however, initial reports on effectiveness are inconclusive (Montell, 2002). As institutions look to corporate models for guidance in an increasingly constrained fiscal environment, tenure seems likely to continue as an issue for administrators and board members concerned about high costs, institutional flexibility, and effective accountability mechanisms (Gilland, 1997).

## Other Stakeholders

Although discussions of governance have historically focused on governing boards, administration, and full-time faculty, other stakeholders have now emerged. Nonacademic staffs outnumber the faculty in many institutions yet do not have a comparable voice in governance. The same is true for non-tenure-eligible faculty, part-time faculty, adjunct faculty, and teaching or graduate assistants. Graduate assistants and adjunct faculty are, increasingly, the targets of organizing efforts by a variety of national unions, both in the public and private sectors. Included among the concerns promoting organization are difficulties in maintaining accountability for academic standards and performance when the workforce consists of exploited part-time people, many of whom do not even have office space, let alone the most marginal opportunity to participate in institutional governance.

## Governance and Accountability

Institutions of higher education have historically enjoyed considerable autonomy but are now facing a general decline in public trust. The growing popularity of performance indicators and outcome measurements forces institutions to concentrate on addressing accountability concerns when evaluating governance practices (Scott, 2001b). Effective faculty involvement in governance is both an important goal and a major challenge. Increasingly, faculty capacity to be directly involved in key decisions affecting institutional management has been questioned, as issues have become more complex and the time for resolving them shorter. Faculty members increasingly complain that participation in governance diverts them from teaching, research, and other scholarly activities. Many campuses have diluted the faculty role in governance by involving nonfaculty staff members and students; in some institutions, the involvement of nonfaculty members exceeds that of faculty. For these reasons, as well as changing faculty demographics, it is difficult to be sanguine about faculty governance as an approach for improving accountability. The role of "loyal opposition" seems more likely for faculty at most institutions.

The key question at the institutional level is whether the governance design promotes effective decision making and accountability processes. Faculty responsiveness to institutional efforts at improving accountability depends on the evaluation and rewards structure. The fragmentation of faculty members into academic disciplines and professional schools, combined with a growing emphasis on responding to the market, has contributed to an academic culture in which faculty loyalties are primarily to their disciplines, secondarily to their department or school, and last to their institution. The increasing specialization of faculty, the pressure of the market for their skills, and the meritocratic reward structure have dissolved institutional loyalty and stimulated more of a self-seeking attitude on the part of many faculty members (Duderstadt, 2001). Promotion and merit systems based primarily on publishing and research often divert attention from academic responsibilities commonly associated with such accountability measures as teaching productivity and service to institution and community.

Achieving a balanced accountability system under these conditions requires trust among faculty, administrators, state boards, elected policymakers, state budget officials, the media, and the public. Criteria for evaluating individual accountability should emerge directly from the institutional objectives. Delineating roles and establishing clear areas of responsibility and communication are prerequisites to better mechanisms for accountability.

## Conclusion

Governance and accountability are inextricably linked. Governance consists of the structures, processes, and related values that support a culture of mutual dependency. State governments provide the legal authority and contribute significantly to the resource base that makes the enterprise possible. Higher education systems provide vital services to taxpayers, including contributions to the knowledge base, preparation of a skilled workforce, economic development, and reinforcement of the values that preserve societal cohesion. For all of this to work, there must be ways of resolving conflicts among stakeholders equitably and promoting efficiency in the use of scarce resources. Management, however competent and empowered, cannot, in the absence of effective governance structures, impose accountability on professionals who prize autonomy above material gain.

In this chapter, we have described some of the characteristics of governance systems that seem to promote performance on those indicators that typically matter most to the policy community. Performance is, of course, the best evidence of accountability. In this concluding section, we summarize the characteristics of governance systems that promote accountability.

To begin, someone in a position of legal authority—a governor, the legislature, or an interface agency—must decide and communicate the outcomes for which higher education is to be held accountable. Beyond identifying the outcomes, there must be agreement on how they will be measured and what constitutes acceptable performance. System accountability is strengthened when elected leaders identify a small number of priorities for improving performance and communicate their expectations to the general public, as well as to institutional providers. Priorities should be reviewed regularly and modified as necessary to reflect new needs or changes in political leadership. The governance procedures through which priorities are established and reviewed should provide for balanced input from all stakeholders and should explicitly take into account federal issues and initiatives.

Next, states must evaluate the capacity of their higher education systems to achieve current priorities. Such issues as the availability and use of community colleges, the role of independent institutions, the efficacy of articulation and transfer policies, and the degree to which system design promotes collaboration, communication, and accountability should be evaluated periodically and the system modified as necessary to achieve new priorities in ways that encourage system synergy and efficiency. Comprehensive and planned systems of differentiated higher education institutions perform with greater effectiveness and versatility than those that reflect the historic accumulation of institutional aspirations.

System accountability is enhanced by an agency in the interface between state government and higher education providers that is charged primarily with representing the public interest. Ideally, such an agency is dominated neither by state government nor institutional allegiances and is able to provide leadership in crafting systemwide strategies for responding to public priorities without controlling or dominating the ways in which individual institutions choose to respond. Such interface agencies typically have a role in mission changes, program approval, resource allocation, information, and articulation. Of these, the most important function arguably involves information.

Effective accountability requires some agency, independent of the higher education community, with its own database and sufficient staff to generate credible reports on institutional performance in areas identified as important to the achievement of state priorities. Accountability reports should be generated on a regular basis and should be available both to elected officials and to the general public. Illinois and New Jersey have used an arrangement in which an independent interface agency generates a systemwide report, while each institution produces its own report in a format established by the agency. Beyond reporting on accountability, systems and their member institutions must use the results as a basis for developing improvement strategies.

Perhaps the most important step states can take to promote accountability is to align fiscal policies with preferred outcomes. Many state funding formulas continue to emphasize competition for new enrollments long after the priority has shifted to completion. The most common approach to encouraging institutional attention to state priorities is incentive funding. Unfortunately, such funds are usually made available only in good fiscal times when institutions are least in need of additional resources. Incentive funding is invariably the first casualty of hard times, making institutions leery of creating special programs that may soon have to be supported out of general revenues (see Chapter Ten). And market incentives work only if institutions are sufficiently free from regulation (tuition caps, for example) to respond effectively.

System leadership and synergy is especially important in pursuing initiatives related to distance education and economic development and in improving K–12 performance. Although individual institutions have developed excellent interventions in each of these areas, states make the most progress in improving performance when they create structures and processes that facilitate the collaboration of multiple actors across the bureaucratic boundaries of systems and governmental agencies. Apart from the complexities of coordinating multiple organizations, such efforts commonly involve the requirement for investments in infrastructure or personnel that can only be managed efficiently from an overall state perspective.

Finally, states must continuously seek, through the political process, the appropriate balance among market incentives, regulation, and deference to professional expertise. This is a central task of the governance structure. As needs and priorities change, so too does the most effective balance point. It is nonsense to talk about the market as a panacea. Federal and state governments create or recognize, subsidize, and regulate both markets and professions. The question is always about which combination of regulation and market incentives is most likely to enhance accountability to contemporary priorities, given a particular system design and set of fiscal strategies.

# Chapter Four

# Accountability and Accreditation

## Can Reforms Match Increasing Demands?

*Ralph A. Wolff*

For more than a century, accreditation has played a central role in promoting accountability and quality assurance in American higher education. Its success and responsiveness to emerging needs has led to a significant expansion of the number and types of accreditation agencies in the United States, as well as the adoption of American-style accreditation in a number of countries throughout the world. The power and influence of accreditation arises from several key characteristics: (1) it uses a peer-review process that is well adapted to the academic culture; (2) unlike any other process of external review, it encompasses *all* higher education institutions in the United States; and (3) it focuses heavily on institutional development and improvement.

Accreditation stands as a bulwark for quality in an environment where institutions are buffeted by state priorities to increase access, improve graduation rates, and operate with less financial support (at least in the public sector). Simultaneously, colleges and universities must respond to powerful market forces to increase competitiveness and improve rankings based on reputation and satisfaction.

I want to thank Fred Volkwein of Penn State University for his contribution to this chapter.

Market forces have also produced new types of institutions seeking accreditation, such as those operating entirely online, proprietary institutions, and single-purpose freestanding professional schools. The demography of higher education has also changed dramatically, with a significant proportion of students who are older than the traditional eighteen to twenty-two age range and substantial increases in the number of part-time and contract faculty carrying large portions of the instructional load. Although accrediting agencies have adapted so they can address many of these changes and guide institutions in ensuring quality, the accrediting process has many critics and is under increased pressure and scrutiny to demonstrate greater accountability and to respond to increasing public interest in the process.

Within the Accountability Triangle described in Chapter One, accreditation has evolved to meet academic needs and has maintained its role as primarily an *academic* and *nongovernmental* enterprise. It is largely a creature of accredited colleges and universities, as its financial support depends primarily on institutional dues, and accrediting standards are developed and approved by the institutions themselves. Increasingly, however, this internal focus has been criticized, and accreditation has been pressed to address more demonstrably public priorities that are advanced, primarily by the federal government and secondarily by the states. Market forces have also affected accreditation, primarily through the significant expansion of institutional and student diversity, requiring the development of the capacity to evaluate an ever-increasing number of institutions, disciplines, and modalities of instruction. The increased number of accrediting agencies has also begun to create a more competitive market within the accrediting community. In recent years, national accrediting agencies have been created or have expanded their scope of functioning so that they provide institutional accreditation along with the regional commissions. Moreover, competition has spread to specialized accreditation, with more than one accrediting agency now operating in such fields as business and education.

Through these changes, accreditation has been moving from the "academic concerns" corner of the Accountability Triangle toward the center, reflecting its attempts to respond to public priorities and market forces. How far it has moved is open to debate, and it remains to be seen whether this shift in emphasis will satisfy the many challenges and concerns still facing accreditation.

## An Overview of Challenges, Criticism, and Changes

Over the years, accrediting agencies have demonstrated a remarkable resilience and have introduced many changes to accrediting standards and practices. In just the past few years, several accrediting agencies have developed radically new approaches to accreditation, redefined their relationship to institutions, identified new markers of quality, and begun to review evidence of institutional and educational effectiveness much more systematically. These efforts were designed to respond to criticisms and to turn the accrediting process into a more vigorous, dynamic force for institutional change. In these new forms, accreditation has the potential for playing a new and major role in redefining accountability, with increased emphasis on effectiveness and student learning outcomes. The new processes, however, are just now being instituted in several of the regional and specialized accrediting agencies and are not fully understood by institutions or embedded in their practices. As a result, they are not well known to policymakers, who still hold traditional views (and concerns) about the accrediting process.

These changes are taking place within an environment of greater accountability for all education and as part of efforts to increase the accountability of the entire higher education community. With the passage of the No Child Left Behind Act, Congress set new measures of accountability for grades K–12. Recent legislation has also heightened scrutiny of teacher training programs for higher education and established new procedures for accountability and public reporting of program results. Over the past decade, each renewal of the Reauthorization of the Higher Education Act, which sets support levels and programs for student and institutional aid, has established greater expectations for both higher education institutions and accrediting agencies. Because accreditation reaches across all institutions, some leaders in Congress see accreditation as a ready method to increase accountability in higher education.

Increasing demands have challenged accrediting agencies to redefine their roles and relationships with institutions, address public concerns more directly, and monitor institutional performance in relation to internal academic needs, external federal and state policy concerns, and market forces. They have significantly heightened the public purpose of accreditation and shifted accreditation from private, academically centered organizations to nongovernmental agencies that are increasingly being relied upon by consumers and federal and state policymakers. With the call for greater accountability, even more responsibilities for accrediting agencies are being considered. They raise the critical question whether accreditation can, or even should, assume such additional roles and responsibilities.

This chapter reviews the historical foundations of accreditation, describes some of the major criticisms of the process, and analyzes the recent reforms undertaken by several of the leading accrediting agencies. It then explores several policy issues affecting the role of accreditation in addressing accountability, particularly the need to satisfy government priorities and market forces.

## Foundations of Accreditation in the United States

Accreditation in the United States was founded on the principles of independence of public and private institutions, academic freedom, self-regulation, and voluntarism (Harcleroad, 1983). Leading college presidents formed the six regional accrediting bodies between 1885 (New England) and 1924 (Western). At first, they established standards for course equivalencies, initially to facilitate admissions from secondary school and the transfer of credits from one postsecondary institution to another. Over the years, voluntary accreditation and the standards grew in strength and complexity, especially after World War II and passage of the GI Bill, followed by Title IV of the Higher Education Act.

Accreditation agencies operate through three different types of organizations: regional, national, and specialized (also called professional or programmatic). Regional accreditation developed first, and while several regional associations represent clear geographical areas (such as the New England Association), the geographical scope of each region results more from historical development than conscious planning. There are six regions—Middle States, New England, North Central, Northwest, Southern, and Western—but eight accrediting commissions. The New England Association has two postsecondary commissions,[1] and the Western Association has one commission for community and junior colleges and another for senior colleges and universities. The regionals vary in the number of institutions accredited from under 200 to over 1,100; together, these institutions serve over fourteen million students. Questions often arise as to why the regional accrediting bodies do not merge into one national group. The best response is that each reflects and represents the culture of its region, and the existence of regional approaches provides rich opportunities for experimentation and adaptation. Institutions feel a much closer connection to their regional accrediting bodies and have actively resisted consolidation or elimination of regional structures.

As the oldest and best-known vehicle for providing external accountability and quality assurance, regional accreditation is institutional in scope and based on self-review and peer assessment. Comprehensive reviews are conducted on a periodic basis, on cycles of six to ten years among the regional commissions, covering finances, governance, faculty-staff relations, institutional achievements, student services, and student learning outcomes.

National accrediting agencies operate throughout the United States, and the U.S. Department of Education (USDE) and the Council for Higher Education Accreditation (CHEA) recognize six such associations. Five agencies limit their scope to specific types of institutions—distance education providers, rabbinical schools, and Christian and other theological colleges and schools. The sixth agency accredits over six hundred independent career schools, colleges, and organizations operating in the United States and abroad. Other national accrediting agencies operate but are not recognized. As the proprietary sector has grown, many have sought national accreditation, increasing the number, size, and influence of these organizations.

Specialized or professional accreditation agencies review specific disciplines or professions and have become an increasingly important part of the academic quality and professional licensing system. These agencies began first in some of the oldest disciplines like medicine, law, business, and theology and now include more than one hundred fields of study. Institutions are eager to meet the standards set by these professional organizations because accredited programs are seen as being of higher quality.

## The Triad: Connecting Accreditation with State and Federal Processes

Accreditation operates within what is called *the triad* of overlapping *state, federal,* and *accreditation* interests. Under the triad, states have the responsibility to license institutions using minimum standards to protect against consumer fraud, the federal government to recognize accrediting agencies and ensure compliance with Title IV on financial aid, and accrediting agencies to ensure quality and effectiveness. As nongovernmental entities with no funding from state and federal governments, accreditation agencies have attempted to maintain a balance between their independent, self-determined responsibilities to address quality issues (which governmental agencies rely on them to do) and the direct oversight played by the federal government through legislation and regulation in the process of recognizing accreditation agencies.

The growing centrality of the federal role within the triad has had a significant impact on accrediting agencies and higher education institutions. For example, accreditation has increasingly become less voluntary for any institution seeking eligibility for federal student and institutional aid. The coupling of nongovernmental accreditation with federal aid has made accreditation critical for most institutions and, while raising the importance of accreditation, has correspondingly reduced the independence of accrediting agencies.

Accreditation also plays a role in the state oversight of higher education. In some states, such as New Mexico and Colorado, accreditation is required to operate. In other states, such as California, accredited institutions receive less regulation or oversight from state agencies. Even in states with strong review approaches, such as New York or Illinois, licensure differs from accreditation: *licensure* is required to operate and typically focuses on minimum standards and the establishment of need; *accreditation* standards typically go beyond minimum state licensing and increasingly require demonstration of effective educational processes and outcomes, concentrating on improvement over time.

Concurrently with expanded federal oversight in the 1990s, many states imposed accountability measures of their own. For example, Florida adopted rising junior examinations, and Virginia required documentation of program review and student learning outcomes. In such states, the lines between accreditation and state reviews become increasingly blurred, and accrediting agencies have adapted their process to account for these state requirements.

## Review and Recognition of Accrediting Agencies

Accrediting agencies themselves are subject to periodic external review and approval, which is called *recognition*. Recognition processes, just as accreditation standards do for institutions, shape the orientation and practices of accrediting agencies, and in the past twenty years they have established significant new areas of accountability. At the federal level, recognition occurs through the U.S. Department of Education. With the passage of the National Defense Education Act in 1958, the link between accreditation and eligibility for federal financial aid was established. Until the creation of the USDE as a separate cabinet-level agency, the Office of Education reviewed accreditation agencies and listed those recognized. Although originally a perfunctory act, starting in 1969 and with increasing detail thereafter, the department has established formal criteria for review of accrediting agencies (Volkwein, Shibley, Mockiene, and Volkwein, 2003).

In its review of accrediting agencies, the USDE has been shifting from an emphasis primarily driven by its financial responsibilities under Title IV to protect against fraud and abuse in financial aid programs to a much larger agenda addressing matters of quality and educational effectiveness. In a conversation with the author, a senior USDE official indicated that the agenda with Congress and the Department has now changed dramatically from focusing on minimum standards to assuring quality. This has been an emerging agenda over the past several years, and is not likely to change. Congress wants to see more evidence of the effectiveness of higher education institutions. The USDE recognition process reflects this shift and now places greater emphasis on indicators of effectiveness, especially student academic achievement. In turn, accreditors have put far greater emphasis on the assessment of student learning as a significant element of accountability in the accreditation process.

Alongside the federal recognition process exists a nongovernmental process, which occurs through the Council for Higher Education Accreditation (CHEA). This body acts as a voice for accreditation nationally and internationally and develops policy themes for the higher education and accreditation communities. CHEA recognition has had more impact on new specialized accrediting agencies than on national or regional agencies, though it has issued a number of papers and monographs to improve the practice of accreditation in all forms.

## Reauthorization Acts: Shaping the Policy Agenda

Every four years, Congress renews the Higher Education Act and uses this renewal process to engage higher education policy, as well as set financial aid policies and awards. With the 1992 Reauthorization Act, Congress signaled its dissatisfaction with accreditation as a form of accountability. It criticized the proprietary sector for not dealing with loan default rates and instances of fraud and faulted regional accreditation for failing to address student academic achievement and learning outcomes more effectively. This dissatisfaction led to attempts by state and federal legislators to sever the link between accreditation and financial aid eligibility, which in turn led to the short-lived creation of State Postsecondary Review Entities (SPREs) under the 1992 Reauthorization Act. Each state was required to set outcomes for higher education and to become involved, under certain circumstances, in determining institutional financial aid eligibility in the place of accrediting agencies. Although Congress later repealed the SPRE legislation, the 1992 and 1998 Reauthorization Acts added substantial new responsibilities for accrediting agencies, and the USDE followed with added regulations to meet to obtain recognition. Throughout this process, the federal side of the triad has expanded to become the driving force.

These episodes reflect a strong challenge to the core credibility and reliability of accreditation. Accreditation agencies were reminded that "to continue the privilege of self-regulation, we must give greater credence to the public's concern about higher education. We must address issues of educational quality much more directly and explicitly" (Wolff, 1993, p. 24). Although the threat in 1992 may have been to replace nongovernmental accreditation, in actuality, the result has been many changes by accrediting agencies, particularly the regionals, and increased reliance on nongovernmental accreditation reviews by federal and state agencies.

## Questions About the Effectiveness of Accreditation

Accreditation has survived and even improved as a result of the challenges it faced during the 1990s, but questions about its effectiveness continue to be raised by policymakers, members of the public, and many within the academic community. A review of several key questions about the effectiveness of accreditation provides a foundation for discussion of both the significant reforms already made by several agencies and the significant accountability issues that remain unresolved.

• *Is accreditation taken seriously by the academic community?* Accreditation plays a significant role for new institutions seeking accreditation and for many smaller institutions with limited resources. Unfortunately, many well-established liberal arts colleges and elite universities ignore accreditation and view it as, at best, a necessary nuisance. At times, higher education institutions and organizations give lip service to the importance of accreditation as a credible form of self-regulation while privately giving little attention to the process when their own institution comes up for review. For accreditation to maintain its credibility, it will need to have broader support within the academic community and greater understanding of its new responsibilities. Initiatives by several of the regional accrediting associations have responded to these challenges by developing new review models that are tailored to the needs of large and well-established institutions and are focused on issues of greatest importance. In the Western region, for example, research universities played a significant role in developing and supporting a new and more effective review process for all institutions in the region.

• *Is accreditation cost-effective and value-adding?* One of the chief criticisms of accreditation, particularly within the academic community, is its cost and burden. Although institutions pay annual dues to their regional accreditor, which are relatively low, the primary cost of accreditation comes from undertaking a self-study and paying the expenses of an external review team. Thus, cost issues must be seen in relation to the value of the exercise and the cumulative impact of accreditation (or for many institutions, multiple accreditations) on the institution.

When accreditation is seen primarily as a compliance-driven exercise to demonstrate the achievement of minimum standards and no more, it becomes like a trip to the dentist: a necessary task but one that should take as little time and cause as little pain as possible. Accrediting agencies (especially the regionals) have become much more conscious of the value added by the accreditation review process and are emphasizing the role of accreditation as an agent of change. The cost of accreditation is more acceptable when the process is seen as a stimulus for much-needed cultural change within the institution.

A recent study of twenty-two regional and specialized accreditation reviews using data from Middle States, the Accrediting Board for Engineering and Technology (ABET), and Association to Advance Collegiate Schools of Business (AACSB) reaccreditations at four universities revealed that the campus costs of each reaccreditation ranged from $41,000 to over $500,000, with $181,000 as the average (Volkwein, Shibley, Mockiene, and Volkwein, 2003). An unpublished study conducted by the Senior College Commission of WASC (Western Association of Schools and Colleges from 1998 to 2000) found that institutional costs varied from $45,000 to $180,000, with an average for larger institutions around $125,000 and far less for smaller institutions. Early research on the new model established by this commission has shown promise in reducing costs and burden and in increasing the value and effectiveness of the process.

Within the academic community, there is general agreement that the costs of self-regulation are substantially lower than if state or federal governments were to assume this function. The staffs managing this complex enterprise are remarkably small and rely heavily on volunteer services. The seven regional commissions accredit nearly three thousand institutions serving over fourteen million students, with a combined professional staff of only forty-six full-time members and fifty-seven support staff.

• *Does accreditation apply effective standards of quality to ensure institutional accountability?* All accrediting associations maintain a set of standards for the evaluation of institutions and programs. While serving as an external framework for evaluation across all institutions or programs, accrediting agencies apply their standards to fit each institution's mission and context. From the institution's standpoint, this approach is entirely appropriate because each institution wishes to be evaluated within its own setting. From the standpoint of many policymakers and consumers, however, there is a greater need for consistency across institutions. As stated in a report of the National Association of Independent Colleges and Universities (NAICU) on accountability: "The accreditation process has been the mechanism for judgments about institutional quality. It has been designed to provide standards without standardization. Outcomes are evaluated within the context of mission and the circumstances of each institution. Judgments about quality of diverse institutions require many indicators and measures, both quantitative and qualitative. The process relies on peer review because evaluations are based on informed judgments, not formulas. In this way, accreditation deals with the complexity of the enterprise" (National Association of Independent Colleges and Universities, 1994).

Policymakers have questioned whether accreditation focuses on the right issues and sufficiently addresses the public interest in accountability. Increasingly, accreditation is expected to apply standards beyond minimum levels to a definition of accountability that ensures greater institutional responsibility for student learning outcomes. Critics also complain that accreditation gives too little attention to comparative performance within and across institutions. Many expect accrediting agencies to set expectations across all institutions for the performance of graduates at each degree level, especially for the baccalaureate degree.

Accrediting agencies have been remarkably successful in balancing these tensions between internal institutional interests and increasing external accountability. Given the significant diversity of institutional types, sponsorship, and mission, no single set of standards can ensure the same results in every case. Nor can a single metric of effectiveness fit the diverse world of higher education. A one-size-fits-all approach is neither appropriate nor effective for American higher education, yet all of the regional accrediting agencies and many of the specialized agencies have made a dramatic shift in emphasis toward educational effectiveness and student learning outcomes. This has moved accreditation beyond the gatekeeping role for new institutions to a requirement that established institutions demonstrate accountability for more effective assessment of student learning.

• *Does accreditation act appropriately to terminate accreditation or require needed change?* A key indicator of effectiveness is the rigor or "toughness" of accrediting actions. One of the most persistent challenges to accreditation is whether the peer-review process is capable of imposing negative actions where warranted or terminating institutional or program accreditation. Although institutions are disaccredited and placed on sanction, more frequently they are placed on a shorter review cycle and subjected to heightened monitoring. These actions are less visible to the public and not well understood. Most often institutions respond and recover, but much of the work of accrediting agencies is done behind the scenes and leads to significant institutional change. Although accrediting agencies urge more focus on the "cure rate" than on its "kill rate" to measure effectiveness, the issue of rigor is unlikely to be resolved without greater disclosure of both institutional performance and accrediting actions—an issue that is further developed later in the chapter.

• *Does accreditation lead to long-term institutional change?* Too often, institutions engage in a large production process to prepare for an accreditation review, only to have much of the results of the work evaporate after the evaluation team has left and the accrediting commission has acted. Critics have questioned whether accreditation actions and follow-up lead to real and needed institutional change. Such concerns have focused primarily on the need to improve retention and graduation rates and the quality of both general education and the baccalaureate-degree experience. Despite accrediting agency emphasis on student learning assessment to improve the quality of education, critics see little significant culture change within institutions.

## Accrediting Response: A Decade of Significant Shifts

Over the past five years, several of the regional accrediting commissions and a few of the specialized associations have undertaken comprehensive self-reviews and instituted major reforms in their practices. The Pew Charitable Trusts stimulated much of this reform through the award of major grants to the Senior College Commission of WASC, the Higher Learning Commission of the North Central Association, and the Southern Association (WASC, Senior, also received several grants for its accreditation reform efforts from the James A. Irvine Foundation). In addition, Pew funded a major grant to the Council of Regional Accrediting Commissions (C-RAC) to support dissemination of the reforms occasioned by the earlier grants and to support a common emphasis by all regional accreditation on student learning assessment.

These reform efforts began with some fundamental questions about the long-term effectiveness of accreditation practices. As the saying goes, "Insanity is doing the same thing over and over again and expecting different results." Several accrediting agencies actively involved their regions in a dialogue about whether the accrediting process was fulfilling the highest expectations for institutional review and improvement. This dialogue led to an active questioning of past practice and the need for significantly new approaches. For example, the Western (Senior) Commission engaged in a multiyear public study of quality assurance, leading to the publication of a folio of white papers on possible new approaches to accreditation, participation in the Baldrige process, travel to Hong Kong and England to study firsthand their academic audit models, and the review of other international forms of quality assurance. The Southern Association conducted a number of regional meetings to assess whether the several hundred "must" statements in its accrediting standards should be continued. Each of these processes actively engaged institutional communities in redefining the accrediting process.

As a result of these significant efforts, new approaches to accreditation have been adopted by the Senior College Commission of WASC for all of its institutions, by the optional Accreditation Quality Improvement Program (AQIP) of the Higher Learning Commission of North Central, and by a new approach taken by the Southern Association. The Middle States Association and the Community College Commission of WASC have also adopted new standards, each reflecting a significantly greater emphasis on student learning. In addition, ABET has embarked on an ambitious redefinition of its standards to emphasize outcomes assessment, which has had a major impact on engineering programs in the United States and internationally.

These new approaches reflect four significant shifts away from historical or traditional patterns of accreditation, which are discussed in the next sections.

## First Shift: From Add-On to Value-Added

Accreditation has often been an episodic exercise leading to a volcanic eruption of activity every ten years, involving the formation of informal self-study committees and the preparation of large reports, often with many useful recommendations. When the self-study process operates outside normal institutional processes, problems typically arise in getting institutional attention to the self-study and the accreditation team's evaluation and recommendations. To address this concern, several approaches have the accrediting process focus on embedded institutional processes and practices. The AQIP model of North Central builds on and improves existing institutional systems and has developed a review process embedded within institutional quality assurance and improvement processes. Similarly, the new WASC (Senior) model intends to build a "culture of evidence" and has all institutions construct their self-reviews around existing evidence and present portfolios of data and evidence with reflective essays.

## Second Shift: From Inputs and Processes to Learning Outcomes

Both institutions and accrediting agencies are challenged by competing definitions of quality and excellence. Despite the lore of accreditation placing undue emphasis on quantitative measures such as the number of books in the library or faculty-student ratios, all regional and many of the specialized accrediting agencies have long ago moved to a model of review that eschews quantitative measures and favors a more qualitative review process linking institutional missions, resources, structures, and processes. The new models being adopted by several of the regional accrediting associations reflect a greater degree of sophistication in defining and addressing quality through standards of accreditation and review processes. Most accrediting agencies now place attention on three major dimensions of quality: inputs, processes, and outcomes or results, especially with respect to student learning. Figure 4.1 illustrates the dimensions of quality as the overlapping characteristics of inputs, processes, and outcomes.

### Figure 4.1. Dimensions of Quality

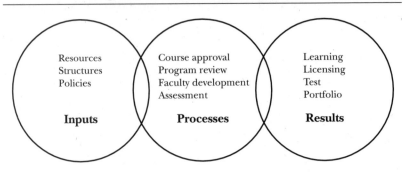

Traditional accreditation practices have emphasized inputs and processes, with some attention to assessment efforts. Inputs such as student and faculty characteristics and financial, physical, and technological resources have always played a major role in defining quality, and they continue to do so. Although critical, they do not guarantee educational effectiveness. The WASC (Senior) Commission has experimented with academic audit models and is now incorporating some of the academic audit principles into its reviews (see Chapter Eight). The AQIP process draws heavily on the Baldrige model of quality processes and on the need for ongoing systems of quality review. At the same time, there must now be increased attention to the actual results of the educational process.

Accrediting agencies have stressed student learning outcomes assessment for more than a decade and have led the national effort to improve the assessment of student learning (see Chapter Five). All too often, however, assessment became reified as a set of activities—an end in itself. Increasingly, the new accreditation approaches call for the actual demonstration of learning results. Such an approach is a major step forward for accreditation but still may not satisfy those interested in a system that allows for institutional comparisons of learning results.

The new standards of the Middle States Association and of the Accrediting Commission for Community and Junior Colleges of WASC call for learning outcomes and, to the extent possible, alignment of outcomes at the course, program, and institutional levels. The WASC (Senior) model consciously addresses each of these three dimensions of quality in its standards and in a new review process and is developing new protocols for looking at learning results. ABET, which is on the forefront on the outcomes-based accreditation movement, is also attempting to determine the extent to which outcomes-based accreditation contributes to better student learning and preparation for careers in engineering. This focus on assessment and accreditation has become so widespread that several national organizations, such as the American Association for Higher Education (AAHE) and the American Association of Colleges and Universities (AAC&U), are bringing accrediting bodies and educational institutions together for the purpose of strengthening their shared responsibilities for student learning.

Building on these reform efforts within regional accreditation, the Council of Regional Accrediting Commissions developed common principles of good practice for accrediting bodies and their member institutions to strengthen the evidence of student learning. The principles have been endorsed by each of the regional accrediting commissions; they make an assessment of student learning results central to both accrediting commission and institutional practice (Council of Regional Accrediting Commissions, 2003). CHEA has also promulgated a policy statement on the mutual responsibilities of institutions and accrediting agencies for student learning (Council for Higher Education Accreditation, 2003).

Regional and specialized accreditors alike are investing heavily in evaluator training to ensure that each review is less personality driven and more evidence based, especially with respect to student learning. It is not always clear how to evaluate student learning from an institutional or programmatic perspective. As a result, new training guides are being developed to assist teams in evaluating student learning outcomes, though many definitional and organizational questions remain. Examples include the Middle States Association's *Student Learning Assessment: Options and Resources* (2003), the Western Association of Schools and Colleges (Senior) *Evidence Guide* (2002), and the Council of Regional Accrediting Commissions' *Regional Accreditation and Student Learning: A Guide for Institutions and Evaluators* (2003).

## Third Shift: From Single, Comprehensive Visits to New Visit Processes

Any change in accrediting standards is only as effective as the processes used to apply them. Research conducted by WASC (Senior) showed the overwhelming challenge for teams to give equal attention to both institutional capacity and educational effectiveness within a single accrediting visit of four days, only two of which are spent on campus. To maximize the effectiveness of the review process, there has been considerable effort in some agencies to revise the cycle and focus of reviews, to clarify the purpose of each review, and to focus attention on site-visit issues warranting the greatest attention. The Southern Association has innovated with an off-site review panel that evaluates a compliance report prior to a comprehensive site visit and identifies (or clears away) issues of compliance to be addressed at the time of the review. This step allows site-visit teams to focus on areas of needed improvement. The AQIP process of North Central aims to answer two overarching questions: (1) Are you doing the right things—the things that are most important in order to achieve your institution's goals? (2) Are you doing things right—effectively, efficiently—in ways that truly satisfy the needs of those you serve?

The WASC (Senior) model is equally if not more radical, in that it applies to all institutions accredited by the commission rather than as an option for those interested. It is made up of three parts: (1) a Proposal, (2) a Preparatory Review, and (3) an Educational Effectiveness Review.

The Institutional Proposal sets out a plan of work and treats the accreditation review cycle as an institutional research inquiry focused on improving student learning and building organizational learning systems. The proposal is submitted two and one-half years ahead of the first review and is evaluated by a peer-review panel. Most proposals are revised before acceptance to ensure that the work plan will lead to meaningful institutional review and change.

The Preparatory Review follows. It focuses on issues of institutional capacity; a year later, an Educational Effectiveness Review addresses issues of educational quality and student learning. Using practices from the Baldrige process, a team conference call precedes each site visit to identify site-visit issues.

These visit process reforms are having a significant impact on the review process by focusing issues and clarifying team roles. In each region where such innovations are being implemented, they are proving very successful in improving the effectiveness of visits.

## Fourth Shift: From Conservator of Traditional Values to Leadership in Institutional Development

A fourth major theme is the dramatic change in the role of accrediting agencies. Rather than serving as conservators of past practices, accrediting agencies are becoming leaders in their regions (in some cases, like ABET, in their disciplines) in student learning assessment, information literacy, and strategic planning. Progressive campus leaders increasingly are seizing the regional reaccreditation process as a "chariot for change" (Ratcliff, Lubinescu, and Gaffney, 2001). Each of the regional commissions now run well-attended workshops and annual meetings on "how to" assess learning and establish learning-centered programs and institutions. In addition, all are producing supplemental documents to their standards of accreditation to give institutions and evaluation teams additional support for addressing student learning and other key issues.

## Future Challenges to Accreditation as a Form of Accountability

These accreditation reforms are quite new and are only now becoming fully implemented. As a result, they are not well known in the public policy community or even fully understood by the higher education community. Yet, even as they become more widely known, questions about the role, purpose, and effectiveness of accreditation will continue. Competition for federal and state resources will lead to more probing questions about higher education. Policymakers will continue to look to accreditation to establish greater accountability. Much of the debate about the role of accreditation occurs during the revision process to Part H of the Higher Education Act, which sets forth the criteria for the recognition of accrediting agencies. Four areas are likely to attract the most attention in the reauthorization process: (1) greater accountability for outcomes,

(2) distance education, (3) transfer of credit, and (4) disclosure of accreditation actions.

## Greater Accountability for Outcomes

As attention shifts away from exclusive reliance on resources and reputation toward greater reliance on outcomes, a number of significant policy issues emerge. First is the question, Who will determine what educational outcomes are appropriate? Should this be done through federal or state legislation or regulation or by institutions themselves? Within the current regulatory framework, institutions are called upon to set their own educational goals, and these are evaluated by accrediting agencies. This approach maintains institutional diversity and autonomy, which is viewed by the higher education community as fundamental to the success of the American higher education system. A decision to establish areas in which each institution needs to demonstrate effective performance of its graduates would significantly alter this tradition.

A related question is, Are there effective measures that should apply to all institutions or programs to ensure effective outcomes? Already the USDE requires all specialized accrediting agencies to identify at least one outcome metric that will be used to trigger further review of accredited programs, such as a minimum pass rate on a licensing exam over a two- or three-year period. To institutional accreditors, a single, or even several, predefined and universally applied metrics of effectiveness are impractical and inappropriate, given the range of institutional types and large number of degree programs offered by institutions. Still, many critics call for accreditation to define the minimum skills students should have upon graduation and to ensure that graduates can function "at the college level." Higher education and accrediting agencies will need to become much clearer about the skills and competencies required for a degree beyond the accumulation of credit for graduation and ensure that graduates consistently acquire these skills in order to graduate.

In the future, it is likely that initial attention will be placed on performance outcomes and a greater disclosure by institutions of outcomes such as graduation rates and, where appropriate, job-placement rates. Such data must recognize differences of institutional type because graduation rates over a six-year period will differ significantly between, for example, a commuter institution with primarily part-time students and that of a residential liberal arts college or research university. And some people question whether the appropriate outcome of all degree programs is employment upon graduation. With respect to all of these issues, the best way to respond is by making more information from institutions and accrediting agencies public and by making these issues a greater part of the accreditation review process.

## Distance Education

The rapid expansion of both the number of students and institutions engaged in distance education has led to continuing debate about whether such programs should be supported by federal financial aid. This, in turn, has raised continuing accountability concerns about the accreditation of distance education: Can distance education programs and institutions be effectively reviewed under current accreditation practices? Can concerns about fraud and abuse and the rapid growth of these suspect programs be addressed by accrediting agencies?

Current law prohibits financial aid availability for programs when 50 percent or more of the instruction is provided through distance education (the 50 percent rule), though distance education programs and institutions are already being accredited, even without such aid. Legislation has been introduced to eliminate the 50 percent rule, but regardless of the outcome, accreditation will be an increasingly important vehicle for ensuring the quality and integrity of distance education programs and institutions. Under current USDE recognition procedures, in order to accredit distance education programs, each agency must now demonstrate its ability to review distance education effectively, and all of the regional accrediting commissions have done so. As the demand for accountability of these programs increases, so too will be the call for separate and specific standards and procedures to ensure their quality.

Regional agencies hold the view that adequate accountability already exists, and separate accrediting standards are inappropriate and unnecessary. To them, distance education is primarily another modality of instruction, which already is being well reviewed under existing accreditation standards and processes. To reinforce this view, all of the regional accrediting commissions have adopted a common policy statement on distance education and produced a set of best practices to guide institutions and evaluation teams in the development and review of these programs. In addition, all agencies require some form of prior review and approval of distance education programs as part of their substantive change procedures and include distance education in all comprehensive institutional reviews. Nonetheless, these accountability issues are likely to remain active as distance education continues to grow and quality assurance questions remain.

## Transfer of Credit

One of the initial reasons for regional accreditation was to facilitate the recognition of credit for transfer between institutions. With the dramatic increase in both the number of students who enroll in multiple institutions and in significantly different types of institutions, transfer of credit has become an increasingly challenging policy issue. Although a number of policy issues relate to transfer, one has emerged recently over the transfer of credit between nationally accredited career and technical schools and regionally accredited institutions.

Many regionally accredited institutions grant transfer credit only to students from regionally accredited institutions. Several national accrediting agencies have pressed this as an important policy issue for legislative attention, arguing that their USDE recognition should qualify their students' course credits to be equally as deserving of transfer as those from regionally accredited institutions. The issue is seen as another area where higher education is not attentive to the public desire for greater student mobility between institutions.

In response to these concerns, the leadership of CHEA has developed a policy statement on the transfer of credit, which has been adopted by all regional and several national accrediting commissions. The statement calls for transfer-of-credit policies to promote responsibly the transfer of credit and calls for institutional polices to rely no longer exclusively on the source of accreditation in making transfer decisions. This issue reflects the emerging tension between publicly mandated policy and institutional autonomy. Regionally accredited institutions believe that this matter is not appropriate for legislative intervention and that the CHEA policy sufficiently addresses the concern. Nonetheless, it is likely that this issue will continue and be the source of some legislative enactment.

## Disclosure of Accreditation Actions

Critics of accreditation repeatedly complain that the lack of transparency in the accrediting process undermines its integrity and credibility. Although accrediting actions are publicly reported, team reports and the content of commission action letters are not publicly disclosed. Even so, most public institutions operate under public sunshine laws that require that the documents be publicly available, and many private institutions act on their own to post accreditation documents on their Web sites. As reflected in the public disclosure requirements of the No Child Left Behind Act, there is a philosophy that greater disclosure will create, in and of itself, an impetus for quality assurance and change. Many academics, however, believe that the ability to write critical reports and focus institutions on improvement efforts will be seriously limited by making all elements of the process public. These issues are not easily resolved, and they divide the academic and policymaking community.

In support of further disclosure is the experience of most public institutions that have learned to live with greater public access and transparency. It is argued that policymakers and the public will not trust accreditation without being able to see the underlying reports on which decisions are based. The accreditation review process generates a wealth of information that is seen only by the review team, the accreditation commission, and the institution itself, which unduly limits the use of these resources by consumers or policymakers. Usually, the only public outcome seen by important stakeholders (such as parents, students, elected officials, and the media) is a list of accredited, sanctioned, and disaccredited institutions and programs, with the dates of their last and next reviews. According to this argument, current reporting and public disclosure protocols address only the question of meeting minimum standards and do not reflect the important shift of accreditation toward improvement and accountability for student learning outcomes.

At the same time, there are important reasons to maintain the current approach of limited disclosure. Private institutions are much more market sensitive and thus are vulnerable to critical findings. There is a much clearer and more direct linkage in the case of disclosure of documents of the impact on finances and enrollment at these institutions. Disclosure of those could lead to the unintended result of seriously damaging institutions and undermining their ability to respond to needed change, especially when an institution is reaccredited and found to be operating well above minimum standards. Still, experience has shown that the average consumer tends to magnify *any* problem into a threat of imminent loss of accreditation.

In other countries, accreditation evaluations are typically sponsored by governmental agencies, and the reports are public. As a result, critical comments and findings are often removed or restated. American accrediting reports, because they are not made public, are much freer to include critical comments. Paradoxically, therefore, publicizing accreditation reports in the United States might well lead to fewer critical comments and "softer" actions.

Moreover, self-study and team reports are only parts of the evidentiary record leading to an accrediting decision. At times, accrediting commissions do not accept all of the findings of the visiting team or reach different conclusions. It is the accrediting commission action and the reasons for the action that are most important. At the same time, accrediting actions are often seriously misunderstood. Consumers and policymakers often draw dire conclusions from common requests for progress reports or interim visits, questioning whether they signal (erroneously) the imminent loss of accreditation. Another problem faced by making reports public is potential legal consequences. Institutions may claim economic damage from reports, challenging their accuracy and suing for consequential damages; already one case has arisen. Even if unsuccessful, such legal threats could have a chilling effect on teams and accrediting commissions.

Disclosure and transparency are two of the most important issues facing accreditation. As stated in the NAICU Report on Accountability: "However, [accrediting] processes and outcomes have been largely invisible to the public, and higher education has been reluctant to apply negative sanctions to problem institutions. Public confidence in accreditation will require better communication about the process and its results" (National Association of Independent Colleges and Universities, 1994).

Accrediting agencies need to pay far greater attention to public information and make their actions easier to understand. No longer can agencies ask for trust without providing more information. The middle ground in such an important debate may well be expanded disclosure of the reasons for each accrediting action and greater explanation of the follow-up action that institutions are expected to take. Such summaries could include the major findings of the commission and major areas of needed attention. Such summaries are also recommended by CHEA as an additional step needed to be taken by accrediting associations. "Providing additional information to students, government, and the public would significantly strengthen the role of accreditation in society. Making additional information about accreditation findings available would contribute to the view that self-regulation in higher education is additionally effective and that further government regulation of colleges and universities is not needed" (Eaton, 2003).

Accrediting agencies will need to work with institutions to make more information public about such important areas as graduation rates and placement rates in employment and graduate school and to give, within each institution's context, a better understanding of measures of effectiveness.

Both higher education institutions and accrediting agencies are ultimately accountable to the public that decisions are fair, consistent, and based on appropriate and rigorous findings of quality and effectiveness. As accreditation places more emphasis on student learning, there will need to be disclosure as well about how the accrediting agency expects institutions to demonstrate student academic achievement and to report findings about the effectiveness of the institution's educational quality. It is likely that interim steps will need to be taken over the next several years to increase reporting toward an eventual system of increased public information.

## Conclusion

Accreditation remains a vital part of the American accountability system for higher education. The process is deeply embedded in the fabric of campus life, and while many institutions might complain about a particular agency or review, the support for accreditation within the higher education community overall is strong, and the process continues to be considered an important bulwark against governmental regulation and control. The last fifty years have led to a major expansion in the diversity of both higher education institutions and accrediting agencies. The last quarter century has led to a significant increase in the role and use of accreditation as an accountability agent in addressing federal concerns about institutional and program quality and integrity. Accreditation as an agent of accountability has shifted significantly from one of *process* (that is, everyone goes through a review) to one of *outcomes,* with an increasing focus on student success and learning.

The privilege of self-regulation is not assured, however. Increased attention to the accountability concerns of states and the federal government and of increasing consumer demands for quality will occur over the coming years. Depending on how the issues cited in this chapter are resolved, however, the course of accreditation, as well as some of the core values and characteristics of the American higher education system, will be shaped. Over the coming years, as accountability will inevitably be increased, the question will be, *At what cost will accountability be increased?* It is possible that accreditation and the very fundamental principle of self-regulation will be dramatically changed. As one commentator has stated:

> Current legislative proposals, if enacted, would significantly alter accreditation, sometimes in dramatic fashion. Through these proposals, Congress could begin to take over judgments for academic quality that have, for centuries, been the responsibilities of our colleges and universities. For example, Congress, working with the United States Department of Education (USDE), could be in a position to determine conditions for transfer of credit, to decide what counts as quality in distance education or to prescribe acceptable student learning outcomes. . . . To challenge self regulation in this manner is to challenge some of higher education's most cherished core academic values: our institutional autonomy, academic freedom and the centrality of institutional mission. (Eaton, 2004)

Such an outcome is not preordained. Accreditation has demonstrated its resilience to challenges in the past and is likely to do so in the future. Accreditation will need to ensure that the changes already under way become embedded in agency and institutional practice. Looking to the future, these changes cannot be seen as an end; they are only the beginning of reforms to address public concerns with a clearer sense of the public purpose and responsibilities of accreditation. To maintain vitality and credibility, accrediting agencies need to communicate more effectively to the academic community about the need to respond to accountability concerns and to the policymaking community about how accrediting reforms respond to their concerns.

Accreditation will continue to provide an important gatekeeping function for new institutions, but even more important will be changing the agenda for review of the large and well-established institutions where most students are enrolled. The new systems of review will need to be refined and improved and the focus on student learning maintained, even through years of constrained financial resources. Accreditation will also need to develop greater commitment and engagement from elite liberal arts and research universities so that its base of support within the academic community is more broadly based. And to ensure the external understanding and credulity of the process, public information and disclosure about the accrediting process will need to be increased. As the debates about the form of increased accountability continue, accreditation will undoubtedly remain as a major force of accountability. In the future, however, it will need to do more to demonstrate and document its own accountability as well.

### Notes

1. A decision has been made, however, to transfer over the next several years the degree-granting institutions from the New England Technical and Vocational Commission to the Commission on Colleges, leaving New England with only one college commisssion.

# Chapter Five

# Can Assessment Serve Accountability?

## It Depends on the Question

*Peter T. Ewell*

Accountability and assessment have been closely linked since the latter's emergence as an identifiable topic of policy discussion in the mid-1980s. Since that time, some have felt the two to be entirely antithetical; others have argued that the purposes of accountability can be effectively served by a properly designed assessment approach. The answer one chooses depends in large part on definition, as the terms *accountability* and *assessment* encompass an enormous expanse of conceptual territory.

For the purposes of this chapter, *accountability* will refer to the constellation of mechanisms that colleges and universities employ to demonstrate to their external publics that they are responsible stewards of the resources invested in them, that they are soundly managed, and that they produce the kinds of results that they are expected to produce. Clearly, this embraces many things, ranging from the responsible use of funds through the visible signs of rational planning and management to educational outcomes. Partly as a result, most conceptual treatments of accountability begin by narrowing the scope of discussion to the intersection of a particular set of institutional actions or products with a particular set of stakeholders: "*Who* is accountable *to whom* for *what?*" (see Jones and Ewell, 1987, p. 2; Chapter One). The "who" in this construction is generally taken to mean individual colleges and universities, though it sometimes addresses systems of institutions or the totality of post-secondary education in a state. The "to whom" is a great deal more multifaceted, with government actors (state and federal) usually occupying center stage, together with other affected constituencies—students, employers, and the wider public—who have various stakes in higher education's success.

The connection with assessment comes with the "for what" question. Prior to the 1980s, most conceptions of accountability for higher education centered largely on costs and access. Indeed, part of the stimulus for developing assessment techniques in the early 1980s was the fact that new kinds of "for what" questions were being formulated by policymakers at that time, centered on a view of higher education as a *societal,* as well as an individual, benefit.

From a definitional standpoint, the concept of *assessment* is far murkier. Indeed, acceptable definitions of the term have ranged from the predominant usage in K–12 educational settings of large-scale standardized testing intended almost exclusively to discharge accountability to the original use of the term in higher education, modeled on corporate assessment centers, where the purpose is to judge individual performances in complex settings. Both definitions are legitimate and, to add to the field's confusion, both remain in use.

For purposes of this chapter, however, I adopt what has become the most common meaning of assessment in national higher education discourse: a program of locally designed and operated evaluation research intended to determine the effects of a college or university on its students, centered on learning outcomes, and engaged in principally for the purpose of improving teaching and learning (AAHE Assessment Forum, 1992). In adopting this definition, topics of several other chapters in this volume might equally be considered assessment. Foremost among them are standardized testing (Chapter Six) and student-alumni surveys (Chapter Seven)—data-gathering approaches that institutions have frequently adopted as part of their local assessment programs. Requirements to establish and maintain locally developed assessment programs have also become common among accrediting organizations (Chapter Four). Additional definitional overlaps with topics covered elsewhere in this volume are equally inevitable, and I make no apologies for them. But to try to minimize these, I keep the discussion confined to the *institutional* and *programmatic* referents of assessment as a process and avoid examining particular approaches to gathering evidence about program effectiveness.

As Burke points out in the opening chapter, "accountability" has many faces, and these have changed over the years as the relationship between higher education and society has changed. The role of assessment within this conversation has mirrored these changes, so it is virtually impossible to avoid devoting much of this chapter to recounting history. I do so in two sections—"Round I," which addresses the early state mandates on assessment that emerged in the period 1986 to 1991, and "Round II," which addresses the more recent requirements for reporting evidence of student learning outcomes adopted by the regional accrediting organizations in the period 1995 to date. Only in the light of this history is it possible to examine the particular kinds of accountability questions that might be answered by the definition of *assessment* that this chapter adopts. With this matter addressed, it becomes pertinent to try to determine the nature and array of policies that might promote effective institutional practice in assessment and to describe how the resulting approaches might actually discharge public accountability "to whom" and "for what."

## Some History

The relationship between assessment and accountability has evolved considerably over the past two decades. On the one hand, it is probably safe to claim that had the two concepts not been visibly linked at the outset, assessment as we know it would never have gotten off the ground. On the other, it is equally clear that assessment has far from fully succeeded as an accountability device and has, in fact, been substantially replaced by some of the more direct accountability approaches addressed by other chapters in this volume. The story of how this evolution occurred is worth telling because it illustrates many facets of a single core dilemma: Can a process that is based essentially on institutional self-regulation consistently and reliably assure stakeholders that they can count on a public enterprise? What history tells us is "sometimes," depending on both underlying environmental conditions and the particular kinds of accountability questions being posed.

## Assessment as Accountability: Round I

In the mid-1980s, two antithetical "ideologies" of assessment arose almost simultaneously in higher education discourse (Ewell, 2002a). The first came from inside the academy as a partial response to the growing curricular reform movements of the late 1970s and early 1980s. Its tenets were most clearly stated in an influential national report, *Involvement in Learning,* issued by the Study Group on the Conditions of Excellence in Higher Education (National Institute of Education, 1984), which argued that breakthrough improvements in undergraduate education could be achieved by establishing high expectations, deploying active and engaging pedagogies, and providing frequent feedback about performance. The second ideology had roots outside the academy, based on strong state interest in pursuing educational reform in the wake of the influential K–12 reform report, *A Nation at Risk* (National Commission on Excellence in Education, 1983). Its tenets also were embodied in a high-visibility report, this time by the National Governors Association, titled *A Time for Results* (Alexander, Clinton, and Kean, 1986). Based largely on policymakers' contemporary beliefs about how to enact reform in K–12 settings, this report argued that colleges and universities should be held accountable for establishing clear standards for performance with respect to student learning and that the results of student assessments should be publicly reported and coupled with consequential actions. I have deemed these two positions "ideologies" because they were at the time (and remain) far more than just policy proposals. Instead, both are systems of interlocking ideas that embody both an ultimate reform ideal and a well-articulated theory of change about how to get there (Ewell, 1989).

The central premise of assessment as an institutional process advocated by *Involvement in Learning* was that colleges and universities could become capable "learning organizations" (though this popular term had not yet been coined) and that concrete information about student performance, if collected carefully and systematically using the best available techniques of educational research and the social sciences, could become drivers of institutional improvement. This approach harbored several important assumptions. The first and probably most important was that academics would innately embrace verifiable evidence as a legitimate point of departure for policy because it was also the defining point of departure for scholarship. A second assumption was that institutions of higher education could develop effective systems to collect, manage, and interpret information about student performance, together with decision-making systems capable of acting on it.

Simultaneously naïve and powerful, like all ideological constructs, these two key assumptions proved not only individually deficient but in conflict as well. Faculty frequently proved distinctly anti-intellectual when it came to examining evidence about performance that might question their professional authority to determine what was best to teach and how to teach it. The deliberative decision-making structures of colleges and universities, in turn, were far more inclined to deliver policies based on conflict avoidance than on the principles of rational management. And even when they accepted assessment as a form of scholarship, faculty were little inclined to buy into what looked to them like a "business" model of running a complex, inquiry-driven enterprise.

The central assumption embedded in *A Time for Results,* in turn, was that publicly reported information about student learning outcomes would provide a basis on which to steer institutions toward improved performance and public purposes. Often forgotten in our current climate of consequential performance-based educational policy is the fact that the activist governors behind *A Time for Results* were strong advocates of higher education who were willing to invest substantially in its development (Ewell, 1997a). The rhetoric of the time for governors was that investments in higher education represented not just an individual benefit for residents of their states but a *public good*—the key to building a strongly competitive workforce and an informed citizenry.

A first assumption here was that college and university leaders (and, by implication, line faculty) would embrace such a public-service mission as part of their reason for existing. Most of the former did so rhetorically, perceiving accurately that it led to greater state investment. But few of them changed the paths of their institutions very much to pursue this ideal. A second key assumption was that institutions would respond to the challenge in more or less similar ways. What happened instead was that a few took up the challenge immediately, while others adopted a posture of "wait and see" (Hutchings and Marchese, 1990). The result for state leaders was a dilemma of how to respond, not to actual differences in institutional outcomes but to quite different levels of institutional cooperation.

The first round of state action in the wake of *A Time for Results* came quickly in the period 1986–1989, and its dynamics were revealing (Ewell and Boyer, 1988). States usually opened with a policy proposal for common outcomes testing for college students that they already understood through their experience with K–12 testing. Reinforcing this tendency was the fact that the few extant state assessment programs for public colleges and universities at the time were already test based, though of very different kinds and purposes (Ewell, 2001). Florida's College Level Academic Skills Test (CLAST) was a "rising junior" examination put in place largely to manage transitions from community colleges to public four-year institutions in a state that had invested heavily in a "two-plus-two" approach in the 1970s. Tennessee's performance funding system, in contrast, was a then-pioneering attempt to base some portion of resource allocations to public institutions on outcomes (along with other dimensions of performance). Mandatory student writing assessments in such systems as the State University System of Georgia and the California State University System, meanwhile, offered additional contemporary examples of common assessments administered in public university settings. These precedents made it likely that state authorities would open any conversation about assessment with a testing proposal, not so much because they felt this was an appropriate approach to accountability for higher education but because it was the only approach they knew.

Because of the influence of *Involvement in Learning*, however, college and university leaders had a reasonable alternative to offer. If public institutions were to agree to undertake serious local assessment programs, use the results to make visible improvements, and report publicly on what they found, surely the state's need for learning-based accountability could be met. In the relatively benign funding climate of the mid-1980s, with lead governors championing higher education as a public investment, it seemed like a good idea to many public officials. Sometimes state leaders initiated such proposals themselves. In Virginia and Missouri, for example, they came from state higher education executive offices; in states like Colorado and South Carolina, they were written directly into law (Ewell and Boyer, 1988). Sometimes they were the result of a protracted set of negotiations, as in Washington where an original testing proposal was converted to a full-scale pilot then dropped when it became clear that the resulting program was neither useful nor cheap (Thorndike, 1990).

Whatever their origins, such "institution-centered" state assessment mandates had been adopted by some two-thirds of the states by 1990 (Ewell, Finney, and Lenth, 1990). Virtually all first required public institutions to prepare "assessment plans" for approval by the governing or coordinating board. Within these plans, institutions were to (1) develop statements of student learning outcomes for general education and for each major program, (2) propose concrete evidence-gathering mechanisms on student performance against these goals, (3) create organizational pathways to use the resulting information to improve curriculum and pedagogy, and (4) prepare a public report summarizing both assessment results and what was done with them. In return, about half the states established additional funding to pay for the process.

In the period 1986 to 1990, the result was the first full-scale field test of the proposition that assessment, as defined in this chapter, could simultaneously serve institutional improvement and public accountability. Certainly, many proponents of this approach believed that it could (Ewell, 1987). State policymakers sincerely wanted their public institutions to change things for the better. Unlike K–12, which was seen as genuinely underperforming, most public officials' criticisms of higher education were more about lack of responsiveness. Meanwhile, corporate excitement about continuous quality improvement (CQI) was growing, and the institution-centered approach resonated well with state officials who looked kindly on this approach to management. If colleges and universities could show that they conducted their affairs rationally and could report coherently to state policymakers in language that both they and the public could understand, a central premise of accountability—that taxpayer investments were being spent wisely and yielded good returns—could be met.

Similarly, college and university leaders had reason at the time to be satisfied with the deal. They had avoided being saddled with a testing mandate that they were convinced would do nothing for their institutions except make them look bad. And they had been handed a potentially powerful tool for improvement that a small but significant minority believed might really make a difference in guiding undergraduate reform. All they would have to do in return was do it.

As institutions struggled to enact assessment under the terms of this bargain, though, the difficulties they encountered were less technical than cultural. The first stemmed largely from the fact that few faculties, despite the apparently scholarly mantle of *Involvement in Learning*, were ready to accept assessment as a natural part of academic discourse and governance. Part of the issue here was language. Even without government overtones, the early terminology of assessment was drawn largely from education and the social sciences, which were not the highest-ranked entries in the disciplinary pecking orders at most universities (Ewell, 2002a). Far more of the problem stemmed from the fact that assessment inherently questioned the premise that individual faculty members should decide on their own what to teach and how to do so. Parallel national calls for undergraduate reform like the Association of American Colleges and Universities' *Integrity in the College Curriculum* (1985) and dozens of similar proposals to restructure general education were, at the same time, assaulting this premise; assessment was seen by many faculty as just another management fad. And because these values tended to permeate the academy in direct proportion to institutional size and prestige, successful examples of sincere adoption tended initially to be drawn from institutions that few faculty cared to be associated with. A significant result was increasingly uneven development; some institutions enacted meaningful programs, while others stonewalled.

From the state perspective, of course, stonewalling blew the original accountability deal. In a relatively benign resource environment in which the primary state policy goal was seen as developing higher education into an engine of economic development, the notion of institutional self-regulation and continuous improvement made a great deal of sense to state policymakers. They were content—in some cases eager—to base college and university accountability on the periodic assurance that institutions were taking clear responsibility for improvement. But they could not continue to abide widespread noncompliance, especially when it was clear that some institutions had, in fact, been able to develop viable and vital assessment programs in the time allowed. By 1990, moreover, additional circumstances had begun eroding the initial success of the institution-centered approach.

One was the challenge of public communication. The fact that no two institutions used the same outcomes metrics meant that it was very difficult for state authorities to make succinct public statements about aggregate college and university performance (Ewell, 1991). Another development apparent by 1990 was that a new recession meant a new accountability conversation. Budget cuts yielded far less rhetoric about investing in higher education as a public good and far more about gaining efficiencies in a large and expensive public enterprise. One clear casualty was the state assessment mandates of the mid-1980s. Although states did not take them off the books, most simply ceased enforcing such requirements, substituting instead an increasing regimen of process-oriented performance indicators and performance-funding schemes throughout the early 1990s (Ruppert, 1994; Ewell, 1996; Ewell and Ries, 2000; Chapter Ten).

The rise and fall of state interest in institution-centered assessment as a policy tool in the 1980s has several lessons. First, states must be given considerable credit for sustaining a national movement that would probably otherwise have stalled. Most of the early activity in assessment happened in response to state mandates and, in many cases, was enhanced by state funding to support networks, technical assistance, and direct institutional subsidies. By the time states withdrew active support, assessment programs were well established administratively at most public colleges and universities, although the question of whether or not they were having any real impact on institutional behaviors remained open. Using the broadest construction of "accountability," government efforts to steer institutions had clearly induced them to do things that they otherwise would not have done. But from a narrower perspective, the "for what" in the accountability question had changed. "Assessment" was perfectly capable of discharging accountability so long as "for what" meant institutions establishing and maintaining viable self-regulatory and self-improvement processes. It was far less capable of answering "for what" questions centered on actual outcomes and performance.

## Assessment as Accountability: Round II

By the mid-1990s, regional accreditation had largely replaced states as the primary external driver of campus assessment (Ewell, 1993). Accreditation, of course, had already been a player in this arena for a decade—a fact signaled most directly by the adoption of "institutional effectiveness" as a new criterion for recognition by the Southern Association of Colleges and Schools (SACS) in 1986. Changes in federal requirements for accreditors in 1990 directing them to pay more attention to student learning outcomes ensured greater attention to the issue with the passage of time. All eight regional accrediting commissions and the majority of specialized accrediting organizations now have formal criteria that establish the collection and use of information about student learning as a condition of institutional recognition (see Chapter Four).

It is important to begin recounting this second historical encounter between assessment and accountability by noting that the basic nature of accountability represented by accreditors and state authorities is quite different. With respect to public institutions, states are deeply and directly interested in the specifics of institutional performance, based on their position as "owner-operators" of these enterprises. At the same time, they are interested in ensuring the quality and integrity of college and university outcomes on behalf of employers and taxpayers. The object of accountability for accreditation, however, has been much more directed toward the viability and effectiveness of colleges and universities as *organizations*. This focus makes the match between the kinds of accountability questions addressed by accreditors and classic institution-centered assessment far closer than with the accountability questions typically posed by states. The fact that accreditation is at least nominally voluntary, based on peer review and owned by the academy, reinforces this basic compatibility. But a basic alignment of purposes has not made the relationship between assessment and accreditation any less complex.

Accrediting organizations began the 1990s with an approach to assessment that strongly resembled the institution-centered paradigm that states were just then beginning to abandon. Indeed, in cases like Wisconsin and North Dakota, policymakers essentially "delegated" responsibility for continuing the initiative to their regional accreditor (Ewell, 1991). Under the new accrediting requirements that emerged in the early 1990s, institutions were asked to establish learning outcomes, deploy evidence-gathering tools of their own choosing, and use the results to make improvements. Indeed, some accrediting organizations followed the former state path to the letter by asking colleges and universities to prepare assessment plans for formal approval. The principal impact here was on independent institutions, which until this point had been largely able to sit out assessment or, in a few notable cases like Alverno College or King's College, to approach it on their own terms.

Once a visible assessment infrastructure was in place, however, the focus for accrediting organizations tended to shift markedly toward processes and away from outcomes. Much more emphasis, for instance, was placed on how institutions made use of the information they collected than on what this information suggested about how much students had actually learned. This orientation was equally typical of the requirement to establish formal statements of learning outcomes. Here, essentially, accreditors were content that institutions had such statements. They had little to say about their content, implied level, or appropriateness. Nor, so long as these goals for learning were visibly used to guide assessment, did they ask deeper questions about whether faculty used these goals to align their teaching and learning practices across classrooms or incorporated them into their regular grading standards or assignments.

Accreditation's focus on the viability of the assessment *process* in this period, like that of states in the decade before, certainly had the beneficial effect of stimulating more systematic institutional attention to evidence-based planning and decision making. Colleges and universities have unquestionably made greater and more visible investments in information gathering, and most can now point to formal structures and processes like assessment that render them more "businesslike" (Peterson and Vaughan, 2002). But a predictable result was reinforcement of faculty perceptions of assessment as an *administrative* process. And as accrediting organizations adopted what seemed like increasingly formulaic assessment requirements, institutions began questioning what they were getting out of the process. Faced by growing resource constraints, many were pressuring regional accreditors to adopt more flexible approaches that would enable them to harness the required ritual of accreditation to attack problems of local interest (see Chapter Four).

The result over the last five years has been a considerable change in accreditation practice—and, in particular, some specific amendments to the classic assessment "recipe" of the 1990s. Partly underwritten by foundation support (The Pew Charitable Trusts, for example, invested heavily in four of the eight regionals in 1998–2002), most institutional accrediting organizations have adopted new standards and review processes (Eaton, 2001; Chapter Four). One clear trend has been to separate visibly the compliance from the "self-study" functions of accreditation. Up until this point, accreditors had always tried to have it both ways: the central acts of self-study and review were supposed simultaneously to discharge accountability and foster internal improvement. Now most regional accrediting organizations essentially run two processes, trying first to quickly identify and resolve any substantive issues of compliance up front, thus freeing scarce institutional energy and attention for more creative analyses of fewer topics in greater depth. A concomitant change in most regions has been away from the comprehensive self-study toward the assembly of existing information as the evidentiary basis for review. One largely unintended consequence of these changes has been to "professionalize" accreditation. On the one hand, review teams are smaller and their members more highly trained. On the other, the numbers of individuals involved in accreditation at the institutional level are fewer, and they are more likely to be administrators. And these developments may only further faculty perceptions of assessment as principally an administrative responsibility.

A second major trend in the recent "reinvention" of regional accreditation has contrasting implications. This is a far more visible focus on the teaching and learning process as accreditation's central topic for inquiry. Many of the changes in review standards adopted by the regionals in the past few years eliminated language about institutional structures and resources, substituting new language about learning and the evidence for learning (Chapter Four). At least as important, the actual words used to describe the effectiveness of teaching and learning and, by implication, what is expected of assessment also changed. The language used in the standards of the 1980s centered largely on establishing goals and collecting evidence periodically to determine if goals are met—the "classic" evaluative approach to assessment that relies on external processes of verification. The language now being adopted by accreditors emphasizes *standards* for learning that are embedded directly into the curriculum and used to align day-to-day teaching and learning activities. The emphasis here moves sharply away from an externally applied "superstructure" of data gathering and reporting. Assessment designed to meet these new standards, in contrast, must focus far more on constructing assignments and exercises that are built directly into the curriculum, designed to do double duty in judging individual student performance and generating aggregate data about institutional performance. This development is important because it also shifts the terms of the underlying accountability question—For what? Rather than the existence of "assessment" as a process being advanced as evidence of accountability, the alignment of the institution's actual teaching and learning with the established standards of performance on regular assignments becomes the stuff of accountability.

It is probably too early to tell whether accreditation will truly become less focused on institutional management processes and more on academic standards and curricular alignment. But if it does, the process of assessment by itself will have increasingly less utility as an accountability device because, once again, the terms of the underlying question will have changed. So long as the central focus of "accountable for what?" remained responsible management and good organizational practice, the presence of a strong and vital assessment system aimed at institutional improvement did the trick. But the kinds of evidence produced by such a system remain as ill suited to providing public information about actual college and university performance now as they were a decade ago (Jones, 2002).

Whatever the underlying accountability question, a clear result is the curious cultural and perceptual position of assessment at most colleges and universities today (Ewell, 2002b). On the one hand, institutions are doing assessment because somebody is telling them to. And precisely because institutional engagement in the process is prescribed by outside bodies, faculty members rarely engage the process in a sincere way. Most, at least at first, treat it as a compliance exercise and leave it to their administrations to deal with. On the other hand, if the "for what" question really *is* about colleges and universities taking collective responsibility for evidence-based self-improvement, compliance-oriented behavior is the worst kind of outcome. In the past, policymakers have been genuinely surprised when institutions exhibit such behavior or actively resist assessment. As a result, they are far more likely to change the accountability question and look for hard-edged evidence of specific performance next time.

## Some Policy Implications

The shifting policy aims and outcomes of this multifaceted story suggest that effective approaches to using assessment to discharge accountability require clear separation between measures designed to steer institutional behaviors on the one hand and policies designed to encourage and support good practice on the other. First, the tension of motives involved in mandated assessment probably represents a permanent condition. Most faculty members will not genuinely embrace an assessment process that they perceive government has imposed on them, even if government's sincere intent, as it arguably was in the late 1980s, is to promote improvement. The situation with respect to accreditation also tends in this direction but is less clear-cut. So long as accrediting organizations follow the current path of allowing institutions to tailor required assessment processes to address local problems, accountability and improvement can both be served. But if the need to require specific standards of student achievement because of federal recognition becomes sufficiently paramount that accreditors begin to make accreditation decisions on the basis of assessment evidence, the dynamic of faculty ambivalence will be rekindled.

In the wake of No Child Left Behind, moreover, there is considerable likelihood that state and federal authorities will demand direct and easily comparable measures of learning in any case. Certainly, proposals for state- or systemwide testing in higher education have been on the rise in the past two years, with new testing initiatives in place in the City University of New York (CUNY) and under consideration at the University of Texas. Tempering this experience, Colorado, Utah, and Massachusetts have experienced a drawn-out process of first demanding a testing program, in some cases experimenting with one, then largely abandoning the effort in favor of easier to implement (and pay for) indicators of institutional performance (Ewell, 2001). But none of these initiatives has proven capable of reenergizing the institution-centered assessment approach that was so characteristic of state accountability policy in the late 1980s. The dominant and increasingly insistent political agenda of K–12 reform, together with a difficult and probably enduring fiscal problem for higher education, appear to demand more direct approaches to examining student outcomes than classic assessment can deliver.

Finally, two decades of actual experience with assessment have taught us that institutions will only engage in it meaningfully and over the long term if the payoffs of the process are palpable at all organizational levels. This suggests that improvement-oriented assessment processes should be removed, structurally and perceptually, from accountability. Furthermore, such efforts will only be sustained if assessment findings yield investments of resources directed toward addressing identified deficiencies instead of producing negative sanctions for doing a "bad" job. Many states underwrote the costs of assessment programs themselves in the 1980s, but few systematically addressed the matter of how to direct additional resources to places where assessment results said they were needed. If assessment is to become a meaningful tool for the "good practice" answer to accountability's "for what" question, states must find ways to more systematically invest both in assessment itself and in needed improvements.

Taken together, these conditions imply a multifaceted state approach to accountability that includes attention to assessment but comprises other initiatives as well. More specifically, a systematic state approach might consist of three clearly differentiated elements:

1. *A set of authentic "educational capital" measures collected at the state level to benchmark progress and to identify particular populations or regions that have deficiencies in collegiate learning.* Educational capital in this sense means broad-based college-level abilities like quantitative literacy, advanced oral and written communication skills, and critical thinking and problem-solving capacities (Miller, 2002). *Authentic* in this case means that the assessments used to capture these abilities would be anchored in real-world task or problem situations that require individuals to do more than simply select the "right"

answer. These measures would emphatically *not* be collected to compare institutions and would be comparable in scope and design to K–12's National Assessment of Educational Progress (NAEP). This approach is currently being pursued in conjunction with *Measuring Up* by the National Center for Public Policy in Higher Education through the Pew Forum on Collegiate Learning (see Chapter Nine).

2. *A limited set of performance indicators for public institutions (and perhaps for independent institutions participating in state-based student financial aid programs as well).* These indicators would *not* attempt to measure student learning directly and compare institutional outcomes. Instead, they would be focused on such matters as access, efficiency, and good practice, perhaps linked to a limited performance- or incentive-funding scheme. Though much maligned, performance indicators are valid and workable so long as they are based on clear definitions and measures and so long as they correspond to the legitimate state interests (Burke and Minassians, 2003; Burke and Associates, 2002). An important function of such indicators would be to hold institutions accountable for specific performances that are easily tracked. With direct accountability in this sense addressed, both states and institutions would be free to be more flexible with respect to accountability for institutional practices aimed at instructional improvement.

3. *Indirect incentives and support designed to promote local assessment and improvement efforts.* These initiatives would be directed toward rekindling the institution-centered assessment approaches that states mandated in the late 1980s and that are still the core of what accrediting organizations require. In fact, states might work directly in partnership with regional accrediting organizations by explicitly endorsing their provisions, helping institutions to meet them, and arranging joint visits to institutions. But the point would be less to "check up" on institutions than to provide them with resources and assistance to pursue activities that are seen by state authorities to be desirable for their own sake.

Only the last of these components is about *assessment* as defined in this chapter. In pursuing this path, states might engage in a number of potentially high-yield activities that would require only modest investments. One might be state investment in assessment-support networks to provide resources and technical assistance, share approaches among institutions, develop common examinations or assignments in similar disciplines, and hold periodic conferences and workshops. The Washington [state] and Virginia Assessment Groups (WAG and VAG) provide excellent examples of such assessment-support networks that have paid substantial dividends to states.

Another avenue might be increased state attention to centralized data-collection and data-sharing capacities, the results of which could be made available to institutions. One approach might be to harness the rapidly expanding capacity of state unit-record data systems. Such systems now exist in the vast majority of states, and they contain a wide array of data on student enrollments and course-taking patterns for public institutions (Ewell, Schild, and Paulson, 2003). The principal reason states run such data systems is to monitor enrollments, develop allocation formulae, construct performance indicators, and track student progress for scholarship recipients. But they are not well mined for management information by state agencies, and, once transmitted to the state, the resulting data are not fed back to institutions in a useful or usable form. Such data can be extremely useful in supporting local institutional assessment efforts by providing information on where students have gone after withdrawal and how well they performed if they transferred.

These kinds of activities require entities and policy structures quite different from those associated with direct regulation. For example, one hallmark of such a policy approach might be the deliberate use of "quasi-public" bodies to run grant and technical assistance programs or to serve as "safe" ways for institutions to share data among themselves. Successful examples of state-sponsored data sharing under protected conditions in the area of employment outcomes have already been pioneered in states like Florida and Texas (Seppanen, 1995). Third-party bodies underwritten by the state might also serve as granting agencies designed to enhance local assessment capacity. Likewise, they might sponsor awards for institutional quality assurance programs designed to improve undergraduate education.

Similarly, states might underwrite voluntary institutional consortia to promote assessment data sharing and the development of common approaches to gathering evidence of student learning.

Successful examples of data-sharing consortia already exist, including the Consortium for Financing Higher Education (COFHE), the Higher Education Data Sharing (HEDS) Consortium, and the Association of American Universities Information Exchange, though they rarely contain data about outcomes beyond common alumni survey results. Access to data, moreover, is strictly limited to member institutions. Other voluntary assessment consortia (for example, the Project for Area Concentration Achievement Testing at Austin Peay State University) have successfully developed common capstone examinations in a range of disciplines (Golden, 1991). Organizations like these allow scarce institutional resources to be combined to create high-quality examinations, tasks, and portfolios that institutions could not afford to develop on their own.

Building assessment-based transfer mechanisms among networks of institutions located in a single geographic region might be especially suited for consortial work of this kind. Credit transfer is currently a hot topic among state policymakers because of rapidly growing patterns of multi-institutional attendance. Course-based articulation systems are increasingly challenged to keep up with the growing complexity of student enrollment behavior. An alternative is to establish competency-based benchmarks for transfer in key abilities like writing or quantitative skills, worked out in concert by faculty drawn from member institutions and assessed through agreed-upon instruments or aligned grading standards in key courses. One among many examples here is the Quality in Undergraduate Education (QUE) initiative, funded by the Knight Collaborative and The Pew Charitable Trusts. In this project, pairs of two-year and four-year institutions that constitute substantial enrollment "feeders" of one another are establishing aligned standards and portfolio-based assessment mechanisms to support seamless transfer. Widespread creation of such voluntary networks is in the interest of the state and, because of the strong institutional commitment that such efforts engender, might represent a more effective articulation policy than directly mandating transferability.

Another indirect approach would be to de-emphasize or abandon one-size-fits-all program review policies, which have become largely formulaic in many states and are a challenge to run in tight budget times. By concentrating on a disembodied notion of quality, most state-level academic program review processes decouple programs from both market conditions and state needs. And using funding mechanisms that treat all programs alike reinforces this lack of connection. An alternative would take advantage of the current trend toward market-driven accountability by subsidizing differentially programs that are visibly targeted toward state needs (Jones, 2002). This would help stimulate institution-based assessment and quality improvement efforts because such initiatives only are undertaken genuinely by institutions when they see that the resulting information can help them create a better educational product. Experience in other sectors suggests that market forces stimulate institutions to invest in information, while information tends to be suppressed (or distorted) in more regulatory reporting environments (Scott, 2001a).

All these examples center on states investing in institutional capacity for assessment or harnessing existing incentives for institutions to engage in it without dictating how they do it. Institutions ultimately do assessment because it pays off in the form of increased learning productivity and market advantage. The secret to making the process work is to keep the incentives positive and to separate visibly such initiatives from other state policy mechanisms designed to address a different accountability question.

## How Accountability Is Discharged

For a variety of reasons, higher education's accountability challenge has always been different from that faced by K–12 education. Elementary and secondary schools are being called to account because of shortfalls in performance that are highly visible and of considerable concern to the public. Prominent stakeholders voice few such deep-seated complaints about higher education. Rather than a "crisis of specific performance," higher education has for the past twenty years experienced what can best be termed a "crisis of confidence" in the eyes of external stakeholders; the point is not so much that outcomes are visibly deficient as the fact that no one seems to know *what* they are. Institution-centered assessment would go a long way toward addressing this "crisis of confidence" if it were done sincerely and effectively. Resisting assessment, however, is clearly a recipe for more (and cruder) government pressure to measure student learning directly.

But experience has demonstrated that simply mandating an assessment process, absent clear incentives to use the resulting information, will yield little beyond narrow, compliance-oriented behavior. Furthermore, it forces institutions to adopt evidence-gathering procedures that absorb scarce resources and rarely connect well with internal planning and management processes. Alternatives to this counterproductive assessment-as-accountability impasse must, above all, emphasize transparency with respect to sharing and using information. And this approach can be actively fostered through state efforts to develop institutional assessment capacity and to provide comparative performance benchmarks.

In a complex informational environment in which institutions can directly display such information, accountability for "good practice" can be well served. Tools like Web-based portfolios, designed explicitly for public access, now provide institutions with an effective vehicle for achieving this kind of transparency (Cambridge, Kahn, Yancey, and Tompkins, 2001). These media allow institutions to make information about performance available and have the additional advantage of allowing stakeholders actively to observe an institution's efforts to go about the business of quality improvement.

Accreditation is increasingly taking advantage of such approaches, and state government could do so as well. What the institution must commit to—no easy task to be sure—is conducting its inquiries about student learning out in the open, where all who care to can see them.

Positioned in this way, assessment can constitute a significant mechanism for discharging accountability but only if the "for what" question remains focused on the degree to which the institution takes responsibility for examining systematically its own effectiveness and acting on the results. This is fundamentally a *management* question, not an outcomes question. So long as external stakeholders want a simple and reassuring answer to the outcomes question, assessment, as this chapter has defined it, will not be sufficient. More direct policy tools like those described by other chapters in this volume will be required. This is why a multifaceted accountability approach represents the best path to follow. Indeed, if the brief historical excursion provided by the first half of this chapter tells us anything at all, it is that accountability questions for higher education can shift quickly and unpredictably. Arguably, higher education began its adventure with assessment in the mid-1980s under an accountability aegis centered principally on trust and good management practice. But when the majority of colleges and universities responded uncertainly or halfheartedly and when resource conditions deteriorated, the central accountability question changed quickly to one that assessment could not answer.

Despite shifting political and environmental conditions, both of accountability's "for what" questions are important. *Real* accountability for learning is based fundamentally on two factors. The first is a sound educational product, demonstrated directly through assessing student learning outcomes or indirectly by tracking graduate success. The second is an organizational habit of doing business effectively and out in the open so that potential investors and customers, as well as regulators, can be assured that an institution is spending the resources entrusted to it appropriately and is on-task with respect to quality improvement. State governments must respect and stick to indirect policy approaches for the second kind of accountability to be successful. They may do so in partnership with accrediting organizations, where this matter is the central concern. They may pursue it on their own by developing programs to foster and extend institutional assessment capacity and by leveraging available information resources. Under current conditions, moreover, they are not likely to lose interest in seeking crisper and more direct answers to the question of what college graduates actually know and can do. But decoupling local assessment processes from any perceived linkage with this second accountability question is the only way state policies can seriously hope to steer institutions toward meaningful assessment for improvement.

# Chapter Six

# Standardized Testing and Accountability

## Finding the Way and the Will

*T. Dary Erwin*

Is standardized testing the answer to our accountability problems or the bane of higher education? Are standardized tests useful tools for improving higher education or impediments to educational progress for institutions and students alike? Given the emotion and editorializing aroused, can officials, academics, and citizens broach, study, and discuss the topic of standardized tests as an effective and appropriate accountability tool? This passion points to the importance of the topic and the need to deal with strengths and weaknesses of standardized tests.

Perhaps it is time to assess the common evaluation method of standardized tests, particularly for accountability purposes. This chapter presents varying perspectives on standardized testing; describes the components of such tests, including criteria for their evaluation; and offers recommendations for their use in higher education accountability.

## Three Perspectives Toward Standardized Testing

Following the Accountability Triangle presented in Chapter One, it is helpful to portray three varying perspectives about standardized tests from the vantage point of state priorities, academic concerns, and market forces.

## State Priorities

Governors, legislators, and business leaders have long been interested in applying standardized testing in higher education. Beginning in 1986 (Alexander, Clinton, and Kean, 1986), with *A Time for Results,* to the more recent *Closing the Gaps with Higher Productivity* (National Governors Association, 2003), governors and legislators have long been frustrated with the absence of college learning measures and with the lack of cooperation from academics in evaluating the knowledge and skills students should gain from college. Initially, state governments mandated surrogate input measures of resources; later, they required reporting of output indicators such as retention and graduation rates. Government and other officials recognized that these input and output measures failed to capture what students learn or how they develop in college. Attempts to link appropriations to institutional performance in student learning have stumbled because of the lack of valid methods for measuring directly the knowledge and skills that students acquire in college.

In the last two decades, the amount of information requested by government and educational institutions about student progress has increased. In the 1980s, states, seeking to understand more about the educational process, initially queried colleges for outcome information. Today, the federal government's No Child Left Behind legislation requires that "each state must measure every public school student's progress in reading and math in each of grades 3 through 8 and at least once during grades 10 through 12" (U.S. Department of Education, 2003, p. 1). This legislation, which is aimed at grades K–12, leads some government officials to believe that tests should also track student learning during the college years.

State officials want information on quality, including student-learning data, to answer several questions. The first is, "Are we getting what we're paying for?" They want to know whether taxpayers are getting an appropriate return on their investment, which in undergraduate education means the growth and level of student knowledge and skills. Although state funding is rapidly dropping, governors and legislators still want to know where the money goes. Administrators and budget analysts can easily estimate the costs of operating buildings and physical plant, but they have more difficulty determining the impact of college on student learning. The growth of distance education poses additional pressures for developing direct methods for assessing student learning—methods that determine competency rather than how much seat time is spent in class (see Bankirer and Testa, 1999). Pascarella and Terenzini (1991) summarize basic research showing that students can derive special benefits from on-campus learning and development, but few colleges offer evidence from standardized tests that students actually gain in knowledge, skills, and personal development on their specific campuses.

Second, state officials, elected and appointed, want to know, "How does higher education contribute, specifically, to state priorities such as building a competitive workforce, producing informed citizens, and preparing better teachers?" How do colleges and universities assess their accomplishments on these state priorities? Global and anecdotal boasts of achievement seem lame, with little or no supporting data.

Third, state officials ask, "What advances in general and specialized knowledge and skills have students made during the college years?" In terms of learning, colleges and universities rarely point to direct assessment data (Erwin, 2003), and, unless mandated, institutions do not use the same testing instrument. Administrators often yield to faculty who develop their own classroom tests, which do not permit comparisons among institutions. Few colleges or universities have direct measures of program effectiveness in specific majors or general education. This posture may keep peace on campus, but it does little to address the question, "What and how much did our graduates learn during their college years?" Unless mandated by states, the use of common test data is unlikely across all institutions. But without comparable data about student learning, it is impossible to draw defensible conclusions about student learning for a state's system of higher education. This absence of data on student learning prevents funding for public colleges and universities based on their quality of undergraduate education and their contribution to the educational and human capital of a state. Moreover, it will fail to justify increased funding for higher education in the coming decade, compared to health care and K–12 education, where data are better (National Governors Association, 2003).

Although their information did not come from state officials themselves, the National Center for Public Policy and Higher Education (2000, 2002) published two report cards that may encourage states to move toward better measures of student learning (Chapter Nine). In both reports, every state received a grade of "incomplete" for student learning because of the lack of common standards and comparable data. This troubling "incomplete" for higher education highlights the inability or unwillingness to generate comparable and acceptable indicators of student learning.

Even though the focus here is on the state perspective, it should be pointed out that the U.S. Department of Education flirted with developing a standardized set of tests for college learning outcomes for use in national policies—tests that would have been similar to the long-administered tests of K–12 learning, the National Assessment of Educational Progress (NAEP). In the early 1990s, the National Education Goals for college students proposed a common national test of critical thinking, problem-solving, and communication skills (Corrallo, 1991). The U.S. Department of Education later withdrew its call for proposals to have a national test battery, but the shadow of the event still lurks in the background. A similar call for a standardized test is being heard during reauthorization hearings of the pending Higher Education Act, but the expense and logistics deter lawmakers from moving concretely in this direction. The discussion in Congress once again reinforces the perception that standardized tests are a potential policy tool for higher education, although higher education remains constitutionally a state program.

## Academic Concerns

Although proponents of standardized testing are found at all levels of government, even the mention of such testing produces a reaction in many professors that is similar to hearing fingernails run across a chalkboard. There are many reasons for this discomfort with standardized testing on campuses. First, faculty members are anxious about measurement itself. Some faculty claim that standardized tests judge "what I do" inaccurately. They discount the validity of tests written by others, including experts. Many professors also view standardized tests as valid only for evaluating lower-level skills and not for higher-order skills and discipline-based knowledge. Some argue that such tests contain built-in biases against minorities.

Professors often claim that "standardized testing infringes on my academic freedom to teach what I want in my way." This concern arises generally because of fears about "teaching to a test" and "being accountable for things I cannot control." This response resembles the complaints of some K–12 teachers that test scores of disadvantaged children deflate class averages. Professors who teach very specialized courses fear that standardized testing might eliminate such offerings from general education or academic majors because the specialized material they teach would not appear on the tests. This last point is particularly true at large universities, where general education components contain many course alternatives from which students choose.

Second, many faculty and administrators fear a "change in the rules" related to the traditional focus, even the funding, of higher education and their departments. Colleges and universities largely allocate resources according to the enrollment-based model (the more students, the more money) to institutions and academic departments. Now professors may fear that standardized testing might shift some funding from enrollments to increases in the knowledge and skills of students in general education and academic majors. Some also worry that states and campuses may reallocate money from existing programs to support the new funding model. Such a shift violates the tacit principle on some campuses that "nothing new should start until you fully fund all existing programs." Equally unsettling to academics are the attacks on the peer-review system of program and institutional accreditation, derisively referred to by critics as "scratching-the-back syndrome."

A third reason for resistance to testing relates to faculty members' worry about their own changing roles. Some fear a loss of independence ("Someone else determines the curriculum with the test") and a loss of self-determinism ("It won't be my test"). They also worry that administrators may use test data for decisions on tenure and promotion, although information about student learning has seldom been part of the personnel-review process. Moreover, some professors view testing as an intrusion into "how I spend my time." Overall, even mentioning standardized testing raises feelings of insecurity and resistance in many members of the campus community.

In addition to faculty members, some presidents and provosts have mixed feelings about closer scrutiny of how much students learn in their colleges or universities. Besides feeling a similar loss of independence that some professors experience, presidents in particular fear possible public relations nightmares. Many worry about explaining test results to reporters who love negative news. Presidents and provosts feel caught in the middle between external advocates and a reluctant faculty, both of whom are outspoken but on different sides of the issue of testing for accountability. Finally, presidents and chancellors of public colleges and universities fear the use of test data in state funding rather than the customary enrollment and base budgets (Ross, 2003). Their private counterparts worry whether those data might affect student recruitment and fundraising.

## Market Forces

Market forces constitute the emerging phenomenon for higher education. Continued restraint in public funding for higher education (National Governors Association, 2003) means that market forces now fill spaces usually occupied by the states (Shaw, 1998). The precipitous rise in tuition now pushes colleges and universities to do a far better job of explaining "what they are asking people to pay for, and what the value of it is" (Chauncey, 1995, p. 30). This push for outcome information resembles the pressure that forced the food industry to place nutrition information on packages. Instead of the government serving as an intermediary, different constituent groups are asking for this information directly and publicly.

Prospective students and their parents constitute one consumer group that seeks additional information to help them make college choices. College guides publish some available data, but little of this information captures the benefits that students gain from attending a particular institution. Much of the available information in the admissions process presents inputs such as the entering characteristics of freshmen classes and campus resources in faculty-student ratios and class size. Given soaring tuition, students and especially their parents have become more sophisticated in their questioning about the comparative advantages of college campuses. At present, the best answers they can get are anecdotes or perceptual information from current students or alumni on their learning and development during the college years. Typical questions often raised by parents press for answers that include student-learning outcomes. Is private higher education worth the extra cost? Will my daughter or son learn or develop more from a private than from a public college or university? Which distance education course or program offers the most benefits? Will students learn as much from technologically delivered as from traditional campus-based education? How well does this college prepare students with the educational background and interest of my son or daughter for a profitable career and a worthwhile life?

Employers, of course, are another type of consumer requesting better information about their prospective employees and the effectiveness of the colleges and universities where they recruit. They can easily assess most of the specialized information taught in a student's major. In contrast, the broad knowledge, reasoning, and analytical skills acquired in general education remain the great unknown. Although employers usually rank communication, analytical, and collaborative skills as most desirable, evaluation of their acquisition by graduates remains uncertain. Unfortunately, transcripts do not furnish the desired information about these and other marketable skills in a meaningful way. Therefore, employers welcome comparable, objective information about marketable skill sets. As a corollary, these outside groups want colleges and universities to "screen out" students from graduation, usually by means of tests that determine competency.

Continuing education, while always an important issue, has become a necessity in today's rapidly changing workforce and society. The marketplace recognizes that traditional college degrees will not last a lifetime in a knowledge and information era in which the most perishable commodities are not bottles and cans but data and skills (Langenberg, 1997). Increasingly, colleges and universities provide short courses and modules culminating in certificates of competency. In time, baccalaureate degrees will not have credibility in the world of work without demonstrating the acquisition of desired knowledge and skills. That result has long been true in professions such as law, medicine, and nursing; soon entry into most careers will require some direct validation of competencies.

Degrees, like the new technical certifications, will gain more acceptance in the marketplace when they are supported by objective evidence of their worth. Information from standardized testing represents the most credible evidence to knowledgeable consumers and employers.

The growth of student transfers will accelerate this trend. Now student transcripts frequently carry credits from multiple postsecondary education providers. States and institutions alike grapple with the process and evaluation of transfer credit. In such cases, which college or university is ultimately responsible for certifying student learning? Should the last attending institution certify all prior learning because it grants the diploma? Moreover, how does a student represent his or her learning from prior institutions? By moving to objective certification of learning, standardized test data could resolve these troubling questions of quality and responsibility (National Governors Association, 2003).

General education presents particular problems for validating student learning. Although advocates of higher education have long lauded the value of a liberal education, it means different things to different people. Certainly, little data support its systematic acquisition by college students. Standardized tests could measure the knowledge, skills, and development supposedly conveyed in general education, such as communication, quantitative reasoning, and critical thinking.

The public media would also welcome standardized test data that could verify the quality and extent of student learning from particular colleges or universities. Every fall, criticisms abound in the academic community and on campuses that fared poorly in the *U.S. News & World Report* ranking of colleges and universities (see Chapters Eleven and Twelve). These ranks rely on resource inputs of students, faculty, and funding, along with perceived reputations. They provide little information about the extent or quality of student learning.

In the absence of data on student learning, internal and external groups will continue to report or review what is available: inputs on entering students and resources spent, outputs on student retention and graduation, and reputational surveys as outcome measures. All of these inadequate measures would drift to the back of the line if objective data on student learning became available.

Where does standardized testing currently place on the Accountability Triangle presented in Chapter One? At present, it fits state priorities best, although market forces would welcome improved information on graduate knowledge and skills. Academic concerns generally question standardized testing of student learning. Despite this resistance, the academic community could gain advantages by contributing to the tests' composition and controlling their use rather than opposing the concept.

## Types of Tests

The conflict between external and internal groups over standardized testing has generated much heat but little light on a series of critical questions. What are standardized tests? What makes a good test? What are some popular tests in use? and What are their strengths and weaknesses? This section seeks to answer those questions in a language that state and campus policymakers can understand. It begins with the all-too-common caveat that standardized tests are neither as good as some outside champions claim nor as bad as some inside critics charge.

In measurement, there are essentially two broad classes of test response formats: (1) selective response and (2) constructed response. Selective response formats are testing instruments that display alternative options from which test takers usually select an optimum answer. Multiple-choice tests are the most common example of the selected response format. Constructed response formats require the test taker to produce, perform, demonstrate a process, or exhibit a personal characteristic; responses are then scored by a rating scale or rubric or a checklist (Erwin, 1991). A test may contain either selective response or constructed response or both formats. Although not generally understood as such, an essay measuring writing ability administered under uniform conditions and rated by multiple readers using the same scoring rubric is still a standardized test. In addition, tests may seek optimal and typical responses from students. Optimal tests are usually achievement tests, and typical tests are often developmental inventories in postsecondary education.

The word *standardized* implies several features: primarily the same (or equivalent) test items; uniform rules for test administering and scoring; a domain or the content, knowledge, or skills being measured; and the type of scale used for scoring and reporting. Test designers often use the word *standardized* in the sense that, if done professionally, a test evaluates all students in the same way at the same time. What they really want is insurance of fairness and consistency in the testing process and validity of the resulting data. Standardization is particularly important in high-stakes testing, that is, when resources such as institutional funding or student progression or promotion depend on the test results. Users of test results demand the confidence that a test or assessment evaluated all students or institutions similarly and that examiners can generalize the results for a given group (for example, college graduates from a particular institution). The capacity of standardized tests for generalization contrasts with classroom tests that are unique to each instructor and cannot be aggregated to represent students in a program, institution, system, or state.

A critical meaning of *standardization* also relates to the domain or knowledge area covered in the test. *Domain* pertains to the content or knowledge, skills, and developmental characteristics that a program or service attempts to convey. *Domain* answers the question, What do we want students to learn? In K–12 testing programs, school districts, or more likely a state education agency, determine the domain centrally. At the collegiate level, the academic community has never agreed on the domain of general education, although some discipline groups have adopted a domain for academic majors. Some states, such as Maryland, have mandated course titles for general education, but these actions lack the detailed determination of content required for a domain that can serve as a blueprint for a test. General education is especially important because it represents the knowledge and skill that college graduates should acquire regardless of major. Agreement on the learning objectives is elusive at every level: nation, state, system, or institution.

Often critics blame problems on a particular test or method, when the fault really flows from an undefined and ambiguous domain. This flaw has hampered the design of many collegiate tests because "one has to know what the test should cover before developing the questions." If this domain or content does not exist in sufficient detail, then test writers must conceptualize the objectives and write questions to address them. This point will be raised again when we discuss test validity. In determining the general education domain, it is wise to include some outsiders whose views may differ from those of faculty and higher education experts. For example, "good" writing on some campuses may stress literary analysis, whereas business leaders might deem good writing as preparing correspondence or memoranda. All too often, test makers gloss over the first and critical step of domain determination and find that the results do not address the questions of policymakers, such as "can college graduates write effectively for the workplace and society?"

Another meaning of standardization relates to the methods of reporting scores. Commonly, test designers place standardized test scores on a "standard" scale, which the public more easily understands. For example, each subscore of the SAT-I ranges from 200 to 800, but students do not answer 200 or more questions on the verbal and mathematical sections. The correct number of test items answered, also called raw scores, is typically converted into a more easily remembered metric such as 200–800 or 10–90 point ranges. (Other scoring systems such as item response theory use complicated scaling algorithms, but these procedures are beyond the scope of this chapter.)

Scores sometimes use percentiles or ranks. For example, if a student is scoring at the 45th percentile on tests, it means that score is equal to or better than 45 percent of the students in the standardization sample, also sometimes called a norm group. The "45th percentile" does *not* mean that the student answered 45 percent of the test questions correctly or that an optimum standard can be determined from a particular percentile.

In contrast to K–12, no collegiate tests of general education or the major exist that have nationally representative percentiles or norms. Test publishers sometimes distribute "user-based norms," which are essentially percentiles calculated from student or institutional responses. Unfortunately, user-based norms are not representative of any larger group. Test reviewers should view norms with caution, as people often draw misinformed conclusions from them.

Another, more technical issue associated with standardization scoring pertains to the "equating" process. If a test has multiple forms, each test form should be "equated" or adjusted for each form's varying difficulty and, perhaps, length; failure to do so can lead to distorted results. For example, one institution under a state mandate became aware that no one had equated the test forms, which resulted in uneven difficulty. Unknown to state policymakers, that institution gave the hardest test form to entering freshmen and the easiest test form to late sophomores. The late sophomores always scored better than the entering freshmen because of a poor equating process, not because the students learned more during their first two years of college.

Policymakers and educators should attach or assign narrative meaning to parts of any score distribution. The term for this narrative is *criterion-referenced interpretation*. Selecting a cutoff score in competency testing, for example, is one popular application. In summary, there are several meanings to the term *standardized test*. Users of test information need to know these variations to draw proper and careful conclusions from test results. They should pay particular attention to the meaning attached to the test scores themselves.

## Quality in a Test

Three related but broader areas also determine the quality of any given test: reliability, validity, and feasibility; the first two involve technical issues. Decision makers can waste much time, money, and energy by skipping over consideration of reliability, validity, and feasibility. Skipping the first two areas can discredit the whole testing process, whereas ignoring the last area results in a belated and often costly discovery that a project is impractical or impossible.

To begin to understand what reliability and validity signify, let us start with a simple story. Imagine that I wish to determine your ability as a bird-watcher. I post you on the top of a hill and ask you to identify an object in the distance. By focusing the lens of your binoculars, you improve the reliability of your bird-watching. Validity involves discerning whether the object in view is a bird, a hawk, or a falcon. Standardized testing requires both reliability and validity. Human behavior is complex, and no exact ways exist for determining whether a person knows something or not. Test designers use these concepts to estimate how much error a score contains (reliability) and how well a test reflects a domain or content of interest (validity).

Reliability has values ranging from 0.00 to 1.00; the higher the value, the clearer, more consistent, and more homogeneous the test. Values should reach at least .70 for program evaluation purposes and at least .80 or higher for use with individual students. If the test uses a constructed response format, then test evaluators should calculate inter-rater reliability, since raters represent another layer of possible error. (For readers who wish a more detailed and technical treatment of reliability, see Feldt and Brennan [1993].)

Validity is an equally complex topic. Readers can regard validity evidence much as a judge would in a judicial proceeding. No one piece of evidence is conclusive, and an accumulation of evidence helps build the case for test worth or validity. For tests of learning, potential users of test information should have domain experts systematically match each test item under consideration for adoption with a particular learning objective in the adopted domain. State or campus policymakers should never choose or administer a test without first insisting on a close match between test questions and domain objectives. This chapter introduced the subject of construct validity under the conditions for standardization, but it is equally important when reviewing the focus and value of a particular test. Again, it is presumed that the domain has specific learning objectives.

Other types of validity evidence include positive relationships or correlations with other measured constructs of similar meaning, along with expected negative relationships with other test constructs of different meaning. For example, one would expect a test of American history to have a positive correlation or relationship with a reading test, but if the relationship becomes too high, say a correlation coefficient of .60 or higher, then that test really measures reading ability, not American history. Tests of general education and the major should reflect what students have learned in college, not the verbal and mathematical abilities they bring to college. Messick (1993) describes more complex validity notions.

Although not a property of tests, feasibility represents a critical consideration when choosing testing instruments. Costs and logistics of administration and scoring are major determinants of test adoption, in addition to the reliability and validity evidence. For instance, some researchers, such as Bennett (1993), report that constructed response formats cost about three to five times that of multiple-choice tests. Another consideration is whether proctors administer testing instruments under similar conditions with adequate test security. Test scores can be influenced simply by what proctors say just before test administration.

Another aspect of feasibility is the motivation of the participants to take the exercise seriously. Data from the best testing instruments in the world become useless if participants, whether students or staff, are poorly motivated. Occasionally, a large-scale state plan will test a sample of undergraduates—a practice that often leads to poor student motivation. The students naturally wonder, "Why am I picked to take a test for three hours and my roommate isn't?" It also follows that having a chief executive officer agree for an institution to participate in an assessment project does not guarantee that the faculty and staff agree to participate seriously. One disgruntled faculty member can easily spread a cloud of negativism that poisons the efforts of his or her colleagues and their students.

In considering test formats, there is some evidence in the literature (Sundre and Kitsantas, 2004) that students perform more poorly on constructed response than selective response formats. The latter can take more effort on the student's part than selecting among alternative answers.

## New Proprietary Instruments

Usually driven by higher education policy, testing instruments generally fall into five topical areas: (1) entering basic skills, (2) general education, (3) the major, (4) student development, and (5) the campus environment. In the 1980s, entering basic skills appeared as an initial area of interest. The public, as well as colleges, complained about the basic skills in communication (primarily writing and reading) and mathematics that entering freshmen brought with them from high school. For example, New Jersey has long used basic skills tests that entering freshmen must pass. The adoption of high school competency tests has softened the demand for entering basic collegiate skill tests.

### General Education

General education, or the curriculum required for the college-educated person, remains the most important area to policymakers because it is the imprint that all colleges should make on all their students, regardless of major. As mentioned previously, higher education has not agreed on its definition and meaning, primarily because faculty, divided by discipline, cannot agree on the most critical knowledge and skills or the learning domain. Some instruments of general education strive for a skill-oriented approach, such as rising junior exams (Arenson, 2003), whereas others try to measure both content and skills. The College Basic Academic Subjects Examination (University of Missouri-Columbia, 2003) purports to measure the four subject areas of English (writing, reading, and literature), mathematics, natural science, and social science, as well as three higher-order thinking skills of interpretive, strategic, and adaptive reasoning abilities. Educational Testing Service (ETS) markets the Academic Profile (AP), which reports three content-related subscales in the humanities, social sciences, and natural sciences and four skills of critical thinking, reading, writing, and mathematics (2003a). Designed by the American College Testing Program (2003a), the Collegiate Assessment of Academic Proficiency (CAAP) reports on five areas: reading, writing, mathematics, science, and critical thinking. Both the AP and CAAP have had problems of too high correlation with general verbal and mathematical abilities, which, as noted earlier, means they fail to test the intended domain of knowledge and skills. ACT also produces another test battery called WorkKeys that is primarily a diagnostic tool for job skill development. Scores are available in applied mathematics, applied technology, business writing, listening, locating information, observation, readiness, reading for information, teamwork, writing, and workforce productivity solutions (American College Testing Program, 2003b).

Because of dissatisfaction with these older general education tests, several newer testing efforts are emerging. First, the RAND Corporation (Klein, 2003) has recently adopted or designed several test measures targeted toward general education. Others include (1) the Graduate Record Examination's Analytical Writing score (Educational Testing Service, 2003b), (2) ETS's Tasks in Critical Thinking (TCT), and (3) reasoning performance tasks similar to the Law School Admissions Test. Erwin and Sebrell (2003) note that some problems have been identified with the TCT. The TCT is a constructed response test that has been very costly to administer and score; also the original TCT was too long for students to complete in its entirety, and individual student scores were not usually reported, which reduced student motivation.

Another proposal for testing general education is the expanded version of the National Assessment of Adult Literacy (NAAL) from the National Center for Education Statistics (2003b) of the U.S. Department of Education. The content areas of prose, document, and quantitative literacy make up the NAAL's tasks; a random selection of adults across the United States takes the test on a sample of tasks. Using an advanced measurement procedure called item response theory, the scoring produces no individual scores but generalizes them to the U.S. population as a whole (National Center for Education Statistics, 2003b). Although well designed from a measurement point of view, NAAL hardly covers the full range of knowledge and skills expected in general education because of its roots as a very basic literacy test for the general population.

## Undergraduate Major Tests

Standardized testing also focuses on undergraduate majors. The two most available proprietary instruments are ETS's Major Field Achievement Tests (MFAT; Educational Testing Service, 2003c) and the Area Concentration Achievement Tests (ACAT; 2003). Originally, most of the MFAT represented revisions of the Graduate Record Examination advanced tests with questions of very high difficulty removed to accommodate a typical graduating senior, who is not necessarily bound for graduate school. ETS currently markets the MFAT tests in biology, business, chemistry, computer science, criminal justice, economics, education, English literature, history, mathematics, music, physics, political science, psychology, and sociology. The ACAT offers either a pool of test items or a single test in majors of agriculture, art, biology, criminal justice, geology, history, literature in English, neuroscience, political science, psychology, and social work. Some of the MFATs lack sufficient subscores for diagnostic uses, and the ACAT test needs more reliability data. Users of these tests should carefully match their questions with the learning objectives of the major programs. Generally, policymakers consider major tests important for accountability but less so than general education because student majors are only subsets of the total number of graduates. Professions and disciplines are the primary audience, unless state policymakers regard a particular major such as teacher education as a problem area for accountability.

## Student Development

Student development focuses around personal characteristics, psychosocial maturity, or "how students change as persons" during college. The Student Development Task and Lifestyle Assessment (Winston, Miller, and Cooper, 1999) is one of the older development options, and it has five subscales: (1) Establishing and Clarifying Purpose (with subtasks Career Planning, Lifestyle Planning, Educational Involvement, and Cultural Participation); (2) Developing Autonomy (with subtasks Emotional Autonomy, Academic Autonomy, Instrumental Autonomy, and Interdependence); (3) Developing Mature Interpersonal Relationships (with subtasks Tolerance and Peer Relationships); (4) Salubrious Lifestyle (health and wellness practices); and (5) Response Bias (which is used to identify response patterns that suggest that a student is attempting to present an unrealistically positive image of himself or herself). Deborah Liddell (1990) published the Moral Orientation Measure—an instrument purporting to measure care and justice. James Madison University (2003a) distributes several developmental tests on curiosity, identity, and ethical decision making. As one example, the Scale of Service Learning and Involvement (James Madison University, 2003b) contains three subscales in (1) Exploration—an early developmental phase of social responsibility, focusing on the initial involvement in voluntary activities during which respondents explore; (2) Realization—a second stage of development of social responsibility reflecting attitudes about personal growth that can result from volunteer experiences, as well as early commitments to specific populations or issues; and (3) Activation—an evolving understanding of broad social issues and a personal commitment to action based on perceived injustices.

Other instruments exist, and interested readers should consult the *Mental Measurements Yearbook* from the Buros Institute of Mental Measurements at the University of Nebraska. Before adopting any of these or other tests, potential users should consult assessment and text experts and review the technical test manual for specific reliability and validity information.

## Need for Clarity

If policymakers demand data on student learning in college, what form should it take? As stated earlier, most constituents and stakeholders of higher education want comparable data. After the original state mandates for statewide testing in Tennessee, New Jersey, and Florida, the next round of state policies, such as those of Virginia and South Carolina, allowed institutions to provide their own instrumentation, which remained unique to each campus and not comparable. Although leaders of colleges and universities prefer institution-specific approaches, state policymakers want comparable data for their states.

However, some groups outside higher education want a single score for a college or university that somehow represents the sum total of what their students learned. This approach represents the *single number* fallacy—the belief that test designers can reduce all of undergraduate education to one score from a two-hour test. A single number would be misleading, as well as inadequate. Undergraduate education, particularly general education, contains many facets and components. An array of scores would answer better the needs of constituents because of the multifaceted tasks of the workplace and society. In addition, if a stakeholder wants to generalize about one component of general education, say technology skills, a reliable score must be planned for and obtained. Moreover, each score must have an adequate number of test items, in whatever form it takes—selective or constructed formats—to result in a reliable score. Most of us consider unfair the extreme example of graduation that depends on one answer to one test question. In professional terms, basing an assessment of student learning in general education or in an academic major on a single number is also unacceptable. Depending on how many learning constructs a test must measure, two hours is also far too short to provide a reliable set of scores for general education.

While they reject the single-score fallacy, some constituents seek an overall "scorecard" for higher education. Many faculty members take issue with the scorecard approach because they claim that a test cannot reduce the complex nature of general education to a few numbers. Critics outside higher education counter that providing too many numbers or too much narrative obfuscates the issue, with the consequence that few readers would derive any meaning about an institution or higher education as a whole.

Similarly, the concept of competency is popular with many stakeholders of higher education. A competency system implies that a standard can be set, at which a given score or above indicates proficiency. Often that set score determines whether a student advances to a higher grade level. Reporting competence is simple because the result is merely the number or percentage of takers who score at or below that standard. The problem comes in setting the standard or cutoff score (Erwin and Wise, 2001), for there is no foolproof way to set a standard. Moreover, reviewers often readjust preliminary standards set by content experts for political considerations. Beside competency, the other main analytical strategy is measuring longitudinal change or "value-added" in student learning during the college years. This approach calculates the difference between test results of entering students compared with their scores on the same or similar tests later in college or just before graduation. Although there are some technical issues to consider (Feldt and Brennan, 1993), value-added helps capture a college's impact on its students by measuring their growth from admission to a later period in college or at graduation.

Policymakers must weigh the external interest in clarity about the level of student learning against the campus need for improvement of student learning (see Chapter Five). Accountability asks for a few meaningful scores, whereas improvement requires many scores for diagnostic purposes. The differing needs explain the tension between external accountability and institutional improvement (Chapter One); it is a long-standing tension and one that is likely to persist for some time. Ideally, both sides could have their needs fulfilled with diagnostic subscores that sum to a composite score for accountability purposes. Data and clearer definitions of various educational constructs serve the quest for clarity.

## Recommendations

The term *standardized testing* evokes strong emotions; exactly which emotions depends on the group. Whereas some public officials perceive standardized tests as the answer to accountability, academic groups often see them as presenting a precise but inaccurate representation of student development and learning. Such strong feelings often arise from either personal experience or a misunderstanding of the nature and value of standardized tests. Periodicals such as *Fair Test* regularly assert that standardized tests have almost no redeeming value, yet testing companies exist because these examinations are in demand. In spite of criticism of tests, their use has proliferated over the past decades. What follows are recommendations to state and campus policymakers that can help make standardized tests more valuable and effective for institutional improvement and accountability.

## Focus on the Main Issue: General Education

It is time to focus on and create reliable and valid measures of student learning and development in general education. One of the most telling criticisms leveled against the higher education community is our failure to develop acceptable measures of student learning and continued use of surrogates. For instance, the *Measuring Up* project is considering the National Survey of Student Engagement (NSSE), alumni surveys, and graduate admissions data as a beginning for assessing student learning, yet none of these are direct measures of learning (Chapter Nine). It is also considering an expanded NAAL, which focuses on basic skills and fails to cover the complexity and diversity of learning in general education. Part of the problem lies in the lack of consensus about the scope and content of general education, which is the major imprint on every college graduate. It is time to make more substantial progress on new conceptual models and new instruments, especially for undergraduate education. The higher education community needs to agree on the domain or knowledge and skills that should be conveyed in general education and to develop direct methods for assessing their achievement.

## Use Computing Technology

Although academics devote considerable attention to research and instruction using technology, very few scholars show the same interests in using technology in developing tests of student learning. Computer-based tests (CBTs) provide a new range of options previously unavailable (Erwin and DeMars, 2002). This technology allows the posing of novel test questions with the multimedia capabilities of the microcomputer. At my own institution, we have CBTs in the arts, oral communication, American history and government, scientific reasoning, and quantitative reasoning. Test questions exhibit visual art, play music, present small-group processes, replay famous speeches, present diagrams, and display real-life applications using numbers. New CBTs help in presenting innovative tests items that could not be administered in the past. Other CBTs allow for complex branching, based on prior responses such as adaptive test items programmed to report student ability, learning style, demographic group, or any other established set of guidelines and algorithms. Unfortunately, tests of learning and development during the college years have not advanced as existing technology has progressed.

Related to CBT is the promising area of automated computer scoring of constructed responses (Burstein and others, 1998; Clauser and others, 1997). Early research (Shermis, Mzumara, Olson, and Harrington, 2001) demonstrates more reliable and valid information on computer scoring of writing ability than that generated by human raters. An even more advanced approach called latent semantic analysis (Landauer, Foltz, and Laham, 1998) shows great potential for rating general education content, as well as writing ability. Some higher education audiences have been reluctant to use these approaches, but their time-saving potential deserves closer attention.

## Use Advanced Measurement Techniques

Standardized tests also have greater potential for use than has been realized in practice in higher education because they currently use designs of elementary technical procedures. A review of all proprietary instruments for the U.S. Department of Education (Erwin, 2000) in critical thinking, problem solving, and written communication revealed that very few instruments used advanced measurement techniques such as item response theory, structural equation modeling, or generalizability measurement theory. External demands for standardized tests will not go away, and it is important to note that many sophisticated advancements in testing (see James

Madison University, 2003b, for definitions of terms) have not found their way into college-level assessment instruments. Any type of testing inevitably has a technical side of measurement, and accountability must recognize this part of evaluation and assessments. Just look at the lawsuits and heartaches associated with poor measurement practices in K–12 tests that illustrate a trail of tears and frustrations (Steinberg and Henriques, 2001).

## Use Cognitive Psychology

Another criticism of standardized tests concerns their limited ability to test higher-order thinking skills. Standardized tests can assess more than recall and lower-level cognitive skills. Combining stage theory from developmental psychology and the "smart tests" of CBT offer new tools for designing tests for higher cognitive skills. Embretson (1999), Haladyna (1997), and Pellegrino, Chudowsky, and Glaser (2001) all propose strategies in designing tests of higher-order thinking skills. Similarly, our conceptual models of what to assess may need further expansion. Discrete knowledge can be fleeting, and often developmental thinking, sometimes called "habits of mind," may be helpful. For instance, when lack of agreement regarding specific knowledge occurred in the fine arts component of general education, we established five stages of "esthetic development" to capture the cognitive complexity in evaluating the arts.

## Include the Affective Domain

Although much testing has been limited to measuring cognitive skills, future standardized tests should give feedback about the affective development of students that is attributable to their college education. Often misconceived as having political bents (such as right or left wing), the affective side of postsecondary education is critical for societal needs: civic engagement, ethical decision making, tolerance for different people, curiosity of lifelong learners, autonomy, confidence, emotional resilience, altruism, and empathy, to name a few. The business community generally values these attributes as interpersonal skills, yet politicians remain hesitant to endorse them. All constructs have measurement errors, whether testing students' discrete knowledge or measuring their affective views. At the least, institutional researchers should study the impact of on-campus programs and services on nurturing the personal development of students.

## Conclusion

The higher education community and test companies can do better than current practice in creating and refining tests of student learning and development. But at the same time, federal and state governments and private foundations should provide sufficient resources to design new instruments that test student learning, especially in general education. Just as important, they should also support comprehensive efforts of the academic community to develop an acceptable domain for general education. As a nation, we regularly endorse and sponsor research on a myriad of scientific, technical, and practical topics. Surely, because of the value that it can bring to individuals, states, and society, higher education deserves similar support. The issue of meaningful and more accurate learning and development information is too important to leave to a few researchers and test companies. Certainly, it requires a maximum intellectual effort from the academic community and substantial funding from the federal and state governments.

Currently, standardized testing does not respond well to any of the three corners of the Accountability Triangle: state priorities, academic concerns, and market forces. It is time that standardized testing moves to meet all three needs. We can find ways for tests to satisfy accountability and improvement, as well as reliability, validity, and feasibility. The real question is whether we in the academic community can find the will.

# Chapter Seven

# Imagine Asking the Client
## Using Student and Alumni Surveys for Accountability in Higher Education
*George D. Kuh*

When he was mayor of New York City, Ed Koch routinely asked people when moving around the city, "How am I doin'?" Koch did this to stay in touch with his constituents' issues, problems, and concerns. It also gave him an idea of how he and his administration were performing. In accountability systems, feedback directly from clients can serve a similar function. Moreover, for the reasons Burke discussed in Chapter One, postsecondary institutions increasingly are expected to present evidence that demonstrates responsible, effective use of resources.

Surveys of current and former students are among the multiple sources of information that authorities recommend including in a comprehensive performance reporting and quality assurance system (Banta, Rudolph, Van Dyke, and Fisher, 1996; Bogue and Hall, 2003; Ewell, 1984, 1997b; Peterson and Vaughan, 2002). Furthermore, without information from these major groups of institutional stakeholders, it is not possible to determine how well a college or university is achieving its educational purposes (Astin, 1991). Indeed, institutions are obliged to be accountable to their students, as well as other stakeholders, and obtaining input from students and graduates and publicly reporting their experiences is one way to do this.

In this chapter, I examine issues related to using student and alumni surveys as part of an accountability framework. First, I articulate a rationale for obtaining information directly from currently enrolled students and graduates and then describe a handful of instruments that can be used for such purposes. Next, I discuss how survey results might be most appropriately used for quality assurance and institutional improvement. Then I discuss why information from surveys of students and graduates is not often used for quality assurance purposes. I close with some suggestions for using survey results effectively. Many of the examples cited come from my experience directing the National Survey of Student Engagement—an annual survey of the extent to which college students take part in effective educational practices.

## The Student Voice and Accountability

For more than two decades, the assessment bandwagon has been rolling across the landscape of U.S. colleges and universities. Once assessment was thought to be a fad (Ewell, 2002a); now all the regional accrediting associations and many field-specific organizations expect institutions to provide evidence of student learning and other measures of the quality of the student experience. Indeed, during the past decade almost every college and university has assessed some aspect of its educational program (Peterson and Vaughan, 2002; Chapter Five). For several reasons, surveys are the method of choice for collecting information about the student experience.

First, surveys are relatively inexpensive to develop and administer compared with other quality assurance measures such as actuarial data that require separate collection and reporting or objective tests of learning or various proficiencies. Because different types of surveys are readily available, they can be used widely within an institution or across groups of colleges and universities within a state system or consortium, providing data for benchmarking and other forms of peer comparisons. Moreover, student reports are the only feasible, cost-effective source of certain kinds of information from a large enough number of students for the findings to be generalizable within and across institutions. Some outcomes of interest—attitudes and values or gains in social or practical competence, for example—cannot be measured by achievement tests. For many indicators of educational practice, student reports are often the only meaningful source of data. In the vast majority of cases, it would be prohibitively expensive and logistically impossible to discover how large numbers of students across a range of different types of institutions use their time, interact with peers and faculty members, and engage in other educationally purposeful activities. Finally, student voices have a magnetic appeal to policymakers at various levels—legislators, commissioners, and governing board members. When survey data corroborate anecdotes, the message is all but irresistible.

## Selected Surveys and Accountability Applications

In this section, I briefly review several of the widely used student and alumni surveys and illustrate their potential use as quality assurance and institutional improvement measures. I draw on Borden and Zak-Owens's (2001) analysis of more than two dozen assessment tools that have been used with large numbers of students at different types of colleges and universities. Borden and Zak-Owens also reviewed other instruments that could potentially be used for purposes of accountability and quality assurance, including direct measures of learning outcomes and proficiencies and faculty behaviors, some of which are available from the American College Testing Program and Educational Testing Service.

### Entering Students

For several reasons, more is known about students as they start college than at any other subsequent time. First, institutions obtain a lot of information from students as part of the admissions process. Second, the organizations that administer the ACT and SAT college entrance examinations also gather a good deal of information from students. For example, College Board's Student Descriptive Questionnaire asks about high school record and course-taking patterns, family background, and other student characteristics. The ACT Freshman Class Profile Service summarizes an informative array of student characteristics. These sources provide rich baseline information about who matriculates to what kinds of institutions, allowing between-institution and within-system comparisons of student characteristics. This kind of information is essential in order to hold constant student ability, student enrollment patterns, place of residence, and other characteristics in analyses of student and institutional performance. I'll return to this point later.

The third reason we know a good deal about students when they begin their collegiate studies is because of the Cooperative Institutional Research Program (CIRP). Based at UCLA's Higher Education Research Institute (HERI), CIRP is the nation's largest and longest-running (thirty-three years) annual survey of undergraduates. Each year, several hundred thousand entering college students answer CIRP questions about their background and attitudes, providing a comprehensive portrait of the precollege experiences of entering undergraduate cohorts. The College Student Expectations Questionnaire (CSXQ), housed at the Indiana University Center for Postsecondary Research, also collects information from students as they start college, focusing on their expectations for what they think their undergraduate experience will be like. The one-hundred-item instrument asks about the amount of time and energy they intend to spend on various matters, including studying, attending cultural events, interacting with peers, and so forth.

## Characteristics and Experiences of Enrolled Students

The voluminous research on college student development indicates that what students *do* when they get to college is more important to their learning (and, arguably, the educational effectiveness of an institution) than *who they are* or what they bring with them to postsecondary education (Pascarella and Terenzini, 1991). That is, after controlling for entering ability and institutional characteristics, student learning is primarily a function of the time and energy students devote to their studies and other educationally purposeful activities. Educationally effective colleges and universities employ pedagogical practices and organize the curriculum and other learning opportunities in ways that induce students to devote more effort to educationally purposeful activities than they might otherwise.

One of the most widely used instruments intended to assess the quality of student educational experiences is the National Survey of Student Engagement (NSSE), which is housed at the Indiana University Center for Postsecondary Research. The NSSE asks students at four-year colleges and universities to report the frequency with which they engage in dozens of activities that are empirically linked with desired outcomes of college. The questions represent a combination of activities that students can do on their own, such as studying, discussing ideas from class with their peers, and participating in extracurricular programs, as well as activities that institutions require, such as the amount of reading and writing and the nature of intellectual work emphasized in classes. Responding to these and other questions requires that students reflect on what they are putting into and getting out of their studies. The very act of completing a survey like NSSE is an effective educational practice in that it encourages students to think about how they spend their time and reflect on the consequences of their behavior during the past year.

Other enrolled-student surveys for four-year institutions include the Your First College Year (YFCY) survey and the College Student Survey (CSS), both administered by UCLA. Students complete the former at the end of the first year of school and the latter at some subsequent point, typically in the final semester of the senior year. Both can be linked to responses to the CIRP to estimate value-added, or the impact of college on student learning by matching responses from when students started college with those provided near the end of the first year (YFCY) or as seniors (CSS).

The College Student Experiences Questionnaire (CSEQ) is the companion instrument to the CSXQ and is administered in the spring semester of the first or subsequent college years. In addition to reporting how frequently they engage in a range of educationally purposeful activities, students estimate the extent to which they have made progress toward twenty-five desired outcomes of college, including writing ability, independent learning, working effectively with people from different backgrounds, and vocational skills. As with the CIRP and its follow-up surveys, using a combination of CSXQ and CSEQ or the Community College Student Experiences Questionnaire (CCSEQ) can document the degree to which student expectations are met through their subsequent behavior and how their behavior changes over time. When used as part of a longitudinal design, the results represent the impact of college on students. Institutional effectiveness can be inferred by examining student performance associated with targeted priority areas, such as particular programs of study or certain activities valued by the institution and state; participation in community service is an example.

Two-year colleges have available the "Faces of the Future" survey, developed by the American Association of Community Colleges and the American College Testing Program; the survey collects demographic information about students. The Community College Survey of Student Engagement (CCSSE) obtains complementary data about student engagement in effective educational practices by collecting much of the same information as the NSSE. Both CCSSE and NSSE have been used in experiments in a handful of states to provide evidence of student learning for the *Measuring Up* state-by-state report card.

As Zemsky (Chapter Twelve) and others (see Peterson and Vaughan, 2002) point out, the results from most surveys are not frequently made public, even though hundreds of schools use surveys such as NSSE, YFCY, CSS, and the CSEQ. However, this information has great promise for performance reporting and quality assurance, and it is likely that more schools will use such instruments in the future. In fact, some governing boards and state oversight agencies are incorporating NSSE results as a performance indicator—a use that was anticipated in its design. Longwood College incorporates its NSSE results as part of an institution-specific set of performance measures that the Virginia State Council of Higher Education requires. The Kentucky Postsecondary Council combines NSSE data with a locally developed alumni satisfaction survey to inform one of its five key indicators of progress toward preparing Kentuckians for life and work; another NSSE question contributes to Kentucky's civic engagement measure. In addition, Kentucky uses the actual and predicted engagement scores calculated by NSSE to compare the performance of Kentucky public universities against the national average.

The University of Texas System uses NSSE to meet its state's mandate to obtain information from its "customers." An accountability portfolio is presented annually to the state legislature and features an analysis of the experiences of first-generation students. The South Dakota University System incorporates its campuses' NSSE results in analyses of first- to second-year persistence rates and combines student engagement information with results from the required general education proficiency exam to assess the efficacy of curricular requirements.

Other systems using NSSE items as a performance indicator include the New Hampshire state universities, Texas A&M University, the University of Wisconsin, and the University of North Carolina. Some states, such as North Carolina, make NSSE results available via the Internet. However, to date no state has featured its student engagement data; typically, it is difficult to locate, and only someone looking hard for such information is likely to find it.

## Student Satisfaction

Generally speaking, students who are more satisfied devote more effort to their studies and are more likely to persist to graduation. Assuming that questions about satisfaction are appropriately worded, student reports about their experiences can provide insight into the quality of programs and services, pointing to places where institutional performance is unacceptable, especially if corroborated with other evidence, for example, when courses are not available to meet student demand and delay graduation, when academic advisers provide poor advice, or when students get the proverbial runaround when trying to solve problems. Some institutions and state systems expect student satisfaction measures to be included in institutional performance reporting schemes; Indiana University–Purdue University Indianapolis (IUPUI), University of Tennessee, and the University of Wisconsin are examples.

About 80 to 85 percent of all college graduates say they are "very" or at least "somewhat" satisfied with the quality of their experience. Thus, the variation among schools is not nearly as great as one might think in this regard and is probably constrained enough to call into question the legitimate use of global satisfaction questions in performance reporting and other forms of accountability approaches. However, experience shows that specific questions about student satisfaction with advising and with major-field program of study might differentiate among universities in a state system (Banta and Moffett, 1987). Locally developed student satisfaction surveys are widely used for assessing these areas and other related purposes like monitoring persistence and educational attainment of various groups and informing strategic planning. The most commonly used nationally normed satisfaction instrument is from Noel-Levitz (http://www.noellevitz.com/pdfs/2003_SSI_Report.pdf). Other instruments with different foci (such as CSEQ and NSSE) contain several satisfaction items.

Student satisfaction can be tricky to assess and interpret because it can refer both to students' expectations about a program and their judgments about its delivery. Those who say they are very satisfied may indicate that they either "have expected high quality and received it, or that they expected low quality and received it" (Van Liere and Lyons, 1986, p. 86). Thus, attempts to measure satisfaction must, at a minimum, distinguish between expectations and evaluations. Also, adjustments need to be made in analyzing satisfaction information to make sure the responses of students who do not use certain programs and services are properly handled. Such adjustments are important because such students have no firsthand experience with the programs and services they are asked to evaluate.

## Alumni Surveys

As with student satisfaction surveys, many institutions use locally developed alumni questionnaires. Institutional advancement and alumni association officers use these surveys primarily to gauge alumni loyalty and to generate goodwill among graduates and friends of the school. But in recent years, incorporating feedback from graduates in performance accountability systems seems to be increasing. For example, the University of Wisconsin surveys its graduates and uses some of this information in its performance indicator system. In 2002, more than a dozen alumni survey items were adapted with permission from the NSSE undergraduate survey in order to compare the experiences of currently enrolled students and graduates.

To respond to market forces, Robert Zemsky and Susan Shaman at the University of Pennsylvania developed the College Results Instrument (CRI) to create a national database that consumers could use to help them choose a college. CRI questions ask college graduates about their occupation and income; educational attainment; job skills; perceived competencies and deficiencies in the areas of communication, quantitative reasoning, and information gathering; engagement in lifelong learning and values reflecting arts and culture; civic engagement; physical fitness; and religion. In 1999, about eighty colleges and universities administered the CRI to samples of their alumni via a secure Web site. Information about its use since 2000 is sketchy after the instrument was turned over to Peterson's—the college guide publisher. Little use was made of the results, for reasons explained later (Rowles, 2003).

## Combining Student and Alumni Survey Data: The Tennessee Experience

Arguably, the best-designed and most comprehensively documented example of using student and alumni surveys in performance reporting and quality assurance is the University of Tennessee, where such measures have been used for more than two decades. Through 2002, the process allocated a total of more than $350 million in performance funding (Bogue and Hall, 2003). Starting with the 1979 pilot, an institution could earn up to 100 points allocated across various categories; 20 percent of the formula was based on input from graduates about their experiences (Banta, 1988). Each point of the 100-point performance funding scheme was worth as much as $60,000 at U.T.-Knoxville in the 1980s and 1990s (personal communication with George Kuh, July 31, 2003). By 1992, state colleges and universities had adopted common surveys that were used with currently enrolled students and alumni in alternating years. Information from students and alumni now constitutes 15 percent of the performance evaluation scheme. Tennessee recently added an "implementation" requirement and is monitoring what institutions do in terms of modifying policies and practices based on the results of surveys and other sources of information (Bogue and Hall, 2003).

The University of Tennessee used its student and alumni survey results to convince administrators and faculty members to focus on advising (one dean added a full-time adviser), increase opportunities for student-faculty interaction, improve publications for prospective students, increase the number of student organizations, and encourage more faculty involvement in career planning and placement of graduates (Banta, 1985, 1986; Banta and Fisher,

1986). Some units did targeted follow-up surveys to learn more about the experiences of students in their majors, both currently enrolled students and graduates (Banta, 1985). Faculty members and administrators were generally interested in the feedback from the surveys, in part because the specificity of the items clearly identified areas where improvements in educational practice, programs, and services could be made. This is contrasted with test scores, which are more difficult to translate into action steps (Banta, Rudolph, Van Dyke, and Fisher, 1996).

The Tennessee experience suggests some valuable lessons, most of which I incorporate later in the section on using survey results effectively. It's worth noting here that simply collecting data does not itself result in program improvements or quality assurance. Careful attention to instrument development and data utilization are also key steps in the process because "they represent the means of linking assessment to institutional missions and goals" (Pike and Banta, 1987, p. 33). "The assessment process in Tennessee grew gradually, without considerable controversy, in large part due to careful planning, involving key faculty stakeholders from the beginning, and permitting institutions to set their own goals and methods of monitoring in areas of interest to the state, such as increasing minority enrollment and retention/graduation rates" (Banta, Rudolph, Van Dyke, and Fisher, 1996, p. 44).

## Factors Limiting Use of Survey Data in Accountability

Although surveys are commonly used to obtain information directly from students and alumni, as mentioned earlier, survey results are not necessarily used in quality assurance protocols. When such data are reported publicly, it is often difficult for external audiences to compare results of two or more schools. Some notable exceptions will be discussed later, along with some conditions that will likely prompt more public reporting of survey results.

There are at least five reasons that survey results are not widely used in quality assurance programs and publicly reported. The first relates to concerns about validity and reliability. Two of the more pressing issues are whether students give honest, trustworthy answers and whether their responses reflect something meaningful about student learning and institutional effectiveness. Some faculty members and academic administrators do not consider under-graduates knowledgeable enough to render informed judgments about teaching and learning. This is due, in no small part, to the omnipresent end-of-term course evaluation forms that typically co-mingle questions addressing areas with which students have direct experience ("The concepts presented in this class are understand-able") with items about the instructor's substantive expertise ("The instructor is knowledgeable about this field"). Faculty members be-come understandably concerned if it appears that student opinions are being used to evaluate quality in areas where they are unquali-fied to judge.

Yet under the right conditions, student self-reports of their be-havior and college experiences are both valid and reliable (Baird, 1976; Berdie, 1971; Gershuny and Robinson, 1988; Kuh and oth-ers, 2001; Pace, 1985; Pike, 1995; Pohlman and Beggs, 1974; Turn-er and Martin, 1984). The most important factors are whether respondents have the information to provide accurate answers (Wentland and Smith, 1993) and whether they are willing to do so (Aaker, Kumar, and Day, 1998). People generally tend to respond accurately when questioned about their past behavior within a reasonably recent period of time (Converse and Presser, 1989; Sin-gleton, Straits, and Straits, 1993) and when the items avoid sensi-tive, potentially embarrassing matters (Bradburn and Sudman, 1988). All things considered, self-reports are likely to be valid and appropriate for use in quality assurance and performance improve-ment systems, provided five general conditions are met (Bradburn and Sudman, 1988; Brandt, 1958; Converse and Presser, 1989; DeNisi and Shaw, 1977; Hansford and Hattie, 1982; Laing, Swayer, and Noble, 1989; Lowman and Williams, 1987; Pace, 1985; Pike, 1995). The conditions are as follows: (1) the information requested is known to the respondents; (2) the questions are phrased clearly and unambiguously; (3) the questions refer to recent activities; (4) the respondents think the questions merit a serious and thoughtful response; and (5) answering the questions does not threaten, em-barrass, or violate the privacy of the respondent or encourage the respondent to answer in socially desirable ways. Most of the in-struments mentioned earlier meet these criteria (Borden and Zak-Owens, 2001).

Flagging survey response rates threaten internal validity; now surveys are becoming more problematic as students are bombarded with them, both through "snail mail" and e-mail, asking about almost every possible type of activity. Question topics range from preferences in toiletries, to alcohol attitudes and consumption, to spiritual beliefs and diversity experiences, to satisfaction with campus food and recreational facilities. Students on some large campuses receive more than a dozen surveys in a single semester! As a result, few schools or national survey research programs report greater than 40 percent average institutional response rates for currently enrolled students. The few campuses that routinely exceed such response rates make participation a condition for course registration or graduation. Even though experts maintain that reliable institutional point estimates can be based on as few as thirty-five to forty respondents, and margins of error can be reduced by increasing sample sizes, a widely held view persists that respondents and nonrespondents differ in important, systematic ways. Although small differences may well exist, most of the evidence suggests that on the questions about the student experience, these differences usually are not great enough to alter the conclusions one might draw from the results, provided best practices in survey administration are followed. They include carefully crafting and field-testing questions, formatting the survey instrument attractively, random sampling, conducting repeated follow-ups of nonrespondents, and so forth. To illustrate, the Indiana University Center for Survey Research contacted by telephone about 550 randomly selected nonrespondents to the 2001 NSSE from twenty-one different four-year colleges and universities. Their answers to selected NSSE questions did not differ in any appreciable way from those who responded to the survey that year (Kuh, 2002).

The second reason that survey results are not always reported publicly is that the purposes for survey results are often confounded, which limits the utility of the information. Two common purposes are assessment and accountability—concepts that are sometimes equated but can mean very different things (Chapter Five). According to Wellman (2003), assessment is intended to measure processes such as student and faculty behaviors, college outcomes, and various other institutional activities. The value of such information is that it stimulates self-analysis and points to areas where institutions can improve, as well as areas where performance is acceptable or outstanding. Accountability efforts differ in that they intentionally connect assessment results with institutional or system goals and publicly report this information within *and* beyond the institution—to government officials, policymakers, consumers, and so forth (Wellman, 2003). Indeed, Wellman argues that accountability systems can work only if data are made public.

Assessment and accountability are not mutually exclusive or incompatible, yet striking an appropriate balance between the two purposes is tricky. In this sense, assessment and accountability are not unlike aptitude and achievement; the same instrument can be used to estimate either, but the meaning of the results depends on the use to which the data are put.

The third reason that institutions do not often report or use student survey data is that many institutions are disappointingly inept at converting information into action, that is, taking concrete steps that can lead to improved student learning and institutional effectiveness. In part, this is because many surveys and other sources of quality assurance and institutional improvement do not themselves present results in a way that points to actions the institution might take to drive the results in a positive direction. In addition, colleges and universities are not organized to make use of such information (Peterson and Vaughan, 2002), as Massy and Zemsky point out in their chapters (Chapters Eight and Twelve); that is, institutions do not often enact policies, programs, or practices that address shortcomings identified by the results. This is especially problematic when putting the results from alumni surveys to good use because of the time lag between former students' experience and current conditions on campus.

For example, results from the CRI do not separate the effects of undergraduate study from postcollege experiences. In addition, in the absence of some sort of precollege measure, it is not possible to determine what effect the institution had on the performance of its graduates some years later. Students start college with different levels of knowledge and competence, and these differences are not reflected in alumni self-reports about how much students gained from college (Pascarella, 2001a). Sometimes the amount of elapsed time between college graduation and completion of the survey makes it all but impossible to determine how much of a graduate's success to attribute to attending a particular college and how much to what an individual learned in the workplace and other life experiences after graduating from college. In the CRI example, alumni completed the survey six years after graduation. It's not surprising, then, that faculty members express concern about what the results mean and what they are to do with the data. In fact, when Rowles (2003) looked at five institutions that participated in the CRI in 1999, none had used their results in any meaningful way. Only one institution indicated an interest in incorporating its relatively positive results in its strategic plan.

The fourth (and arguably least important) reason that survey results tend not to get much attention inside or outside higher education is that, as Zemsky argues (Chapter Twelve), so-called medallion institutions do not use or publicly report this information. Thus, the popular media do not give nearly as much attention to student survey results as they do to other indicators on which medallions do well, such as rankings based primarily on reputation and resources. Although the vast majority of private medallions do not administer quasi-public surveys such as NSSE, some "public ivies" do, including the University of Michigan, University of Virginia, Miami of Ohio, and the College of William and Mary. Although the majority of Ivy League schools and other members of the thirty-plus-member Consortium for Financing Higher Education (COFHE) do not use NSSE, many administer surveys such as the CSEQ, which is the conceptual base on which NSSE is grounded. The extent to which COFHE member schools use this information for purposes of quality assurance and improvement is unknown, though conversations with institutional research officers from some of these colleges and universities suggest that they know a good deal about their students and their educational experiences.

The NSSE project offers a promising contrast to the CRI experience. From the beginning, NSSE set out to promote the use of student engagement results. In addition to featuring nascent examples of how schools were using the data in its annual reports (NSSE, 2001, 2002), the project sends out periodic requests to participating institutions to obtain more information about data use and its impact on policy and practice. The most recent example is that the executive officers of the Council of Independent Colleges and the American Association of State Colleges and Universities sent out e-mails cosigned by the NSSE director inviting schools to share their use of NSSE data for quality assurance and institutional improvement. More than eighty institutions had responded by the time this chapter was drafted. Although a few schools candidly admitted they were not using the data in any systematic way, most were sharing it with various groups on campus, some quite widely with groups beyond the campus as well.

A few institutions have featured or organized their regional accreditation reports around student engagement (California Lutheran University, Juniata College, Ohio University, Radford University). At Illinois State University, University of Charleston, and University of Southern Indiana, the results are being widely disseminated and routinely used in almost every facet of institutional policy and planning. Fresno Pacific University and Oral Roberts University are among the schools using NSSE data in ongoing program reviews. Other institutions have used their data to identify priorities for fundraising and foundation support (Madonna University, St. Xavier University). Still others find student engagement to be associated with persistence and achievement and are developing programs to enhance student engagement with an eye toward improving student success rates (California State University Chico, Dordt College, Indiana University Bloomington, Towson University, University of Wisconsin-Green Bay, University of Wisconsin-Stevens Point, University of Missouri-St. Louis, and University of Montana).

The final reason schools do not report student engagement results is that they worry that the results will embarrass the institution or be misinterpreted or be used in ways that will do harm to the institution. There is little evidence that public embarrassment will, by itself, guide improvement efforts. Also, as mentioned earlier, just because a school appears to be below average, many students at that institution are more highly engaged than average or below-average students at other institutions with higher mean scores. As discussed later, there are many ways student engagement and other survey data can be misused, and it seems prudent to go slowly in testing how such information can be most productively introduced into the public domain.

## Issues Complicating Using Survey Results for Quality Assurance

Public perceptions of collegiate quality are substantially swayed by institutional reputations and other vestiges of prestige, as contrasted with various performance measures (Bogue and Hall, 2003;

Ewell, 2002a; Kuh, 2001). In this context, as Zemsky notes (Chapter Twelve), student and alumni surveys can be an antidote to reputation and prestige. Indeed, Zemsky's medallion institutions have more to lose in reporting survey results because they are supposed to be good at everything. But no school is perfect. No single institution of the more than eight hundred colleges and universities participating in NSSE, for example, performs at or near the top in each of the five benchmarks of effective educational practice.

One of the more dramatic findings from the NSSE project thus far is that substantial within-institutional differences in various measures of the student experience are the rule at most institutions. On average, these within-school differences usually are greater (even for ability measures)—and sometimes much greater—than between-school differences. This indicates that although institutional mean scores of campuses of a state university system may be large enough to differ statistically, every institution has a substantial number of students performing well below its campus average. Furthermore, comparing institutional average benchmark scores tells only a small part of a university's performance. Some institutions may have an average score that places them only two or three points on a scale away from the overall system average but have more students operating below the mean score than other institutions because a few high or low scorers skew the distributions. Similar performance patterns characterize clusters of small, independent colleges. That is, the greater within-school variance, compared with between-school differences, is not confined to larger state-supported institutions.

Another nettlesome issue is how to distribute accountability fairly for transfer student performance. NSSE data show that, although transfers generally find their institutions as academically challenging as do their nontransfer peers and report comparable grades, they are generally less involved in other educationally engaging activities at the school from which they are about to graduate (Kuh, 2003). Does the performance of transfer students at the time of graduation belong to the current institution, the institutions that transfer students attended previously, or to the individual student? More than half of all undergraduates start college at a school different from the one they currently attend. At some universities, the proportion of graduating seniors who are transfers exceeds 70 percent; more than 25 percent of students are attending two or more schools concurrently.

## Managing the Message and the Media

Publicly reporting student and alumni survey results is a potential media event, such as the annual stir that occurs when *The Princeton Review* releases its "party school" list. Because every institution has an insatiable appetite for positive media coverage, schools themselves can get caught up in making news by reporting student survey results in order to attract more applicants or change the characteristics of the applicant pool or compete for foundation support. In fact, the initial discussions out of which the NSSE project evolved emphasized the need for alternative indicators of quality to rankings. But because rankings can be misused and often hide as much information as they disclose, the NSSE project goes to great lengths to discourage using student engagement results in rankings and features a "no-ranking" policy on its Web site (http://www.indiana.edu/~nsse/html/usingst.shtml). Nonetheless, a college president recently wrote an op-ed piece for a regional newspaper that included the following statement: "The highly regarded National Survey of Student Engagement, the best quantitative indicator of undergraduate education available, *ranks* [our] academic program in the highest percentile among the roughly 500 participating schools across the country" (italics added for emphasis).

NSSE does no such thing! At the same time, it would be worse, certainly, if some individual or group created rankings from the information NSSE publishes in its annual report or from what participating schools may be willing to release. These scenarios are at odds with the purposes of any serious accountability agenda.

## Using Survey Results for Quality Assurance and Institutional Improvement

Designed appropriately, student and alumni surveys can yield instructive information for benchmarking—one approach to quality assurance. Such data may have immediate relevance and applicability for institutional improvement and can also be used for external accountability, such as within a state system for comparing performance on vetted indicators of quality or efficiency. This kind of normative application should take into account student and institutional factors that can affect the results, such as student ability and institutional size. For example, institutions that have a substantial proportion of high-ability, full-time-enrolled students usually have higher graduation rates than institutions that attract lower-ability students who attend part-time and commute to college. Adjustments should be made for these and other factors to level the playing field and produce fair, reasonable, and defensible comparative data.

As mentioned earlier, one promising approach is to develop residual models where the predicted graduation rate, based on relevant factors such as student ability and institutional selectivity, is compared with actual performance. NSSE has done this by calculating predicted and actual scores for its five benchmarks of effective educational practice at the institutional level.

Benchmarking and other forms of performance indicators are not restricted to the public sector. Independent colleges and universities are also feeling the press to respond to their constituents' expanding appetite for accountability. Council of Independent Colleges member schools are reviewing ways to "make the case" for private higher education; student and alumni surveys will almost certainly be a part of this effort (R. Ekman, personal communication with George Kuh, June 22, 2003). The Lutheran Education Conference of North America (LECNA) contracted with Hardwick-Day to compare Lutheran college alumni with graduates of public universities as to the nature and perceived benefits of their college experiences (www.lutherancolleges.org). Lutheran college graduates were generally more satisfied overall and more likely to report that their school emphasized value formation and religious practice than their counterparts who attended public institutions. Thus, it is not surprising that independent institutions feature these results on their Web sites and in communications with prospective students and alumni.

In the remainder of this section, I offer some guidelines for using information from students and alumni for quality assurance purposes.

• *Select or design surveys and questions that measure established institutional goals for student learning and campus programs and services and that are also compatible with state priorities.* To do this correctly, considerable planning, patience, persistence, and incentives are required to get people to the table. Once assembled, the purposes for surveying students and alumni need to be determined. Why do we want this kind of information? For what purposes will we use the data? Who else besides key institutional decision makers will see the results? It is essential that both assessment experts and people representing various units and perspectives on the student experience be involved. This will give credibility to the process and go a long way toward ensuring that the right things get measured. As others have observed, institutions measure what they value and value what they measure, so both espoused and enacted institutional and program values and goals should be reflected in the survey questions. At the same time, technical expertise is essential to selecting instruments with acceptable psychometric properties and to employing analytical strategies that will answer key questions.

• *Ensure that surveys are psychometrically sound and that the results do not systematically disadvantage certain types of institutions.* To resonate with policymakers and institutional leaders, survey questions must have face validity, be relevant to the educational programs and character of students attending the institution, and withstand the scrutiny of a discerning (and potentially skeptical) faculty. Even well-constructed surveys designed by experts, such as NSSE, which has good psychometric properties (Kuh and others, 2001), are not perfect. For example, prior to 2003, NSSE questions may have underestimated engagement on the part of students majoring in math, science, and the performing arts because the survey contains few questions that directly tap the activities characteristic of study in those fields. Changes made to the survey in 2003 are intended to ameliorate this problem.

Another concern is how to take into account systematic differences in student characteristics to estimate accurately the educational effectiveness of various types of institutions. For example, student satisfaction questions should be sensitive to the range of services and institutional functions used by different types of students, such as adult learners and commuters. Another related challenge that will grow in importance is adequately and accurately capturing the experiences of e-learners—students who are enrolled in distance education programs or who attend "virtual" universities.

Most surveys are designed with traditional-age, full-time, residential students in mind. This complicates efforts to estimate performance of institutions in state systems that have a flagship residential campus and other campuses populated by part-time commuting students. Too often, such comparisons fail to take into account institutional differences in student ability, attendance patterns, and place of residence, which are positively linked to engagement and learning. Schools have little or no control over these factors and should not be penalized in quality assurance programs. In addition, the goals and nature of experiences that these students want and have probably differ substantially. As mentioned earlier, controlling for these and other relevant factors, such as size, program mix, and educational expenditures per student, levels the playing field somewhat. This approach resembles efforts to calculate retention and graduation rates nationally after taking into account institutional characteristics.

• *Involve representatives from different constituent groups in interpreting survey results.* Indeed, "improving the quality of the undergraduate experience demands cooperation by the two groups on campus who spend the most time with students: faculty members and student affairs professionals" (Banta and Kuh, 1998, p. 42). The warrant is compelling: students learn more and are more likely to persist to graduation when their in-class and out-of-class experiences are meaningful and complementary (Pascarella and Terenzini, 1991).

Faculty members and student affairs professionals bring different perspectives to the table to understand and interpret the meaning of results. Two of the more important conditions that characterize productive collaborations on assessment are (1) participation by academic and student affairs professionals in the design and assessment of curricular programs and (2) intentional efforts to develop a shared understanding of student learning and personal development among faculty, student affairs professionals, and others (Banta and Kuh, 1998). These conditions are not conceptually complex nor do they require additional resources or expertise in planning, program design, and assessment beyond that typically found on most college or university campuses. Alumni affairs personnel and local community members can offer insights into the meaning and potential uses of key survey findings.

Last but not least, the views of students and alumni themselves should be represented in vetting the results and when discussing possible changes. Student involvement can also help encourage higher levels of participation in subsequent survey cycles. At Norfolk State University, students prepared stories about their school's NSSE results for the student paper, using their own language to call attention to important findings. At Oregon State University (OSU), first-year students in the Leaders of Positive Innovation Program provided feedback to the administration about NSSE results and subsequently conducted their own research, which resulted in recommendations to the provost's council about ways to increase faculty-student interaction and build involvement in campus clubs.

• *Survey enough students that the data have meaning at the department level.* As mentioned earlier, reliable institutional point estimates can be obtained from forty to fifty respondents. But decisions about programs and resources based on only a few dozen students typically do not carry much political clout with faculty members and academic administrators. Moreover, faculty members are much more likely to pay attention to survey results if they know that reasonable numbers of *their* students are among the respondents. Therefore, to report findings by major field, a sampling scheme is needed that will produce an adequate number of respondents to make the analysis worthwhile. Toward this end, in 2002, Texas State University (formerly Southwest Texas State University) systematically sampled large numbers of students in thirteen departments to ensure that enough students completed the NSSE survey to enable faculty members to be confident about the results. Southern Illinois University-Edwardsville also surveys substantial numbers of students enrolled in first-year seminars, as well as students in certain colleges and departments, to stimulate the interest of deans and department chairs in using the data.

Providing information about students in their classes to large numbers of faculty members is one step toward developing an institutional culture in which data are routinely shared and used for a variety of purposes, including decision making (Kuh and Banta, 2000; Peterson and Vaughan, 2002). DePaul University is one such institution. Its NSSE data, along with other information about the student experience, are available on a password-protected Web site that faculty members, administrators, and selected others can visit to learn about student and institutional performance. Indiana University–Purdue University Indianapolis (IUPUI) uses NSSE with locally developed surveys to monitor the effectiveness of its university college and student satisfaction with various services and the campus environment. A key feature in the IUPUI accountability system is that units annually report on how they are using their results to improve. The vice chancellor for institutional planning and assessment is a key actor in this process; she attends budget hearings to ask questions related to program quality and improvement.

•   *Use multiple sources of information.* Well-designed surveys can obtain certain kinds of information not readily available through other means. At the same time, survey results cannot and should not be the only source of information about the student experience used in an accountability or quality assurance approach. Moreover, when survey results can be corroborated with other evidence (and results from valid, reliable surveys almost always are), the results are much more likely to be taken seriously and promptly acted upon.

At the same time, student self-reports of their learning in substantive areas are not valid proxies for objective measures of student achievement and development. That is, these data cannot be used reliably to represent or compare student learning outcomes, either at the national level or between different types of institutions. This is because self-reported gains may be confounded by students' entering ability levels or their response tendencies or both (for example, students vary in the degree to which they are open to change as a result of attending college (Pascarella, 2001a). There are statistical procedures to ameliorate these problems, such as regressing these results on measures of entering ability to produce residual gain scores, as recommended by Pascarella (2001a). Though gain scores are not necessarily related to measures of entering ability (Pike, 1996, 1999b, 2000), it is not possible to determine conclusively whether consistencies in students' responses represent a source of error or true relationships among outcome dimensions (Pike, 1999a). Such technical issues aside, individual institutions often rely on student self-reported gains to identify potential areas of improvement, as self-reports are generally reliable in areas about which students have a good deal of experience or knowledge, such as reading and writing ability.

•   *Make survey results available to external audiences later rather than sooner.* Running throughout this and several other chapters in this book is the sense that many institutions are ill prepared to make good use of the results from quality assurance efforts. Indeed, colleges and universities are among the least adept organizations at converting data into action. That does not mean, however, that more good than harm will come from publicly reporting all findings from a quality assurance program. Indeed, the potential for mischief is all too real when external groups obtain such information. That worry aside, it is also the case that institutional leaders and others often are unfamiliar with evidence about the quality of the student experience. As a result, on learning about such results they need time and space to corroborate survey results with other data and gather perspectives from various constituent groups as to what reasonable steps to take to address the issues the survey data reveal.

Two points warrant emphasis. First, it is unwise to make results available before the institution has had a chance to carefully and thoroughly examine them internally and to establish a plan for addressing areas where performance is less than desirable. It would be a shame if premature public release of survey data places the institution in an embarrassing position and detracts or distracts from getting about the improvement business. Second, when reporting results publicly, the meaning of and implications behind every key number or pattern of responses should be explained, to the extent possible. Utmost care should be taken to communicate survey results in a way that does not mislead or allow consumers to misinterpret and draw erroneous conclusions. If the school does not explain what the numbers mean, someone else will.

Some administrators are paranoid about releasing data, even internally. I visited one campus where the provost met me at the airport. As we talked about her campus and my consultation (topics we should have discussed before my arrival!), she asked me not to present all of her university's student engagement results to various groups. "The campus," she said, "isn't ready to deal with the data." But it was too late, at least as far as I was concerned. My first presentation was only an hour away, and the PowerPoint displays were already prepared. We all were pleasantly surprised to discover that there was keen interest in data (perhaps because people saw so little information most of the time) and that deans and faculty members alike found the institution's student engagement results to be provocative and instructive, though some areas of performance were not necessarily flattering or affirming. Too often, we

underestimate our collective capacity to absorb and deal constructively with unpleasant news.

How much time should an institution have to improve? It is a
fair question, and my answer will not surprise academics but will
surely disappoint those who expect colleges and universities to respond more quickly to changing circumstances. Realistically, and
assuming the steps previously outlined in this section are implemented in short order (within a year), a college needs at least three
years to begin to see changes in the performance of its students.
This is because there is typically a four- to six-month lag between
surveying students or alumni and the time the data are reported in
one or more consumable formats to flag areas of concern. It will
take the remainder of that academic year (year one) to determine
what might be appropriate interventions. The second year is best
spent designing and field-testing interventions (changes in programs and practices, new programs) and tweaking the interventions
before full implementation. So, it's not until the end of year three,
after students have been exposed to the modified policies and practices, that the indicators may begin to show improvement. This said,
it is also the case that no single intervention or program will likely
have a dramatic, immediate impact on the quality of the undergraduate experience. Rather, much good research shows that it is
a complementary set of activities that is most likely to have the desired effects (Pascarella and Terenzini, 1991).

## Closing Thoughts

On the one hand, student and alumni surveys are relatively weak
measures of many dimensions of student learning. On the other
hand, they can be instructive, reliable measures of student engagement and satisfaction, which are moderately correlated with
many desirable outcomes of college. Moreover, surveys can provide information about certain aspects of the collegiate experience
that cannot easily be obtained by other means.

Ideally, survey results should move closer to the center of
Burke's Accountability Triangle. This could happen if schools or
systems perceive a market advantage and begin systematically releasing their results and encouraging their peers to do so. At the
same time, making public the results from all surveys presents a

mild to moderate risk to most schools because no institution performs at the highest levels on all measures. For this reason, it would be unfortunate if all student and alumni surveys moved much closer to the market forces corner of the triangle. Although survey data can and should serve the market, the potential for manipulating the results or selectively reporting results to create a certain image in the public is so great that the value of the data themselves for purposes of institutional improvement could well be compromised should institutions or others succeed at manipulating or gaming responses. In this situation, no one benefits. Institutions lose a potentially instructive opportunity to learn about their strengths and shortcomings, as experienced by key customers. Prospective students are misled by poor-quality data, and all surveys get tainted with the specter that students cannot be trusted.

A culture of individual professorial and professional autonomy is deeply rooted in academe. This does not mean colleges are constitutionally opposed to quality assurance and improvement, just that it is terribly difficult to mobilize and sustain the level of effort needed. Such efforts are all but impossible without one or more local champions who can muster the collective will. Also necessary is credible, trustworthy information that documents institutional performance in areas that affect educational quality. Well-designed and -implemented student and alumni surveys are indispensable to this task.

# Chapter Eight

# Academic Audit for Accountability and Improvement

*William F. Massy*

Authors throughout this volume cite the tension between account-ability and improvement. Accountability-oriented interventions as-sure external stakeholders that higher education institutions are delivering quality education. Improvement-oriented interventions help institutions develop more robust quality assurance and im-provement processes. This chapter describes how higher education oversight agencies and individual schools can use academic audit to further both objectives simultaneously.

As originated by the university community in the United King-dom, academic audit examined an institution's quality assurance and improvement processes rather than the delivered quality of education itself (Westerheijden, Brennan, and Maassen, 1994). Audit was regarded as institution friendly, for reasons that will be described presently. The idea was adopted by New Zealand, Aus-tralia, Hong Kong, Sweden, and, to some degree, Denmark (Massy, 2000). Sweden switched to assessment a few years ago, but England reaffirmed its faith in audit in 2001. In the United States, audit has been piloted by the Senior College Council of the Western Asso-ciation of Schools and Colleges (WASC), which is the Western re-gional accreditation agency, and by the University of Missouri's systemwide administration. A recent article in the *Chronicle of Higher Education* has boosted interest in audit (Massy, 2003c). Audit also is being considered for the K–12 environment (Education Commission of the States, 2003).

Champions (including the author) of audit include David Dill of the University of North Carolina, who has studied the subject intensely, and David Woodhouse, executive director of the Australian Universities Quality Agency and former director of the New Zealand Academic Audit Unit. There are as many versions of audit as there are implementations. The versions described here are based on my development of audit applications in Hong Kong and Missouri. These experiences convinced me that audit is unique in being able to combine stakeholders' accountability and improvement agendas. I believe that the tension between accountability and improvement can be largely mitigated by adopting the principles of academic audit.

## Education Quality Processes

Familiarity with education quality processes is a prerequisite for understanding the audit methodology. These processes represent the subject matter of audit—the scope of and criteria for answering audit questions. One cannot understand academic audit without knowing the questions it asks and the answers it seeks. The following descriptions were adapted from Massy (2003a, Chapters Six and Seven) and Massy (2003b).

Education quality processes are *organized activities dedicated to improving and ensuring educational quality.* They systematize a university's approach to quality instead of leaving it mainly to unmonitored individual initiative. They provide what pioneers in higher education quality, David Dill and Frans van Vught, call "a framework for quality management in higher education . . . drawn from insights in Deming's approach, but grounded in the context of academic operations" (van Vught, 1994; Dill, 1992). I describe the processes from five perspectives: (1) quality process domains, (2) quality principles, (3) use of evidence, (4) responsibility for quality processes, and (5) quality process maturity.

## Quality Process Domains

Quality processes span five interrelated domains of activity; none of the five are optional. Exemplary practice in one domain does not automatically produce good performance elsewhere, although failure in one makes progress harder in the others. I outline the five domains in terms of the kinds of questions an auditor might ask.

1. *Learning objectives.* What should a graduate know and be able to do? How do teachers build on their students' prior knowledge and capability? How do they contribute to students' employment prospects, capacity to make social contributions, and quality of life?

2. *Curricular design.* What is being taught, in what order, and from what perspective? What course materials are used? How do the materials relate to other parts of the student's program and further the program's learning objectives?

3. *Teaching and learning activities.* How are teaching and learning activities organized? What methods are used for first exposure to materials, for answering questions and providing interpretation, for stimulating involvement, and for providing feedback on student work? Is learning active? Is technology being exploited effectively?

4. *Student learning assessment.* What measures and indicators are used to assess student learning? Are they constructively aligned with learning objectives? Do they compare beginning and ending performance? Who is responsible for learning assessment, and how do the results spur student and teacher improvement?

5. *Implementation quality assurance.* How do department and program leaders assure themselves and others that content is being delivered as intended, that teaching and learning activities are being implemented consistently, and that learning assessments are performed as planned and their results used effectively?

Few institutions cover all five domains in an organized way. Curriculum committees—the traditional mainstay of quality assurance—focus on Domain 2. Unfortunately, they usually pay more attention to disciplinary tenets than to student needs and wants—needs and wants that could be identified by putting more effort into Domain 1. Student course evaluations fall under Domain 5, but more powerful methods like peer review of teaching usually are conspicuous by their absence. State-mandated assessment programs focus on Domain 4, but assessment does not work well when divorced from the other four domains. Technology forces consideration of Domain 3, but this can reach full effectiveness only when embedded in a systematic program of education quality process development.

## Education Quality Principles

Suppose a department or program wants to improve its quality processes. Where should it look for ideas? What kinds of practices should it adopt? My research at the National Center for Postsecondary Improvement identified seven commonsense principles that can help answer these questions. The principles have their roots in business, government, and health care, but the exemplary practices come from academe.

1. *Define education quality in terms of outcomes.* The quality of student learning, not teaching by itself, is what ultimately matters. Learning should pertain to what is or will become important for the program's students. Exemplary departments collect evidence about what their students need and then work to meet these needs.
2. *Focus on the processes of teaching, learning, and assessment.* Departments should carefully analyze how professors teach, how students learn, and how both parties approach assessment. Professors should talk with their students, consult the literature, collect and discuss evidence about what works and what does not, and be quick to adopt successful innovations.
3. *Strive for coherence across all educational activities.* Departments should view learning through the lens of the student's entire educational experience. Objectives, curricula, teaching and learning activities, student assessment, and quality assurance should relate to each other seamlessly.
4. *Work collaboratively to achieve mutual involvement and support.* Professors should demonstrate collegiality in teaching, just as they do in research. Departments should encourage teamwork in order to reinforce collegiality, bring multiple talents to bear on difficult problems, and provide quality assurance through peer accountability.
5. *Base decisions on evidence wherever possible.* Departmental teams should collect data on student preparation, learning styles, and

probable requirements for employment. They should obtain feedback from current and past students and, where applicable, from employers. They should embrace the principles of evidence discussed in the next section.

6. *Identify and learn from best practice.* Departments should benchmark examples of good practice and adapt the best ones to their own circumstances. They should compare good versus average or poor-performing methods and students, collect evidence about the causes of the differences, and strive to move poor performers toward the average and average performers toward exemplars.

7. *Make continuous improvement a high priority.* Departments should strive to improve the quality of teaching and learning on a regular basis. Although many professors will continue to place strong emphasis on research, they should spend enough discretionary time on education quality processes to maintain momentum for improvement. Personnel committees should include the results of such work, along with research and teaching performance, as criteria for promotion and tenure.

Although primarily intended to improve practice, the principles can also be used by auditors as criteria for determining quality process maturity. For example, an auditor might find a lack of collegiality, inadequate use of evidence, or indifference to the identification and exploitation of best practice. Exemplary practice might include the careful articulation of desired outcomes arrived at through collegial analysis informed by evidence, followed by careful design of teaching, learning, and assessment processes based on best practice and improved continuously through feedback from assessment results and consultations with students. Auditors have little difficulty distinguishing between the good, the bad, and the ugly when it comes to the application of these criteria.

## Use of Evidence in Quality Processes

Better use of evidence has become the most widely discussed idea for improving teaching and learning since *Scholarship Reconsidered.* The aforementioned quality principles make several references to evidence usage. Indeed, evidence usage lies at the heart of quality process effectiveness. WASC's *Evidence Guide* provides an excellent description of how those responsible for quality processes can improve their use of evidence. It points out that "evidence is the substance of what is advanced to support a claim that something is true"—for example, the claim that an institution's educational quality is high (Western Association of Schools and Colleges, 2002, pp. 7–8). Space limitations preclude recounting the *Evidence Guide's* many good examples, but just listing the characteristics of good evidence conveys the message that many quality claims fall short on these criteria.

- *Evidence is intentional and purposeful.* Information about quality should focus on what the institution does and how well it does it, not on traditional measures like books in the library and student-faculty ratios. Reliance on anecdotal information should be avoided.
- *Evidence entails interpretation and reflection.* Considered judgments are required because the data do not "speak for themselves."
- *Evidence is integrated and holistic.* The weight of the evidence is what matters, not simply lists of facts.
- *Evidence can be both quantitative and qualitative.* Quality metrics can include considered judgments, as well as numbers.
- *Evidence can be either direct or indirect.* Large-scale data collection exercises may not be needed. Data based on samples or unobtrusive observations may well suffice.

The *Evidence Guide* also presents four principles for using evidence when assessing student performance, such as discharging one's responsibilities under quality process Domain 4:

1. *Evidence should cover knowledge and skills taught throughout the program's curriculum.* The unit of analysis should be the cumulative experience of the student at the time of graduation, not simply averages based on work done in individual courses.
2. *Evidence should involve multiple judgments of student performance.* Departmental assessments should represent the considered judgment of a faculty team, not a single individual. They should be discussed by the team members before finalization.
3. *Evidence should provide information on multiple dimensions of student performance.* There should be more than a single summa-

tive performance measure. Information should instead be collected on a variety of performance dimensions. Reports should include profiles of the relevant student population, not simply averages or data for the top few percent of the class.

4. *Evidence should involve more than surveys or self-reports of competence or growth by students.* Surveys asking students to rate their satisfaction, strengths and weaknesses, or areas of perceived growth, though helpful, are not adequate as the primary metric for educational quality.

Few professors would dream of violating such principles in their research and scholarship. However, this is not the norm on the educational side of the enterprise. Universities usually do not urge improvement or reward performance, and academic people are too busy to invest the needed time without external stimulus. As is true in other aspects of quality process improvement, the better use of evidence requires programs that are reinforced continuously up and down the academic hierarchy.

## Responsibility for Quality Processes

Education quality processes form part of the larger system outlined in Table 8.1. The system starts with teaching and learning—the subjects of quality process work. Professors and the students with whom they work bear the primary responsibility for teaching and learning. Quality processes are depicted as the second, third, and fourth activities in the list. They begin at the department or program level because professors are closest to the teaching and learning action. Chairs also play key roles because they are close enough to professors to see that the requisite tasks get performed effectively.

School- and institution-level education quality processes stimulate, support, and ensure the soundness of departmental and program processes. The responsible parties provide leadership, resources, rewards and incentives, information and skill development, and interdepartmental venues for discourse on quality processes. They also evaluate the lower-level processes from time to time (for example, through academic audit) and take action, where needed, to improve performance.

Deans, presidents, and provosts should be proactive when it comes to quality, but they should not disempower the professors

**Table 8.1. The Higher Education Quality System**

| Level | Activity | Primary Responsibility |
|---|---|---|
| 1 | Teaching and learning | Faculty and students |
| 2 | Department and program *quality processes* | Faculty and department chairs |
| 3 | School *quality processes* | Deans |
| 4 | Institutional *quality processes* | Presidents, provosts, and faculty senates |
| 5 | Institutional *quality oversight* | Governing boards |
| 6 | External *quality oversight* | State coordinating boards, accreditation agencies |

directly responsible for producing it. Such leaders should manage *for* quality, which is different in philosophy and practice from the direct management (some would say micromanagement) *of* quality (Barnett, 1992; van Vught, 1994). Professors rightly ridicule the idea that "teaching police" can ensure quality. Managing for quality involves a lighter touch—one that does not disempower professors or impinge on academic freedom. The principles of audit described herein provide good examples of managing *for* quality.

Quality oversight, depicted by the last two lines in Table 8.1, energizes and ensures the effectiveness of quality processes at the departmental, school, and institutional levels. Contrary to much current practice, education quality oversight should begin with trustees and regents. By establishing the quality process agenda and monitoring progress, boards can spur improvement without micromanagement. State higher education coordinating boards and accreditation agencies can and should do the same. Initiatives for quality process improvement can begin anywhere, but the system works best when all levels are mature and proactive.

## Quality Process Maturity

Suppose a department has begun working on quality principles and a more robust use of evidence. What language can it use to gauge progress? For that matter, by what criteria can deans, presidents or provosts, trustees, and oversight agencies gauge the progress of the entities for which they are responsible?

The so-called capability-maturity model provides a useful language for evaluating quality process maturity. Developed by engineers to track the capacity of R&D teams to manage complex systems, the model applies equally well to education quality processes. "Low maturity" implies a lack of attention to such processes, whereas "high maturity" indicates strong and systematic attention. Academic departments can use the criteria as benchmarks for evaluating their progress up the quality process maturity curve; so can deans, presidents and provosts, boards, and oversight agencies.

The model lays out five levels of quality process maturity at the department or program level. Similar criteria have been developed for the supervisory and oversight levels (Massy, 2003a). As with the quality domains and principles, the maturity criteria were used successfully by auditors in Hong Kong.

1. *No effort* means the department does not have organized education quality processes. Quality and quality assurance remain in the hands of individual professors.
2. *Firefighting* means the department responds to problems but mostly with ad hoc methods. The five domains are not covered systematically, and the quality and evidentiary principles receive little attention.
3. With *informal effort*, one sees individual initiatives and experimentation with the principles in one or more domains. Coverage remains spotty, however, and the department has yet to become a "learning organization" with respect to education quality processes.
4. With *organized effort*, departments plan and track quality process initiatives in all five domains. Emergent norms point effort toward the quality and evidentiary principles, and methods for gauging performance are under development.
5. With *mature effort*, the quality principles have become embedded in the departmental culture, and the idea of regular improvement in all five domains is a well-accepted way of life. The department has accepted planning, tracking, and performance evaluation of quality processes as key elements of peer accountability and collegiality.

The levels can be assigned numerical scores and perhaps even used as inputs to formulaic incentive systems, but I believe they are better used qualitatively. Suppose a dean, president or provost, board, or oversight agency has made clear that quality process improvement is a high priority. Now imagine the tough-minded discussions that could occur between department chairs and deans, or between chairs and professors, if performance has been evaluated as unsatisfactory. What chair would feel comfortable defending a "no effort" or "firefighting" assessment to the dean? What dean would feel comfortable defending such assessments to the provost? What institution would feel comfortable defending them to the quality assurance agency, students, and the public?

## Academic Audit

Academic audit evaluates the maturity of a department's, institution's, or system's education quality processes. Although the maturity descriptors suggested in the previous section may or may not be used, the bottom line is the same: units with mature processes will score well on audit, and those with immature processes will score poorly. Furthermore, units with mature quality processes will produce meaningful student learning assessment data that can be vetted by academic audit.

I will introduce the audit methodology as it applies to an institution's improvement agenda, the University of Missouri System serving as a case in point. Then I will fuse the improvement and accountability agendas using Hong Kong's University Grants Committee (an oversight body) as exemplar. The discussion sequence is for expositional convenience; the Hong Kong process was implemented first and influenced the design of the Missouri process. I will conclude this section by describing the kinds of information provided by audit.

## Departmental Audit

Education quality processes begin at the department level, so the department is a good place to start our discussion. Audit can supplement or perhaps eventually replace the program reviews now required of many departments. That, in fact, was the University of Missouri's motivation in launching its pilot program in the fall of 2001.

The pilot involved one department or program on each of the university's four campuses: Psychology at Columbia, Communications at Kansas City, Physics at Rolla, and the undergraduate Honors College at St. Louis. Participation was voluntary, with the units being exempted from the upcoming round of program reviews. Local leadership was provided by the department or program chair or, in the case of Columbia's large Psychology Department, the director of undergraduate education. The system-level associate vice president for academic affairs led the project overall.

Following a kickoff meeting of the local and systemwide leadership group, the author and project leader visited each campus in November 2001 for half-day meetings on education quality processes and the audit methodology. A "Question and Answer" paper distributed in advance informed the discussions. We asked participants to reflect on what they were doing to assure and improve education quality in each of the aforementioned five domains and how they "knew what they knew" about their performance. The discussions were informal and wide-ranging, and although we encountered some initial skepticism, every group embraced the idea that improvement was possible and that the audit exercise was likely to be helpful.

Each unit agreed to work on its processes during the ensuing academic year and then prepare a self-evaluation document (SED) as a precursor to audit. Our "SED Guidance Notes" suggested that the unit try to identify exemplary accomplishments in each of the five domains and then, for each, ask whether and how the various quality principles contributed to the success. (Reflection on the principles of evidence would be included if the exercise were fielded today.) Then we asked the unit to reflect on how the lessons learned might trigger additional improvements, especially in domains that had not received much focus previously. Finally, we asked the unit to commit, as part of its SED, to implementing the most promising of these improvements.

The strategy of inviting units to articulate their successes in quality process language and then use their descriptions to identify additional areas for improvement proved useful. So did the focusing effect of deadlines and our request for an action commitment.

Monthly telephone meetings with the unit leaders sustained momentum and communicated emergent ideas, as did a face-to-face meeting held in May 2002 to discuss the units' draft SEDs. Final documents were submitted in the fall of 2002, just prior to the audit visits.

Teams of six to eight auditors spent one day at each of the four pilot departments. Team members were mostly faculty from other University of Missouri campuses, not necessarily in the discipline of the unit being audited. The aforementioned unit leaders served on audit teams for the other campuses, but most auditors had no prior exposure to the audit process. One day of "auditor training" proved sufficient to enable the teams to operate on their own without the aid of a consultant. The audit visit consisted of a plenary opening session, two rounds of breakout discussions, and a plenary closing session. The breakout sessions pursued areas of interest identified from the SEDs and explored whether students felt their views of quality were being taken into account. The visit was billed as a "set of structured conversations, among peers and with students, about education quality processes," and most participants felt that is exactly what took place. Team chairs wrote reports on the conversations, which after review by the unit leader for factual accuracy were shared with the audited department, dean, provost, and vice president for academic affairs.

An evaluation in March 2003 concluded that the project had been successful. What follows are some comments from faculty who participated in the audit.

"We all learned a lot. People on both sides of the table were thinking outside their disciplines."

"We identified some real problems. For example, the curriculum is haphazard—'chaotic' as one department member put it. And we generated some good, tangible ideas for improvement."

"In retrospect, as a result of the process, we collectively learned more about what we actually do (indeed, some members learned for the first time what some of their colleagues do), and because students were included in the audit process, we received some valuable perspective on how they view our attempts to provide a quality education."

"Even if no one beyond ourselves reads the final report, we are a better department for having stepped back to ask fundamental questions."

"I note that as a result of its participation in the audit process, the Physics Department now has a clearer vision of the changes it needs to make in order to improve what is generally regarded on campus as an effective educational program serving the needs of a diverse body of physics students."

It is noteworthy that even educationally effective departments can benefit from audit. Moreover, by evaluating someone else's efforts, the auditors also gained new ideas about how to improve quality in their own departments.

Stephen W. Lehmkuhle, Missouri's vice president of academic affairs, summed the experience up this way: "Sharing experiences among faculty from all four campuses as well as working together on this unique audit . . . builds bridges in many ways . . . some related to the audit . . . others just come up as they talk" (Massy, 2003c, p. B16). Missouri is expanding the pilot to include additional departments during the 2003–2004 academic year. The scope will include additional subjects now covered in program review, but the essential focus on education quality processes will be retained.

## Oversight Audit

Although audit can spur improvement at the institutional level, its roots lie in quality oversight, that is, holding institutions accountable for quality. Its power lies in the convergence between the improvement and accountability agendas and indeed between the agendas of the oversight agencies and the institutions themselves. Nowhere is this clearer than in Hong Kong, where the University Grants Committee (UGC) has twice audited the universities under its jurisdiction. Hong Kong's Teaching and Learning Quality Process Review (TLQPR), as it dubbed its exercise, has been described in detail elsewhere (Massy and French, 2001). Hence, I will limit my discussion to the differences between these oversight-level audits and the departmental audits conducted at Missouri.

Hong Kong's first TLQPR began in 1996 with briefing documents that described our emergent ideas about education quality processes and the role of audit. This was followed by UGC-sponsored orientation sessions at each university—sessions that proved particularly useful because the institutions differed in their familiarity with quality processes. The first audit round allowed four to six months between the orientation session and submission of the institution's SED. Orientation sessions were not needed in the second round because the institutions already were familiar with education quality processes. (Campus administrations ran extensive preparation exercises, however.) The SEDs described the institution's education quality processes at levels 2, 3, and 4 in Table 8.1. The audit panel reviewed the draft and provided feedback prior to finalization, then used the SED as a basis for the audit visit.

So far, the TLQPR process is very similar to the departmental audit process described for Missouri. However, the multi-institution context and fusion of the accountability and improvement agendas dictated some variations. First, the TLQPR panels were much larger than the departmental audit panels: eighteen people in round one and twelve in round two, as compared to six at Missouri. This allowed us to involve both Hong Kong academics and overseas experts and to populate more breakout groups. We used an "intact panel," whereby all members visited all institutions. This maximized the degree of learning among panel members and facilitated informal comparisons among institutions.

Second, the UGC decided at the outset that the TLQPR reports would be made public, both as an accountability measure and to facilitate the exchange of good practice among institutions. The institutions published their own reports, in Chinese as well as in English, along with comments on the findings. All publications were accessible on the Web and in booklet form. The wide dissemination of audit findings represents a sine qua non of accountability.

The biggest difference between departmental and institution-level audits lies in the necessity for the latter to examine quality processes at each level in the quality process hierarchy. This requirement does not arise in department audits, which by definition focus on the second level of Table 8.1. The need to look at departmental, school, and institutional processes, plus the large number of schools and departments in most universities, dictates some kind of sampling. Fortunately, the requisite schemes are not difficult to implement.

Time constraints related to international travel limited the Hong Kong audit visits to a little over one and one-half days each. This allowed for three sets of breakout sessions. Three panel members were assigned to each session in the first-round TLQPRs, for a total of six sessions per set or eighteen sessions total. Round two utilized two panel members per group, also for a total of eighteen sessions. The typical visit sampled about a dozen departments, four schools, and two special units like the teacher development office. We made sure to include multiple departments in most if not all the schools sampled. Institution-level quality processes, such as the work of quality assurance committees, were covered in plenary sessions. Group interviews with all the deans proved particularly valuable for understanding the relation between school-level and institution-level processes, including the deans' sense of responsibility for educational quality and the ways they propagated this feeling to the departments.

Finally, the UGC let it be known before the first TLQPR that the results might "inform funding" in some way. This was controversial because the then-current conventional wisdom held that such a linkage would poison our improvement agenda and perhaps lead institutions to dissemble in their responses. In fact, it worked the other way around. Although no formulaic linkage was ever suggested, the knowledge that something tangible might be on the line increased the TLQPR's saliency and thus its benefits. In this case, the audit "informed funding" for only one institution: the single university that refused to make improving its education quality processes a high priority. The UGC withheld a modest sum until the school changed its priorities. The turnaround took less than a year, and now that institution has exemplary quality processes.

The feedback on Hong Kong's TLQPR has been positive. A team from the Center for Higher Education Policy Studies (CHEPS) at the University of Twente, Netherlands, evaluated the first round and concluded, "The TLQPR was the right process at the right time." They urged the UGC to "keep up the beat" with a second round. The second round now has been completed, with salutary results. Not only was the process again judged effective by participants on both sides of the table, a striking amount of improvement was observed between the first and second rounds. Panelists felt that all institutions are serious about their quality processes, and many, if not most of the units sampled, exhibited "organized effort"—to use the maturity scale introduced earlier. (Those of us who participated in first-round TLQPR felt that "firefighting" or at best "informal effort" characterized the situation at that time.) Some institutions have developed their own "internal academic audit" programs (like Missouri's). The UGC has resolved to maintain its focus on education quality processes by embedding academic audit as an identifiable component of the integrated quality assurance methodology now under development.

## Information Provided by Audits

Audit can provide two kinds of information: (1) information about the department's or institution's education quality processes and, because these processes include student learning assessment, (2) information about the quality of education actually delivered. First-time audits usually focus on process because the audited entities probably lack maturity in their approach to learning assessment. This was the case in Hong Kong and to a lesser extent in Missouri. Increasing maturity brings the capacity to assess student learning, however, and subsequent rounds of audit should evaluate the fitness for the purpose of such assessments and the use being made of them, as well as on quality processes. The following description projects today's audit experience to a mature audit system.

Audit reports should describe the entity's work in all five quality process domains: learning objectives, curricular design, teaching and learning activities, student learning assessment, and implementation quality assurance. Exemplary activities should be identified, both to commend the unit and to help disseminate good practice. Student assessment results should be reported when the methodologies are mature enough to make that meaningful, and the auditors should state explicitly where and why such results could not be reported. Areas of shortfall should be flagged as needing improvement. Finally, the audit panel or subpanel should evaluate the overall maturity of the unit's quality processes. The evaluations can be reported directly, or they may inform "softer" summative language for use in the public audit reports.

Institution-level audit reports should describe average quality process maturity at the department and program levels, as well as variations from the average. For example, maturity may be uniformly high, or it may be good on average but with significant numbers of units requiring improvement. Institution- and school-level processes, as well as campus-level processes for multicampus institutions, should be described. For example, do exemplary activities at the department level mostly arise spontaneously, or are they influenced by policies and purposeful activities at the decanal and provostial levels? If spontaneous, what steps is the institution taking to sustain, enhance, and propagate the exemplary practices? What are the deans doing to improve education quality processes in units that lack maturity? For example, do the deans know about variations among their departments and, if so, what are they doing to spur on the laggards?

Programs with mature education quality processes will, by definition, have meaningful methods for student learning assessment. For example, departments may assess the learning achieved by graduates in the major, and general education committees may do the same for "graduates" of that program. The auditors will ask respondents to describe their assessment methods, including use of evidence, and explain why they were adopted. Self-assessed shortfalls and plans for improvement also will be noted. The auditors will probe for examples of how professors use assessment results to improve teaching and learning. Such usage represents an important quality process in its own right, and it provides evidence about whether assessment is taken seriously. Positioning student learning assessment as central to the department's efforts to improve education quality represents an important characteristic of audit.

Whether external entities can design and implement valid student learning assessments remains controversial. The Collegiate Results Survey described by Zemsky in Chapter Twelve and the National Survey of Student Engagement described by Kuh in Chapter Seven represent good first steps, but they have not been widely adopted. Moreover, even when adopted the results are seldom made public or even used intensively by faculty. Audit sidesteps external assessment by requiring those closest to the action (departmental and program faculty) to assess student learning as part of their own education quality processes. Given the difficulties encountered by state external assessment programs, described by Peter Ewell in Chapter Five, this would appear to be a significant advantage.

Assessment design should follow naturally from the determination of desired learning outcomes (another education quality process domain) because outcomes that cannot be assessed are too fuzzy to be meaningful. Once assessment is in place, the results can be used to assure and improve quality. This launches a virtuous circle, wherein good results reinforce professors' improvement efforts, and poor results stimulate remedial action. External assessments can help, and, indeed, a robust local assessment program would do well to use them when available. However, quality information would not be limited to things that can be assessed externally.

The controversy about student learning assessment boils down to whether the task should be performed externally or delegated to departments, programs, and institutions. Few experts doubt the importance of learning assessment, and most agree that assessment at the grassroots level would be very desirable. But getting institutions to step up to the responsibility has been a major problem. Audit offers a new and more promising approach. It embeds student learning assessment in a comprehensive and useful program of quality process improvement where such assessments benefit the initiating department in the first instance.

## Audit Characteristics

I summarize the characteristics of audit in terms of (1) tensions between internal interests and external concerns, (2) strengths and weaknesses of the approach, and (3) the Accountability Triangle described in Chapter One. The methodology to be described represents a slight extension of the methods used in Hong Kong and Missouri. I believe it reflects the state of the art. The approaches used in Australia, New Zealand, and the United Kingdom differ somewhat, but the same basic principles apply.

### Tensions Between Internal Interests and External Concerns

Authors of chapters in this volume were asked to address the following eight questions pertaining to the tensions between interests internal to the academy and the concerns of external stakeholders. I answer each briefly, based on the material previously presented.

1. *Institutional improvement versus external accountability.* I believe audit to be unique among accountability methods in being able to accomplish both purposes simultaneously. The structured conversations between auditors and respondents are mainly formative. However, the process can turn summative if respondents do not take the conversations seriously or have not done their homework.

2. *Peer review versus external regulation.* Audit is based on peer review, not regulation. Entities can design their quality processes as they see fit, so long as they cover the aforementioned five domains and can defend their decisions to peers using good logic and rules of evidence.

3. *Inputs and processes versus outputs and outcomes.* Audit focuses on processes but does not ignore outcomes. Inputs are taken as given, with respondents expected to achieve the best quality possible, given their resources. Mature quality processes put strong emphasis on student learning assessment, which brings outcomes into the picture. The audit model delegates responsibility for measuring outcomes to institutions as described in the previous section, then follows up to hold institutions accountable for so doing.

4. *Reputation versus responsiveness.* Audit focuses on responsiveness to the needs of students and other education-oriented stakeholders. Reputation means nothing because professors who teach are expected to embrace good-quality processes regardless of their research prowess.

5. *Consultation versus evaluation.* Audits are conducted as consultations—the structured conversations described earlier. However, auditors do evaluate the quality of the conversations and the supporting examples and evidence. They ask whether decisions are well thought through and flow logically from the evidence, not whether they conform to a fixed template or what the auditor would have done if confronted with similar circumstances.

6. *Prestige versus performance.* Audits look at performance. Prestige does not enter the equation.

7. *Trust versus evidence.* Audit is based on the mantra, "Trust but check." It views faculty as professionals who should be trusted to make good educational decisions on behalf of their students.

However, faculty members confront many different pressures and objectives. Audit checks to see whether educational decisions are in fact being made carefully and boosts the incentives for so doing.

8. *Qualitative versus quantitative evidence.* Audit is a qualitative process. However, some of the evidence unearthed in audit, including student learning assessments, may well be quantitative.

## Strengths and Weaknesses

Audit's overriding advantage is that it fuses the improvement and accountability agendas. To many, its major disadvantage is that it does not directly measure student learning, student outcomes, or similar output dimensions. Since the beginning, audit has been tagged as dealing only with process and therefore is suspect as an accountability instrument. I have argued in this chapter that the "process versus outcomes" dichotomy is misguided. The real question is whether institutions and the departments and programs within them are to be held accountable for assessing student learning and student outcomes or whether that task must be shouldered by an external agency. This is not the place to evaluate external assessment. What does seem clear is that external assessment programs should not disempower local academics with respect to assessment or relieve them of responsibility for this key quality process domain. From this perspective, audit's focus on education quality processes, including student learning assessment, is no disadvantage at all.

Audit's second disadvantage is that it requires on-site visits, just like subject-level assessments, accreditation, and program reviews. These are labor intensive for both institutions and auditors. Desk checks of performance indicators require no such visits. Student examinations pose their own design and logistical challenges, but they do not require site visits to institutions.

Audit's third disadvantage is that the quality process idea is new to most institutions and faculty. This makes it harder to gain acceptance than if such processes were broadly familiar. The first goal of audit must be to educate about quality processes. However, that goal in and of itself represents an important milestone on the road to better educational provision. Faculty who are climbing the maturity curve usually welcome greater clarity about quality process domains, principles, and approaches to the use of evidence. Others recognize the value of these ideas and show willingness to work on improvement. Those who resist because they use poor processes and are unwilling to improve should not be afforded great weight in evaluating the audit methodology.

Audit offers some advantages of a very practical nature. First, audits can be conducted anywhere in the accountability hierarchy. In fact, audit programs that coexist at multiple levels generate synergies rather than conflict or waste. I mentioned, for example, that certain Hong Kong institutions have established internal academic audit programs to maintain momentum in quality process improvement during the years between UGC audits. A robust internal audit program benefits the institution directly. It also facilitates the UGC's external audits and provides powerful evidence that the institution takes education quality seriously.

Second, audits can be conducted at the institution or campus level, as in Hong Kong, rather than at the disciplinary level. External assessments usually need to be performed at the disciplinary level, as with the United Kingdom's subject-level evaluations, for example. The economies associated with a single institution-level visit that incorporates schools and departments through sampling are obvious.

Third, auditors need not be expert in any particular academic discipline. In Missouri, the departmental auditors generally came from different disciplines, and in Hong Kong the limited overlap of disciplines in the subpanels that sampled departments was mostly coincidental. Disciplinary knowledge is not a prerequisite for conversations about education quality processes. Indeed, too much disciplinary knowledge tempts auditors to advocate their own preconceived views about how things should be done. The ability to choose auditors without regard to academic discipline simplifies the design of audits at all levels.

Fourth, audit generally costs less than subject-level assessment when viewed across a higher education system and no more than program review when performed by a single institution. At the system level, suppose there are X number of institutions and an average of Y number of subjects per institution. Subject-level review requires X x Y visits and audit requires only Y visits of roughly similar length. Audit teams may be larger than assessment teams in order to staff sampling subgroups, but the smaller number of visits more than compensates for the difference. Within institutions, the number of audit and program review visits is about the same. However, program reviewers usually come from outside the institution, whereas most if not all auditors can be internal. This allows one to use larger audit teams for the same or less cost as program review.

Finally, and of overwhelming importance, responses to academic audit are almost impossible to fake. Respondents who are fully engaged with education quality processes will talk the auditor's ear off. They will describe what they are doing, how it is working, and how they plan to improve their performance. Examples of good practice will flow easily, and evidence will be produced when requested. Respondents who are unfamiliar with quality processes or give only lip service to them will soon sputter into generalities. Their use of evidence will violate rules of good practice if, indeed, they use evidence at all. Even inexperienced auditors can tell the difference between systematic and evidence-based quality processes and responses that essentially say, "We know quality when we see it, and you should trust us to get things right." Experienced auditors can differentiate among maturity levels, no matter how hard respondents try to gloss over their shortcomings. Audit's ability to detect puffery, coupled with its down-to-earth questions and inherently consultative nature, are what allows it to fuse the accountability and improvement agendas.

Audit does not rely on regulation or evaluate against predetermined templates, so it sidesteps the resistance so often associated with accountability initiatives. Because audit is less intrusive than other methods, it is said to have a "light touch." The Missouri and Hong Kong experiences demonstrate that many professors actually welcome audit as validating things they have been doing anyway. Audit raises the profile of such activities, provides a language with which to discuss them, and offers ideas for improvement. There is no reason why audit cannot benefit private as well as public institutions, and, indeed, all kinds of institutions may soon be able to opt for audit in regional accreditation. In short, audit holds promise for all kinds of stakeholders and for institutional improvement agendas.

## The Accountability Triangle

The Accountability Triangle shown in Figure 1.1 (Chapter One) has been a unifying theme of this book. Where audit fits on the diagram depends on context. I would position Hong Kong's TLQPRs in the upper-left part of the triangle, although not close to the apex. They were motivated by governmental priorities, but the UGC's extensive consultations brought professional factors strongly forward. Making the reports public allowed them to inform the marketplace. Missouri's pilot project was motivated mainly by internal academic concerns, and its reports were not made public.

Imagine, now, a well-developed system of academic audits that has been around long enough for institutions to climb the quality process maturity curve. Such institutions will routinely assess student learning and the outcomes enjoyed by graduates. They will do this mainly for their own purposes, that is, to provide the feedback they need to assure and continuously improve quality. But once the assessment data are available, schools that can document good quality will almost surely use the data publicly. Prospective students and parents will come to expect such reports, and publishers of college guides will begin to supply the information whenever they can get

**Figure 8.1.  Locating Audit on the Accountability Triangle**

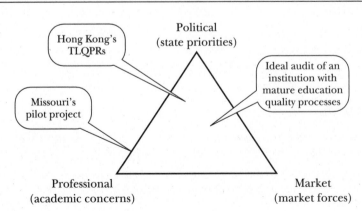

it. Institutions of lower quality will be pressed to report their data, as even mediocre data may play better than no data at all.

This situation is depicted by the "Ideal Audit" callout at the right of Figure 8.1. It points to the center of the triangle because this audit would serve all three purposes simultaneously. In addition to serving political and professional interests, audit would vet the education quality data supplied to the marketplace. As in financial audits, the institutions produce the data, but auditors review their methodology. The auditors cannot determine whether the results are right in every detail, but they can enforce generally accepted principles and usually prevent material misrepresentation.

Consider where such a program might lead. The following scenario might seem far-fetched, but it is not beyond the realm of possibility.

> Institutions across the higher education spectrum are spurred to produce meaningful grassroots student learning assessments, which are vetted by auditors from time to time. Those with good assessment results use them in recruiting, fundraising, and political lobbying. College choice publications take note of these data because some readers find them interesting, if for no other reason. Some elite institutions try to discredit the reported assessment methodologies, but this only triggers a long-overdue debate about measurement versus reputation. Such institutions are challenged to justify their reputations with real data, and soon those with good stories to tell begin to tell them. Eventually, all institutions are expected to publish audited assessment reports, perhaps as a condition for accreditation, just like public corporations are expected to publish audited financial reports.

Whether one buys into the scenario described, the first step—using audit to spur institutions to improve their education quality processes—seems to me to be eminently worthwhile.

## Conclusion

Academic audit has come a long way since its U.K. beginnings in the early 1990s. There it was largely a paper exercise; auditors concentrated on whether formal quality assurance procedures were being followed and documented. Sweden and Hong Kong broadened the concept to include the entire scope of education quality processes. Modern audit implementations shun formalisms, are down-to-earth and collegial in character, and are usually accepted by academics.

Two further innovations appear desirable. First, the quality process construct might be extended to include all aspects of academic activity, including research, scholarship, and doctoral education. This is on the agenda in both Hong Kong and Missouri. A second innovation would bring the economics of teaching within the audit scope. Massy (2003a, Chapter Ten) describes how faculty can analyze and improve the economics of teaching. This is an important subject for departmental consideration, especially as costs escalate and information technology brings so many new options to the table. The subject is beyond our scope here, but it requires no stretch of the imagination to add value-for-money improvement to the accountability agenda and use audit as a vehicle for spurring departments and institutions to get the job done.

# Chapter Nine

# State-by-State Report Cards

## Public Purposes and Accountability for a New Century

*Patrick M. Callan and Joni E. Finney*

The concept of accountability is hardly new in higher education. Colleges and universities have been accountable throughout their history—accountable to religious orders; directly to students in the medieval days; and, most recently, to governors, legislators, and their sharp-penciled staffs. In each era, higher education has been accountable, and, in each, the fundamental questions have been the same: Accountable for what? Accountable to whom? The answers to these questions have varied over time, as colleges and universities have responded to the changing needs of their social, economic, and demographic environment. The current restructuring of national and international economies has major educational consequences for the United States, as well as for its economic competitors; most workers require at least two years of education and training beyond high school (Carnevale and Desrochers, 2003).

This new requirement for greatly expanded educational capital—the nation's reservoir of knowledge and skills—will require new forms of accountability that are explicitly redesigned for higher education's critical role in a knowledge-based global economy. We believe this accountability will require clear articulation of state public purposes, an emphasis on demonstrable educational outcomes most relevant to those purposes, better linkages of accountability with public finance, and an initial policy focus on the educational progress of the citizenry rather than on individual colleges and universities.[1]

In this chapter, we first examine aspects of accountability at the state level since World War II, focusing on the transition from the early decades of phenomenal growth to the more recent era of "institutional maintenance." In the second section, we describe our view of the "new accountability" and state our rationale for it. In the third section, we suggest how state report cards can stimulate and inform public accountability. Accountability does not exist in a vacuum, and its linkage with public finance and with governance is emphasized in the final section.

## From Capacity Building to Institutional Maintenance

With few exceptions, the transition of higher education from one dominant societal environment to another is a slow process that defies exact dating. A major exception is the era of growth that began with enactment of the GI Bill in 1944 (officially, the Servicemen's Readjustment Act of 1944). Public support for broad college opportunity dates from that enactment, and public policies for higher education were driven by a social environment that demanded growth. Beginning with the influx of veterans, this now-historic expansion of colleges and universities changed the very definition of higher education. The primary focus of the states was on enlarging capacity to accommodate first the veterans and later the baby boomers. For at least three decades, three themes dominated governing and financing state higher education: (1) institutional expansion to accommodate the new enrollments, (2) efforts to rationalize growth through explicit institutional missions for public colleges and universities, and (3) design of statewide governing and coordinating structures. During this era of capacity building, state and federal policies and financial support created and sustained the remarkable array of colleges and universities that the United States enjoys today.

Under the GI Bill, thousands of people benefited from a college education who could not otherwise have even considered it. Moreover, the experience of that generation raised the aspirations of those who followed. In 1950, 34 percent of Americans had earned a high school diploma, and 6 percent had earned a bachelor's degree.

In each successive decade, the proportion of Americans graduating from high school and earning a bachelor's degree increased dramatically (see Table 9.1). Expanded institutional capacity stimulated demand for higher education and grew with it. In the five decades from 1950 to 2000, 1,046 public institutions were established, as were 1,186 private colleges or universities (National Center for Education Statistics, 2003c).

During this period of expansion, at least six major developments were directly or indirectly relevant to questions of public accountability. They remain relevant today, for the accountability measures developed during this era of expansion have, for the most part, remained a legacy of the past.

The public institutions were given fairly clear delineation of their responsibilities that, in general, guide them today: vocational, technical, and general education at the community colleges; general and professional education at the state colleges and regional universities,

**Table 9.1. Percentage of Population Completing
High School or College**

|  | Percent Completing High School | Percent Completing College |
|---|---|---|
| 1940 | 25 | 5 |
| 1950 | 34 | 6 |
| 1960[1] | 44 | 8 |
| 1970 | 55 | 11 |
| 1980 | 69 | 17 |
| 1990 | 77 | 21 |
| 2000 | 84 | 26 |

[1] The actual year was 1959.

*Note:* From 1940 to 1990, the percentages are for the U.S. population aged twenty-five or older who completed four or more years of high school or college. In 2000, the percentages are for the U.S. population aged twenty-five and older who have a high school diploma or equivalent and who have completed a bachelor's degree. Numbers are rounded.

*Source:* U.S. Bureau of the Census, March 2003.

with limited graduate education; and general, professional, and graduate education and research at the research universities.

Major universities, particularly those that had been active in wartime research, greatly expanded their research capacity with financial support from federal governmental agencies and private foundations. State support for research was less in the form of direct appropriations than in recognition of differential faculty workloads across public institutions.

Normal colleges that had only prepared teachers were given broader regional educational missions, first in offering liberal arts courses, then bachelor's and master's degrees; then they were renamed as "state colleges." Many aspired to be research universities, and some succeeded. Most became "universities" in name, and virtually all have become the primary educators of the American professional workforce.

The expansion of community colleges and their separation from public school district governance across the country was certainly one of the most outwardly visible areas of growth in American higher education. Many are now the primary entry level for four-year colleges and universities, and their offerings rapidly respond to local manpower needs through their vocational and technical programs.

To rationalize growth and expenditures, states organized their higher education systems in a variety of patterns. Some consolidated their public colleges and universities, including community colleges, into multicampus systems under governing boards (New York). Others established separate governing mechanisms for multicampus "systems" of community colleges, state colleges, and the research institutions (California). Still others created smaller such systems within states (Illinois). Yet another model was individual governing boards for each college or university (Michigan; see Chapter Three).

A notable feature of the postwar scene was the interposition of relatively independent state coordinating agencies between elected officials and the higher education institutions. In all but a few states (for example, Michigan), the objectives of rational growth and avoidance of unnecessary program duplication depended on coordination by a state higher education agency. Strictly speaking, each state's pattern is unique to that state, but, broadly speaking, they fall into three categories: (1) single boards, (2) regulatory agencies, and (3) advisory agencies. In single-board states, these agencies usually, but not always, had the same responsibilities and authority as the governing boards of single or multicampus institutions. In other states, the coordinating board was a separate agency to which the state had delegated authority, and these agencies could be classified as either advisory or regulatory—the latter having specified power, for example, to give final approval to new academic programs and to present aggregated or consolidated budgets to the state. The new state structures did not connect higher education with elementary and secondary education, and some of them severed previous linkages between K–12 schooling and higher education (for example, California).

These developments took place during a period in which state governments, the public, and higher education leaders shared the value of institutional creation and expansion of higher education capacity and enrollment as a very high priority of public policy. At the same time, concerns about economy and quality prevented unrestricted growth. Under the rubric of "rational growth," the structures and processes designed to accommodate expansion contained restrictions or limitations on it. The latter were—and still are—found, for example, in mission statements, provisions barring program duplication, and admissions standards. Across states, these developments, or slight variations of them, resulted in differing state funding and operational processes and procedures, including approaches to public accountability. Accountability measures were consistent with the state structures and processes that implemented them, and these measures focused on institutions, fiscal controls, program growth, and student enrollment. States sometimes required accountability to advance particular policy priorities. For example, beginning in the late 1960s, states started monitoring educational equity—the gaps in service to minority students and those from economically disadvantaged backgrounds. (For a more complete discussion of state structures and accountability, see Chapter Three.)

During most of the first four postwar decades, public policymakers and colleges and universities shared important priorities. There was general consensus on policies of growth and the financing of it. Accountability measures reflected a shared reliance on inputs, on enrollments, on compliance with statutory and administrative regulations and controls, and on proxies for educational quality, particularly on regional and professional accreditation. The globally envied capacity and quality of American higher education was achieved during these early postwar decades when shared values meant that state and federal public policies could be generally characterized by deference to the higher education community in most matters related to educational quality (for example, accreditation). Until recently, state policymakers did not deem explicit public accountability for educational performance necessary.

This hugely successful institution-building era ended after the peak years in which baby boom enrollees completed college. New campuses continued to be built, and existing ones continued to grow, particularly in states experiencing substantial population increases. But the great era of expansion tapered off by the early 1980s. The agenda of equity remained a daunting challenge, and opportunities for the most needy had not been adequately addressed. For the most part, however, lack of institutional capacity was not the major impediment to college participation for most Americans in the 1980s and 1990s.

The most recent decades have seen continued growth, along with many public policies addressing the needs of those still underserved by higher education, but none was comparable in magnitude or public support to the overarching policy imperatives of the earlier institution-building era. The period from the early 1980s through the end of the century can best be characterized as a time of "institutional maintenance" by the states rather than one of major policy initiatives comparable to those of the postwar expansion of higher education. That is, state policies and financing were directed primarily at maintaining the institutional assets rather than on new initiatives or on attempts to influence the priorities or outcomes of colleges and universities. Even in the absence of bold policy initiatives, states continued their financial support of higher education, which increased from $21 billion in 1980 to $40 billion in 1990 and over $60 billion by 2002 (Palmer and Gillian, 2003; National Association of State Universities and Land-Grant Colleges, 2002). State appropriations per student, adjusted for inflation, grew by 24 percent from 1980 to 2000, even as higher education's share of state expenditures decreased (National

Center for Public Policy and Higher Education, 2003a). Other sources of institutional revenue also increased; inflation-adjusted federal support of public colleges and universities grew by 69 percent, and tuition and fees increased by 117 percent (National Center for Public Policy and Higher Education, 2003a). Institutional maintenance, even in the absence of major new policy directions, was not inexpensive.

Accountability measures established in the era of growth continued into the period of maintenance, but their applicability was increasingly questioned by state executive and legislative agencies. The general consensus on such matters as responsibility for funding higher education eroded as colleges and universities competed for funding against the legitimate needs of other state services: welfare, Medicaid, corrections, and the public schools. State budget authorities began asking what the state was getting for its appropriations—questions that could not be answered by such traditional input measures as student-faculty ratios or accreditation reports. Increased state interest in performance budgeting began in this period (see Chapter Ten).

## Why a New Accountability Is Needed

America's educational capital—its educated public—has always been a foundation of the nation's success. Federal policy recognized this in the 1862 Morrill Act for the establishment of land grant colleges, and state policies implemented it. This was an enormous achievement, but it was only the beginning. The GI Bill broadened opportunity enormously following World War II, and so did the growth of community colleges. By any real-world standard, these were tremendous achievements, and they greatly raised the level of educational attainment across the United States. The history of higher education in this country has been one of continual, albeit sporadic, broadening of educational opportunities and of revising our expectations of colleges and universities, usually in response to economic and societal changes such as industrialization, the civil rights movement, war, and the cold war.

American higher education in the four decades after World War II developed on the premise that education and training beyond high school should be both expanded and limited—that, in

effect, college opportunity could be equitably rationed to a selected part of the population and so rationed without detriment
to individuals or society. Based on this premise, the resulting state
systems had characteristics that sought both equity of opportunity
and selectivity—for example, relative ease of entry to some form
of postsecondary education, high attrition rates, and meritocratic
principles to govern access to selective institutions. As the nation
and colleges focused increasingly on equity, the policy emphasis
was on the equitable rationing of college opportunity, that is,
rationing that would minimize and, ultimately, eliminate the influences of gender, race, and income in allocating college opportunities. By any historical standard, this uniquely American system
produced a remarkable, if uneven, increase in higher education
enrollment, participation, and attainment in the postwar decades.
The underlying premise was successful for its time. Only by hind-
sight, if at all, could it be seen as a shortcoming. The expansion of
higher education participation and the raising of national educational attainment levels was one of the success stories of post–World
War II America—a success made possible by federal and state policies, by the expansion of institutional capacity, and by the ability
of the labor market to absorb better-educated workers. In the last
half of the twentieth century, the United States was the world
leader in the expansion of educational opportunity and participation, and it reaped significant economic and societal benefits.

To grasp the next major transition in American higher education, as with the transitions of the late nineteenth and mid-
twentieth centuries, one must look first not to the academy but to
external forces that shape society's needs for education and training beyond high school. At the turn of the century, there was little
doubt that the most powerful and pervasive of these was the changing structure of employment, a global phenomenon induced by
the knowledge-based economy. Most employment that supports a
middle-class standard of living now requires education and training beyond the high school level. Over the past two decades, the
inflation-adjusted income of Americans with high school education
or less has decreased, while the income advantages of college-
educated workers have increased dramatically, even as the numbers
of workers with education and training beyond high school has increased by 20 percentage points (Carnevale and Desrochers, 2003,

p. 47). Economists Anthony Carnevale and Donna Desrochers have called this phenomenon, beginning in the 1980s, a "dramatic switching point between the old blue-collar economy and the new knowledge economy" (2003, p. 4).

For individuals, college-level education and training is a necessary condition for employment that enables full participation in the restructured knowledge economy. The knowledge-based economy punishes undereducated individuals and nations, states, and communities as well. Economic growth requires educational capital on an unprecedented scale. Those societies that are most successful in broadly raising educational attainment have the advantage in the international competition for those businesses and jobs that reap the benefits of the knowledge economy. These economic lessons have not been lost on the rest of the world.

The United States no longer leads the world in several important educational indicators of the educational status of young adults. According to the most recent international comparisons produced by the Organisation for Economic Co-operation and Development (OECD), the United States has been overtaken in the proportion of the population twenty-five years and younger who enroll in some form of postsecondary education, who achieve a postsecondary degree of any kind, and who hold a bachelor's degree. The United States has not regressed in absolute terms, but its rate of progress lags behind other nations on these measures. The awareness of the relationship of education and training beyond high school to the economic prospects of individuals and societies is more acute in some other nations, including many of our economic competitors (Organisation for Economic Co-operation and Development, 2003).

Just as the United States lags behind other nations in the higher education of its young population, workforce projections indicate that the nation's need for more workers at higher levels of knowledge and skills threatens to outpace supply. Demographic and manpower studies project low growth of the labor force over the next two decades as baby boomers retire and as the number of jobs that require college-educated workers increases. Even conservative projections forecast a significant shortage of qualified workers between now and 2020 in jobs that will require at least some college. A *BusinessWeek* analysis (Bernstein, 2002) describes the prospective postrecession labor market as a seller's market and warns employ-ers of an impending "wrenching manpower and skills shortage," especially of college-educated workers. The analysis projected a shortage of workers with some college-level skills of fourteen mil-lion by 2020.

The labor market projections suggest that the sorting functions of education, including discontinuities within education (for ex-ample, high school to college, two-year college to four-year college, college enrollment to program or degree completion) that may have contributed to efficiency may be dysfunctional at a time when ratcheting up the knowledge and skill levels of more Americans is vital to economic competitiveness and a high standard of living. Can the nation afford to lose the 33 percent of the ninth-graders who do not complete high school or to send only 38 percent of those who graduate on to college? Can we afford to have 26 percent of those students complete their second year and see only 18 percent graduate with a bachelor's degree within a reasonable amount of time (Ewell, Jones, and Kelly, 2003)?

Many educators and their supporters and patrons have always believed that what the country needs is more of what education of-fers. However, never before have the economic and demographic "facts of life" pointed to the conclusion that most Americans need education and training beyond high school and that the economy will require college-level education throughout the workforce as a necessary condition of national prosperity. The highest state and national priorities should be designed to raise—significantly raise—the level of educational attainment of the population. This will re-quire public policies, including public accountability and finance, that go far beyond the earlier and highly successful initiatives of the past.

Changing societal conditions require reexamination of the public purposes of higher education, of how these purposes can be served, and of relevant criteria for public accountability. If so-cietal needs require a significant increase in college participation and attainment, then change and innovation in both public policy and practice are likely to be needed: twenty-first-century reforms will be required that would parallel the quantitative and qualita-tive magnitude of the initiatives of the post–World War II decades. Achieving such change in higher education will be no less daunting than creating an elementary-secondary education system that "leaves no child behind." Ultimately, the challenge may be to incorporate college-level education and training as an imperative to "leave no person behind."

The current legacy of post–World War II policies is unlikely to meet three closely related imperatives: (1) to produce the opportunities for individuals in the restructured labor markets, (2) to meet the needed national, state, and community demands for competitive workforces, and (3) to maintain a high quality of life and healthy democracy. The leaky educational pipeline will not suffice to afford sufficient numbers of Americans with a middle-class standard of living, nor will it produce the knowledge and skills needed by the economy. Past measures of accountability focus almost exclusively on individual colleges and universities, are heavily procedural and even managerial in character, and usually fail to focus on the most critical public purposes and outcomes that are the rationale for public investment in higher education.

Within American federalism, the primary public policy responsibility for elementary, secondary, and higher education resides with the states, and it is to the states that public colleges and universities will continue to be publicly accountable. Explicit public policy goals and sustained policy attention by the states and higher education leaders are necessary conditions for increasing educational attainment. State policy will not, in itself, guarantee the desired educational attainment, but without a deliberately designed policy infrastructure, the needed attainment is unlikely. Such infrastructure would set clear performance goals for states and institutions, monitor progress, and use public finance as an incentive to leverage improved performance. Redesigning state policy to address the economic and societal conditions of the twenty-first century is a daunting task—one that must reach myriad elements of higher education, including finance and accountability. In the absence of a supportive public policy framework, educational change on a large scale is unlikely.

The balancing of institutional and public interests will be critical and difficult at a time when higher education is so central to the welfare of most individuals and of society. Requirements for public accountability will be more explicit than the traditional reliance on professional judgment and input measures, and both will have to be supplemented, or in some instances replaced, by evidence of performance and results. Leadership within the higher education community *and* among public policymakers for expanding access and attainment is essential. Absent such joint leadership, counterproductive public policy interventions in the name of public accountability are likely; the misuse of standardized testing is an example. And as long as most public funding is allocated to institutional maintenance rather than performance, the implicit policy message will reinforce the status quo.

## State Report Cards: A First Step

In 2003, state policies and practices for higher education, including those for accountability, are largely patched-up versions of legacies from the periods of expansion and institutional maintenance in the last half of the twentieth century. These policies and practices are not likely to meet the needs of the new environment of the twenty-first century. In most states, new policies will have to be designed around the goal and expectation of nearly universal high school completion, followed by at least two years of education and training beyond high school.

We suggest that the new accountability begin with the educational needs of the state—with explicitly stating the public purposes and goals of the higher education system and devising measures by which the state can monitor its progress toward achieving those purposes. The state interest in raising the levels of knowledge and skills in its population is a central public purpose. It is in the context of public needs that states should define the roles and assess the contributions of colleges and universities and establish priorities for financial support.

We would argue that a major deficiency of most state accountability systems of recent years, including most state-mandated assessment programs, performance funding, and budgeting systems, is that they have been designed around *institutional* purposes and effectiveness rather than around *public* purposes and needs. Existing indicators and measures may be adequate proxies for institutional effectiveness or health, but they often offer little to the public and to state authorities who seek to understand what differences colleges and universities, individually and collectively, make in addressing public needs and filling educational gaps.

The first order of issues for state public policies, including accountability and funding, must center on the educational condition of the state's populace. In "Reinventing Accountability" (Chapter Ten), Burke discusses the growing interest in institutional performance measures that may reach state priorities. If, as we believe, greatly expanded "educational capital" will be among the highest public priorities, then interest in performance measures is likely to continue, and accountability measures may well be extended to include performance of the entire state education system.

A transition in public policy seems required—one that is *away from* public policies that implicitly equate the functioning of colleges with state public purposes and *toward* policies that explicitly place expansion of the state's educational capital—the educational attainment of its populace—at the forefront. Institutional performance alone is an inadequate barometer of state performance, for effective institutions can and do exist in the midst of significant unmet educational needs. The first step in the new accountability is to take the educational temperature of the state in order to measure how many are being educated and how well, compared with current and prospective state needs and goals. The state policy agenda, the mechanisms of public finance, and institutional accountability should follow from the assessment of educational capital.

To assist states in this transition, the National Center for Public Policy and Higher Education designed and published two state-by-state report cards, *Measuring Up 2000* and *Measuring Up 2002*. Each offers a comparative assessment of the performance of each state in key categories relevant to state educational capital. In designing the report cards, the National Center took cognizance of existing report cards in other areas of state responsibility, including public school education, the condition of children, and state participation in the new economy. The ones deemed most effective shared several characteristics that were incorporated into the *Measuring Up* report cards on higher education:

- They placed primary emphasis on results, outcomes, and performance rather than on measuring effort or process.

- They relied most heavily on quantitative measures rather than on the opinions or judgments of the authors or sponsors.
- They were prepared by independent organizations that were not connected directly to the providers of public services or the responsible state policymakers.
- They presented, interpreted, and distributed findings to a broad public (with substantial media attention) that included but was not limited to specialists, professionals, and policymakers.
- They were repeated at regular intervals to monitor progress or regression.
- They began with the most reliable, timely, and relevant information available and worked to refine and improve data and methodology in each successive iteration.

Because the state is the unit of analysis of the *Measuring Up* studies, the reports, in effect, evaluate how well the people of the state are served by higher education, not whether the state has good colleges and universities (as we believe all states do). As part of this perspective, the report cards recognize that, from the state's perspective, the quality of higher education depends on the effectiveness of its elementary and secondary schools in preparing its young residents for college. A challenge for state policymakers, as well as for educators, is to view the entire educational system from the perspective of those who must negotiate its levels and structures. For students, the continuum of learning should be the central reality, not the organizational boxes that typically divide education for the purposes of administration, policy, funding, accountability, and regulation. Hence, the first category of *Measuring Up*, "Preparation," encourages policymakers to adopt a "K–16" perspective.

A second underlying premise of *Measuring Up* is that higher education performance, as it affects the residents of each state, depends on the contributions of *all* the diverse higher education institutions in the state—public and private, two- and four-year, academic and vocational-technical, campus based and distance, nonprofit and for-profit. Whatever the institutions, all are part of the picture of state performance painted by *Measuring Up*. Whatever the array, a state can have policy approaches that encourage institutional performance to improve the aggregated performance of the state overall.

In keeping with the fundamental shift of the policy paradigm from institutional maintenance to educational capital, the indicators and categories used in the state-by-state report cards measure the progress of the states in raising the educational levels of their populations, not the success of particular colleges and universities. *Measuring Up* evaluates and grades each state on answers to these questions:

*Preparation.*  How well are students prepared for education beyond high school?

*Participation.*  How much opportunity is provided for students to enroll in postsecondary education?

*Affordability.*  After accounting for college costs and student financial aid, what proportion of family income in each state is required to support a year of college attendance?

*Completion.*  How many students actually get degrees and certificates?

*Benefits.*  What economic, civic, and social gains does the state derive from its college-educated populace?

*Learning.*  What is known about student learning in comparison with other states? (All states were given an "Incomplete" in this category in *Measuring Up 2000* and *2002*.)

The answers to the questions that are posed for each category (except Learning) are provided by publicly available, quantitative data through the indicators shown in Table 9.2.

These six graded categories and their indicators comprise a state policy framework for education and training beyond high school. (As states have developed their own report cards, several have added categories that incorporate state policy priorities, including research, graduate and professional education, and economic development.) Each category represents an aspect of education over which the state, regardless of its institutional configuration, can exercise substantial policy influence. For each category, with the exception of student learning, there are sufficient data to compare performance across states.

Grades in each category are derived by benchmarking all states against those that perform best in that category. The "A" through "F" grades awarded, therefore, evaluate each state against

# Table 9.2. Fifty-State Report Card: Performance Categories and Indicators

**Preparation:** *How well are students prepared for education beyond high school?*

| | | | |
|---|---|---|---|
| High school credential | Math course credits | Science course credits | 8th-grade algebra |
| Math proficiency | Reading proficiency | Science proficiency | Writing proficiency |
| Low-level math proficiency | Advanced placement exam | Upper-level math | College entrance exam |

**Participation:** *How much opportunity is provided for students to enroll in postsecondary education?*

| | | |
|---|---|---|
| High school to college rate | Young adult enrollment | Working-age adult enrollment |

**Affordability:** *After accounting for college costs and student financial aid, what proportion of family income in each state is required to support a year of college attendance?*

| | | | | |
|---|---|---|---|---|
| Family ability to pay at community colleges | Family ability to pay at public 4-year colleges | Family ability to pay at private 4-year colleges | Need-based financial aid | Low-priced colleges |
| Low student debt | | | | |

**Completion:** *How many students actually get degrees and certificates?*

| | | | | |
|---|---|---|---|---|
| Students returning at 2-year colleges | Students returning at 4-year colleges | B.A. degree completion within 5 years | B.A. degree completion within 6 years | All degree completion |

**Benefits:** *What economic, civic, and social gain does the state derive from its college-educated populace?*

| | | | |
|---|---|---|---|
| Adults with B.A. degree or higher | Increased income from B.A. degree | Increased income from some college or associates degree | Population voting |
| Quantitative literacy | Prose literacy | Document literacy | Charitable contributions |

**Learning:** *What is known about student learning in comparison with other states?*

All states were given an "Incomplete" in this category in *Measuring Up* 2000 and 2002 because of the lack of relevant indicators across states.

a real-world standard that has been achieved by the highest-performing state. This grading methodology was selected over others that were considered, such as setting an arbitrary standard or grading on the curve. Hence, both the methodology and the title of *Measuring Up* were chosen to encourage high, but demonstrably achievable, levels of performance.

The state-by-state report cards, which are issued biennially by the National Center, remain a work in progress; the next iteration will be released in 2004. Several states, however, have found them to be helpful diagnostic tools. Combined with more detailed state data and using the National Center's state-by-state report card as a template, a state report card can highlight the strengths and weaknesses of a state's higher education system; can shift the focus of policy leaders away from an institutional agenda and toward a public agenda based on educational purposes, needs, and gaps; and can bring about a parallel policy shift toward performance and away from institutional inputs and processes.[2]

## Accountability and Beyond

Effective accountability requires that states define public purposes and needs and that they carefully design accountability procedures to monitor progress toward achieving these purposes and meeting these needs. The new accountability, as proposed here, requires first the articulation of public purposes and then the capacity to monitor progress or regression. Without explicit recognition of statewide public policy priorities, such as those set forth in the *Measuring Up* report cards, state policies (including policies for institutional accountability) tend to exist in a vacuum, often as means disconnected from ends.

We disagree with those who criticize current performance budgeting systems for their ineffectiveness in reaching departments and faculty. If these systems are ineffective, it may well be because institutional leaders often see their role as buffering their internal academic constituencies from what are seen as inappropriate state intrusions. These leaders will, we believe, respond quite differently to explicitly annunciated state policy goals and policy priorities. Accountability for state and institutional performance, accompanied by redesigned and substantial public finance incentives, would hold the institutions responsible to the states and the public for results; would allocate resources accordingly; and would expect institutional leaders to interpret, translate, and apply statewide accountability provisions internally. If the accountability and public finance systems are appropriately designed and linked, then governing boards, presidents, provosts, deans, and even department heads will find it in their best interest to respond to public purposes and incentives. States will find it in their best interest to adopt a sustained focus on performance and to eschew issues of institutional management and procedure.

Much of the state and national discussion of public accountability and finance has centered on the technical aspects of protocols, indicators, and measures. In our experience, most states have the capacity to address these technical issues. Where states have floundered in recent years is not over intractable technical issues but rather over the overarching policy questions of the public purposes of education and the relationship of institutional performance to those purposes. In the absence of articulation of state purposes and needs, we doubt that any system of accountability, no matter how sophisticated its construction, will have significant influence on states or on the colleges and universities for which states are responsible.

We do not underestimate the great political and educational difficulties of modifying the nation's immense and historically successful higher education policy infrastructure. But this challenge can be met. The expansion of educational attainment that we believe necessary has its precedents in expansions of educational attainment in the Morrill Act and the GI Bill. Accountability is a means to an end. In this era of a global, knowledge-based economy, the end that we foresee will be an unprecedented increase in educational capital and attainment. Public accountability in this new environment must connect to public purposes and priorities, as well as to colleges and universities.

## Notes

1.  For a more extensive discussion of educational capital and its relationship to college-level learning, see Callan and Finney, 2002.
2.  For a description of one approach to accountability that delineates state, system, and institutional accountability measures and their relationships, see Shulock, 2003.

# Chapter Ten

# Reinventing Accountability

## From Bureaucratic Rules to Performance Results

*Joseph C. Burke*

The 1990s saw a dramatic shift in the concept of accountability from complying with rules to producing results. *Reinventing Government,* published early in the decade, proclaimed a new manifesto for public managers (Osborne and Gaebler, 1992). They must manage for priority results rather than comply with bureaucratic rules and must transform their agencies from provider- to customer-driven organizations. Public bodies, like private business, could improve performance while decentralizing operations by being tight on setting goals and assessing results and loose on the means of achieving priorities.

The new accountability for government and business, which demanded both direction and decentralization, suited the new era of knowledge and information fueled by the creativity and ingenuity of knowledge workers. A number of governors and legislators concluded that what was good for business and government should also apply to the knowledge industry of higher education. At the end of the 1990s, the North Dakota Roundtable report confirmed the changing concept of accountability for higher education: "North Dakota's definition of accountability is a 1980s definition directed almost entirely at financial accountability. The accounting measures are for means rather than ends. . . . There is a need to move from micro-management to . . . strong accountability for ends rather than means" (North Dakota Roundtable, 2000, p. 15).

The decade produced a "performance phenomenon for higher education" (Ruppert, 1995, p. 11). The new accountability shifted the focus from academic concerns to state priorities, but by the end of the decade the momentum had moved toward market forces, which produced its own problems. As so often happens, reinventing accountability in higher education proved easier to proclaim than to practice.

Developments early in the decade encouraged the move from bureaucratic compliance to performance programs. First, critics, mostly from government and business, complained about the quality and quantity of faculty teaching and student learning, the preoccupation with graduate studies and research, the neglect of undergraduate education, the burgeoning of administration and support staff, and the growth of "mission creep" and "program sprawl." They charged that public campuses accepted too many unqualified students, graduated too few of those admitted, permitted too many of them to take too long to earn degrees, and produced too many graduates without the knowledge and skills for life and work in a knowledge and information era (Burke and Associates, 2002; Burke and Minassians, 2002b).

The performance programs of the 1990s would turn these public criticisms into policy goals. Second, more and more governors and legislators realized that the economic success of their states depended increasingly on the ability of their public colleges and universities to produce knowledge workers for the new economy. Finally, the economic recession early in the 1990s reduced state revenues and depressed state funding for higher education. The net effect of these developments meant that public higher education had to raise quality, reduce costs, and respond to new state needs. The times demanded programs that pushed public higher education to do both more and better with less. Public colleges and universities had always opted to do more. Now state priorities—not campus concerns—would determine what that "more" should be.

## The Performance Trio

Advocates of performance funding, budgeting, and reporting thought the adage, "What gets measured is what gets valued" was only half right. Only what gets funded, budgeted, or possibly reported, they claimed, could attract attention on college campuses and in state capitols and affect higher education performance. Although examples of these three performance programs preceded the 1990s, they flourished during that decade. Decentralization with direction characterized all three initiatives. In many instances, coordinating or consolidated governing boards for higher education struck a bargain with state officials, trading more accountability for more autonomy. The deals decentralized more authority over personnel, budgets, and operations to campus leaders in return for accepting accountability for increased productivity, improved performance, and enhanced responsiveness to state priorities (Blumenstyk, 1991). In classic "reinventing government" theory, the performance programs adopted priorities and assessed results but allowed campus leaders to choose the means of reaching these ends. Responding to public criticism, all three programs focused on undergraduate education and slighted research and especially graduate studies (Burke and Associates, 2002; Burke and Minassians, 2002b).

## Definitions

Confusion among state and campus policymakers about the differences of performance reporting, budgeting, and funding demands definitions and descriptions of each of these programs.

• *Performance reporting* relies on publicity to push colleges and universities to pursue state priorities and improve institutional performance. It rests on the assumption that institutions and individuals perform better when they know their results will become public. State coordinating or consolidated governing boards report periodically statewide and often institutional results, mostly for public higher education, although some, such as Alabama, Illinois, Missouri, and Tennessee, include limited data for private colleges and universities (see Chapter Two). Public institutions often report separately on their own performance. The reports usually go to governors, legislators, and campus leaders, and they increasingly appear on the Web sites of coordinating or system boards and individual institutions. Some reports include information directed to prospective students and their parents. Performance reporting has no formal link to state funding or budgeting. Campus leaders view reporting as the least objectionable of the performance programs, while state officials, pressed for funding from all sides, naturally favor a program that promises accountability without allocations (Burke and Minassians, 2002a).

- *Performance funding* and *performance budgeting* add institutional results to the traditional considerations in state budgeting, such as current costs, student enrollments, and inflationary increases. The latter represent input factors that ignore outputs and outcomes, such as the quantity and quality of graduates and the range and benefits of services to states and society. Some states previously adopted programs that front-ended funding to encourage desired campus activities. Performance funding and budgeting depart from these earlier efforts by allocating resources for achieved rather than promised results (Burke and Associates, 2002; Burke and Serban, 1998).

- *Performance funding* ties specified state funding directly and tightly to campus performance on individual indicators. It focuses on the distribution phase of the budget process. The relationship between funding and performance is tight, automatic, and formulaic. If a public college or university achieves a prescribed target or an improvement level on defined indicators, it receives a designated amount or percentage of state funding.

- *Performance budgeting* allows governors, legislators, and higher education boards to consider campus achievement on performance indicators as one factor in determining allocations for public colleges and universities. Performance budgeting concentrates on budget preparation and presentation and often neglects, or even ignores, the distribution phase of budgeting. In performance budgeting, the possibility of additional funding due to good or improved performance depends solely on the judgment and discretion of state, coordinating, or system officials.

The advantages and disadvantages of each of these programs is the reverse of the other. Performance budgeting is flexible but uncertain; performance funding is certain but inflexible. Despite these definitions, confusion often arises in distinguishing between the two programs. Moreover, at times, the connection between state budgets and campus performance in performance budgeting almost disappears. The allocations determined by either program are usually quite small, and current costs, student enrollments, and inflationary increases still set the lion's share of state funding for public colleges and universities.

## Initiation Methods

Methods of initiation matter, for they determine the participation of state and campus policymakers. The three initiation methods differ in critical ways.

1. *Mandated-Prescribed:* State legislation both mandates the program and prescribes the performance indicators.
2. *Mandated-Not Prescribed:* Legislation mandates the program but allows state coordinating agencies, in consultation with campus leaders, to propose the indicators.
3. *Nonmandated:* Coordinating or system boards, in collaboration with campus officials, adopt the plan without legislation.

Mandates, and especially prescriptions, clearly undermine program support in the academic community. Imposed by state officials, they ignore or slight the importance of consultation with coordinating, system, and campus leaders. Conversely, nonmandated programs leave state policymakers without a sense of ownership of the initiatives. No consultation means no consent on college campuses and in state capitols.

Whatever the method of initiation, the longevity and effectiveness of performance programs depend on the combined and continuing support of state, coordinating, and campus officials. Even nonmandated programs are often something less than voluntary. A coordinating official in Arkansas, who asked to remain anonymous, admitted about their nonmandated program in performance funding: "We did it to ourselves before they did it to us" (Burke and Associates, 2002, p. 219).

Legislation mandated many of the early programs in performance funding and budgeting and, in the case of performance funding, also prescribed the indicators. Mandates for the funding programs have diminished over the decade. Our annual survey of state higher education finance officers (SHEFOs) in June 2003 showed 53 percent of the current funding programs as nonmandated, and of the mandated plans, only 27 percent prescribed the indicators. Performance budgeting had 57 percent mandated, but just 10 percent prescribed indicators. Legislative mandates seemed more the rule in performance reporting, with two-thirds started by statute, but less than a quarter of them dictated the indicators (Burke and Minassians, 2003).

## Performance Programs: Common Components

Performance funding, budgeting, and reporting share some common components (Burke and Associates, 2002; Burke and Minassians, 2002b; Burke and Serban, 1998):

- *Program purposes,* avowed or implied, include demonstrating external accountability, improving institutional performance, and meeting state needs. Increasing state funding often constitutes an unannounced goal for coordinating boards and campus leaders.
- *Program goals* reflect external complaints and demands; or interest in access, affordability, and diversity in admissions; quality, productivity, and efficiency in programs and services; workforce and economic development; and, more recently, teacher education and college and school K–16 collaborations and partnerships.
- *Performance indicators* measure the level of achievement on program goals. Performance funding, given the tight tie to allocations, usually confines the number of measures to around ten to twelve, although South Carolina's program has no fewer than thirty-seven. Lacking the direct link to funding, performance budgeting has a longer list of measures. Our study of twenty-nine performance reporting plans suggests an average of forty but as many as eighty indicators (Burke and Minassians, 2002b).
- *Success standards* use improved performance for institutions, comparisons with the results of state or national peers, set targets by campus, or a combination of these criteria; most use a combination. Success standards are required in performance funding, frequent in performance budgeting, and less common in performance reporting.

The remaining components apply only to performance funding.

- *Funding levels* provide a percentage, or a specified amount, of state operating allocations for campuses. The levels generally range from half of 1 percent of state general fund support to about 5 or 6 percent; they average around 2 percent.
- *Funding sources* normally call for additional or reallocated resources or a combination of the two. Nearly all of the programs in performance funding allot some additional monies beyond base budgets.
- *Allocation methods* consist of base budget increases or annual bonuses based on performance. Most programs increase the budget base.

Surveys of state and campus leaders on performance funding suggest that the greatest problems are selection of the performance indicators, followed by using inappropriate success criteria, measuring the results of higher education, and changing state priorities. Performance reporting and budgeting shared all these difficulties but without the high stakes of deciding specific funding (Burke and Associates, 2002; Burke and Serban, 1998).

## The Triumph of Performance Reporting

All three programs flourished during the 1990s, but the early years of the twenty-first century saw the decline of performance funding and budgeting and the triumph of performance reporting as the preferred approach to accountability. Our annual surveys of state higher education finance officers (SHEFOs) show that performance funding nearly doubled from ten programs in 1997 to nineteen in 2001 (Burke and Minassians, 2002a, 2003). Performance budgeting more than doubled from sixteen to twenty-eight programs from 1997 to 2000. The recession that began in 2001 and lingered on through the early years of the new decade contributed to the decline of both programs. By 2003, the number of performance funding efforts had fallen to fifteen and performance budgeting to twenty-one. In a startling contrast, performance reporting grew from thirty initiatives in 2000—just two more than performance budgeting—to no fewer than forty-six in 2003 (see Table 10.1). The anticipation, as well as the publication of *Measuring Up 2000: The State-by-State Report Card for Higher Education,* clearly encouraged the expansion of performance reporting (National Center for Public Policy and Higher Education, 2000, 2002; Chapter Nine).

If performance reporting rapidly added programs, performance funding charted a more volatile course. These funding programs proved easier to start than to sustain. Beneath the steady increase in number of performance funding initiatives lay lots of volatility. The tie to funding provoked hostility from college and university leaders, who favored base funding and feared budget

### Table 10.1.  Performance Programs 2003

| | | |
|---|---|---|
| Performance Reporting | 46 states (92%) | Alabama, Alaska, Arizona, Arkansas, California, Colorado, Connecticut, Florida, Georgia, Hawaii, Idaho, Illinois, Indiana, Iowa, Kansas, Kentucky, Louisiana, Maine, Maryland, Massachusetts, Michigan, Minnesota, Mississippi, Missouri, Montana, Nebraska, New Hampshire, New Jersey, New Mexico, North Carolina, North Dakota, Ohio, Oklahoma, Oregon, Pennsylvania, South Carolina, South Dakota, Tennessee, Texas, Utah, Vermont, Virginia, Washington, West Virginia, Wisconsin, Wyoming |
| Performance Budgeting | 21 states (42%) | California, Connecticut, Florida, Georgia, Hawaii, Idaho, Iowa, Kansas, Louisiana, Maine, Maryland, Michigan, Minnesota, Mississippi, Nebraska, Nevada, New Mexico, Oklahoma, Texas, Utah, Wisconsin |
| Performance Funding | 15 states (30%) | Colorado, Connecticut, Florida, Idaho, Kansas, Louisiana, New York,* Ohio, Oklahoma, Oregon, Pennsylvania, South Carolina, South Dakota, Tennessee, Texas |

*SUNY System only.

instability. Its popularity in state capitols also dropped when revenues fell, campuses complained, and success seemed less than instant. Arkansas offers a classic case of volatility. The coordinating board adopted a nonmandated program in 1996, but the legislature abolished the funding a year later when the community colleges complained about their share of the allocation. The Arkansas legislature mandated a new funding program in 2001, only to abandon it again in the following year. Colorado phased out its 1996 funding program in 1998 and then adopted a revised initiative in 2000. The California community college system started performance funding in 1998 but dropped it by 2002. In addition, Kentucky, Minnesota, Missouri, and Washington once had but later abandoned their funding programs.

The dilemma of performance funding contrasts desirability with difficulty. Its attractiveness in theory is matched by its difficulty in practice (Burke and Associates, 2002, Chapter Ten). For a time, performance reporting seemed a "halfway stop" on the road to performance budgeting or funding. Reported results would arouse the attention of state policymakers, who would eventually turn to funding to lever campus action on public priorities. Some statistics supported this suggestion. More than two-thirds of the states with performance funding and budgeting in 1999 also had performance reporting. Moreover, the adoption of performance reporting preceded the initiation of 44 percent of the performance funding and 49 percent of the performance budgeting programs. Our 2003 SHEFO survey confirms a conclusion suspected the previous year (Burke and Minassians, 2002a, 2003). Far from being a precursor for other performance programs, performance reporting is now the preferred approach to accountability, perceived by policymakers as the less controversial and less costly alternative to performance funding or budgeting. Indeed, some legislators see it as a no-cost approach to accountability.

## Performance Indicator Preferences

Our studies of the indicators used in twenty-nine performance reports in 2001 and in eleven performance funding programs in 1998 allows some comparison of the measures used in both approaches (Burke and Minassians, 2002b; Burke and Serban, 1998). These studies identified 158 generic indicators used in one or more of the performance reports and 66 in performance funding programs (Burke and Minassians, 2002b, Chapter Nine; Burke and Serban, 1998, Chapter Four). Both programs exhibited a limited number of widely used indicators, although the performance reports shared more common measures than those for performance funding. Table 10.2 ranks the top sixteen indicators for both programs according to their usage. The two programs share only six of their sixteen most popular measures.

### Table 10.2.  Most Popular Indicators

| Performance Reporting (29 States) | | Performance Funding (11 States) | |
|---|---|---|---|
| Graduation and retention | 24 states | Graduation and retention | 10 states |
| Racial enrollment | 21 | Job placement | 8 |
| Sponsored research | 20 | Student transfers | 6 |
| Student transfers | 19 | Faculty workload | 5 |
| Tuition and fees | 18 | Institutional choice | 5 |
| Financial aid | 17 | Time-to-degree | 5 |
| Degrees awarded | 16 | Licensure scores | 4 |
| Licensure scores | 16 | Workforce and economic development | 4 |
| College participation rate | 16 | Faculty and staff diversity | 3 |
| Enrollment by degree level | 14 | K–16 linkages | 3 |
| Remedial activity effectiveness | 14 | Noninstructional staff costs | 3 |
| State operating funding | 14 | Program duplication | 3 |
| Enrollment trends | 13 | Satisfaction surveys | 3 |
| Job placement | 13 | Sponsored research | 3 |
| Technology and distance learning | 13 | Standardized test scores | 3 |
| Enrollment, resident | 12 | Technology and distance learning | 3 |

The two programs stress some of the same indicators, such as graduation, transfer, and job placement rates, licensure test scores, sponsored research, and technology or distance learning. Despite these similarities, indicators for performance reporting revealed more interest in access, affordability, and diversity, with measures on enrollment trends, student diversity, tuition and fees, and financial aid. Performance funding would naturally not reward increased access, since state budgets for public colleges and universities already funded enrollments in regular allocations. In addition, this funding program would not add money for increased financial aid because the states funded some of this aid. Performance funding paid more attention to efficiency measures such as faculty workload and time-to-degree.

## Performance Indicators and Policy Lags

In part, these differences reflected shifting state priorities. Issues and the indicators they beget are products of perceived problems at particular points of time. Problems emerge and recede ever more quickly, while policies respond and retreat ever more slowly. State initiatives usually lag behind policy issues, for problems often outrun policies (Burke, Minassians, and Yang, 2002).

Performance funding for higher education became popular in the first half of the 1990s (Burke and Associates, 2002). Program expansion after a period of national economic recession and restricted revenues naturally promoted measures of productivity in response to restrained revenues. As the economy and funding recovered, the second half of the decade and the early years of the new century generated new concerns when performance reporting began its expansion. They centered on student access in the face of the baby boom echo and the workforce training and economic development in reaction to the new economy. The latest policy concerns moved the focus away from efficiency and productivity and toward state priorities in teacher training and college-school collaborations.

Although the performance reports react to emerging issues in state capitols, their indicators often trail the latest public concerns. For example, only nine of the twenty-nine performance reports in our study have an indicator on the pressing issue of teacher training and just seven on K–16 collaboration, yet every list compiled of leading state priorities for higher education includes those two topics (Chronicle of Higher Education, 2001, 2002; Association of Governing Boards, 2002, 2003a; Coulter, 2003; Ruppert, 2001).

Although policy issues have time limits, they also reveal recurring themes. The record of reporting results in the early 1990s suggests that the recession in the early years of the new century, with state budget shortfalls and higher education funding cuts, may revive the interest in efficiency and productivity indicators, which the reports never completely abandoned. Although capitol critics consider policy responses to emerging issues as too slow, policy lags are inevitable. Even when higher education leaders are willing and able to design new indicators that respond to emerging issues, this time-consuming process means that performance measures will always lag behind policy needs. Delays are endemic in state government, and the complexities of academic governance stretch the response time. Slow responses also serve the useful purpose of testing whether an emerging issue represents a continuing trend or a momentary fad. These policy lags may explain the continuing complaint of government and business leaders that higher education is not responsive to state and business needs. State capitols and public campuses operate on different time clocks, which a cynic not affiliated with either might describe as slow and slower.

## Indicator Types, Values, and Models of Excellence

The indicator types, policy values, and models of excellence these measures imply reveal something of the intent and aims of the policymakers who adopted them. They also show that policymakers seldom made serious efforts to tailor the indicators to fit the approved differences in operations and goals of two- and four-year institutions.

The following analyses of indicator types, values, and models of excellence discuss first the percentages for the total number of indicators—158 for performance reporting and 66 for performance funding—and then the percentages for each program, considering only the 16 most popular measures (see Table 10.2). The reporting indicators come from those found in the 29 reports studied in the 2002 publication (Burke and Minassians, 2002b). The funding indicators were used in 11 performance funding programs in the 1998 study (Burke and Serban, 1998).

## Indicator Types

The rhetoric of performance programs claims that they shift the focus of colleges and universities from provider-driven resource input and process indicators to customer-centered output and outcome indicators. The reality shows something different. Figure 10.1 gives the percentages of indicator types for the 168 reporting indicators by institutional sector—combined they show 36 percent input, as opposed to just 23 percent output and 18 percent outcome measures. Moreover, inputs constituted half of the sixteen most popular indicators for performance reporting shown in Table 10.2. The total number of performance funding measures also shows a slighting of outcomes (12 percent) and outputs (19 percent), but this time in favor of an astonishing 48 percent for process indicators. Considering only the most common indicators, the reality of performance funding comes a bit closer to the rhetoric. Outcomes with five items matched the number of process measures and combined with outputs equal half of the sixteen most-used funding indicators (refer to Table 10.2).

The accent on access and affordability explains the heavy use of input indicators for reporting, which include items on enrollment, tuition, and financial aid. The reliance on process indicators in performance funding has a more complex explanation. In part, these indicators reflect the adoption of the process measures found in best practices in undergraduate education. Moreover, many of them (faculty and course availability, academic advisement, and class size) serve as surrogates for the absence of acceptable outcome measures of student learning (Burke and Associates, 2002; Burke and Minassians, 2002b). Only three of the eleven funding programs in the study used student and alumni surveys, and just three standardized test scores in general education, for learning outcomes, although four incorporated licensure test scores in professional fields.

## Shift from Internal to External Focus

As expected, the indicators in both reporting and funding programs shifted from the internal focus of the assessment movement of the 1980s to the external emphasis of state priorities of the 1990s.

## Figure 10.1.  Type of Indicators
## by Two- and Four-Year Institutions

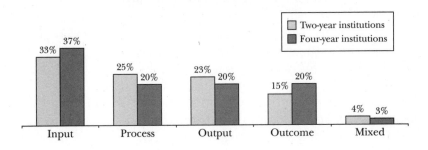

Looking at all the indicators, over two-thirds of those in performance reporting and nearly the same percentage in performance funding suggested external interests of society, as opposed to internal concerns of academe. External motivation for performance reporting rose to three-quarters of the most popular measures. Clearly, in both of the performance programs, traditional internal academic concerns lost out to external state priorities. Performance reporting also shows more attention to market forces, reflecting the interests of students and other clients.

## Policy Values

Indicators also imply the core policy values of quality, efficiency, equity, and choice. Indicators of quality include items like SAT or ACT scores, program reviews, or licensure test scores. Efficiency suggests a cost-benefit relationship, as in measures such as time to degree or graduation rates. Student, faculty, and staff by race or gender would constitute equity indicators. Campus choice of one or several mission-centered measures constituted the most obvious choice indicator.

Efficiency and quality indicators are nearly equal in the total numbers of performance reporting measures (Figure 10.2). Although performance funding has a higher percentage of efficiency than quality indicators, no less than 20 percent of the total number reflects a mixture of efficiency and quality, for example, course availability or licensure test scores, which reflect both values. In contrast, the sixteen most popular indicators give efficiency four times as many measures as quality in performance reporting. Quality does much better on the sixteen top indicators for performance funding; four reflect quality measures and four a combined quality and efficiency, whereas six imply efficiency. The two programs differ significantly on equity. Performance reporting has a higher percentage of equity indicators (22 percent) than performance funding (13 percent). Again, timing might explain this disparity. Performance reporting expanded when court cases had ruled against affirmative action in admissions, and many policymakers became concerned about enrollment diversity. Neither program gives much attention to the policy value of choice.

## Models of Excellence

Indicators also imply the models of excellence that policymakers desire for colleges and universities. Our study used a *strategic investment model* based on a cost-benefit analysis reflecting state priorities, such as graduation rates. The *resource-reputation model* is a provider-driven type, concentrating on academic concerns, as in SAT and ACT scores. The market forces of student and other customer demands drive the *client-centered model* that covers measures, such as student satisfaction surveys. The three models parallel the three reference points in the Accountability Triangle introduced in the Preface and Chapter One: state priorities, academic concerns, and market forces.

**Figure 10.2. Performance Reporting
and Funding Indicators by Value**

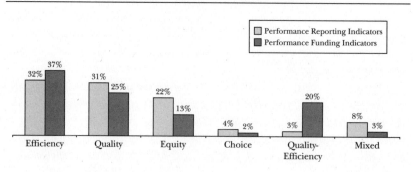

On all the indicators, performance reporting spreads them fairly evenly across strategic investment, client-centered, and a combination of these two models (see Figure 10.3). The total number of measures in performance funding shows similar interest in strategic investment, much less attention to client-centered, and a heavy emphasis (46 percent) on the mixed model of strategic investment and client-centered. The mixed model involves indicators that combine cost-benefit considerations with client service, such as graduation and job placement rates, workforce and economic development, and teacher training and K–16 collaboration. The most popular indicators in performance reporting also tilt heavily toward the mixed model of strategic investment–client services. That model garnered half of the measures for performance reporting and nearly half for performance funding. Neither reporting nor funding devotes much attention to the resource-reputation model on the most common measures. Clearly, these performance programs chose state priorities and market forces over academic concerns. The emphasis on the combination of strategic investment and client-centered suggests some merging of state priorities and market forces. As states cut their support for higher education and raise their role as customers of educational services, state priorities and market forces come closer together.

## Program Performance

To test the performance and effect of the funding and reporting programs, we used two separate surveys, one for performance reporting in 2001 and another for performance funding in 2000. The first questioned governors' aides, legislative chairs of higher education committees or subcommittees, and the SHEFOs in twenty-nine states with performance reporting, as well as directors of institutional research from two- and four-year public campuses in California, Florida, South Carolina, Tennessee, Texas, and Wisconsin (Burke and Minassians, 2002b, Chapter Four). The overall response rate for all positions reached 46 percent. Nearly all of the SHEFOs and over half of the governors' aides from the twenty-nine states responded. The response rate reached 33 percent for legislative chairs, with at least one from sixteen states; over 44 percent

## Figure 10.3. Performance Reporting and Funding Indicators by Model

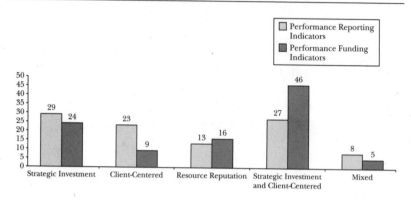

of the surveyed directors of institutional research replied. The funding survey went to presidents, vice presidents, academic deans, and department chairs at all public two- and four-year colleges and universities in Florida, Missouri, Ohio, South Carolina, and Tennessee (Burke and Associates, 2002, Chapter Four). The response rate reached 45 percent.

## Preferred and Achieved Purposes

Contrary to popular opinion, campus leaders appear to accept all four purposes of the performance programs, including external accountability, but they have decided preferences. They clearly favor institutional improvement first, followed closely by increased state funding. They see responding to state needs as trailing in third place and accountability as a distant fourth (Burke and Associates, 2002; Burke and Minassians, 2002b). Despite these preferences, state and campus respondents to both surveys say performance reporting and funding clearly achieved only the purpose of demonstrating accountability while having, at best, only a minimal impact on increasing state funding or improving institutional performance. The average responses from all of the positions in each survey ranked the achievement of external accountability first, meeting state needs second, improved performance a distant third, and increased state funding as little more than an also-ran (Burke and Minassians, 2002b; Burke and Associates, 2002). The only variation came from chairs of education committees on performance reporting. They rated responding to state needs first and demonstrating accountability second. Although campus and state leaders might well disagree on the relative importance of demonstrating accountability and responding to state needs, the poor rating of improving institutional performance must have disappointed both groups.

## Symbolic Usefulness

The surveys suggest that respondents considered performance reports and funding more useful in general than in particular. All parties—governors' aides, legislative chairs, SHEFOs, and institutional researchers—call the reports generally useful to themselves and to their government branch, agency, or campus. But they usually found the report results less useful for budgeting, planning, and conducting studies. If performance reporting is useful to state and campus policymakers, it seems reasonable to assume that it would have a positive impact on improving policies. The mean scores for all respondent groups on usefulness and improvement dash this assumption. Although mean scores on the program usefulness of performance reporting are not as high as desired, those on policy improvement are consistently lower (Burke and Minassians, 2002b). Table 10.3 shows statistically significant differences between the answers of the four groups of respondents on program usefulness compared to policy improvement. This result may suggest that the use of performance reporting, especially on campus, reflects what political scientists call "symbolic policies." Such policies have little real impact on organizations or their participants, for they only appear to apply principles and purposes, such as accountability (Anderson, 1997). They allow organizational leaders to get the credit for compliance with external demands without creating controversy with internal constituents.

A survey of campus leaders on the use of performance funding results on nine campus activities found moderate use in most areas and extensive use only in institutional planning and student outcomes assessment. Respondents from two-year colleges suggest significantly more use of performance results in campus activities

### Table 10.3. Program Usefulness
### Compared to Policy Improvement

|  | Legislative Chairs | Governors' Aides | Institutional Researchers | SHEFOs |
|---|---|---|---|---|
| Program Usefulness | 3.21 | 3.40 | 3.24 | 3.41 |
| Policy Improvement | 2.89 | 3.07 | 2.46 | 2.85 |
| Differences | 0.32 | 0.33 | 0.78 | 0.56 |

*Note:* High = 5; Low = 1.

than those from four-year colleges and universities. Senior campus officers from all campus types perceive more use of performance results than deans and chairs in campus decision making. Respondents also believe that performance funding has only a minimal impact on most of the goals often set in performance funding plans. Overall, they think that the program has a moderate impact only on *mission focus* and *administrative efficiency* and a minimal effect on other common goals and activities. Significantly, performance funding had the most impact on the objectives largely controlled by senior administrators and a minimal effect on outcomes mainly dependent on faculty activities (Burke and Associates, 2002).

## Impact on Improving Performance

Our annual survey of SHEFOs in June 2003 allowed a later assessment of the effect of performance reporting, budgeting, and funding on improving the performance of public colleges and universities (Burke and Minassians, 2003). None of the three programs shows the desired impact on improvement. In fairness, bad budget years are hardly the best times to test the relative impact of reporting, and especially funding or budgeting, programs on institutional improvement. In our 2000 survey, conducted before the economic downturn, SHEFOs said that 35 percent of funding programs improved performance to a great or considerable effect (Burke, Rosen, Minassians, and Lessard, 2000). That year, finance officers from Tennessee cited "great extent," and Connecticut, Missouri, Ohio, and Oklahoma claimed "considerable extent." By 2003, Missouri had dropped the program, and Ohio, Oklahoma, and South Carolina had reduced its funding. By then, more than half of the SHEFOs said performance funding had minimal or no impact or could not judge the effect. Only 6 percent said "considerable" and 40 percent "moderate" effect.

Despite this less-than-stellar showing, performance funding had more effect on improvement than either budgeting or reporting, perhaps reflecting its close connection to funding. Performance budgeting also showed a declining impact on improvement. Over 10 percent of the responses in 2001 indicated "great" and a third "moderate" extent. In 2003, no SHEFOs claimed great or considerable effect on performance improvement, while the number citing "no extent" nearly doubled from the previous year. "Moderate extent" represented the highest category at 38 percent; those of "minimal" and "no extent" combined for 38 percent; "cannot judge" reached 24 percent.

With so many new programs started in the last three years, it is difficult to assess the trends of the perceived impact of performance reporting on higher education improvement. What is clear is that the Seventh SHEFO Survey in 2003 showed positive effects of about 10 percent for "great" and "considerable extent" combined and a "moderate" impact of just 24 percent, whereas the negative ratings of "minimal" and "no extent" reached nearly 40 percent and the "cannot predict" slipped slightly to 26 percent. An impact on improvement is hardly acceptable when the percent of "minimal" and "no extent" exceed four times the "great" and "considerable" effect, even when a number of the programs are new.

## Reasons for the Modest Impact

With all the attention devoted to performance programs, why have they apparently had only a modest impact on improving policymaking and institutional performance? Our surveys and studies suggest several answers, including lack of familiarity, lack of feedback, fighting over means and forgetting ends, particular program problems, and the tendency to place civic over academic culture.

## Lack of Familiarity

The surveys on performance funding and performance reporting show that both programs become increasingly invisible on campus below the level of vice presidents, where performance counts the most. Nearly 90 percent of the presidents and vice presidents in our survey say they are familiar with the performance funding programs in their state, but over 40 percent of the academic deans and over 60 percent of the department chairs admit little or no familiarity (Burke and Associates, 2002). Even in South Carolina, with its unpopular program of thirty-seven indicators prescribed in statute, more than a quarter of the deans and over 40 percent of the chairs say they are only "somewhat," "slightly," or "not at all" familiar. Despite the longevity of the program in Tennessee, launched in the 1970s, over one-third of deans and more than half of the chairs give the same reply.

The results are even worse for performance reporting. Over 70 percent of the institutional researchers claim that the senior administrators on their campuses are familiar or very familiar with the performance reports. Although it is disappointing that nearly 30 percent of senior campus officers apparently have little or no familiarity with performance reporting, the lack of familiarity of deans and chairs is more disturbing. Forty-five percent of the directors of institutional research claim that academic deans at their institution have little or no familiarity with performance reporting. Even more distressing, 70 percent of the directors say the same for department chairs (Burke and Minassians, 2002b). Although this suggested lack of familiarity of deans and chairs is not surprising, it does undermine the effectiveness of performance programs, which depends largely on the results achieved by the academic units of colleges and universities led by deans and chairs. The significant difference in familiarity of senior officers with performance funding than with performance reporting does suggest that money matters on campus.

## Lack of Feedback

The lament of a coordinating agency board officer from New Mexico tells the tale of the lack of feedback: "We . . . put together a report which we thought would provide more useful information. So far, we have had the same reaction to the latest report that we had to the first two reports, which was silence" (Mercer, 1993, p. A37). None of the performance programs required a reaction to their results from state officials, coordinating or system boards, or campus trustees, and our study suggests that feedback seldom occurred. When performance on required results repeatedly gets no reaction from policymakers, campus compliance becomes routine. This lack of feedback led to the next problem.

## Fighting over Means and Forgetting Ends

State and campus policymakers frequently forget that performance funding, budgeting, or reporting are merely the means for encouraging the ends of improved performance and increased responsiveness to state priorities. The survey results suggest mostly squabbling over the means of selecting performance indicators and success standards and largely silence on the end products of how to use them to improve performance and responsiveness. State and campus policymakers have turned the new accountability for results into the old accountability of compliance. Reforming performance reporting requires the reminder that its power comes not only from publishing *but from using* results. Moreover, making performance funding or budgeting meaningful means using the results to improve performance rather than transferring trifling sums among competing campuses.

## Particular Program Problems

Performance reporting in most states suffered from forbidding formats that discouraged rather than encouraged readers. Many reports ran on for a hundred or more pages, filled with dense tables, little explanation, and few summaries. Too many indicators confused readers on state priorities and their achievement. Most of the reports lacked the concise conclusions and clear recommendations that busy state policymakers want and need. At the same time, their aggregate statistics at the institution level lacked the detailed information desired by prospective students considering enrollment or by businesses or civic groups seeking specific services or research support. In short, the performance reports often seemed too detailed for state policymakers and too general for potential customers.

The flexibility of performance budgeting that allowed but did not require consideration of results in allocations proved more of a defect than an asset. In many states, the consideration seemed largely for show, while in others even the appearance disappeared. Conversely, the tight tie of funds to the performance indicators in performance funding had the liability of severely restricting their number. As a result, funding programs failed to fit the full range of campus types. The close link to funding also caused budget problems because all of the funding programs, except Tennessee, relied on at least some additional state allocations. This requirement puts the performance funding programs at risk in times of budget cuts. In addition, campus complaints about budget instability usually led to inadequate funding. Consequently, the funding in these programs was enough to cause controversies but insufficient to spur reforms.

## Civic over Academic Culture

The performance programs fall clearly on the civic, as opposed to the collegial, side of the cultural dualisms described by Bogue and Hall (2003; Chapter One). Although performance funding and reporting avow both *institutional improvement* and *external accountability* as desired purposes, state and campus leaders claim that these programs have the most impact on external accountability and little effect on institutional improvement. Although performance programs do slight *peer review,* they also diminish regulations by encouraging deregulation. Both also clearly reflect *responsiveness* to external need rather than to academic *reputation.* These programs push *performance* more than *prestige* and side more with *evaluation* than *consultation. Evidence,* not *trust,* and *quantitative,* not *qualitative* data represented the preferences of performance funding, budgeting, and reporting. The indicators of performance reporting and performance funding that combine strategic investment and client-centered models of excellence suggest the possibility of a closer connection of the civic and commercial cultures and state priorities and market forces.

## Future Prospects for Performance Programs

Despite these difficulties, the new accountability for results seems here to stay. The future looks bright for performance reporting, but problems cloud the prospect of performance funding and budgeting. Reporting already covers forty-six states, and SHEFOs in 2003 predict that 80 percent are highly likely and 20 percent likely to continue their effort. Of the four holdout states, finance officers from Delaware, Nevada, and Rhode Island see starting the program as unlikely, and the one from New York cannot predict its future action. In contrast, just 67 percent of the finance officers see continuance of performance funding as highly likely, and 20 percent cannot predict its future, including Ohio and South Carolina that started programs in the mid-1990s. Only 53 percent of the performance budgeting programs appear highly likely to continue.

In spite of problems, performance funding, budgeting, and especially reporting remain the most used approaches in the states to the new accountability for results. Improving these programs is critical, for the taxpayers are unlikely to accept the concept that performance should count in all endeavors except higher education.

## The Accountability Triangle: Connecting the Corners

Where do the performance programs place on the Accountability Triangle, with its three corners of state priorities, academic concerns, and market forces? All three programs stress critical state priorities, so they are closer to state priorities than the other two imperatives. Performance reporting increasingly emphasizes the market issues of student access and affordability, workforce and economic development, teacher training and college-school collaboration. Not surprisingly, these issues also reflect state priorities. Performance reporting and performance funding indicators also include a sizeable percentage of indicators that reflect a combination of strategic investment and client-centered models, reflecting both state priorities and market forces, and show little interest in the resource-reputation model that often appears in academic concerns. Performance reporting comes the closest to the center of the triangle. It still favors state priorities most but has indicators of interest to market forces and is the least objectionable of the performance programs to academic concerns. Performance budgeting also favors state priorities, but its longer list of indicators also has some interest for market forces. Performance funding places near the top of the triangle, with too few indicators of interest to markets and intense hostility from the academic community.

The question is how to move funding, budgeting, and reporting programs more toward the center of the Accountability Triangle, where they can respond better to academic concerns and market forces. Figure 10.4 estimates their current position.

Mandated-Not Prescribed adoption could move more of the programs toward campus concerns by involving campus leaders with coordinating agencies in proposing the indicators and success standards. However, performance funding and, to a lesser extent, performance budgeting probably will never satisfy academic concerns nor have sufficient reach to include diverse market groups. In addition, performance funding, with its direct tie to state allocations, can never include sufficient indicators to reflect diverse market needs. This limitation is less true for performance budgeting, with a looser link to funding. Performance reporting could respond much more to market needs. Performance reports at the institutional level, which increasingly appear on campus Web sites, could include the disaggregated information on campus programs, activities, and ser-

**Figure 10.4. Current Performance Programs**

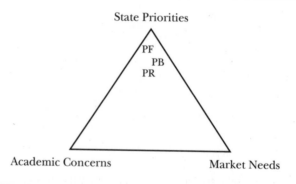

PB = Performance Budgeting, PF = Performance Funding, PR = Performance Reporting.

vices desired by diverse groups of potential students and clients. Flexible Web sites would allow state and campus leaders to acquire the aggregated information needed for policymaking yet permit the wide range of detailed data desired by potential clients about campus programs in instruction, research, and service.

Currently, all the performance programs stress state priorities while slighting in varying degrees market needs and, especially, academic concerns. Several suggestions could help correct those shortcomings. First, representative groups of business, civic, government, and education leaders could develop public agendas for higher education that ensure appropriate consideration of state priorities, campus concerns, and market needs (see Chapter One). Second, a pyramid of indicators—relatively few at the state, more at the college or university system, and still more at the institution level, with a limited set of common measures at each level—could help connect priorities and track performance at every level (Burke and Minassians, 2002b). Finally, none of the performance programs can work unless they connect to performance where it really counts—at the department level. Internal reports of departmental results on relevant parts of the state public agenda could address this problem. With these changes, performance reporting could move to the center of the Accountability Triangle, with appropriate attention to all three of the accountability factors: state priorities, campus concerns, and market forces. Figure 10.5 approximates the program positions on the Accountability Triangle after adopting these changes.

## A Comprehensive Accountability System

The big problem with performance programs, as with all the accountability plans, is that they are isolated initiatives, unconnected to a comprehensive accountability system. Instead of competing initiatives, coupling all three performance programs could create an integrated accountability system that connects state priorities, campus concerns, and market needs.

## Performance Reporting

Performance reporting can supply the accountability template. This initiative can include the full range of state priorities, campus concerns, and market needs because it merely publicizes rather

**Figure 10.5.  Ideal Performance Programs**

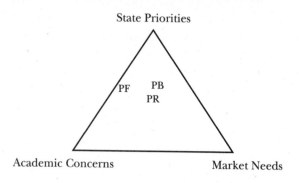

PB = Performance Budgeting, PF = Performance Funding, PR = Performance Reporting.

than funds—or even budgets for—performance results. Its liability is the lack of a required review of report results by state and campus policymakers. One way to ensure this requirement is to link the reporting to the process of developing and reviewing the public agenda for higher education in a state. A representative group of business, civic, government, and education leaders would develop that agenda, which would include consideration of state priorities, academic concerns, and market needs (Chapter One). The agenda would set the goals and indicators for the performance reports at the state, system, and institution levels. In addition, colleges and universities would include relevant indicators in reports from their academic departments—the units most responsible for results on many critical measures. Every five years, a similar group would publicly review the report results and recommend needed improvements.

## Performance Budgeting

Performance budgeting could add financial consequences to those reviews of performance on the public agenda while averting its major problem. The real difficulty with this policy is the uncertainty of whether policymakers really consider campus performance in state budgeting. Tying that consideration to five-year reviews of results on the public agenda could avoid that uncertainty and add financial consequences that raise the visibility of those periodic reviews. The five-year span would also allow adequate time for assessing performance on critical indicators for higher education.

## Performance Funding

In this accountability system, performance funding would become largely a campus-based program. Its problems stem from the size of budget allocations, the number of program goals, and the inevitability of campus opposition to an outside imposition. The allocations are either too large to prevent budget instability or too small to encourage improved performance. In times of state budget cuts, any special allocation becomes an endangered item. Low levels of funding for most of these programs tend to trivialize even a limited number of program priorities with trifling sums. Finally, administration and faculty leaders naturally resist the program as an external imposition that fails to consider academic concerns.

One way to address these problems is to turn performance funding into a special-purpose program with just two indicators that are chosen by campuses. The first would copy Tennessee's indicator that allows a college or university to select a distinctive element in its campus mission that coincides with a list of state priorities. The second would use a device from the Missouri model that encouraged academic departments to select a state priority and then show results that support it. To perpetuate the program in bad, as well as good, economic times, this proposal would use the Tennessee model of allocating a set percentage of the annual operating budget of an institution to fund these two initiatives. Such a proposal would turn performance funding into a campus program stressing academic concerns while still supporting state priorities.

The proposed program would fund only one state indicator—degree or certificate completion. The critical need for human capital in a knowledge and information era makes degree attainment the highest state priority for higher education (Chapter Nine). Currently, state budgets for public colleges and universities fund student enrollment and ignore degree completion. This practice sends the wrong message—that access is everything—at a time when anything less than a certificate or degree has diminishing value in a workforce that is growing ever more sophisticated. States should tie from 3 to 5 percent of their operating funding to actual degree or certificate completion, with actual completion rates compared with projected rates related to admission standards. That funding program should also encourage attainment of baccalaureate degrees by two-year college transfers.

## Recommendations

The following recommendations can do more than increase the connection between the three performance programs and state priorities, academic concerns, and market forces. They can raise visibility of the performance programs in state capitols and on college campuses and increase their impact on policymaking and performance.

- Involve the deans and chairs in developing internal institutional plans that bring reporting, budgeting, and funding down to the school and department levels, which would also make those programs more sensitive to academic concerns.
- Add an indicator to plans for performance funding, budgeting, or reporting showing how colleges and universities have used the results from these programs to improve their performance.
- Require governors, legislative committees, coordination boards and regents, and institutional trustees to react to the results produced in the performance programs and comment on how they intend to use this information in planning and policymaking.
- Include consideration of the results on critical indicators of the performance programs in institutional and specialized accreditation reviews.
- Develop, through summits or commissions of business, government, civic, and education leaders, public agendas for higher education that reflect state priorities, academic concerns, and market forces and conduct five-year reviews of those agendas and higher education performance.

These recommendations may not cure all of the problems of performance programs, but they can connect them to the three accountability requirements of state priorities, academic concerns, and market forces.

# Chapter Eleven

# Resources and Reputation in Higher Education

## Double, Double, Toil and Trouble

*J. Fredericks Volkwein and Stephen D. Grunig*

In Shakespeare's *Macbeth,* the three witches assess the ingredients of a boiling pot to engage in "prophecy by necromantical science." Similarly, in American higher education, we succeed in brewing up a hodgepodge of variables to rate and rank institutions. In order to attract annual customers for their publications, some publishers cause "double toil and trouble" by making changes to their jumbled mixture of a brew every year. In the most widely noticed cauldron, *U.S. News & World Report* (*U.S. News*) has ignited fires of controversy that excite some academic leaders and bewilder others, as published rankings for some campuses ascend and descend with each new edition.

Although Macbeth is confused by the witches' prophecies, he does seek them out and shapes his actions accordingly. Just so, parents, students, trustees, policymakers, and even faculty are strongly influenced by the ratings and guidebooks. Colleges and universities are involved in a metaphysical game in which presidents, deans, and institutional researchers engage in strategic guessing

The authors gratefully acknowledge the research assistance for this chapter supplied by Kyle V. Sweitzer, a research assistant in the Center for the Study of Higher Education at Penn State.

about what areas might be emphasized or de-emphasized in forth-coming ratings. Like Macbeth, the fortunes of institutions seem sub-ject to fate—to the whims of unpredictable revisions in the ratings and rankings from year to year. This chapter attempts to divine what the various brews of ratings and rankings tell us about the ac-countability of colleges and universities. What do they prophesize about that mysterious mixture of quality and performance?

As noted in Burke's Chapter One and elsewhere in this volume, there are at least three separate models, or philosophies, about what constitutes educational excellence (see also Chapter Ten). These models represent the three points on the Accountability Triangle that is the organizing framework for this volume.

First, the academic community traditionally holds to the resource-reputation model. This model emphasizes the impor-tance of financial resources, faculty credentials, student test scores, external funding, and ratings and rankings. Institutional and pro-gram reputation plays an important if not central role in this model because reputational ratings measure beliefs about institutions or programs. But as we discuss next, the beliefs themselves are fre-quently related to quantifiable institutional attributes. Attention often focuses on the ratings, yet it is worth considering the societal value of the institutional attributes that serve as the foundation for the beliefs and ratings.

Second, the civic and government community generally holds to the strategic investment model. This model emphasizes the im-portance of return on investment, cost-benefit analysis, results-oriented and productivity measures such as admissions yield, grad-uation rates, time- to-degree, and expenditures per student. Within this model, reputation ratings are relevant only to the extent that they shape the pride of civic and business leaders and their willing-ness to support and give autonomy to institutions of higher educa-tion. Although state policymakers may have a casual interest in the ratings, they are even more keenly interested in the strength of the institutional attributes that the ratings capture. For example, states generally are concerned about maintaining their technological and scientific competitiveness, and thus their reputations, as a means of developing their industry tax base and employment growth.

Third, many parents, students, and student affairs profession-als cling to a client-centered model. This market-oriented model

emphasizes good customer service, student satisfaction, faculty availability, alumni feedback, low tuition, and high aid. Seymour articulates this model in his book *On Q: Causing Quality in Higher Education*
(1992). He proposes that the first priority of a college or university
should be the assessment and fulfillment of the needs of students,
parents, employers, and other "customers" of higher education. Institutions that possess the highest quality are those that do the most
effective job of meeting the needs of their constituents. Thus, the
organization's customers, rather than the experts, define quality.

## Undergraduate Ratings and Rankings

This section of our chapter describes and examines the undergraduate college ratings and rankings that appear in the leading American publications. These publishers attempt to simplify a complex
world for their readers by describing, grouping, and rating colleges
in a variety of ways. We distinguish between guidebooks that group
colleges into descriptive categories, those that rate institutions, and
those that rank them. Some students and parents confuse these
grouping, rating, and ranking functions. For many students and families, the college choice process is a difficult affair that requires them
to balance a complex array of institutional characteristics with the
particular educational goals, personal needs, values, attitudes, finances, and abilities of the applicant. The factual data and narrative descriptions presented in most guides strike us as providing
helpful information to students and families as they journey through
the college choice and admissions process. However, the reduction
of colleges into simplistic ranks makes the student-institution fit
process sound quick and easy; it is not.

Many publishers collect and print a good deal of information
about colleges and universities but stop short of trying to reduce
the facts to a single rating category, the College Board's *Handbook*
and the *Yale Daily News's Insider's Guide* being perhaps the most
prominent examples. Barron's *Profiles of American Colleges*, Peterson's
*Four-Year Colleges*, and Rugg's *Recommendations on the Colleges* rightly
describe themselves as grouping colleges into admissions categories. *The Fiske Guide to Colleges* and *The Princeton Review* correctly
claim to engage in rating. Literally hundreds of specialty guides
serve particular populations of students—the colleges that are most
wired, disability friendly, conservative, faith based, Hispanic serving,

and so forth. Although the number of guidebook publications has proliferated in recent years, a few of the nation's most venerable guides, like Cass and Birnbaum's and Lovejoy's, appear to be no longer publishing. We describe next as much as we can decipher about the "selectivity," "competitiveness," and "academic" ratings used by these college guides.

Table 11.1 displays some of the salient features of the four leading guides and *U.S. News,* the information they contain, and the nature of the ratings they use to classify colleges. The oldest guidebooks (Barron's and Peterson's) share roughly similar institutional coverage and classify colleges by admissions selectivity. Barron's gathers information on nearly all accredited four-year colleges and constructs a six-category grouping of admissions competitiveness. Peterson's also gathers information on almost all the four-year institutions and asks each college to place itself into one of five categories of admissions "difficulty." Fiske uses a five-star rating system for rating the academic, social, and student life at each campus. *The Princeton Review* gives a 60 to 99 rating to colleges in each of four categories: admissions, academics, quality of life, and financial aid.

Published every other year since the 1950s, Barron's *Profiles of American Colleges* classifies colleges and universities according to the Admissions Selector rating of "competitiveness" of the entering freshman class. Using a relatively consistent standard over the years, the Barron's rating is reported to be a combination of the percent of applicants admitted, high school rank in class or GPA, median test scores on the SAT and ACT, and proportion of each freshman class scoring at or above certain levels on the SAT and ACT. The current 25th edition of Barron's places 64 institutions in the most competitive category, 94 in highly competitive, and 243 institutions in very competitive; the largest category is competitive, with 615 institutions. Finally, Barron's puts 318 colleges in the less competitive and 104 in the noncompetitive categories. Although the exact methodology for calculating these ratings is a bit mysterious, the campus ratings have been reasonably stable over time. In our analyses, they correlate most highly with the average SAT scores for the entering freshman class.

Published by Peterson's annually since 1970, Thomson-Peterson's *Four-Year Colleges* contains an index that classifies colleges according to their self-rated difficulty of admission. Each college selects the level that most closely corresponds to their entrance difficulty,

**Table 11.1. Guidebook Measures**

| Name of Guidebook | Barron's Profiles of American Colleges | Peterson's Four-Year Colleges | The Fiske Guide to Colleges | Princeton Review's The Best 351 Colleges | U.S. News & World Report |
|---|---|---|---|---|---|
| Number of Institutions Rated | 1,650 | 2,100 | 299 | 351 | 1,400 |
| Name of Rating | Admissions selector rating | Entrance difficulty | Three dimensions: Academic, Student life, and Social ratings | Four dimensions: Admissions, Academic, Quality of life, and Financial aid ratings | "Best" colleges in each of ten institutional categories |
| Type of Rating | Nine categories of competitiveness, from most competitive to noncompetitive | Five categories of self-rated entrance difficulty, from most competitive to noncompetitive | One to five stars in each dimension | One to four stars in each dimension | Ranking for top one or two quartiles; alpha list for other quartiles |

| Measures Used in the Ratings | | | | | |
|---|---|---|---|---|---|
| **Student Selectivity** | | | | | |
| (percent freshman applicants admitted) | X | | X | X | 15% (10%) |
| High School GPA | X | | | X | |
| High School Class Rank | X | X | | X | (40%) |
| Average SAT or ACT | X | X | X | X | (50%) |
| **Survey Information:** | | | | | |
| Academic rating | | | X | X | Reputation among administrative peers 25% |
| Quality-of-life rating | | | X | | |
| Quality of social life | | | X | | |
| Financial aid rating | | | | X | |
| **Faculty Resources** | | | | | Six measures = 20% |
| **Financial Resources** | | | | | Per-student spending = 10% |
| Retention-Graduation | | | | | 20% |
| Freshman Retention | | | X | | (20%) |
| Five- or Six-Year Graduation | | | X | | (80%) |
| Alumni Giving | | | | | 5% |
| Predicted vs. Actual Graduation Rate | | | | | 5% |

*Note:* X = Variables used in each rating, according to the publisher.

according to guidelines supplied by the publisher. In the 34th edition, 55 institutions self-rated themselves as fitting the most difficult category, 172 colleges as very difficult, 1,157 as moderately difficult, 313 as minimally difficult, and 240 as noncompetitive.

Fiske and Logue and *The Princeton Review* concentrate their coverage on the 300 or so "best and most interesting" institutions. (Barron's *Best Buys* and Peterson's *Competitive Colleges* pitch themselves to the same audience.) First published in 1982, *The Fiske Guide to Colleges* has become a respected description of the salient features of its 299 institutions (Nicholson, 1991; Walleri and Moss, 1995). *The Fiske Guide* rates colleges in three areas: academics, social life, and quality of life, using a one- to five-star system. The rating may be somewhat subjective, but it does list the average SAT and ACT scores for the freshmen class; the number of applicants, acceptances, and enrollees; a five-year graduation rate; and the percentage of freshmen returning for their sophomore year. We find that these items correlate highly with the five-star ratings.

First published in 1992, *The Princeton Review*'s guide, *The Best 351 Colleges,* is the newest of the guides analyzed in this chapter. (A more comprehensive *Princeton Review* publication, *The Complete Book of Colleges,* covers about 1,200 institutions but describes rather than rates them.) The publishers construct qualitative descriptions from an analysis of 106,000 multiyear survey responses from students. The campus survey of students consists of about seventy items seeking student perceptions "on subjects ranging from the school's administration to their social lives, from the quality of food to the quality of teaching." The publishers appear to favor cute and offbeat comments from students that make entertaining reading. The ratings that appear in *The Review* are of two types: (1) "What's hot and what's not"—the top twenty schools in academics, administration, quality of life, politics, demographics, social life, extracurriculars, parties, and "schools by archetype" and (2) four global ratings, on a 60 to 99 scale, of admissions competitiveness, academics, financial aid, and quality of life.

Because several of the guides use similar measures, if not similar methods, to place colleges in their rating categories, one would expect considerable overlap in their lists. We examined the colleges appearing in the top two (most competitive, most difficult) of the rating categories for Barron's, Peterson's, Fiske, and *The*

*Princeton Review* and found that they generally contain the same colleges. Moreover, when we entered these guidebook ratings for a sample of universities into a database, we found that the correlations among them range from .59 to .80.

Next, we examined the ratings and their component measures to determine which variables exhibit the highest correlations with each rating, as reported in the four guidebooks. In their 1999 study, Baughman and Goldman found a strong relationship between faculty scholarship and Barron's freshman selectivity. Institutions in the "most competitive" Barron's category had four times the publications per 100 faculty members than institutions in the "highly competitive" category and nine times those in the "very competitive" group of colleges. The 37 most selective campuses had 52 times as many publications per faculty as the 365 least selective. Although the causal connection between faculty scholarship and student selectivity is not completely clear, their findings are consistent with Peter Blau's study in *The Organization of Academic Work* (1994). It concluded that large research universities disproportionately attract the most productive faculty, and these productive professors, in turn, attract high proportions of the most talented students.

We examined the correlations between each rating and the reported test scores, acceptance rates, rank in class, and GPA where available for these reports. Our correlations between these ratings and acceptance rates ranged from .56 to .68. The guidebook ratings correlated with high school rank and GPA within a range from .64 to .80. The ratings correlated most with test scores, which ranged from .73 to .90. Almost identical results occurred whether we used the SAT 25th percentile, the 75th percentile, or the midpoint. Therefore, the various guidebook ratings of college competitiveness and academics essentially boil down to a rating of the reported test scores of a recent entering freshman class.

In summary, the chief value in these guides may be in publishing the facts and impressions about each campus and letting consumers decide what is most relevant for them. We fail to see that the selectivity and competitiveness rating categories help very much, except for applicants to the nation's most selective institutions. These admissions ratings no doubt help some students be more realistic about their chances, and they can also be helpful in getting students to shape their college application list to include both likely and aspirational choices. Even so, these ratings of admissions selectivity and competitiveness appear to give students the same information they receive from knowing the average test scores and test score ranges for the previous freshman class.

## Why *U.S. News* Is Different

Fierce competition among the guidebook publishers escalated in the 1980s when *U.S. News* began publishing its annual rankings of undergraduate colleges. Now its fall issue each year, described by many as its "swimsuit issue," is a hot seller and attracts considerable media coverage. Robert Morse and his colleagues at *U.S. News* not only use the largest array of measures but they openly describe their ranking methodology. Although the variables and assigned weights have changed over the years, partly in response to criticism from the academic profession, *U.S. News* now assigns explicit weights to seven indicators and fifteen subfactors in order to rank about 1,400 institutions, as shown in the right-hand column of Table 11.1. This gives the appearance of scientific objectivity, and in a demonstration of marketing cleverness, *U.S. News* has, over the years, gradually increased the number and types of institutions that are ranked rather than merely assigned to quartiles. The 2004 edition of *U.S. News* not only ranks the top 126 national universities and top 110 national liberal arts colleges but creates even more "winners" by creating an additional eight categories of ranked institutions—"Best Universities–Master's" within the North, South, Midwest, and Western regions and "Best Comprehensive Colleges–Bachelor's" in each of four regions. Within these ten ranked groups, the institutions not in the top one or two tiers are grouped roughly by quartile rather than ranked.

Currently and historically, the heaviest weighting in the *U.S. News* rankings is the measure of "academic reputation" or "peer assessment." Distributed to only three officers—president, provost, and admissions director—at over 1,400 four-year colleges, the survey asks each to rate the academic strength of their peer institutions on a scale from 1 (marginal) to 5 (distinguished). Those with insufficient information are asked to mark "don't know."

## What Influences Reputational Ratings?

Although a great deal of scholarly attention has been directed toward analyzing the reputational ratings of graduate programs at major universities, fewer analytical studies have examined reputation at the undergraduate level. We found a handful of studies concluding that two inputs—institutional size and selectivity—are the primary influences on reputational quality (Astin, 1970; Astin and Lee, 1972; Astin and Solomon, 1981; Solomon and Astin, 1981; Volkwein, 1989; Schmitz, 1993; Grunig, 1997; Porter and Toutkoushian, 2002). The earliest of these studies by Astin and his colleagues indicate that institutions with large enrollments and high average SAT and ACT scores for entering freshmen are considered the most prestigious. The more recent studies have generally confirmed these findings and expanded them by finding, in addition, that reputational ratings correlate significantly with the following variables: average high school class standing of entering freshmen; admissions acceptance rates; instructional budget per student; percentage of faculty possessing Ph.D.s, faculty publication rates; average cost of tuition, room, and board; and retention-graduation rates. Generally, these variables explain between 65 percent and 85 percent of the total variance in undergraduate reputational ratings.

## What Is the Impact of Reputational Ratings?

Several empirical studies have examined the impact of the reputation-and-ratings game and the connections to enrollment management and educational quality. We draw several conclusions from this scholarship.

### Increase in Value

Throughout the nation's history, college attendance has steadily increased, and in the past twenty-five years alone the college participation rate has grown from about one-third of high school graduates to well over half. This appears to reflect the increasing value of a college education. Studies indicate that attending more selective colleges is associated with higher graduate degree attainment and higher postcollege earnings (Brewer, Eide, and Ehrenberg, 1999; Ehrenberg and Smith, 2003; Hoxby, 1998). Moreover, Geiger (2004), among others, has commented on the "peer effect," or the desire by high-ability students to cluster together. Thus, we see a national obsession with becoming the best by attending the best. Americans are naturally competitive, as any casual observer of our reality television programming and sports events will conclude. Parents of talented students and some who are not so talented are increasingly engaged in the passionate pursuit of the highest-ranked institutions. The most prestigious institutions, in turn, have a keen interest in maintaining their market position, and they engage in high levels of spending to compete for higher student quality. Roger Geiger describes this as the selectivity sweepstakes (2002). Admissions directors are akin to NFL or NCAA coaches competing for state, regional, and national championships. We also know that this competition is gradually altering the structure of higher education along the lines of the market taxonomy described by Zemsky and his research colleagues (Chapter Twelve). The relatively small number of medallion and name-brand colleges compete fiercely for the equally small proportion of talented student "zoomers."

## Diversity of Choice

American higher education offers its students more diversity of choice than any other nation. Over 4,200 two-year and four-year institutions have widely different missions, histories, governance, structural complexity, financial flexibility, administrative policies, campus climates, residential and curricular options, and student and faculty subcultures. Thus, the guidebook and publisher ratings appear to fill a public appetite for information to help applicants sort and sift the dizzying array of choices. Many families approach the college choice decision knowing that the total four-year cost, even with financial aid, will almost certainly exceed $40,000 and may exceed $100,000 at many private colleges.

In reality, however, fewer than one hundred institutions are selective enough to admit fewer than half their freshman applicants. Based on current information in the guidebooks discussed here, we estimate that 90 percent of the nation's two-year and four-year college campuses in 2002 admitted at least 85 percent of their freshman applicants, and the transfer admissions picture is even less competitive. Although this picture is different in some states, surveys suggest that over 70 percent of students get admitted to their first-choice school and over 90 percent to one of their first two choices.

Thus, prospective students have many good options, and the frenzy over the difficulty of gaining college admission is largely marketing hype and limited to a small proportion of institutions. Sophisticated marketing and recruitment strategies aimed at reputation building are now in widespread use among the majority of all types of institutions of higher education. Proliferating guidebooks and publications that rate and rank colleges feed the American appetite for becoming the best by attending the best. Consequently, prospective students in the upper quartile of the talent pool typically receive an avalanche of promotional materials and even telephone calls from college students, alumni, and faculty who have been enlisted in the conversion of enrollment management from "tell" to "yell" to "sell," as Moll has described it (1994). There is no best college, only a good student-institution fit. For each student, there are literally hundreds of institutions where happiness and academic success is likely. We think the college search process should be about examining the strengths and weaknesses of each college and finding a good fit, not selecting "the best" or most prestigious.

## Changes in Rank

We know that *U.S. News* ranks are extremely sensitive to changes in the weights for each measure, and when weightings change, the danger of distorting public perception increases. *U.S. News* college rankings change from year to year, based in rare cases on "dirty data" but more frequently on responsive enhancements to the methodology following criticism from the profession. In his 2001 analysis of *U.S. News* scores, Dichev (2001) reports that 90 percent of the variation in scores over time was due to variation in the weights and only 10 percent to changes in the indicators themselves.

However, relatively minor changes in the measures and their weights can produce relatively large changes in rank. Machung reports that twenty of the top twenty-five universities shifted ranks between 1993 and 1997: "Nobody gets to stay at the top too long" (1998, p. 15). In his study of 140 liberal arts colleges, McGuire (1995) asked a panel of 129 presidents and academic deans to assign weights to the fifteen *U.S. News* measures and found that twelve of the fifteen weights were roughly similar to those used by *U.S. News.* (The three that were significantly different are the weights for student-faculty ratio, faculty compensation, and reputation.) The weights assigned by this panel of experts produced a change in rank for 88 percent of the institutions, and for 15 percent the change was large enough to move them into a different quartile. Other authors, like Ehrenberg (2003), have described numerous institutions that experienced dramatic year-to-year changes in rank due to altered, omitted, or misinterpreted data when nothing else at the institution changed much. Monks and Ehrenberg (1999) examined the impact of shifts in rank over a period of eleven years at thirty COFHE (Consortium for Financing Higher Education) institutions. They conclude that a less favorable ranking in *U.S. News* leads the institution to accept a greater percentage of its applicants and to experience a decrease in its admissions yield rate, resulting in a decline in average freshman SAT scores and additional investment in student financial aid.

Although rankings influence decisions by students and parents, the *U.S. News* rankings appear to have an even more powerful influence on trustees, alumni, faculty, large donors, and college presidents, provosts, and deans (Ehrenberg, 2000, 2003; Hossler, 2000; Hossler and Foley, 1995; Litten and Hall, 1989; Machung, 1998; McGuire, 1995; Monks and Ehrenberg, 1999; Walleri and Moss, 1995). Indeed, these scholars have documented an array of questionable institutional behaviors encouraged, in particular, by the *U.S. News* ranks. Because even small changes in reported statistics produce artificially high changes in rank, the system encourages tinkering with data like class size, alumni giving, admissions yield, and faculty resources. For example, the current *U.S. News* methodology does the following:

- Rewards colleges that generate large populations of applicants that have little chance of being admitted

- Encourages colleges to enlarge the early decision process (when students might make a decision before they are ready) as a means of reducing the regular admissions acceptance rate and increasing the yield
- Encourages institutions to make admissions test scores optional because mostly high-scoring test takers will submit them
- Favors those colleges with fewer high schools reporting class rank
- Rewards colleges that keep the freshman class small and enlarge their transfer population
- Rewards colleges that use financial aid funds to buy talented students and penalizes those who admit students from low-income, at-risk, and underserved populations requiring high aid
- Encourages institutions to raise full-time faculty salaries, even if the market does not necessitate it, and penalizes those state institutions where the state picks up the fringe benefits
- Fails to reward institutions for efficiencies like forming collaborations or consortia with other institutions for the purpose of sharing curricula, faculty, and other resources
- Rewards institutions with expensive research and professional programs, especially if the institutions are located in high cost-of-living areas requiring high salaries
- Penalizes those who unilaterally reduce costs
- Penalizes those who keep most classes at midrange (thirty to fifty) and favors those with a bimodal distribution of class sizes (some enormously large lecture classes and lots of smaller classes under twenty)
- Penalizes colleges whose students leave after a year or two to attend higher-rated colleges
- Penalizes those who count all former students as alumni, whether or not they graduated or have accurate addresses
- Penalizes those who concentrate their development efforts on a few large individual donors and corporations rather than solicit alumni donors widely
- Encourages colleges to send costly publicity materials to their peer institutions as a means of influencing the reputation ratings

Finally, some of the worst problems with the integrity of the data on which the earlier ratings and rankings were based have been substantially addressed. The Association for Institutional Research Higher Education Data Policy Committee led a national effort during the 1990s to develop a Common Data Set and uniform national templates for counting and reporting enrollments, resources, and personnel. This collaborative process included the National Center for Education Statistics, college guide publishers, and secondary school counselors, as well as academics. In addition, the publishers of ratings and rankings have invested considerable resources to ensure the accuracy and completeness of the information they receive. The problem now is less with the accuracy of the data (although this may still be a problem for some colleges with poor information systems) and more with how data are manipulated by the publishers.

Perhaps the greatest problem with reputation ratings in particular is that they constitute academic "beauty contests" where looks count more than substance. College characteristics like financial support and admissions selectivity are superficial substitutes for knowing the quality of the educational experience that students receive. We know from the research by Astin (1985), Banta and Associates (2002), Pace (1979), Kuh (2001), Pascarella and Terenzini (1991), and Upcraft and Schuh (1996), among others, that what happens to students after enrollment is far more important than the characteristics students bring with them. "Within-college experiences tend to count substantially more than between-college characteristics" (Pascarella, 2001b, p. 20). The Higher Education Data Sharing (HEDS) Consortium undertook an exercise among its members and developed an array of domains and measures of quality for institutions of higher education (Trainer and Sapp, 2000). Most of these HEDS measures overlap with those of *U.S. News,* except for academic reputation (notably absent from the HEDS list) and measures of student outcomes, skill enhancement, academic achievement, and faculty-student interaction (notably absent from the *U.S. News* list).

In response to some of these criticisms and a desire to be more outcomes oriented, *U.S. News* in recent years has included a graduation rate performance indicator that calculates the predicted six-year graduation rate (based largely on freshman student selectivity) and compares it to the actual rate. The difference between the predicted and actual rate is an appealing performance indicator, but Porter and Toutkoushian (2002) analyzed the *U.S. News* data and examined potential problems: sample definition and selection, variable precision, model specification, missing data, and confidence intervals. He concluded that only 9 of 198 institutions had an actual graduation rate that differs significantly from the predicted one. In other words, current *U.S. News* methodology overstates the differences between actual and predicted graduation rates.

The research literature yields a fairly consistent picture of what matters most in college—student effort and engagement in the classroom, peer relations, faculty interaction, and other enriching experiences. Bob Pace summarized several decades of research with the observation that students tend to learn what they study, and the more they study, the more they learn. For example, analyzing a series of studies in the State University of New York, Volkwein and his research colleagues found that student classroom experiences were the most powerful contributors to various measures of student outcomes in twenty-one of thirty-three studies. Classroom engagement and vitality was the best predictor of intellectual growth in ten of eleven studies, and in the eleventh it was a significant secondary contributor. The vitality of the classroom experience was also the most important influence in one study of openness and tolerance, in one study of responsibility and self-control, in two studies of overall satisfaction, in four studies of freshman goal clarity, in two studies of student commitment, and in one study of the length of enrollment (Volkwein, 2003). In their massive review of the literature in 1991, Pascarella and Terenzini concluded that the amount of energy and effort students invest in their own education is much more important than the reputation or selectivity of the college they attend. George Kuh's NSSE data on student engagement also indicates that the variation within institutions is far greater than the variation between or among them (see Chapter Seven); the rankings of undergraduate colleges have only the most indirect and ephemeral connection to actual student educational experiences. We suspect that comparable students at the 3rd and 33rd or even the 93rd ranked colleges can have substantially similar undergraduate experiences (Pascarella, 2001b; Kuh, 2003).

It is particularly troublesome when presidents and provosts are asked to rate the academic quality of other colleges, and this becomes *the* major variable in a published ranking. Such judgments are likely to be based on superficial, outdated, or perhaps even biased impressions of competing institutions. As Zemsky suggests, such rankings do not establish reputations as much as they reinforce them as measures of market position (Chapter Twelve). Pascarella argues that it is both overly simplistic and misleading to reduce all these numbers down into a single rank and to pretend that this reflects educational quality. Such a scorecard mentality hides the fact that there are *many* good institutions and many good faculty and students and educational opportunities within each campus.

## Ways to Improve the Brew

Current reputation and selectivity data largely measure institutional wealth and resources, so the *U.S. News* ranking game stimulates colleges to build more and spend more while the search for convenient indicators of educational quality continues. Comparison measurement, like grading students on the curve, unduly limits the list of achievers. Only one institution can be ranked number one, and only ten can be in the top ten, even though dozens, if not hundreds, may deserve to be recognized for their educational quality. We know that "an excellent undergraduate education is most likely to occur at those colleges and universities that maximize good practices and enhance students' academic and social engagement or effort" (Pascarella, 2001b, p. 22). Elsewhere in this volume, Kuh and Zemsky describe the development of several instruments that are now in use at hundreds of colleges and are designed to assess the quality of the student educational experience and to supply better consumer information (Chapters Seven and Twelve). We refer the reader to their chapters for descriptions of the College Student Experiences Questionnaire, the National Survey of Student Engagement, the College Student Survey, and the College Results Instrument. Such instruments, among others, have the potential to replace, eventually, the reputation-and-resources approach to the ratings game, especially if they are used to identify and describe effective institutions rather than to rank them.

Many have argued for a greater emphasis on student outcomes, but this is not without problems as well. Porter and Toutkoushian's analysis shows the limitations of comparing the predicted versus actual graduation rate (2002). Likewise, student and alumni performance on standardized tests substantially replicates the statistical profile of entering students. Input is the best predictor of output. Information from students and alumni must be treated carefully in quality assurance, and we find ourselves in substantial agreement with the guidelines articulated by Pascarella in his 2001b *Change* article and by Kuh in Chapter Seven. The measurement of effective practices must not only be linked to institutional goals for student development but must be compatible with state and national priorities. And evidence should be collected not only from multiple sources but also in large enough quantities to have both external face validity and internal usefulness for academic departments and student subpopulations. Not only can we document effective institutional practices based on student self-reports, but we should enhance the validity of those perceptions by controlling for the influence of precollege differences and by basing them as fully as possible on low-inference, factual data. We must also obtain high response rates by representatives from different constituent groups of students and alumni. For example, the student experiences and educational outcomes of community college and transfer students have been greatly underexamined thus far.

The current *U.S. News* rankings are expressions of market position and a scorecard value system. There is no room in the current system to recognize the four thousand or so institutions that serve low-income, at-risk, and underserved populations of students. Nor is there any performance reward for institutional improvement and lower-cost operations. Significant change in academic organizations takes three to four years to become visible, so yearly surveys and annual published rankings seem to be produced solely for the purpose of boosting sales. Colleges change glacially, not year to year, so the biennial publication of Barron's is a practice that should be lengthened and extended to the other publications as well.

## Rating and Ranking Graduate and Professional Programs

Efforts to measure the performance of doctoral programs have generally centered on peer comparisons with similar programs at other institutions. Although a variety of measures can and do serve as the basis for these comparisons, reputational ratings, like those of the National Research Council (NRC), have long been the gold standard. Using reputational ratings by informed peers produces assessments that academics and prospective students alike generally accept as valid. Even so, we have a national tradition of eagerly awaiting the publication of the graduate ratings every decade or so yet also criticizing the rating process for years afterward. (An excellent summary of this history is contained in a *Higher Education Handbook* chapter by Webster [1992].)

Like its predecessors in 1966, 1970, and 1982, the 1995 NRC study gathered reputational ratings by asking faculty members in similar departments at other doctorate-granting institutions to consider the "scholarly competence and achievements of the faculty" within the rated program. Respondents indicated whether the "scholarly quality of program faculty" could best be described as "distinguished," "strong," "good," "adequate," "marginal," or "not sufficient for doctoral education." Those unfamiliar with a program could decline to evaluate it. These various ratings have demonstrated consistency over time and high reliability, averaging around .98 (Astin, 1985; Goldberger, Maher, and Flattau, 1995).

Always eager to open a new market, *U.S. News* in the past decade has developed its own process for collecting judgments about graduate program quality. It now ranks graduate programs in the professional disciplines of business, education, engineering, law, and medicine every year. Graduate programs in fine arts, health fields, library science, public affairs, the sciences, social sciences, and humanities are covered every two to five years. The rankings in the major professional schools use both survey opinion about program quality and program statistical indicators, whereas the rankings in professional school subfields and in the arts and sciences are calculated solely on survey opinion. *U.S. News* sends the reputational opinion surveys to a dean and a senior faculty member in each discipline on each campus (usually only two surveys per discipline, per institution) and sends surveys to selected professionals in each field who are part of the hiring process for graduates. Each survey respondent judges the overall "academic quality of programs" in their field on a scale from 1 (marginal) to 5 (outstanding). The *U.S. News* quantitative indicators attempt to measure the quality of a program's faculty, research, and students. For the professional school rankings, the surveys receive 40 percent of the total score. For the departments and program areas *within* these professional schools, rankings are based entirely on the reputational ratings. Thus, the *U.S. News* ratings of graduate program quality, compared to those of the NRC, not only occur with unnecessary frequency but are based on a rather thin population of respondents.

## Uses and Misuses of the Professional School and Graduate Program Reputational Ratings

Graduate and professional program ratings, if collected scientifically, have many appropriate internal and external uses. Unlike the "best college" rankings for undergraduate education, the graduate and professional program ratings and rankings receive less criticism and are widely perceived to have legitimacy, especially as indicators of faculty scholarly quality and research productivity rather than as "educational quality." Inside the university, deans and faculty alike believe in the value of "knowing where we stand" and "staying competitive" in the eyes of respected colleagues. Rankings influence university planning and resource allocation decisions by identifying those fields to be developed as centers of excellence, to be resurrected from obscurity, or even to be phased out. Comparing current with past ratings can alert universities to departments that are in serious decline, as well as highlight areas of significant improvement. Finally, reputational ratings serve as marketing and recruitment tools for departments and professional schools. For prospective graduate students, faculty, and deans alike, the ratings constitute valuable information that influences their application and acceptance decisions.

Using faculty reputation ratings for accountability purposes seems less problematic for judging the research mission than it does for judging undergraduate education. Outside the campus, national organizations like the Association of American Universities and the National Academy use the rankings to determine those who are worthy of membership. Foundation and government officials often consider these ratings as a basis for awarding grants and contracts. State and university system officials employ ratings information not only to judge quality but to target economic development opportunities, as well as to discontinue weak programs, as happened in the State University of New York (Volkwein, 1984). Examined over time, these ratings help both national and university policymakers assess how the nation's doctoral programs are faring. The improvement in the ratings of doctoral program quality from 1966, 1970, and 1982 to 1995 suggests that the United States is getting a good return on its investment in graduate education and research.

However, these professional school and graduate program reputational ratings are not without their problems:

- The ratings appear to be influenced by various types of rater bias. Previous studies have found that raters rank institutions more highly if they are very familiar with or graduated from an institution, which gives an advantage to the largest schools with the most graduates. Correlations between faculty reputation and program size in the 1982 and 1995 national studies generally varied between .60 and .80.
- Studies have suggested that ratings are subject to time lag. Some programs are *living on* their past reputation, while others are *living down* their past reputation. Overall, the NRC reputational ratings have been relatively impervious to change, with median intercorrelation of .93 in the overall ratings since 1966 (Astin, 1985; Webster, 1992).
- Reputational ratings are subject to a prestige bias, or "halo effect." There is similarity in the ratings of graduate programs from the same institution.
- Graduate programs with excellent but narrowly focused strengths are often disadvantaged in the ratings game, as are interdisciplinary programs and those in relatively young fields.
- Raters may not always know enough about the programs they are rating. The 1995 NRC study attempted to solve this problem by supplying each survey recipient with a list of the faculty in each program being rated.

In their 1997 book *The Rise of American Research Universities,* Graham and Diamond found dramatic differences in institutional rankings, especially among "rising" public universities, when they employed per-capita measures of faculty research funding, faculty publications, and citations. Previous studies have relied on total funding, publications, and citations (rather than per-capita measures), thus favoring larger programs and institutions.

Concerns about the use of these reputational ratings raise thorny questions: What exactly do the graduate ratings measure? What constitutes the knowledge base of those ratings? And most important for this chapter, Are they useful for accountability to stakeholders? We have already given a partial answer to this last question. Answering the first two questions is both simple and complicated. In simple terms, the NRC and *U.S. News* graduate program surveys measure prevailing beliefs about the scholarly quality of individual programs. But it's less clear how those beliefs are formed.

An analysis of institutional and departmental characteristics and their relationships to NRC reputational ratings provides some clarity. Reputational ratings are strongly correlated with a large number of both departmental and institutional variables. The *departmental* variables found to be significantly correlated with ratings of faculty and program quality include the following: number of faculty in the department, number of doctorates granted, annual research spending, number of articles published, number of doctoral students, percentage of faculty holding research grants from selected government agencies, percentage of postdoctoral fellows, and the average number of published articles per faculty member (Abbott, 1972; Abbott and Barlow, 1972; Drew, 1975; Guba and Clark, 1978; Elton and Rodgers, 1971; Elton and Rose, 1972; Geiger and Feller, 1995; Hagstrom, 1971; Hartman, 1969; Knudsen and Vaughn, 1969; Morse, Donohue, Sanoff, and Shapiro, 1994; Tan, 1992). In the aggregate, these variables reflect the size of the department, its resources, and its research and scholarly activity.

The *institutional* variables found to be significantly correlated with ratings of faculty quality include the following: the age and size of the university, average salary for full professors, total annual research expenditures of the institution, institution's share of national R&D expenditures, annual number of doctorates conferred, total number of full-time faculty, average number of faculty and graduate students in each department, average SAT scores of entering freshmen, student-faculty ratio, number of library volumes, percentage of faculty with doctorates, total publications, and publications per faculty member (Abbott, 1972; Brown, 1967; Conrad and Blackburn, 1986; Geiger and Feller, 1995; Grunig, 1997; Hagstrom,

1971; Hartman, 1969; Morgan, Kearney, and Regens, 1976; Porter and Toutkoushian, 2002; Toutkoushian, Porter, Danielson, and Hollis, 2003; Volkwein 1986, 1989; Volkwein and Malik, 1997).

## Simplifying the Reputation Recipe

As noted earlier, we found a handful of studies concluding that two factors—institutional size and selectivity—are the primary influences on reputational quality. The Grunig study is especially illustrative. His factor analysis of twenty variables for a population of public and private research universities also identified these same two underlying institutional dimensions. Because his 1997 study analyzes public and private institutions separately, with similar results, we combined the two populations in preparation for this chapter. For public and private universities alike, the most significant common factor is "size/resources," which has high loadings for institutional and department variables generally associated with the enrollment size, resources, and research activity of the institution. For these 127 universities, the second common factor, "selectivity," has high loadings for variables associated with average SAT scores of entering freshmen, acceptance rates of freshman applicants, student-faculty ratios, percentage of faculty with doctorates, instructional and student services expenditures per FTE student, and average salaries of full professors.

Next, we examined the extent to which these two factors explain academic prestige. Our analysis indicates that the clusters of variables reflecting the size and selectivity of public and private universities strongly influence their combined NRC reputational ratings of the scholarly quality of graduate program faculty. The size/resources and selectivity factors, taken together, explain 84.2 percent of the total variance in average NRC ratings. The size/resources factor, considered by itself, explains 51.4 percent of the total variance in faculty NRC ratings, and the selectivity factor explains an additional 32.8 percent.

Surprisingly, these same two size and selectivity factors explain 83.8 percent of the total variance in the *U.S. News* undergraduate reputational ratings. The size/resource factor by itself explains 33.1 percent of the total variance in *U.S. News* ratings, and selectivity uniquely explains another 50.7 percent. Thus, the size and selectivity of public and private universities contribute significantly not only to the NRC ratings of faculty scholarly reputation but to ratings of undergraduate academic prestige, as collected by *U.S. News* from presidents, provosts, and admissions directors. Selectivity appears to be more important in explaining differences in undergraduate educational reputation, whereas size/resources play a larger role in explaining differences in aggregate NRC ratings of faculty.

We also uncovered a number of studies finding a strong relationship between reputation and faculty scholarship. Thus, we decided to examine the relationship between academic prestige and the available quantitative measures of research and scholarly performance and selectivity and size from the NRC and Graham-Diamond and *U.S. News* datasets. Table 11.2 displays the results. Both measures of academic prestige are strongly correlated not only with faculty publications but also with publications per faculty; not only with citations but also with citations per faculty; not only with R&D expenditures but also with R&D expenditures per capita; not only with faculty salaries but also with every measure of freshman selectivity and competitiveness. The measures of organizational size and selectivity are influential but not nearly as strong as the measures of research and scholarship.

Although correlation is not necessarily causality, the evidence in Table 11.2 suggests a strong linkage between faculty resources and salaries, faculty productivity, student selectivity, and academic prestige. We see these first six measures in the table as products or outcomes of investing in top salaries and faculty recruitment. Most R&D expenditures result from projects earned competitively by outstanding faculty. Such projects generate important publications that are frequently cited. Thus, it appears that universities tend to get what they pay for in research and scholarship. Although this reflects only indirectly on the quality of training that graduate students receive and connects even less clearly to the undergraduate experience, the resources-and-reputation model appears to be a highly accepted and empirically relevant one among graduate programs and doctoral universities. If research universities are held accountable for their mission attainment, perhaps these measures of research and scholarly productivity and citation impact are legitimate reflections of that mission.

Geiger and Feller (1995) were among the first to observe the connection between the graduate ratings and the abilities of university undergraduates. Still, we are surprised to find a nearly

**Table 11.2. Graduate and Undergraduate Reputation Correlations, with Indicators of Faculty Strength and Freshman Selectivity at Research and Doctoral Universities**

| Indicators of Faculty Strength and Freshman Selectivity | Correlations with 1993 Average NRC Faculty Reputation Ratings[1] | Correlations with 1994 U.S. News Academic Reputation Ratings[1] |
|---|---|---|
| Total faculty publications | .84 | .84 |
| Publications per faculty | .81 | .73 |
| Total citations | .87 | .84 |
| Citations per faculty | .81 | .75 |
| Total R&D expenditures | .79 | .78 |
| R&D expenditures per faculty | .70 | .67 |
| Average salaries for professors | .72 | .62 |
| Total faculty size | .60 | .67 |
| Total enrollment size | .53 | .58 |
| Percentage of freshmen in top 10% of class | .61 | .66 |
| Combined SAT scores 75th % | .66 | .77 |
| Combined SAT scores 25th % | .54 | .64 |
| Admissions acceptance rate | -.53 | -.42 |
| Barron's 1993 competitiveness | .54 | .63 |

Note: N = 128.

[1] Correlation between these two reputation ratings = .91.

perfect correlation ($r = .91$) between the 1993 NRC ratings of academic prestige and the 1994 *U.S. News* ratings of undergraduate academic reputation. It appears that judgments about undergraduate and graduate academic prestige are influenced by the same things—faculty talent (largely indicated by publication counts) and student talent (largely indicated by freshman SAT scores).

## Using the Ratings for Accountability

Although the *Macbeth* witches stir a mysterious and troubling concoction, their prophecies nevertheless come true. Despite all the noise about the ratings, there's an element of truth there. Our analysis clearly suggests that the national reputation ratings, collected approximately once a decade by the National Research Council and annually by *U.S. News*, constitute shared perceptions about faculty talent and student talent. Moreover, although these shared perceptions are statistically associated with university resources in the form of faculty positions, faculty salaries, and student enrollments, our analyses of public and private research universities suggest that rater beliefs, in the aggregate, appear to be based on quantifiable differences in faculty research and scholarly productivity, as well as freshman student selectivity.

The production of faculty research and scholarship, combined with student selectivity, generates reputational quality, though imperfectly, in both undergraduate and graduate education. This conclusion is consistent with Peter Blau's *The Organization of Academic Work* (1994) and Roger Geiger's selectivity sweepstakes—the arms race among universities to enroll the nation's best faculty and brightest students. Our society and each institution place a high value on resource acquisition and growth. Presidents and trustees judge their success on the basis of increased endowments, enrollment growth, distinguished faculty recruited, research funding raised, new programs launched, SAT scores increased, and new buildings constructed. In the aggregate and with some exceptions, the largest and most affluent institutions have the highest salaries and attract the most productive faculty and competitive students.

Thus, looking within the value system of the resource-and-reputation model and recognizing that reputational ratings and rankings essentially are imperfect indicators of faculty and student talent, these measures can be useful to parents, students, academics, admissions recruiters, strategic planners, foundations, government officials, and business consumers. For example, the desire to maintain one's research prowess can be a significant motivator for faculty and a basis for setting priorities by administrators. In choosing between two equally affordable and geographically close colleges, students and parents may be greatly interested in how other people perceive the quality of each college. Likewise, state government policymakers are proud to build and maintain excellence in their state. When corporations consider locating facilities in competing states, they probably consider the caliber of universities. High reputation ratings connote high quality to many people.

It is not entirely clear that reputation ratings capture educational quality, nor do we fully know what quality is or what thing out there does measure it. In a human world, beliefs are important. Nevertheless, numbers eventually matter, and there are at least two number problems; one is the absence of empirical connection between reputation and student educational experiences, and the other is the conversion of ratings into ranks. First, based on decades of solid research, a national set of good practices serves as a model for undergraduate education (Chickering and Gamson, 1987), but we do not know whether such practices influence reputation ratings. Second, we see less problem with collecting and publishing institutional ratings than with converting them into ranks that magnify trivial differences among good institutions and programs. At one extreme, *U.S. News* pretends that it is identifying the "best colleges" and that the ranks represent meaningful differences in educational quality. At the other extreme, critics would have us believe that the *U.S. News* undergraduate rankings are "full of sound and fury, signifying nothing" (*Macbeth,* Act 5, Scene 5). In this imperfect world, the truth probably lies somewhere in between these extremes.

We all yearn to have accountability models reflecting performance rather than prestige. Although both the graduate and undergraduate academic prestige ratings substantially reflect invested resources and market position, the graduate ratings come closer to indicating measurable performance than the undergraduate ratings do. Thus, we place the graduate and undergraduate ratings in slightly different locations within the Burke Accountability Triangle. All reputation ratings are lodged near the academic concerns corner of the Accountability Triangle, but the graduate ratings tend toward the state priorities axis, while the undergraduate ratings tend toward the market forces axis. Moving them more to the middle, or even farther down the line, will be a difficult undertaking, but we believe that the following suggestions will help:

1. *Develop more relevant indicators.* At both graduate and undergraduate levels, we need to expand the use of instruments that measure the student experience, as well as measure development and improvement.

2. *Increase transparency.* Undergraduate ratings in particular can be improved by increasing their transparency and reliability.

Organizations that publish ratings not only must fully disclose their methodology and data sources but must choose a rating methodology and stick with it.

3. *Expand the ratings.* There has been an overconcentration on the campus profile of full-time, tenure-track faculty who teach eighteen- to twenty-two-year-old full-time students in a traditional classroom setting. Even the least complex U.S. college campuses serve diverse populations of students, with a mixed array of faculty resources engaged in separate instructional, research, and outreach activities. Rating systems should be expanded to incorporate more information on the outcomes of transfer students, commuter and adult populations, two-year students, interdisciplinary studies, low-income students, and poorly prepared populations.

4. *Expand the perspective.* Reputational ratings could also be improved by asking for opinions from a wider range of decision makers. *U.S. News* has started to survey the opinions of employers of new graduates and other professionals. This seems like a step in the right direction. Rather than eliminate subjective ratings, it might be useful to widen the scope of people and programs giving opinions about each institution.

5. *Rate, do not rank.* Rate institutions on several mission-congruent dimensions, but do not rank them. The ranks unnecessarily magnify trivial differences among institutions and programs; the tiers of relative quality are more important than the precise place in the hierarchy.

6. *Rate less frequently.* The fortunes of departments rarely change with great speed, and the fortunes of their institutions change even more glacially. Reputational surveys simply do not need to be conducted with great frequency. Moreover, recent improvements in national databases greatly facilitate the annual collection of some types of performance indicators, such as publication counts, revenue and expenditure data, graduation rates, student-faculty ratios, admissions profiles, loan defaults, and campus crime.

The double toil and trouble in the ratings game may boil down to realizing that graduate and undergraduate reputations are mixed together in the same stew and relatively impervious to change for any particular institution without a significant addition or subtraction of resources. Our review of the evidence suggests that academic prestige substantially reflects the scholarly productivity of the faculty and the SAT scores of entering freshmen; neither the graduate nor undergraduate reputation ratings are based on the realities of the student experience. However, the graduate ratings at least seem founded on output measures of research and scholarship that are closely connected to the academic research mission.

# Chapter Twelve

# The Dog That Doesn't Bark
## Why Markets Neither Limit Prices nor Promote Educational Quality
*Robert M. Zemsky*

Starting in the mid-1980s, the Ford Motor Company came to ex-emplify how skillful management could use the workings of the market and questions of quality to achieve and then sustain a competitive advantage. Ford had found itself with a double task: differentiating its products from those produced by other American manufacturers while developing a product of sufficient quality to stem the tide of Japanese imports—what Detroit was openly, if somewhat inelegantly, calling the Japanese invasion. To win in the American market, Ford needed to persuade U.S. consumers that quality was important, and to win against the exports, Ford needed to, in fact, produce a demonstrably better product.

Ford's solution was an ingenious fusing of advertising moxie and human resource management, all neatly packaged in the slogan, "At Ford Quality Is Job 1." The first task was to teach a skeptical workforce that quality would really matter to them in terms of better job security and more opportunity. But if the public did not buy quality, then it mattered little what the workers produced, hence the importance of the advertising campaign, which became a primer in automotive quality. Gambling that its workers and engineers could produce what the advertisements promised, Ford set about the task of teaching the car-buying public what to look for in a quality automobile.

Ford was helped in this campaign by the maturing of a consumer movement that had begun asking tougher questions about safety and reliability and by the willingness of the public to buy and support a growing number of consumer publications that tested the products America was buying. Best known now, but not quite so well known in the early 1980s, was *Consumer Reports,* which unabashedly pitted one product against another. J. D. Power and Associates provided the customer satisfaction data that, when matched with *Consumer Reports* product data, helped in the development of a host of consumer markets in which product and producer quality really mattered.

## Market Accountability for Higher Education

Given that market forces were beginning to reshape other American institutions, it is not surprising that a number of commentators began to see in those forces the possibility that the market would exact the same kind of accountability from the nation's colleges and universities that it was already exacting from American manufacturers. There was even that delicious irony that institutions of higher learning were already pricing their products like cars, complete with sticker prices, discount rates, and accompanying credit packages. Why not expect the public to follow suit and begin looking at colleges as commodities that could be, if not actually tested as *Consumer Reports* tested automobiles, at least compared, even ranked, as to their quality. And, indeed, *U.S. News and World Report,* seizing the opportunity, did just that, first somewhat tentatively in 1983 and then persistently and with an evolving, as well as increasingly complex, methodology annually from 1985 onward.

What was expected of the market was progress on two key fronts. Better-informed consumers, it was argued, would make better decisions, sending the message to colleges and universities that ever-escalating prices would not be tolerated and that educational processes that ignored what the customer wanted and needed would no longer suffice. Faculty would get the message, much like the engineers and workers at Ford, that the way forward lay in a fundamental investment in educational quality. The American Association of Higher Education and, subsequently, the Carnegie Foundation for the Advancement of Teaching placed teaching and learning, with more emphasis on the latter than the former, at the center of a national reform agenda that sought a fundamental re-ordering of higher education's priorities. The National Center for Postsecondary Improvement's *Collegiate Results Instrument* and The Pew Charitable Trusts–initiated *National Survey of Student Engagement* were launched as alternatives to the *U.S. News* rankings; by focus-ing on educational outcomes, they promised even better consumer information. What the government and the media had failed to ac-complish by jawboning, the market, in conjunction with a growing reform movement within higher education, would achieve through the forces of competition.

It didn't happen. The prices that colleges and universities charge have continued to rise substantially faster than the underlying rate of inflation. Even the reform movement itself seems tired, not sure what to do next, no longer quite capable of commanding center stage. Discussions of quality and accountability have, at least within government circles, intensified, but there is scant evidence that much is happening at the institution level.

Why didn't the market have the expected impact? Why didn't market forces impose the kind of accountability on colleges and universities that was being imposed on hospitals and health-care providers, as well as on the manufacturers of consumer products? Many answers are possible; none are necessarily conclusive, but, taken together, they suggest why having market activity play a sup-portive role in the search for accountability will prove problematic at best.

## The Market and Price Accountability

Let's start with the question of price and the fact that the rela-tionship between price, product, and demand is different for dif-ferent purchasers in different parts of the higher education market. The most written-about consumers of higher education are those young people (and their parents) who are interested in full-time undergraduate enrollment, most often at a private or public insti-tution practicing selective admissions. For these consumers, what is being purchased at extraordinary expense is a degree whose value depends on the reputation of the institution, as well as the purchaser's natural abilities and the effort he or she puts into the earning of that degree. Think dance lessons—the quality of the cer-tificate doesn't amount to much if the student doesn't have rhythm and doesn't work at the tasks at hand. That makes this kind of col-lege education very different from an automobile. Automobiles are consumables in the sense that they are not expected to last forever. After one's third or fourth purchase, one is expected to get the hang of how to judge the quality of the product and haggle over its price.[1] For most Americans, purchasing a college education from a selective college or university is a singular event or, if taken from the parents' point of view, a purchase that happens more than once but still not very often and not over the course of a lifetime of pur-chasing.

## The Buying-Selling Transaction

For this select group of higher education's consumers, deciding where to enroll is also a shared experience—in a double sense. On the one hand, the choice of institution is something to be negoti-ated with one's parents or whoever is expected to help pay for the purchase. As such, it is an event in which family forces and tensions can be expected to play as great, if not a greater, role than market forces; questions about price get lost amidst the family drama.

At the same time, the choice of a college is also a transaction in which the selling college has a direct role in the purchaser's choice and hence willingness to pay a premium price. The fact is that the selected college may choose not to sell its product to the would-be purchaser—and in the case of the most sought-after in-stitutions, the decision *not* to sell is made much more often than the decision to sell. The duality of the decision is made more com-plex because the normal rules of supply and demand have been suspended. Although the prices the top institutions charge are high, they are not as high as they could be; that is, most of the medallion institutions at the top of the pecking order could fill their freshman classes at substantially higher prices but choose not to, choosing instead to let the surplus of applications add to their prestige rather than their revenue. To make matters even more convoluted, the price an individual consumer is charged in this part of the market reflects his or her ability to pay; when a selec-tive institution admits and enrolls a so-called full-pay, it will make money on that transaction. If, however, the purchaser is determined to have "financial need," the selling institution may spend considerable amounts of its own funds to educate that customer.

For a second group of young Americans, the choice of a college often follows the path of least resistance. These would-be students are not even sure they want to go to college, but their friends are going, the job market isn't very promising, and, what the heck, they just might like it. These young people develop largely local options, for the most part choosing among reasonably priced privates and even lower-priced public institutions. What makes them price sensitive, as opposed to those youngsters who compete for a place in a medallion institution, is the sense that they are still not sure they know what they want, not even sure they intend to graduate, at least within four or five years. While increasingly all college youth work, in this part of the market work is often as important as college itself.

The third and fastest-growing group of purchasers in the higher education market space sees colleges and universities principally as providers of spot courses and skills. They buy their college education one course at a time, often attending a variety of institutions over a wide span of years. These are higher education's most price-sensitive shoppers, though ironically, they often end up paying higher prices in the sense that the sum of their purchases can easily exceed the cost of tuition had they attended full-time and been eligible for institutionally supplied financial aid.[2]

## How States Encourage Price Increases

In thinking about price and market accountability, it is important to note that state governments, their rhetoric not withstanding, have consistently used market forces to solve their own short-term budgetary shortfalls by driving up the prices that publicly owned colleges and universities charge. This result occurs every time the business cycle reduces state revenues and forces state governments to choose between reducing state services and increasing state taxes. What the governor and legislature rediscover at that moment is that prisoners don't pay rent, Medicaid recipients can't pay much for health care, and public schools can't charge tuition. But, thankfully, publicly funded colleges and universities can. Each time, the college-attending public pays the increase, grumbling to be sure but not enough to reduce enrollments or spur a revolt next election day. The result is that state governments use the robustness of the market, not to control prices or hold public institutions accountable but to raise the revenue they cannot or will not raise through increased taxation.

The net result is the smoke of confusion that encourages most institutions to charge what they think they need to in order to balance their books. So pervasive, in fact, are the pressures to increase rather than reduce or control prices that genuine price cutting—the tried-and-true way to increase volume in a saturated market—is a rarity in higher education. Those few institutions that have announced price cuts are, for the most part, small, struggling privates that provide financial aid discounts to practically all of their students. Thus, the announcement of a price cut is more of an advertising gesture than a real reduction in the amount of money their customers are expected to spend in pursuit of their baccalaureate education (Van Der Werf, 2003).

Given this set of circumstances, it is hard to imagine a scenario in which the adroit management of markets or market forces would lead to a moderating of the price increases that colleges and universities, public as well as private, charge. Indeed, the continued reliance by state agencies on the market to raise revenue in lieu of taxes suggests that the prices colleges and universities charge will continue to rise faster than the underlying rate of inflation into the indefinite future.

## Markets, Quality, and Accountability

Is it perhaps more likely that markets can hold American colleges and universities accountable for the quality of their educational products? Could the educational equivalent of a *Consumer Reports* lead the purchasers of undergraduate degrees and courses to discriminate in favor of those institutions delivering the best demonstrated quality? By the fall of 2001, there were at least three major initiatives promising just that kind of consumer information. The biggest, most successful, and most closely followed consumer guide remained *U.S. News,* with its detailed data on more than fifteen hundred colleges and universities. For the price of the magazine, students and their parents could learn which were the top fifty universities and the top fifty liberal arts colleges—the so-called nifty-fifty national institutions in each category—as well as the relative ranking of regional institutions grouped into competitive tiers. All these data were in the public domain, and when the magazine did not present the detailed data, they were available for a nominal fee on the magazine's Web site.

*U.S. News*'s principal competitors were two research projects: one supported by the federal government through its National Center for Postsecondary Improvement and the other initiated by The Pew Charitable Trusts and developed under George Kuh's leadership at Indiana University. The CRI (College Results Instrument), now a licensed product of Peterson's, the publishers of some of the nation's best college guides, was initially adopted by eighty institutions in the spring of 1999.[3] In all, more than forty thousand college graduates six years beyond their receipt of a baccalaureate degree reported on their current activities, the skills required of them in the workplace, and their principal activities outside work by responding to ten specially crafted scenarios that represented their degree of confidence in performing a host of tasks their college education might have prepared them for.

The NSSE (National Survey of Student Engagement) has been administered over the last four years to a sample of seniors at 730 baccalaureate institutions. Kuh provides a fuller description of the NSSE and its successes in Chapter Seven, but briefly, the instrument focuses on the extent to which the respondents' college experiences reflect agreed-upon best practices leading to a quality undergraduate education. As its name applies, the NSSE seeks to measure the level of engagement on the part of both the student and the faculty in the learning process.

Both the CRI and NSSE promised to do precisely what *U.S. News* had eschewed—to focus on the educational process itself (NSSE) and to ask whether it mattered whether one attended one institution instead of another (CRI). As measurement exercises, both the NSSE and the CRI more than exceeded initial expectations, demonstrating that it was possible to focus on processes and outcomes. As major levers of market-driven change, however, neither the NSSE nor the CRI have had much impact.

Their best efforts notwithstanding, neither the CRI nor the NSSE was able to convince a private medallion university to participate; none of the "ivies" joined; neither did Duke nor Stanford nor the University of Chicago; neither did any other universities belonging to the Consortium for Financing Higher Education (COFHE). A handful of public medallions—the University of Michigan, the University of Illinois, and the University of North Carolina at Chapel Hill—used either the CRI or NSSE, but, in general, public medallions also declined to participate. Among the eight campuses of the University of California offering undergraduate programs, for example, only U.C.-Santa Cruz has participated in the NSSE, and none have participated in the CRI.

## The Problem with Public Accountability

This absence of medallion participation should surprise no one. Already enjoying superior market position, these institutions had nothing to gain and potentially a great deal to lose if their outcomes or levels of engagement were no better than those of institutions charging substantially lower prices. Even institutions that did participate insisted, as part of their formal agreement to administer either the CRI or the NSSE, that they and they alone could make their results public. It was as if the producers of products or services tested by *Consumer Reports* could decide, after they knew how well they had scored in the test, whether or not to make the results public.

In general, higher education as an industry has little inclination to provide the kind of quality-based data that would let the public decide which product or service was best. Just how entrenched this attitude is became clear in an e-mail I recently received as one of the designers of the CRI. The sender, a principal consultant of a major firm offering enrollment-management expertise to colleges and universities, wanted to know if the CRI, now that it was under license to Peterson's, was available under any other terms. "I'd like to learn more about the College Results Instrument for a client. Client doesn't want to give information to Peterson's (fear of ranking) but loves the CRI."

That fear of being publicly ranked and, presumably, held accountable was only half the problem the CRI and NSSE faced. Most institutions that administered the NSSE to their seniors or the CRI to their young alumni were often conflicted as to how to use the measurements the instruments supplied to improve the quality of their educational services and products. The CRI, in part because it was initially sold to presidents and provosts, sought from the outset to build in a process of data utilization through the convening of campus roundtables involving both administrators and faculty. Nichole Rowles, in a recently completed Ph.D. dissertation at the University of Pennsylvania, tracked what happened at five institutions that had administered the CRI and then convened campus roundtables. What she discovered was a continuing chasm between administrative responses to the CRI and faculty responses. The former she characterized as being largely corporate, in that they were committed to using data to improve processes, products, and services. The faculty's response, however, remained largely chaotic, more concerned with relationships than with standards. The members of the faculty directly responsible for the quality of instruction their institution provided were not at all sure what the data meant, whether to accept them as valid, or whether the data suggested any remedies to problems the faculty were not certain actually existed. The chair of the faculty senate, in a case involving a faculty vote to impose a punitive rule that a study conducted by that institution's Office of Institutional Research had demonstrated was unwarranted, told her that it was "a matter of principle, not data." Yet it is hard to imagine an accountability system in which members of the faculty are not the key agents and that employs only those data in accord with the faculty's principles.[4]

## The Dreaded Rankings

Neither of these concerns—the reluctance to stand publicly judged or a refusal to use market data to improve products and services—hampers *U.S. News*. Begun in 1983 as an almost casual experiment, the rankings started out as a kind of "beauty contest" in which college and university presidents were asked which they thought were the best undergraduate institutions in the country. Once the public's appetite for these rankings became palpably obvious, a steady stream of presidents and association spokespersons visited the editors responsible for the survey, telling them that such an important measure of quality should not depend on the vagaries of institutional gossip. *U.S. News* responded by assembling an extraordinary array of data, much of it supplied directly by the institutions themselves.

The more precise and detailed the data requirements became, the clearer it became to institutions how they could improve their rankings: by increasing their six-year graduation rate, by increasing their yield rate, by giving more weight to an applicant's SAT or ACT scores, and by increasing the newsworthiness of the institution. Making sure those things happened was the responsibility of a management that could proceed without worrying too much about faculty sensitivities or principles.

It is hard to overestimate just how important the rankings game and *U.S. News*'s annual reciting of America's Best Colleges has become. No matter how the results are pooh-poohed, everyone pays attention. Everyone's strategic goal is to move up in the rankings: from tier 2 to tier 1 or from there into the top one hundred and, ultimately, the nifty-fifty. But what does it mean? What exactly does *U.S. News* measure?

## What *U.S. News* Measures

What *U.S. News* does *not* measure is the quality of the educational experience. The data *U.S. News* so arduously collect tell us nothing about what actually happens on campus or in the classroom. Some have argued that the rankings reflect institutional prestige. And they do, though that concept is sufficiently amorphous as to lose most of its meaning when one tries to describe the difference between two institutions with similar profiles but ranked twenty places apart.

Over the last decade, Susan Shaman and I have periodically returned to this question of determining precisely what *U.S. News* measures. Our explorations have defined a market structure for higher education that ranges from a relatively small, extraordinarily high-priced medallion market segment at one end of the spectrum to a slightly larger, more moderately priced segment that appeals on convenience and user-friendliness at the other end.

The single largest segment is in the middle of the distribution. The model that produced this structural description of the market and that we employed to predict the prices individual institutions charge used six-year graduation rates as its primary variable, along with admit and yield rates as surrogates for demand. Given that *U.S. News* used the same measures in its ranking scheme, not surprisingly, our market structure and *U.S. News* rankings overlay one another.

We concluded that what *U.S. News* measures is market position: the higher the ranking, the better the market position, the higher the price the institution could charge. Put another way, if you know an institution's *U.S. News* ranking, you also know its market segment and roughly the price it charges (The Learning Alliance, 2003).

What is being measured by our market taxonomy and *U.S. News* rankings? The answer is remarkably simple. What both measure is competitive advantage. The higher ranking or, conversely, the better the market position, the better the institution is able to attract students, faculty, and revenue. That's half the answer; the other half derives from an understanding as to why graduation rate is the best proxy for a *U.S. News* ranking and the market segment designation.

## Zoomers, Amblers, and Bloomers

*U.S. News* itself believes that an institution's graduation rate is an output measure—an index of how well an institution serves its customers, as well as the public. Graduation rates in general are coming to be seen as a critical measure of accountability, such that when leading politicians and media pundits list higher education's most glaring failures, they most often cite just two: (1) the inability of colleges and universities to control their costs and hence limit their price increases and (2) the fact that many more students enroll than graduate. Why, they have taken to asking in increasingly harsh terms, must students, their parents, and the tax-paying public pay so much for a system that fails to deliver what it promises?

Such attacks frequently betray a fundamental misunderstanding as to how the higher education market sorts students and sets prices. In that market, the higher the probability the student has of graduating in four or six years, the higher the price that student is prepared to pay for his or her college education. The market then sorts those students in terms of their probability of graduation, which, not so coincidentally, is correlated with their SAT or ACT scores, their rank in class, their parents' level of education and income, and, certainly not least, their academic and professional ambitions. Those with the highest probability of graduation are best thought of as "zoomers." For them, secondary school is a preparatory experience in much the same way that an Olympic training village prepares athletes for the rigors of Olympic competition. It is primarily in secondary school that these zoomers get ready not just for college but for the rigors of the selection process through which top-ranked institutions pick the students to whom they want to sell their high-priced products and services.

For the nation's medallion institutions, it is a win-win situation. They preserve their competitive advantage in the marketplace principally by enrolling students who are seeking the competitive advantage a medallion degree confers. The top-ranked institutions win precisely because they can choose those students most likely to succeed and most likely to be willing to pay the high prices medallion institutions charge for an undergraduate degree. Why? Because zoomers know that the baccalaureate degree is the next gateway in their run to the professional and academic credentials they have spent their young lives preparing for. The better the undergraduate medallion, the better the law or medical or business or graduate school to which they will win admittance. It is more than worth the price because the prize is great and because they and their parents know that there is very little chance they will not graduate in four, let alone six, years.

Most high school students thinking about college are not zoomers; they are "amblers" in the sense that they are less certain about what the future will hold, less certain they will graduate from the institution in which they initially enroll, less willing to cut their social ties to their home communities, and, not surprisingly, less sure they can afford the high prices medallion and name-brand institutions charge.[5] They are students who attend college on a "try it, see if you like it" basis. Even when they are residential students, they are likely to go home on weekends and maintain jobs more tied to their home than their college towns.

Because most college students are amblers, and the market siphons off most zoomers into a relatively limited number of medallion and name-brand institutions, most colleges and universities face the challenge of turning their amblers into "bloomers"—young, and sometimes not so young, people who discover relatively late the rewards, even the joys, of learning. When enough amblers become bloomers, first the freshman-to-sophomore retention rate rises, followed by a slow but measurable increase in the institution's six-year graduation rate.

*U.S. News* has recognized both the importance and the difficulty of increasing the graduation rate by rewarding extra points to institutions whose actual six-year graduation rate is higher than its predicted rate, with the predicted rate based on the average SAT or ACT score plus average rank in class for an enrolling freshman class. In our terms, this bonus calculation becomes a kind of bloomer index. In terms of the actual rankings, however, this adjustment appears to make little difference, suggesting perhaps that even greater weight ought to be given to this corrector.

At the same time, however, there is simply no evidence that the students who consider these institutions pay much attention to this capacity. Where the graduation rate matters—and even then it is more of a *correlate of* than a well-understood *proxy for* competitive advantage—is among those students and parents interested in medallion and name-brand institutions. The rest of the market seemingly understands that whether they graduate or not is largely up to the students themselves. To be sure, most of these institutions can do a better job converting amblers into bloomers, with smaller classes in the freshman year, more individualized attention, and more willingness to serve vocational interests during the years traditionally devoted to general education. Private institutions in this part of the market have generally done a better job here, not because of market demand but in order to preserve enrollment and lessen marketing costs. What these institutions have learned is that a student retained is a student who goes on paying tuition. Public institutions, despite the use of enrollment-based funding formulas, still do not seem to have the same incentive to increase retention and thereby preserve, or better yet increase, enrollment.

What the faculty and staff of both public and private institutions have learned is that in the end there really is no market advantage accorded to institutions that provide extra-quality education. Indeed, there are plenty of examples of institutions with exemplary teaching programs (Alverno College comes first to mind) that have in fact struggled for enrollments. What foundations and even at times the media find attractive, the market largely discounts. What matters in this market is not quality, as defined by Schulman and his Carnegie Foundation for the Advancement of Teaching, but rather competitive advantage. It is a lesson *U.S. News* has learned well, helping to ensure its dominance as the collegiate consumer magazine of choice.

## The Possibility of a More Managed Market

Given what the market's most skilled shoppers want—a competitive advantage either for themselves or their children—the market for an undergraduate education works remarkably well. As these consumers go about the business of selecting where to apply and, ultimately, where to enroll, they know, precisely because *U.S. News* tells them, which institutions offer the greatest competitive advantage in terms of prestige and ease of entry to a remunerative profession. Parents may grumble about the price, but it is one they are more than willing to pay—a fact that the institutions that enroll their children understand well and do their utmost to promote and protect. All the hallmarks of an efficient market are present: ample consumer information, prices that reflect value, and transactions that make equal sense to consumer and provider.

Could it be otherwise? Could market forces, in concert with public initiatives and institutional practices, somehow be linked or combined to make colleges and universities more accountable in terms of the prices they charge and the kinds of educational experiences they offer? Could, to use Burke's Accountability Triangle, market forces be somehow linked to state priorities and academic concerns to create what some have called managed markets capable of restraining price increases while simultaneously rewarding institutions of demonstrable educational quality?

The first condition that would have to be met for such a triangulation of forces to occur is that the colleges and universities in general and their faculties in particular would have to decide that educational quality is, in fact, Job 1. Much of Massy's recent work describing developments both in this country and abroad has explored the conditions under which faculty will invest in programs promoting educational quality and innovation. As his chapter (Chapter Eight) in this volume makes clear, Massy is an optimist who argues that when the faculty share directly in the benefits deriving from programs of quality improvement, then quality improves. His quality audits thus become an important way of making educational quality Job 1 on American campuses.

What Massy understands as well, however, is that there has to be an alignment of incentives of sufficient value to engage the energies of whole departments and schools. Neither good intentions nor personal pride will suffice. What is required is a clear sense that something untoward is likely to happen unless progress is forthcoming. Then and only then will faculty make the commitment that they—and here it is important to note that it is the faculty and no one else who can deliver the quality that is being sought—must translate into coherent plans of actions (Massy, 2003a, 2003d).

## A State-by-State Report Card

In short, for educational quality to become Job 1 on American college campuses, some entity must help create the demand for quality—must make quality a real and tangible attribute that contributes directly to an institution's competitive advantage in the marketplace. As in the example of the Ford Motor Company, consumers will have to be taught to first recognize, then understand, and, ultimately, value educational quality. Metrics will have to be developed. Consumer information that touts quality rather than competitive advantage will have to become widely available and actually used by the consuming public.

*Measuring Up*—the state-by-state report card compiled by the National Center for Public Policy and Higher Education—represents an important first step in the launching of just such a campaign of public awareness while simultaneously exemplifying the difficulties inherent in using the tools of public policy to shape the market for higher education (Chapter Nine). *Measuring Up* grades each of the fifty states by asking,

How well are students in each state prepared to take advantage of college?

Do state residents have sufficient opportunities to enroll in college-level programs?

How affordable is higher education for students and families in each state?

Do those who enroll make progress toward and complete their certificates and degrees in a timely manner?

What economic and civic benefits accrue to each state from the education of its residents?

What do we know about student learning as a result of education and training beyond high school?

Just three of these questions actually pertain to the questions of quality and accountability that are the subject of this volume, the first being, "Are a state's public and private colleges and universities affordable?" Here, *Measuring Up* answers by looking at both sticker and discounted price, that is, the report takes into account the availability of student financial aid. It is this question of price that has received the greatest political attention and caused those who speak on higher education's behalf the most pain. The truth of the matter, however, is that higher education's price spiral has continued unabated. Why? Because the industry's medallions and name-brand institutions know their prices are not retarding interest in their services and products and because the nation's public institutions have had no choice. What state policymakers know is that among their prime programs, higher education alone has sufficient market power to substitute consumer revenues for public appropriations. To repeat an observation made earlier, neither K–12 schools nor prisons can charge tuitions, more toll roads are a near anathema to the driving public, and Medicaid expenses can only increase as a state's population grows older and has less access to employer-funded health benefits. The one source of substitute revenue readily available to state budget makers is the increase in tuition that colleges and universities have been encouraged to charge, political posturing and the admonitions of *Measuring Up* notwithstanding.

*Measuring Up* has had considerably more success in making states see graduation rates as a prime measure of system and institutional accountability. Like the editors of *U.S. News*, the report's sponsors see graduation rates as an outcome measure—one that testifies to both the efficiency and effectiveness of a state's institutions of higher education. But graduation rates, as we have seen, measure neither efficiency nor effectiveness but competitive advantage. The big winners, ironically, in the focus on graduation rates are those institutions that charge the highest prices and prove the most attractive to those students with the greatest probability of graduating within four to six years of initial matriculation. They are also the institutions that have been the most reluctant to administer instruments like the CRI and NSSE in part, at least, because they have nothing to prove.

That leaves *Measuring Up*'s focus on student learning as a possible spur to institutional accountability. Here, however, the report's sponsors faced the same problem every advocate of educational quality confronts when trying to build a consumer movement that takes quality seriously: there are simply no readily available public data reflecting the quality of either individual institutions or state systems of higher education. No one really knows what students are learning or how well they feel prepared to apply lessons learned in college to a world in which jobs, families, and careers assume center stage. The result is that *Measuring Up* gives every state an "Incomplete" in the learning category.

In *Measuring Up 2002*, Peter Ewell, one of this country's leading and most thoughtful commentators on how student learning ought to be a principal component of institutional quality, talked about the path ahead. "What is needed for the future" he wrote, "is to extend the administration of the NSSE and CCSSE [NSSE's community college companion] to all states, and administer the CRI (or similar surveys) to national samples of college graduates" (Ewell, 2002c, p. 75). Having previously noted efforts funded by The Pew Charitable Trusts to test the usefulness of these and other instruments, Ewell went on to observe:

> Creating new instruments to reliably assess college-level learning will require considerable time and effort. . . . But individual states can improve their ability to monitor their educational capital by taking two steps right now: (1) states that have not participated in existing national surveys such as the NAAL could elect to do so, and (2) states could work proactively to induce testing and licensing authorities to open their databases to researchers seeking to improve the state's store of policy-relevant information. With more data in hand, state leaders could begin to realistically assess the mix of key abilities among their citizens in relation to state economic and workforce development plans. They could use these data to help persuade firms in key industries to locate in their states, direct state investments to remedy identified gaps in workforce skills, and

adjust their plans to respond to changing economic conditions on an ongoing basis. These immediate actions will admittedly not give us the measures we will ultimately need to monitor and improve the nation's store of educational capital. But we have to start somewhere. (Ewell, 2002c, p. 76)

What Ewell is proposing is just a beginning—one that focuses almost exclusively on the makers and consumers of public policy, primarily at the state level. Still to be addressed are the institutions that provide the educational services along with the consumers, whose demand for those products constitutes the market for post-secondary education in the United States.

## In Pursuit of Public Purpose

In addition to those Ewell has proposed, state governments, in partnership with the relevant federal agencies, would have to take at least two additional steps before the consumer information required by a managed market in higher education is in place. The first would be a commitment to pay for the collection, analysis, and distribution of the learning outcomes data the consumers require if they are to make quality choices. Well into the foreseeable future, there will not be sufficient consumer demand for that kind of information to attract the kind of entrepreneurial capital necessary to make the effort self-financing.

Second, governmental agencies will have to find a way to encourage, if not actually require, all institutions to collect and make public data on the learning outcomes of their students and graduates. Ironically perhaps, the governmental initiative at the moment garnering the most attention is a proposal by the Republican congressman who chairs the House Subcommittee on 21st Century Competitiveness. He would punish institutions whose price increases exceed federally established maximums—an imposition of price controls that would neither promote greater accountability nor enhance educational quality. What is required instead, particularly at the federal level, is sustained investment in the collection and analysis of the kinds of learning outcomes data *Measuring Up* has called for.

At the same time, there would have to be far greater willingness on the part of organized higher education in general and the industry's medallion and name-brand institutions in particular to join in the development of consumer information that focuses on learning outcomes as a significant measure of educational quality. These colleges and universities would have to accept voluntarily and publicly the challenge of demonstrating that quality matters. The faculty of these institutions, already largely responsible for the standards defining the quality research outcomes, would have to be persuaded that it was in their own, as well as the public's, interest to have similar standards defining the quality of learning outcomes. The best way to start this process is to have a dozen or more presidents of major institutions publicly commit themselves and their institutions to such an endeavor. The most practical step they could take would be to have their institutions participate in the NSSE and CRI and to pledge to make the results public.

## The Possibility of Reform

The requirements for a managed market in higher education that promotes quality (but probably not price restraint) are relatively straightforward. First, within institutions there would have to be a clear commitment to make quality Job 1. Massy's academic audits have demonstrated that motivated faculty can translate that commitment into concerted action so that whole departments can know just how good the services are that they are delivering. Second, public agencies would have to both lead in and fund the continued development of the instruments necessary to measure learning outcomes and then provide the infrastructure that would allow those data to be converted into the kind of consumer information that students and their families could use when evaluating college choices. Finally, higher education's leaders, particularly those responsible for the nation's most prestigious colleges and universities, would have to stand up and be counted, committing themselves and their institutions to a full and public reporting of educational outcomes.

That leaves the nagging question as to whether higher education's consumers would actually use the information and, by extension, whether those institutions that committed themselves to making quality Job 1 would be rewarded in the marketplace. Those who have championed educational quality and accountability have done so from a largely reformist perspective. Like the faithful who follow the fortunes of the Chicago Cubs and the Boston Red Sox, they are forever hopeful that this time will be different—that the public and public agencies will at last say no to further price hikes, that somehow medallion and name-brand institutions will begin to compete among themselves on the basis of public data that document education quality.

Perhaps. But if the past is our guide, not likely. Implicitly, the reformers have argued for a kind of market failure borne of the absence of good information about costs and educational quality. But if what the consumer wants and the market delivers is competitive advantage, then there is no market failure and no reason to believe that the results of a managed market would be substantially different, particularly given the need of most states to reduce their direct support of their public colleges and universities.

Put another way, in today's market for baccalaureate education, it is the zoomers who give that market its competitive caste. And the market gives them what they want—a substantial leg up in the pursuit of a remunerative profession—along with the information to judge which institutions offer the best prospects for achieving those results. It is, after all, what *U.S. News* does best. For the kind of managed market the reformers envision to work, these young people would have to want to attend and thus be willing to search out institutions with demonstrably better learning outcomes. If it turns out that it is the medallions that produce the best outcomes simply because they enroll the better-prepared, more competitive students, then the whole exercise has been for naught.

Nor is it clear that those young people who amble off to college would be prepared to invest in the kind of sorting of alternatives based on learning outcomes that would be required by a managed market designed to promote educational outcomes. These students and their parents might be interested in learning which institutions had the best track record of converting amblers into bloomers, but that too would depend on their being less ambling when choosing where to enroll. It is the kind of catch-22 that too often bewilders reformers who are certain that they know what is best for nearly everybody.

Finally, one should note that in the market, quality is a tough taskmaster. That certainly is the lesson the Ford Motor Company learned as the number of SUV rollover lawsuits against the company escalated. Then "At Ford Quality Is Job 1" became ripe for deadly parody. Its replacement, announced in the fall of 2002, had all the safety of a sound bite minted on a college campus: "At Ford, the Future Is Now."

## Notes

1. In one of higher education's more interesting coincidences, colleges and universities have for a long time justified their prices by comparing a year in college to the cost of a new car. And for just as long, they have priced their products *like* new cars, that is, by differentiating between sticker price, discount price, and cash price (Shaman and Zemsky, 1984).

2. Susan Shaman, Daniel Shapiro, and I have detailed these market contours, first in a series of reports in *Change* and subsequently in a volume in the Jossey-Bass New Directions for Institutional Research series (Zemsky, Shaman, and Shapiro, 2001).

3. For it own purposes, Peterson's has renamed the CRI the College Results Survey, or CRS.

4. Peterson's, through a joint venture with Marts & Lundy called "Alumni Viewpoint," discovered that there was a much more robust market for the CRI among alumni affairs and development professionals who want to use the results to help them design programs for their alumni.

5. Tom Kane has argued that because of an information deficit, some high-ability students of modest means choose low-priced institutions. For a discussion of these and related issues on the functioning of the higher education marketplace, see Dill and Soo (2003).

# Chapter Thirteen

# The Three Corners of the Accountability Triangle

## Serving All, Submitting to None

*Joseph C. Burke*

Responding to state priorities, academic concerns, and market forces offers a challenge, not a choice, for higher education. Colleges and universities—private and public—must serve all but submit to none of these imperatives. Stressing one and slighting the others loses the equilibrium among these interests. Focusing narrowly on state priorities can subject higher education to political winds without the moderating influences of academic concerns or market forces. Accenting mostly academic concerns can reduce responses to public priorities and market needs. Reacting impulsively to markets can mean chasing consumer whims while ignoring public needs and academic necessities. The three corners of accountability, like the tripartite branches of government, balance each other, ensuring service to all but submission to none of the civic, collegiate, and commercial interests.

Each of the accountability approaches covered in this book initially favored one of the corners in the Accountability Triangle. Accreditation, assessment, reputational ratings, and academic audits reflected mostly academic concerns. State report cards, performance reports, performance funding and budgeting, and standardized testing stressed state priorities. Student and alumni surveys solicited the opinions of current and former customers, but the institutional reluctance to publish their results stifled their usefulness to perspective students and state officials. Although reputational ratings supposedly reflected market forces, they really responded to academic concerns for resources and reputation, not the usual customer concerns for price and quality.

Prior to the 1990s, academic concerns dominated the Accountability Triangle. Market forces appeared in competition for student recruitment, financial aid for all colleges and universities, and budget formulas that rewarded enrollments in public institutions but not in federal or state accountability initiatives. The relation between state governments and public campuses remained largely one of providing funding and accounting for expenditures. Federal and state governments assumed rather than asserted the accountability of private colleges and universities to serve an amorphous "public good."

This relationship shifted in the decade of the 1990s, at least for public institutions. Decentralization meant that public campuses gained more control over their internal operations in return for accepting performance programs that held them responsible for meeting public needs (Chapter Ten). Toward the end of the decade and in the early years of the new century, the emphasis shifted more to market forces. As competition for tax support increased and economic recession reduced public revenues and endowment values, markets brought increasing income to campuses and became almost a surrogate for state priorities. Political concern about access and affordability produced proposals and talk in federal and state capitols of constraining tuition increases in private and public institutions as a condition for financial aid (Chapter Two).

Continuing calls for accountability suggest a perception in government and business circles that the current programs are not working. With all of the accountability programs in place, quantity is not the problem. As so often happens in policymaking, accountability programs couple good concepts with poor coordination and ineffective implementation. In response to complaints, policymakers added new initiatives without connecting them to existing efforts to ensure systemic accountability. Although *coordination* in higher education has become a sullied word in an era enamored with decentralized authority and educational markets, better coordination among programs could improve their impact on both accountability and performance.

The chapters in this book suggest that none of the accountability programs remain static. Most of them are moving in varying degrees toward a second imperative and some even a third, although each retains a partiality for its preferred corner of the Accountability Triangle. This result is understandable. If no person can serve two masters, surely no program can serve two and certainly not three imperatives of accountability when each makes what appear to be conflicting demands. The preferences of the accountability programs for a particular imperative suggest that combinations among them represent the best way of responding to all while submitting to none of the three corners of the Accountability Triangle. What higher education needs is an accountability system in which programs connect rather than compete—a system that links accountability efforts at the state, system, and institution levels.

## Jurisdiction and Governance

Although federal and state governments have considered private colleges and universities vaguely accountable for providing public benefits to society, Zumeta (Chapter Two) notes that neither has exacted much accountability from this sector. This laissez-faire approach toward private, nonprofit colleges and universities persists, despite the substantial financial benefits they receive from the federal and state governments in tax exemption, research support, and student financial aid. Given this sector's contribution to economic competitiveness of states in human capital development, as shown in the *Measuring Up* report cards (Chapter Nine), Zumeta thinks more of the state performance reports in the future may include results from private colleges and universities. Should the rhetoric from Republicans in Congress about tying financial aid to tuition constraint become a reality, Zumeta believes both sectors would suffer. However, private colleges and universities would lose the most because federal financial aid and research grants represent the lion's share of their government funding. He urges state policymakers to rely on markets rather than mandates to ensure accountability for both private and public institutions. Of course, market forces cannot work for accountability in private or public higher education without reliable public information that allows prospective students and other clients to compare campus performances before making their choices. In addition, markets reflect private preferences, which may not sum to public goods.

Richardson and Smalling (Chapter Three) claim that coordinating boards as interfaces between state governments and collegiate institutions can balance better the interests of state priorities, academic concerns, and market forces than system or institutional boards that tend to favor campus desires. State governments, they say, should set public priorities and shape markets to achieve them while allowing institutions to determine their responses and holding them responsible for their results. By directing funding initiatives and setting "rules of the game," policymakers can help ensure that colleges and universities respond to state priorities. Their chapter does not address the problem that coordinating and public governing boards at times pursue the political interests of long-term governors who pack them with supporters. Too often, the power to appoint becomes the power to control. The Association of Governing Boards (AGB) would address this problem with nominating committees of leading citizens to propose candidates for gubernatorial appointment to state coordinating and public governing boards (2003b). This proposal brings broad civic and commercial interests in higher education to balance narrow political considerations.

Richardson and Smalling concentrate mostly on coordination of higher education at the state and, to a lesser extent, institutional levels. Although academic departments receive the least attention in their discussions of accountability, these units are most responsible for academic performance and results. These units form what Clark calls the "disciplinary bottom" that spurs discipline but stifles systemic changes (1983, pp. 205–206). Wergin (2003) details the difficulties of getting outside interests into department deliberations and inside concerns of departments outside to institutional governance. This departmental disconnect erodes accountability efforts, since these units are not only responsible for academic results but are often unaware of, or ignore, accountability programs (see Chapter Ten). The growth of interdisciplinary, entrepreneurial research centers funded by industry and government offers an alternative avenue for market forces and, at times, state priorities (depending on funding sources) to reach the academic core of universities. But these centers may sacrifice the instructional function to applied research and may distort institutional missions.

## Accountability Programs and Clashing Cultures

The accountability approaches covered in this book generally fall on one side or the other of the dualisms flowing from the "collegiate" and "civic" cultures described by Bogue and Hall (2003). Recently, a third rival has emerged—the "commercial" or "entrepreneurial" culture. It moves beyond responding to current demands by anticipating and even creating future market needs and developing the programs and activities to meet them. The civic, collegial, and commercial cultures reflect, respectively, state priorities, academic concerns, and market forces. Chapter One details the conflicts over purposes and means that characterize the collegiate and civic cultures, with the interests of the former listed first:

- Institutional improvement versus external accountability
- Peer review versus external regulation
- Inputs and processes versus outputs and outcomes
- Reputation versus responsiveness
- Consultation versus evaluation
- Prestige versus performance
- Trust versus evidence
- Qualitative versus quantitative evidence

The "commercial" culture shares the "civic" side of these clashes, except on a new one pitting state priorities against market forces. Although some government and business leaders see them as similar, even identical, state priorities should be more limited and lasting, whereas market demands are often more diverse and fleeting. Increasingly, the commercial culture threatens, or at least intrudes on, both the collegiate and the civic interests. However, several of the authors argue that states can manage markets to achieve public priorities by special initiatives (Chapters Two, Three, and Twelve).

The chief clash of cultures comes with *institutional improvement* versus *external accountability*. Although all of the programs in this book claim, or at least imply, both purposes in theory, they favor one or the other in practice. Accreditation and assessment focus primarily on improvement, as noted by Wolff (Chapter Four) and Ewell (Chapter Five). To date, student and alumni surveys influence improvement but not accountability because their results are seldom published and are used primarily for internal purposes (Chapter Seven). Although Kuh claims that more colleges and universities will voluntarily publish survey results in the future, the Community College Survey of Student Engagement (CCSSE) is one of the few that requires publication. Academic audits stress improvement, but Massy (Chapter Eight) argues that they simultaneously seek accountability because their reviews are increasingly being publicized. Report cards, performance reports, and performance funding and budgeting accent external accountability, although all of these programs hope to spur institutional improvement (Chapters Nine and Ten). Markets obviously press for accountability to client demands, but Zemsky (Chapter Twelve) claims that reputational ratings, such as those by *U.S. News & World Report,* have prevented them from affecting the quality or price of colleges and universities. Volkwein and Grunig (Chapter Eleven) agree that reputational ratings reflect faculty research and student selectivity, not accountability or improvement of student learning or experiences. Colleges and universities at the top of the reputational ratings compete over position, not price. A lack of effective and accepted standardized tests of student learning outcomes limit their influence on improvement or accountability, according to Erwin (Chapter Six). The absence of an accepted notion of academic quality in undergraduate education based on results leaves the reputational ratings largely unchallenged.

Program preferences for improvement or accountability usually dictate the clashes over methods in the remaining dualisms. Those favoring the collegiate culture and focusing on institutional improvement generally prefer peer review, inputs and processes, reputation, consultation, prestige, and trust. Programs stressing external accountability generally prefer the civic side of the dualisms. One caveat is that these programs increasingly abandon external regulation in favor of deregulation with direction. They dictate some policy directions but leave the means for achieving them to coordinating and campus leaders. Report cards and performance-based programs accent outputs and outcomes, responsiveness, evaluation, and evidence, especially quantitative, although Burke (Chapter Ten) says that performance reporting includes more input and performance funding more process indicators than expected. Standardized tests could serve both improvement and accountability. Of course, they accent outcomes, evaluation, and quantitative evidence. Currently, without agreement on what constitutes "quality" or the means of measuring it, Erwin (Chapter Six) claims they have little impact on improvement or accountability.

Policymakers often perceive the dualisms of these differing cultures as dichotomies—as mutually exclusive goals or methods. Their policy presentations so exaggerate differences that even the possibility of connections disappears. They reflect the "either-or thinking" in policymaking that sees choice as always desirable, even inevitable.

State and campus policymakers should reject such simplistic thinking. The purposes and means presented here offer challenges rather than choices. An accountability system that neglects institutional improvement would be worthless. Inputs and processes obviously affect outputs and outcomes. In the long run, trust and evidence must connect. And why should policymakers choose between quantitative and qualitative evidence when each adds a distinct dimension to assessment? These clashing propositions also ignore the reality that appropriate choices depend on particular circumstances. Reliance on peer review or external regulation and qualitative or quantitative evidence surely shifts with the issue or problem.

And, finally, dichotomies depend on definitions. Their differences would diminish, for example, if higher education broadened the definition of *reputation* to incorporate responsiveness and that of prestige to include performance. Tensions exist in all of these parings, but we make them dichotomies.

## Accountability Program Differences

Programs differ in focus, drivers, appraisals, and consequences.

### Different Focus: Internal or External

*Program focus* refers to an initiative's general direction, prominent actors, and principal audience. Accreditation, assessment, and academic audits focus primarily on internal campus processes and audiences and rely on peer reviews by members of the academic community. Accreditation and assessment slight the interests of external groups such as governors and legislators and business and civic leaders. The mature forms of audits that insist on public reports and include some student learning information are starting to speak to external, as well as internal, parties (Chapter Eight). Although reputational ratings largely reflect academic concerns and peer impressions, they do influence external groups, especially prospective students and parents and even government and business leaders, enamored with ratings and rankings (Chapter Eleven). Report cards, standardized tests, market forces, and performance reporting, budgeting, and funding focus largely on the external concerns of outside audiences. Student-alumni surveys question consumers who have both inside and outside connections, but the failure to publish results means they address internal rather than external groups. Currently, none of the accountability programs affords an adequate balance of external and internal interests, although Massy argues that academic audits are moving in that direction (Chapter Eight).

Despite these differences, most of the accountability programs in this book initially arose or derived their strength from external pressure. For example, Ewell (Chapter Five) concedes that early mandates caused the spread of assessment. Nonetheless, assessment, accreditation, and, to a lesser extent, audits reflect primarily an *inward accountability* that responds to professional norms and to *downward and professional accountability* that accents participation and collegiality. Report cards, performance reporting, funding budgeting, student-alumni surveys, standardized tests, and markets respond to *outward accountability* to clients and stakeholders, although several of these initiatives have some elements of *upward accountability* to governors, legislators, and the general public. Reputational ratings are external, but their indicators reflect largely the internal aspirations for resources and reputation of the academic community (Chapters Eleven and Twelve).

This internal-external dichotomy is as self-defeating as the philosophical division of mind and body. Every professional service organization, public or private, serves an external clientele. Organizational success requires attention to both the internal concerns of its professionals and the external needs of its clients. In higher education, this means protecting the academic concerns of faculty and staff and providing programs that meet state priorities and market needs. Richardson and Smalling (Chapter Three) champion a coordinating agency for higher education between institutions and governments that can best balance external and internal interests.

## Different Drivers: Information, Publicity, and Resources

Accountability programs use three major drivers—information, publicity, and resources—to ensure responsibility of colleges and universities for their performance. Assessment, student-alumni surveys, and accreditation rely mostly on internal availability of performance information as their accountability driver. They follow the adage that what gets collected is what gets valued and presumably improved through internal use of the information. In contrast, report cards, performance reports, markets, and, to a lesser extent, academic audits depend on publicity to ensure accountability. Only what gets publicized externally gets valued and improved, say their advocates, although academic audits use both internal information and external publicity. Reputational ratings also rely on publicity but mostly as a gauge of prestige rather than performance. Finally, champions of performance funding, budgeting, and markets claim that only initiatives that generate resources really get valued and used to improve performance in colleges or universities.

Of course, all drivers of accountability depend on the availability of information. Most of the chapter authors advocate expanded roles for the federal and state governments and coordinating agencies in supporting data collection on the performance of higher education and its colleges and universities. If information is essential to accountability, publicity is its sine qua non, especially to public service organizations in a democratic society. Advocates of resources as the driver of accountability assert that money matters most on college campuses and in state capitols. Despite the truth in all these claims, the best drivers of accountability often depend on the circumstances. Sometimes internal availability of information is enough to spur improvement, although more substantial change often requires the push of publicity or the force of funding.

## Different Appraisals: Unique or Comparable

Performance appraisals of colleges and universities depend on whether they are viewed as primarily unique or comparable institutions. Some academics consider each college or university as "one of a kind," which makes campus comparisons impossible or at least misleading. Champions of the "unique" argument apparently limit its applications to external appraisals. They constantly (but privately) benchmark their campus activities against competing colleges or universities in internal decision making. Outsiders in government and business counter the "unique" argument by observing that colleges and universities award degrees in the same programs. To protect diversity in higher education, appraisers should accept comparisons only among institutional types, such as two-year colleges, comprehensive institutions, and research universities. Even within these categories, comparisons should carefully consider differences in missions, sizes, and circumstances.

Accreditation, assessment, and, to a lesser extent, academic audits lean toward the unique side of appraisal. Reputational ratings, performance reporting, budgeting and funding, and student-alumni surveys usually cite comparisons in their evaluations, although Kuh (Chapter Seven) warns against their misuse. Markets should encourage comparisons in higher education, but the lack of comparable information on student outcomes and experiences often confounds consumer choices. Report cards rate only state higher education systems, not individual institutions.

As so often happens in such disputes, both sides of this "unique-comparable" debate are partly right and partly wrong. Every college and university has both distinct and comparable characteristics. The old adage that "one size can't fit all colleges and universities" is true, though overused as a defense mechanism against accountability. It is no less true that they share missions and goals, by campus type, that permit a comparison of results on some but certainly not all indicators. In response, performance reports increasingly encourage diversity by allowing institutions to enhance their distinctiveness by choosing one or more indicators that reflect their special mission and goals (Chapter Ten). Once again, either-or thinking is self-defeating. Accountability programs should make comparisons by campus type while encouraging institutional diversity.

## Different Consequences: Soft, Medium, Hard

Finally, accountability programs rely on consequences that some might describe as soft, medium, or hard. Internal availability of information on institutional performance constitutes the softest consequence. External publicity on institutional performance, which would produce public approval or disapproval, constitutes a medium-level consequence. Outside observers often contend that only a loss or gain of resources based on institutional results rises to the level of hard consequences, as in performance funding. Unfortunately, performance funding is often either too little to ensure significant reforms or too large to ensure budget stability (see Chapter Ten).

Despite the talk of policymakers about the need for funding to encourage desired performance, budgeting formulas seldom favor public priorities. For example, in spite of laments about the level of degree attainment, state budgets continue to emphasize student enrollments and neglect degree completions. Moreover, a drop in reputation in academia is often more disturbing on campus than a decline in funding. The loss of reputation seems the faculty's fault, while the fall in funding can be blamed on outsiders. Again, an either-or approach seems foolish. To paraphrase Gilbert and Sullivan, let the consequences fit the circumstances.

Coordination of the consequences is often the wiser course. Accountability should draw on information, publicity, and funding as needed to suit the situation. For example, Kuh (Chapter Seven), who favors some publicity, warns that publishing the results of student-alumni surveys should come "later rather than sooner" to give experts time to correct the surveys, analyze the responses, and prepare improvement plans. In addition, Burke (Chapter Ten) suggests that it makes sense to report on designated indicators to test their validity and reliability before funding them. Clearly, the best focus, drivers, and consequences will shift, depending on time, place, and circumstances, and often they work best in tandem or sequence.

# Program Positions on the Accountability Triangle

Given the equal importance of state priorities, academic concerns, and market forces, the center of the Accountability Triangle seems the ideal spot for an accountability program and certainly for a co-ordinated accountability system. Figure 13.1 estimates the location of each accountability program in light of current trends, though not future possibilities. It suggests that all programs fall short of the ideal. Although influenced by the opinions of the chapter authors, the editor accepts full responsibility for the program placements on the Accountability Triangle.

## Accreditation

Accreditation (AC) considers mostly academic concerns. Its requirement by the federal government for financial aid and states for operating permission justifies the slightly raised position on the

### Figure 13.1. The Academic Triangle

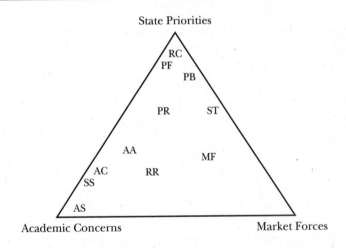

AA = Academic Audits, AC = Accreditation, AS = Assessment, MF = Market Forces, PB = Performance Budgeting, PF = Performance Funding, PR = Performance Reporting, RC = Report Cards, RR = Reputational Ratings, ST = Standardized Tests, SS = Student-Alumni Surveys.

academic concerns–state priority axis. Although administrators and professors often complain about regional accreditation as an unnecessary bureaucratic burden, academics control accrediting organizations, and peer reviewers dominate accreditation teams. Initially, institutional reviews looked only at the inputs of students and resources and the processes of institutional governance and academic operation in relation to campus mission and goals. In the early 1990s, both institutional and program accrediting agencies added an insistence on institutional plans for assessing student learning and later looked more closely at campus results, as well as processes (Chapter Four). In addition, regional commissions, such as the Western Association of Schools and Colleges (Senior), have divided accreditation into two purposes to make the review more acceptable and valuable to colleges and universities. The first is quality assurance, which in most cases is swiftly accomplished largely through profiles of institutional results on the traditional issues of mission, finance, governance, and minimal quality standards. The second—institutional improvement—gets the most attention. It assesses the quality of institutional results that are usually related to some aspect of student learning outcomes, often selected by the college or university for appraisal.

Despite these welcome changes, continuation of the public notice only of accreditation status is of limited value for assessing responsiveness to state priorities and market forces. The growing practices of posting institutional profiles and even accreditation self-studies on institutional Web sites as preludes to team visits represents promising developments, as does the move toward incorporating academic auditing as part of the process (Chapter Four). Still, accreditation can never engage state priorities and market forces without at least a summary publication of the findings of accreditation reviews. Absent publication in some form of review results, regional accreditation remains in the academic concerns corner of the Accountability Triangle. Wolff, though contending that not all findings need be made public, proposes that accrediting agencies issue some explanation of the reasons for their accreditation decisions and move in phases toward some disclosure of their assessment of the educational quality of colleges and universities. The effectiveness of this suggestion for accountability will depend on its acceptance by the academic community and on whether the reasons given for accreditation decisions include information of sufficient interest to government policymakers and higher education clients. Both moves require substantial shifts in the attitude of the academic community. Publication of substantial summaries of the results of regional accreditation reviews would move this program closer to the center of the Accountability Triangle.

Program accreditation also reflects academic concerns, given that academics control their organizations and review teams. Still, the label of professional accreditation has some weight in the marketplace and with policymakers. If its abbreviation appeared on the Accountability Triangle, program accreditation would move a bit toward market forces and state priorities.

## Assessment

Although external pressure has spread assessment to nearly every college or university, Assessment (AS) remains largely an internal operation. States mandated assessment for public institutions, and accrediting agencies required it for both public and private colleges and universities. These actions left the details of assessment to each institution. Assessment reports lack the comparability desired by external officials and potential customers, and faculty resistance to an imposed mandate has inhibited its use for institutional improvement. Ewell (Chapter Five) believes the time has come to loosen the initial link in assessment between institutional improvement and external accountability. He would use assessment directly for improvement and only indirectly for accountability. Ewell hopes that the faculty will embrace assessment once it is no longer a mandate for external accountability. Others would argue that removal of the external pressures could result in less rather than more assessment on campus. The history of assessment, which depended so heavily on external pressures, lends credence to this claim. In any case, a decision to separate assessment from external accountability would mean a move even closer to academic concerns and farther away from state priorities or market forces on the Accountability Triangle.

## Academic Audits

Academic Audits (AA), according to Massy (Chapter Eight), show the greatest potential to respond to academic concerns and state priorities and possibly to market forces as well in the future. Although audits began largely as internal process reviews of quality assurance mechanisms conducted confidentially by academics, they have the flexibility to become an effective and efficient way of protecting professional norms, improving institutional performance, and demonstrating accountability. At a time when Ewell suggests that assessment is moving inward, Massy sees audits, while retaining their academic focus, reaching outward by publishing their reports and in a "mature model" by even including some sense of student learning outcomes. Although admitting it is a stretch, Massy foresees the possibility that academic audits in the future may supply information to markets, as well as to campus and state policymakers. Figure 13.1 places academic audits more than one-third of the way up the axis from academic concerns toward state priorities and only slightly toward market forces.

## Market Forces

Market Forces (MF) obviously influence decisions on instructional, research, and service programs offered by public, as well as private, colleges and universities. The growing importance of tuition and research income accents market forces in an era of restrained government funding and depressed endowment values. Student demands have swelled enrollments in professional programs such as business and information technology and diminished interest in arts and humanities majors. State delegation of authority over tuition to public systems and institutions will increase these market forces, as would the recent interest in funding students rather than institutions.

Despite these trends, Zemsky (Chapter Twelve) insists that market forces in higher education, unlike in business and health care, have neither restrained prices nor improved quality. Instead, reputational rankings led colleges and universities to compete for resources and reputation rather than on price and quality. Although Zemsky's argument centers on what he calls the medallion colleges and universities at the top of the prestige pyramid, his conclusion may be correct for large segments of colleges and universities. "'Positional warfare,' it appears, is occurring on all the rungs of the status ladder," says Kirp (2003a, p. 1). Volkwein and Grunig (Chapter Eleven) reach the same conclusion. The for-profit privates such as the University of Phoenix may, in time, reverse this trend. They use competitive prices and demonstrated quality, as well as convenience, to attract students because they lack the academic aura of traditional prestige.

Although market forces may not restrain prices or improve quality (two prized objectives of state priorities, along with access), state policymakers often urge colleges or universities to respond to markets. As a result, market forces move up somewhat toward state priorities on the Accountability Triangle. They also shift a bit toward academic concerns, which favor increased tuition revenue and accept the competitive market for recruiting the best students.

## Reputational Ratings

Reputational Ratings (RR) reflect the resource-and-reputation model of quality, based on inputs of students, resources, and faculty. According to Volkwein and Grunig (Chapter Eleven), student selectivity and faculty reputation, which neglect student experiences and outcomes, dominate the ratings of graduate programs and undergraduate institutions. So long as the resource input model of quality continues in higher education and remains accepted as a surrogate for quality by student and other markets, reputational ratings will fall on the axis between academic concerns and market forces, although closer to the former than the latter. It moves up slightly toward state priorities, for national rankings of in-state colleges and universities often beguile governors and legislators. It surely says something about the lack of objective assessments of institutional quality that reputational ratings come as close as they do to the center on the Accountability Triangle. It is telling testimony to the impact of the "ratings game" in America and higher education.

## Performance Funding

Performance Funding (PF) stresses state priorities, with little recognition of market forces and academic concerns. Nonmandated programs now constitute most of the funding initiatives (Chapter

Ten). Coordinating agencies initiate them without legislation and usually after some consultation with campus leaders. This consultation moves performance funding only slightly toward academic concerns because of campus resistance to tying budgets to performance. From a policy point of view, the bias of performance funding and performance budgeting toward state priorities makes sense. State priorities are often costly and produce little revenue, whereas market forces bring their own reward in revenue from tuition and research. Chapter Ten proposes moving performance funding closer to academic concerns by making it mostly a campus rather than a state program, which would allow institutional leaders to use a portion of their state funding to further an element of their designated mission. It suggests only a single state component linking a small percentage of funding to campus results on degree completion. However, performance funding currently sits near the top of the Accountability Triangle, though slightly down toward academic concerns because so many programs are nonmandated.

## Performance Budgeting

Performance Budgeting (PB) could move somewhat closer to market forces, since its loose link to funding allows it to include a longer list of performance indicators that could interest perspective students, businesses, and civic organizations. As Chapter Ten suggests, performance budgeting could connect with periodic reviews of progress on a public agenda adopted by states. Absent such a connection, performance budgeting places a bit more toward the market forces but still close to state priorities.

## Performance Reporting

Performance Reporting (PR) also accents state policy goals, and academic leaders resist its initiation, though they prefer it to performance funding or budgeting. Legislation mandates more of its programs, which means less consultation with campus officials. Yet campus leaders find it much less objectionable than performance funding or budgeting. Publication of performance results could interest potential customers, but the bulk and complexity of most of the current reports discourage easy access by policymakers or clients. The aggregation of data, even at the institution level, fails to provide the detailed information desired by potential students or clients interested in academic programs or research or service activities. Chapter Ten claims that the increased appearance of the performance reports on campus Web sites offers the opportunity of providing disaggregated information for potential clients, as well as aggregated data for state policymakers. The connection between performance reporting and academic concerns comes from its preference by campus leaders over performance funding or budgeting. The placement of performance reporting on the Accountability Triangle shows its continued emphasis of state priorities, but it moves closest of all accountability approaches in this book to the center because it includes information for market forces and arouses much less opposition on campus than the other programs that stress state priorities.

## State-by-State Report Cards

State-by-State Report Cards (RC) address state policymakers and state priorities and stress higher education's contribution to the capacity and development of human capital, which has become so critical to a knowledge and information economy. *Measuring Up 2000* and *Measuring Up 2002* graded states but deliberately avoided comparing the results of colleges and universities or connecting state results to campus performance (Chapter Nine). Callan and Finney believe that other accountability efforts have failed because they focused on individual colleges and universities. They call for a "new accountability" that stresses instead state and societal needs. As a result, the aggregated statewide data from the report cards do not directly affect campus concerns or interest market forces. Although Callan and Finney note the efforts of the National Center for Public Policy and Higher Education to develop accountability systems in selected states that connect to institutional accountability, the report cards rest at the peak of the triangle under state priorities. Report cards relate to market forces only in the macro sense of human capital development within a state as a competitive factor in workforce development but not in research, which is not included in the report card indicators.

## Student-Alumni Surveys

Kuh (Chapter Seven) claims that Student-Alumni Surveys (SS) have the potential to respond to all three of the accountability imperatives in the following order: academic concerns first, state priorities second, and market forces a cautious, distant third. These surveys can supply information on both educational processes and results. The National Survey of Student Engagement (NSSE) and its community college version (CCSSE) provide information comparing the level of student participation in college with the best educational practices, as designated in research. Alumni surveys, such as the College Results Instrument (CRI), evaluate student perceptions of their learning and development in colleges and preparation for careers and civic life. Unfortunately, many colleges and universities, including some of the most prestigious, do not participate in these surveys, and most of those that do refuse to authorize their publication for a variety of reasons, including fear that they may reveal institutional faults (Chapters Seven and Twelve). For this reason, student-alumni surveys are used mostly for internal purposes on campuses. As a result, this program places deep in the corner of academic concerns. Kuh believes campus leaders when they see market advantages will begin to publish survey results, which will increase pressures on other institutions for publication. That information would interest state leaders and markets, although Kuh worries that the connection to markets could lead to manipulation of survey results. Despite these predictions, student-alumni surveys currently place just above assessment in the academic concerns corner of the triangle.

## Standardized Tests

Standardized Tests (ST) that measure directly student learning outcomes, says Erwin (Chapter Six), are generally desired by many state and business leaders and derided by most academics. Administrators and professors welcome standardized tests to determine admissions but not to assess the results of undergraduate education. External groups champion their use without recognizing their limitations and complexities. Erwin examines the current standardized tests for assessing specialized training in academic majors and basic skills and liberal learning in general education. He finds all of the current off-the-shelf tests wanting, more so in general education than specialized majors. General education testing lacks an agreement about the domain of the knowledge and skills desired for college graduates, as well as valid and reliable measures of their attainment.

If scores on standardized tests could suggest the extent of student learning in general education and academic majors, they would provide vital information of great interest for state priorities and market forces. Yet agreement in the academic community on the learning domain remains elusive, and commitment of the extensive funding required is missing. The abbreviation for standardized tests appears about a third of the way down the state priority–market forces axis because of the interests of policymakers and, to a lesser extent, business leaders. Unfortunately, this placement suggests desire more than reality.

The failure to publish information on results constitutes an accountability flaw for all the programs that cluster closer to academic concerns. This fault makes them of little use to policymakers or market forces. Some academics consider confidentiality essential to ensure candid internal self-studies and even external peer reviews. They may be right, but confidentiality confines the interest of these programs to academic concerns and excludes public priorities and market forces. Conversely, the accountability programs close to state priorities slight academic concerns and, to a lesser extent, market forces. Figure 13.1 suggests that the accountability programs in this book generally favor state priorities or academic concerns. The slight attention to market forces possibly flows from the conviction that markets, which produce resources, can take care of themselves.

## Connecting Rather Than Competing

If none of the programs respond equally to each of the accountability imperatives of state priorities, academic concerns, and market forces, they could come close in combination. Regional accreditation is the natural carrier for other accountability programs. Accreditation could combine them, and they, in turn, could strengthen accreditation. Regional accreditation has long included assessment of student learning. Including academic audits could strengthen accreditation's connection to outcomes assessment and reinforce the attention to academic quality and student learning. Accreditation could also encourage the use and insist on reviewing results from student and alumni surveys. In addition, accreditation teams could consider the performance of colleges and universities on the critical indicators in the state-by-state report cards and the state performance reports and on their responsiveness to the market needs of their regions and communities. Regional accreditation affords the obvious vehicle for integrating all of these accountability approaches into an effective and efficient system.

But before accreditation can absorb other accountability programs, it must cure its fatal flaw—the failure to reveal some sense of the results of accreditation reviews. Steven Crowe, the executive director of the Higher Learning Commission of the North Central Association, said it all in his keynote address at an annual meeting. "I happen to believe that perhaps the biggest challenge we face after adopting new accrediting standards will be tearing down the walls of confidentiality that have so long separated us from a public now wondering what it is we actually do and why we give so little information about what we know. . . . It's not a viable formula for integrity and accountability in the long run" (2002, p. 20).

Accreditation will become irrelevant as an accountability program unless it issues at least summaries of the findings of the accreditation process. Wolff (Chapter Four) recognizes that publicity could reduce the candor of team reports but proposes releasing the reasons behind the accrediting decisions and, in phases, the effectiveness of educational quality of colleges and universities. Some supporters of institutional accreditation seem to rue its use for accountability by the state and federal governments. The day regional accreditation loses its responsibility for certifying accountability, it will likely lose its support on campus. Campus leaders tolerate institutional accreditation because it is usually required for federal programs and state operations. Program accreditation will continue, for it reflects academic concerns with reputation and prestige and is of interest to student and business markets.

Those markets would show even more interest if program accreditation reported more of the results of their reviews. The public reports from accrediting agencies should assess institutional response to state priorities, academic concerns, and market forces, particularly their service to the public good.

Academic audits already incorporate assessment in a way that follows Ewell's plea to use it directly for institutional improvement and only indirectly for demonstrating accountability. Most important, audits also engage academic departments in the accountability process, whereas other approaches often ignore these critical units. Additional connections among accountability programs are desirable. Standardized tests and student and alumni surveys could provide both quantitative and qualitative data and direct and indirect measures of student learning. A limited list of common indicators could link report cards and performance reports at the state, system, sector, and institution levels and allow policymakers to measure down as well as up the performance chain to track the source of strengths and shortcomings of higher education results in states (Chapter Ten; Burke and Minassians, 2002b). Indeed, the combined information provided by these accountability programs might help base market decisions on institutional performance rather than national ratings of resources and reputation.

## Agreement on Priorities

No accountability system can succeed without broad agreement on higher education priorities. "You can't have accountability without expectations," says Behn. "If you want to hold people accountable, you have to be able to specify what you expect them to do and not do" (2001, p. 7). Agreement on higher education priorities is difficult but not impossible. Governors and legislators change and so do their demands; clients and customers often shift their desires. If these outside groups press for change, academics should stress the long-term needs of the society, as well as the academy. The goals and priorities of accountability systems for higher education should mirror the dual needs of every organization and society, both change and continuity. The goal of accountability is not to satisfy academic, state, and market desires but societal needs.

"Someone in a position of legal authority—a governor, the legislature, or an interface agency," say Richardson and Smalling, "must decide and communicate the outcomes for which higher education is to be held accountable" (Chapter Three). But they recognize that state priorities for higher education have become too important to society and individuals to be left to government or agency officials. No one group can go it alone in accountability. Each segment operating from its favored corner on the Accountability Triangle will not work. Business, civic, government, and education leaders must agree on public priorities. Chapter One calls for the development of a public agenda of what each state needs most from its public and private colleges, endorsed by a representative group of business, civic, government, and education leaders who reflect all three corners of the Accountability Triangle.

## General Education and Student Learning Outcomes

Erwin (Chapter Six) describes the continuing external demand for, and internal resistance to, direct measures of student learning outcomes, especially in general education. Leaders of higher education, along with Ewell (Chapter Five), urge the use of indirect rather than direct measures of student learning for accountability purposes. One favored approach is institutional evidence of implementation of best practices in undergraduate education, such as high expectations, student-faculty interaction, coherent curriculum, time-on-task, and other processes that research suggests contribute to student learning (American Association for Higher Education Assessment Forum, 1992; Ewell and Jones, 1996). Other student-alumni surveys solicit opinions on the presence of best practices and the perception of the knowledge and skills acquired during the college years (Chapter Seven).

Academic leaders acknowledge that these indirect measures fall short of assessing student learning directly, but they usually insist that the diversity of students and institutions and the complexity of general education make impossible the development of direct means of evaluating learning outcomes. Their conclusion may well be correct, but outsiders can legitimately counter that the academic community has never really tried to devise direct methods of assessing student learning in general education. That community has never made a collaborative, comprehensive, and consistent effort to identify the knowledge and skills that general education should convey and to develop the direct methods of assessing their achievement. The time has come for the academic community to make this effort. Identifying the knowledge and skills desirable for all college graduates, whatever their major or their state, surely justifies a national effort.

Such an initiative might not produce acceptable methods for assessing directly learning outcomes, but the attempt could clarify the goals of general education and the integrity of the baccalaureate degree and could help convince external critics that the academic community is willing to make a sincere effort. In any case, we will never know for certain and can never convince outsiders until we try. Such an effort could also forestall the outside push for implementation of inadequate measures and inappropriate comparisons among institutional types. It would also allow the academy to push for a value-added approach that looks at student progress from entry to graduation and rejects the reputational ratings that rest on the proposition that campuses, like computers, are mostly matters of "good in, good out." An academic community that defines higher education "quality" in terms of inputs is unlikely to make the case for a qualitative rather than a quantitative assessment of its performance. An academic community that cannot convince itself of common learning desired of all undergraduates is unlikely to persuade outsiders of its contribution to the common good.

## Accountability Problems

Accountability for higher education currently suffers from a host of problems:

- Lack of agreement on priorities and goals that leaves open-ended the commitments of, and demands on, higher education and leads to "360-degree harassment"
- Disconnect among policymakers, providers, and purchasers in developing accountability programs for higher education
- Split between institutional improvement and external accountability
- Lack of direct methods of measuring undergraduate learning, especially in general education
- Separation among state, system, campus, and departmental accountability efforts
- Isolated programs rather than integrated approaches to accountability

- Symbolic rather than effective implementation of accountability programs

Edward Weber asks the right question: "What does an effective system of accountability look like in a world of decentralized governance, shared powers, collaborative decision processes, results-oriented management, and civic participation?" and, to add a newer and powerful one, market forces (1999, p. 485)? Accountability systems will differ because states are different, but they should share characteristics because the competing pressures of state priorities, academic concerns, and market forces know no boundaries.

## Characteristics of an Effective Accountability System

What follows are some suggested characteristics of an effective accountability system for states:

1. A Public Agenda identifying what the state needs most from higher education, endorsed by a representative group of business, civic, government, and education leaders.
2. An implementation plan balancing public priorities, academic concerns, and market needs that sets priority goals and performance indicators, targets and timetables, coordinated by a statewide board representing all three interests.
3. Private, as well as public, college and university participation in the process and implementation, along with public schools.
4. A focus on external results, not internal operations, of colleges and universities to ensure external accountability while protecting internal autonomy.
5. A commitment to adequate and sustained funding from public and private sources equal to the difficulty and diversity of the Public Agenda, along with readjustment of targets but not goals when budgets must be cut.
6. A balanced approach to funding and tuition in the public sector, coupled with financial aid that encourages access and affordability in both public and private colleges and universities.
7. An appreciation of the contribution to the Public Agenda from all types of colleges and universities based on mission performance, not mission levels.

8. An integrated plan that connects accountability programs and their implementation at the state, system, and institutional levels.

9. Annual performance reports on the progress toward the Public Agenda at the state, system, and institution levels and five-year reviews and agenda revisions when necessary to meet new problems or needs.

10. Internal institutional reports that link departmental results to campus missions and the Public Agenda.

The list ends at ten remembering Premier Clemenceau's retort to President Wilson's 14 Points: "Why God has only ten!" Besides, higher education needs not more accountability tasks but a better system for serving while not submitting to state priorities, academic concerns, and market forces.

These characteristics of an effective accountability system require commitments from the higher education community, federal and state governments, business and civic leaders in each state, and individual colleges and universities.

### National Level: Higher Education Community

- Launch a comprehensive project to identify and disseminate the range of knowledge and skills that undergraduates should acquire in general education, funded by a consortium of private foundations.
- Develop valid, reliable, and feasible methods for measuring directly student acquisition of these knowledge and skills, funded by the consortium of private foundations.
- Make regional accreditation the centerpiece of accountability by incorporating into the process the approaches and findings of other accountability programs.
- Support publication of substantive summaries of accreditation reports on the performance of public and private colleges and universities.
- Develop, publicize, and honor multiple models of excellence for colleges and universities based on institutional types and missions—on performance, not prestige.

## The Federal Government

- Fund the National Center for Education Statistics to collect and publish a fuller range of output and outcomes data for colleges and universities, including learning outcomes, at the state and institutional levels.
- Provide funding to states to support collection of these data by coordinating and system boards and by individual colleges and universities.

## State Level

- Adopt a Public Agenda that articulates the priorities and goals of what each state needs most from higher education, prepared by a representative group of business, civic, government, and education leaders, including those from K–12 education.
- Use every type and sector of college or university in the plan for achieving the Public Agenda.
- Win a commitment from state, business, and civic leaders to supply public and private funding for higher education to support the Public Agenda.
- Readjust targets but not the Public Agenda goals when budgets must be cut.
- Fund public colleges and universities for the level of their performance, as well as the level of their mission.
- Move some of the general fund support (3 to 5 percent) for public colleges and universities from enrollment levels to degree and certificate attainment, using actual completion rates compared with predicted rates based on SAT or ACT scores, high school averages, and ranks in class.
- Review periodically the Public Agenda and revise it when necessary.

## State Higher Education Coordinating Agencies

- Insist that colleges and universities avoid mission creep by sticking to their designated missions.
- Publish and comment on the performance reports of the progress of public and private colleges and universities in achieving the Public Agenda.

- Reorder agency priorities to reallocate funding toward achievement of the state Public Agenda.

### Individual Institutions

- Pursue and report progress toward achieving the Public Agenda according to their designated missions.
- Publish, on campus Web sites, profiles of institutional performance on critical input, process, output, and outcome indicators and institutional results on the Public Agenda.
- Require internal performance reports on the results of academic units and departments on key indicators of the institutional mission and the state Public Agenda.
- Reorder their priorities to reallocate funding toward achievement of the state Public Agenda.

## Conclusion

Accountability in higher education has many faces and has spawned many programs. Despite all this activity, external groups in government and business continually call for more accountability. This book suggests that the call is misplaced. Chapter after chapter describes creative initiatives with desirable objectives. Higher education does not need *more* accountability programs. What it needs is better coordination and effective implementation of the ones already in place. Accountability also demands agreement on what states and their citizens need most from their colleges and universities, public and private.

Deciding on the Public Agenda is too critical to the future success of states and their citizens to leave its determination to long-range duels between government officials and academic champions. It needs the advocacy of business and civic leaders as well. Accountability, especially in times of limited public funding, will only prolong 360-degree harassment if it continues the perception of an open-ended commitment of higher education to meet everyone's desires. Business, civic, government, and education leaders must work toward 360-degree accountability by determining what each state needs most from higher education and by committing to achieving that public agenda—or the "what" of accountability. Only such an agreed-upon accountability can ensure that higher education responds to all while submitting to none of the three corners of the Accountability Triangle of state priorities, academic concerns, and market forces.

# References

Aaker, D. A., Kumar, V., and Day, G. S. *Marketing Research.* (6th ed.) New York: Wiley, 1998.

Abbott, W. F. "University and Departmental Determinants of the Prestige of Sociology Departments." *The American Sociologist,* 1972, *7,* 14–15.

Abbott, W. F., and Barlow, H. M. "Stratification Theory and Organizational Rank: Resources, Functions, and Organizational Prestige in American Universities." *Pacific Sociological Review,* 1972, *15,* 401–424.

Alexander, L., Clinton, B., and Kean, T. H. *A Time for Results: The Governors' 1991 Report on Education.* Washington, D.C.: National Governors Association, 1986.

American Association for Higher Education Assessment Forum. *Principles of Good Practice for Assessing Student Learning.* Washington, D.C.: American Association for Higher Education, 1992.

American College Testing Program. "College Assessment of Academic Proficiency." [http://www.act.org/caap/index.html]. Aug. 2003a.

American College Testing Program. "WorkKeys: Improving the Quality of America's Workforce." [http://www.act.org/workkeys]. Aug. 2003b.

Anderson, E. J. *Public Policy Making.* New York: Houghton Mifflin, 1997.

Arenson, K. W. "Halfway Through College, a Crucial Test to Pass." *New York Times,* July 5, 2003, p. A11.

Association of American Colleges and Universities. *Integrity in the College Curriculum: A Report to the Academic Community.* Washington, D.C.: Association of American Colleges and Universities, 1985.

Association of Governing Boards. *Bridging the Gap Between State Government and Higher Education.* Washington, D.C.: Association of Governing Boards, 1998.

Association of Governing Boards. *AGB Statement on Institutional Governance.* Washington, D.C.: Association of Governing Boards, 2001.

Association of Governing Boards. *Ten Public Policy Issues for Higher Education in 2001–2002.* Washington, D.C.: Association of Governing Boards, 2002.

Association of Governing Boards. *Ten Public Policy Issues for Higher Education in 2003–2004*. Washington, D.C.: Association of Governing Boards, 2003a.

Association of Governing Boards, Merit Screening of Citizens for Gubernatorial Appointment to Public College and University Appointments. Washington, D.C.: Association of Governing Boards, 2003b.

Astin, A. W. "How Colleges Are Rated." *Change,* 1970, *2,* 11–86.

Astin, A. W. *Achieving Educational Excellence.* San Francisco: Jossey-Bass, 1985.

Astin, A. W. *Assessment for Excellence: The Philosophy and Practice of Assessment and Evaluation in Higher Education.* New York: American Council on Education/Macmillan, 1991.

Astin, A. W., and Lee, C.B.T. *The Invisible Colleges.* New York: McGraw-Hill, 1972.

Astin, A. W., and Solomon, L. C. "Are Reputational Ratings Needed to Measure Quality?" *Change,* 1981, *13*(2), 14–19.

Baird, L. L. *Using Self-Reports to Predict Student Performance.* New York: College Board, 1976.

Bankirer, M. W., and Testa, A. "Update on Assessment at Western Governors' University." *Assessment and Accountability Forum,* Spring 1999, *9*(1), 13–14.

Banta, T. W. "Use of Outcomes Information at the University of Tennessee, Knoxville." In P. T. Ewell (ed.), *Assessing Educational Outcomes.* New Directions for Institutional Research, no. 47. San Francisco: Jossey-Bass, 1985.

Banta, T. W. *Performance Funding in Higher Education: A Critical Analysis of Tennessee's Experience.* Boulder, Colo.: National Center for Higher Education Management Systems, 1986.

Banta, T. W. "Assessment as an Instrument of State Funding Policy." In T. W. Banta (ed.), *Implementing Outcomes Assessment: Promise and Perils.* New Directions for Institutional Research, no. 59. San Francisco: Jossey-Bass, 1988.

Banta, T. W., and Associates. *Building a Scholarship of Assessment.* San Francisco: Jossey-Bass, 2002.

Banta, T. W., and Fisher, H. S. "Putting a Premium on Results." *Educational Record,* 1986, 54–58.

Banta, T. W., and Kuh, G. D. "A Missing Link in Assessment: Collaboration Between Academic and Student Affairs." *Change,* 1998, *30*(2), 40–46.

Banta, T. W., and Moffett, M. S. "Performance Funding in Tennessee: Stimulus for Program Improvement." In D. F. Halpern (ed.), *Student Outcomes Assessment: What Institutions Stand to Gain.* New Directions for Higher Education, no. 59. San Francisco: Jossey-Bass, 1987.

Banta, T. W., Rudolph, L. B., Van Dyke, J., and Fisher, H. S. "Performance Funding Comes of Age in Tennessee." *Journal of Higher Education,* 1996, *67*(1), 23–43.

Barnett, R. *Improving Higher Education: Total Quality Care.* London: The Society for Research into Higher Education and The Open University Press, 1992.

Barron. *Profiles of American Colleges.* (25th ed.) Hauppauge, N.Y.: Barron's Educational Series, 2003.

Baughman, J. C., and Goldman, R. N. "College Rankings and Faculty Publications: Are They Related?" *Change,* 1999, *31*(2), 44–50.

Behn, R. D. *Rethinking Democratic Accountability.* Washington, D.C.: Brookings Institution Press, 2001.

Benjamin, R., and Chun, M. "A New Field of Dreams: The Collegiate Learning Assessment Project." *Peer Review,* Summer 2003, *5*(4), 26–29.

Bennett, R. E. "On the Meaning of Constructed Response." In R. E. Bennett and W. C. Ward (eds.), *Construction Versus Choice in Cognitive Measurement in Constructed Response, Performance Testing, and Portfolio Assessment.* Hillsdale, N.J.: Erlbaum, 1993.

Berdahl, R. "Academic Freedom, Autonomy and Accountability in British Universities." *Studies in Higher Education,* 1990, *15*(2), 169–180.

Berdie, R. "Self-Claimed and Tested Knowledge." *Educational and Psychological Measurement,* 1971, *31,* 629–636.

Bernstein, A. "Too Many Workers? Not for Long." *BusinessWeek,* May 20, 2002, pp. 126–130.

Birnbaum, R. *Maintaining Diversity in Higher Education.* San Francisco: Jossey-Bass, 1983.

Blau, P. M. *The Organization of Academic Work.* (2nd ed.) New Brunswick, N.J.: Transaction Publishers, 1994.

Blumenstyk, G. "Florida Bill Offers Campuses Fiscal Autonomy in Return for Accountability." *Chronicle of Higher Education,* Apr. 24, 1991, pp. A22–A23.

Boehner, J. A., and McKeon, H. P. "The College Cost Crisis: A Congressional Analysis of College Costs and Implications for America's Higher Education System." [http://edworkforce.house.gov/issues/108th/education/highereducation/CollegeCostCrisisReport.pdf]. Nov. 2003.

Bogue, E. G., and Hall, K. B. *Quality and Accountability in Higher Education: Improving Policy, Enhancing Performance.* Westport, Conn.: Praeger, 2003.

Bok, D. "Academic Values and the Lure of Profit." *Chronicle of Higher Education,* Apr. 4, 2003a, p. B7.

Bok, D. *Universities in the Marketplace: The Commercialization of Higher Education.* Princeton, N.J.: Princeton University Press, 2003b.

Borden, V., and Zak-Owens, J. *Measuring Quality: Choosing Among Surveys and Other College and University Quality Assessments.* Washington, D.C.: Association for Institutional Research and American Council on Education, 2001.

Bradburn, N. M., and Sudman, S. *Polls and Surveys: Understanding What They Tell Us.* San Francisco: Jossey-Bass, 1988.

Brandt, R. M. "The Accuracy of Self Estimates." *Genetic Psychology Monographs,* 1958, *58,* 55–99.

Breneman, D. W. *Liberal Arts Colleges: Thriving, Surviving, or Endangered?* Washington, D.C.: Brookings Institution, 1994.

Brewer, D. J., Eide, E. R., and Ehrenberg, R. G. "Does It Pay to Attend an Elite Private College? Cross-Cohort Evidence on the Effects of College Type on Earnings." *Journal of Human Resources,* 1999, *34*(1), 104–23.

Brown, D. G. *The Mobile Professors.* Washington, D.C.: American Council on Education, 1967.

Burd, S. "Bush's Next Target?" *Chronicle of Higher Education,* July 11, 2003a, p. A18.

Burd, S. "Education Department Wants to Create Grant Program Linked to Graduation Rates." *Chronicle of Higher Education,* Jan. 3, 2003b, p. A31.

Burd, S. "For-Profit Colleges Want a Little Respect." *Chronicle of Higher Education,* Sept. 5, 2003c, *50*(2), p. A23.

Burke, J. C. "The 'Knowledge Economy': Ohio's Challenge and Choice." Washington, D.C.: Association of Governing Boards, 2003.

Burke, J. C., and Associates. *Funding Public Colleges and Universities for Performance: Popularity, Problems, and Prospects.* Albany, N.Y.: Rockefeller Institute, 2002.

Burke J. C., and Minassians, H. P. *Performance Reporting: The Preferred "No Cost" Accountability Program: The Sixth Annual Report.* Albany, N.Y.: Rockefeller Institute, 2002a.

Burke, J. C., and Minassians, H. P. *Reporting Higher Education Results: Missing Links in the Performance Chain.* New Directions for Institutional Research, no. 116. San Francisco: Jossey-Bass, 2002b.

Burke, J. C., and Minassians, H. P. *Performance Reporting: "Real" Accountability or Accountability "Lite": Seventh Annual Survey 2003.* Albany, N.Y.: Rockefeller Institute, 2003.

Burke, J. C., Minassians, H. P., and Yang, P. "State Performance Reporting Indicators: What Do They Indicate?" *Planning for Higher Education,* 2002, *31*(1), 15–29.

Burke, J. C., Rosen, J. A., Minassians, H. P., and Lessard, T. A. *Performance Funding and Budgeting: An Emerging Merger? The Fourth Annual Survey.* Albany, N.Y.: Rockefeller Institute, 2000.

Burke, J. C., and Serban, A. M. *Performance Funding for Public Higher Education: Fad or Trend.* New Directions for Institutional Research, no. 97. San Francisco: Jossey-Bass, 1998.

Burstein, J., Kukich, K., Wolff, S., Lu, C., and Chodorow, M. "Computer Analysis of Essays." In *Automated Scoring.* Symposium conducted at the annual meeting of the National Council on Measurement in Education, San Diego, Apr. 1998. [http://www.etstechnologies.com/pdfs/ncmefinal.pdf]. Nov. 2003.

Callan P. M., and Finney, J. E. "Assessing Educational Capital: An Imperative for Policy." *Change,* 2002, *34*(4), 25–32.

Cambridge, B. L., Kahn, S., Yancey, K. B., and Tompkins, D. P. *Electronic Portfolios: Emerging Practices in Student, Faculty, and Institutional Learning.* Washington, D.C.: American Association for Higher Education, 2001.

Carnevale, A. P., and Desrochers, D. M. *Standards for What? The Economic Roots of K–16 Reform.* Princeton, N.J.: Educational Testing Service, 2003.

Center for Higher Education and Policy Analysis. *Challenges for Governance: A National Report.* Los Angeles: University of Southern California, 2003.

Chauncey, Jr., H. "A Calm Before the Storm?" *Yale Alumni Magazine,* 1995, *58*(7), 30–31.

Chickering, A. W., and Gamson, Z. F. "Seven Principles for Good Practice in Undergraduate Education." *AAHE Bulletin,* 1987, 7(3), 3–7.

Chronicle of Higher Education. *Almanac 2001–2002.* XLVII, No. 1, 2001.

Chronicle of Higher Education. *Almanac 2002–2003.* XLIX, No. 1, 2002.

Clark, B. R. *The Higher Education System: Academic Organization in Cross-National Perspective.* Berkeley: University of California Press, 1983.

Clauser, B. E., Ross, L. P., Clyman, S. G., Rose, K. M., Margolis, M. J., Nungester, R. J., Piemme, T. E., Chang, L., El-Bayoumi, G., Malakoff, G. L., and Pincetl, P. S. "Development of a Scoring Algorithm to Replace Expert Rating for Scoring a Complex Performance-Based Assessment." *Applied Measurement in Education,* 1997, *10*, 345–358.

College Board. *Trends in College Pricing 2002.* New York: College Board Publications, 2002.

College Board. *College Handbook 2004.* (41st ed.) New York: College Board Publications, 2003.

Conrad, C. F., and Blackburn, R. T. "Current Views of Department Quality: An Empirical Examination." *Review of Higher Education,* 1986, *9*(3), 249–266.

Converse, J. M., and Presser, S. *Survey Questions: Handcrafting the Standardized Questionnaire.* Thousand Oaks, Calif.: Sage, 1989.

Cook, C. E. *Lobbying for Higher Education.* London: Vanderbilt University Press, 1998.

Corbett, D. C. *Australian Public Sector Management*. Sydney, Australia: Allen & Unwin, 1996.

Corrallo, S. "Critical Concerns in Assessing Selected Higher Order Thinking and Communication Skills of College Graduates." *Assessment Update*, 1991, *3*(6), 5–6.

Coulter, T. *Issue Priorities and Trends in State Higher Education*. Denver, Colo.: State Higher Education Executive Officers, May 2003.

Council for Higher Education Accreditation. *Statement of Mutual Responsibilities for Student Learning Outcomes: Accreditation, Institutions and Programs*. Washington, D.C.: Council for Higher Education Accreditation, 2003. [http://chea.org/pdf/StmntStudentLearning Outcomes9–03.pdf]. Jan. 2004.

Council of Regional Accrediting Commissions. *Regional Accreditation and Student Learning: A Guide for Institutions and Evaluators*, 2003.

Couturier, L. K. "Balancing State Control with Society's Needs." *Chronicle of Higher Education*, June 17, 2003, p. B20.

Crowe, S. *Engaging the Future by Restructuring Expectation*. Keynote address to the Higher Learning Commission at the 107th annual meeting, Chicago, Mar. 24, 2002. [http://www.ncahigherlearningcommission. org/restructuring/CrowKeynote.pdf]. Nov. 2003.

*Dartmouth College* v. *Woodward*. 17 U.S. 518 (1819).

Day, P., and Klein, R. *Five Public Services*. London: Travistock Publications, 1987.

DeNisi, A. S., and Shaw, J. B. "Investigation of the Uses of Self-Reports of Abilities." *Journal of Applied Psychology*, 1977, *62*, 641–644.

Department of Veterans Affairs. "The GI Bill: From Roosevelt to Montgomery." [http://www.gibill.va.gov/education/GI_Bill.htm]. Sept. 2003.

Dichev, I. "News or Noise? Estimating the Noise in the *U.S. News* University Rankings." *Research in Higher Education*, 2001, *42*, 237–266.

Dill, D. D. "Quality by Design: Toward a Framework for Academic Quality Management." In J. Smart (ed.), *Higher Education: Handbook of Theory and Research*. New York: Agathon Press, 1992.

Dill, D. D., and Soo, M. *Transparency and Quality in Higher Education Markets*. Paper presented at the Centre for Research in Higher Education Policies/Hedda Seminar Markets in Higher Education: Mature Economies. Douro, Portugal, Oct. 2–6, 2003.

Drew, D. E. *Science Development: An Evaluation Study*. Washington, D.C.: National Academy of Sciences, 1975.

Duderstadt, J. J. "Fire, Ready, Aim!: University Decision-Making During an Era of Rapid Change." In L. E. Weber (ed.), *Governance in Higher Education: The University in a State of Flux*. London: Economica, 2001.

Duderstadt, J. J., and Womack F. W. *The Future of the Public University in America: Beyond the Crossroads.* Baltimore: Johns Hopkins University Press, 2003.

Eaton, J. S. "Regional Accreditation Reform: Who Is Served?" *Change,* 2001, *33*(2), 38–45.

Eaton, J. S. *Is Accreditation Accountable? The Continuing Conversation Between Accreditation and the Federal Government.* Washington, D.C.: Council for Higher Education Accreditation, 2003.

Eaton, J. S. "Letter from the President: Is the Era of Self-Regulation Over?" [http://www.chea.org/pdf/SelfRegulation_0104.pdf]. Jan. 2004.

Education Commission of the States. "Current Status of State Structures, 1997." In C. Lenth (ed.), *State Postsecondary Education Structures Sourcebook.* Denver, Colo.: Education Commission of the States, 1997.

Education Commission of the States. "Accountability—Next Generation Models: Quality Improvement Model." Denver, Colo.: Education Commission of the States, 2003. [http://www.ecs.org/html/issue.asp?issueid=206&subIssueID=130]. Sept. 2003.

Educational Testing Service. "Academic Profile." [http://www.ets.org/hea/acpro/index.html]. Aug. 2003a.

Educational Testing Service. "Interpreting Scores on the GRE Analytical Writing Measure." [http://www.gre.org/interpret.html]. Aug. 2003b.

Educational Testing Service. "Major Field Tests." [http://www.ets.org/hea/mft/index.html]. Aug. 2003c.

Ehrenberg, R. G. *Tuition Rising: Why College Costs So Much.* Cambridge, Mass.: Harvard University Press, 2000.

Ehrenberg, R. G. "Reaching for the Brass Ring: The *U.S. News & World Report* Rankings Competition." *Review of Higher Education,* Winter 2003, *26*(2), 145–162.

Ehrenberg, R. G., and Smith, R. G. *Modern Labor Economics: Theory and Public Policy.* (8th ed.) Boston: Addison-Wesley, 2003.

Elton, C. F., and Rodgers, S. A. "Physics Department Ratings: Another Evaluation." *Science,* 1971, *174*, 565–568.

Elton, C. F., and Rose, H. A. "What Are the Ratings Rating?" *American Psychologist,* 1972, *27*, 197–201.

Embretson, S. E. "Cognitive Psychology Applied to Testing." In F. T. Durso (ed.), *Handbook of Applied Cognition.* New York: Wiley, 1999.

Erwin, T. D. *Assessing Student Learning and Development: A Guide to the Principles, Goals, and Methods of Determining College Outcomes.* San Francisco: Jossey-Bass, 1991.

Erwin, T. D. *The NPEC Sourcebook on Assessment: Definitions and Assessment Methods for Critical Thinking, Problem Solving, and Writing* (Vol. 1). Washington, D.C.: U.S. Department of Education, 2000.

[http://nces.ed.gov/pubsearch/pubsinfo.asp?pubid=2000195].
Sept. 2003.

Erwin, T. D. "The ABC's of Assessment." *Trusteeship,* 2003, *11*(2), 18–23.

Erwin, T. D., and DeMars, C. "Advancing Assessment: Why Not Computer-Based Assessment?" *Assessment Update,* Mar.-Apr. 2002, *14*(2), 1–2, 15.

Erwin, T. D., and Sebrell, K. W. "Assessment of Critical Thinking: One Performance Method Analyzed." *Journal of General Education,* 2003, *52*(1), 50–70.

Erwin, T. D., and Wise, S. L. "Standard Setting." In R. A. Voorhees (ed.), "Measuring What Matters: Competency-Based Models in Higher Education." *New Directions for Institutional Research,* no. 110. San Francisco: Jossey-Bass, 2001.

Ewell, P. T. *The Self-Regarding Institution.* Boulder, Colo.: National Center for Higher Education Management Systems, 1984.

Ewell, P. T. *Assessment, Accountability, and Improvement: Managing the Contradiction.* Washington, D.C.: American Association for Higher Education, 1987.

Ewell, P. T. "Hearts and Minds: Some Reflections on the Ideologies of Assessment." Keynote address at the Fourth National Conference on Assessment in Higher Education. Washington, D.C.: American Association for Higher Education, 1989.

Ewell, P. T. "Assessment and Public Accountability: Back to the Future." *Change,* 1991, *23*(6), 12–17.

Ewell, P. T. "The Role of States and Accreditors in Shaping Assessment Practice." In T. W. Banta (ed.), *Making a Difference: Outcomes of a Decade of Assessment in Higher Education.* San Francisco: Jossey-Bass, 1993.

Ewell, P. T. "The Current Pattern of State-Level Assessment: Results of a National Inventory." *Assessment Update,* 1996, *8*(3), 1–12.

Ewell, P. T. "Accountability and Assessment in a Second Decade: New Looks or Same Old Story." In E. E. Chaffee (ed.), *Assessing Impact: Evidence and Action.* Washington D.C.: American Association for Higher Education, 1997a.

Ewell, P. T. "Organizing for Learning: A New Imperative." *AAHE Bulletin,* 1997b, *50*(4), 10–12.

Ewell, P. T. "Statewide Testing in Higher Education." *Change,* 2001, *33*(2), 21–27.

Ewell, P. T. "An Emerging Scholarship: A Brief History of Assessment." In T. W. Banta (ed.), *Building a Scholarship of Assessment.* San Francisco: Jossey-Bass, 2002a.

Ewell, P. T. *Perpetual Movement: Assessment After Twenty Years.* Washington, D.C.: American Association for Higher Education, 2002b.

Ewell, P. T. "Grading Student Learning: You Have to Start Somewhere." In *Measuring Up 2002*. San Jose, Calif.: National Center for Public Policy and Higher Education, 2002c.

Ewell, P. T., and Boyer, C. M. "Acting Out State-Mandated Assessment: Evidence from Five States." *Change*, 1988, *20*(4), 40–47.

Ewell, P. T., Finney, J. E., and Lenth, C. "Filling in the Mosaic: The Emerging Pattern of State-Based Assessment." *AAHE Bulletin*, 1990, *42*, 3–7.

Ewell, P. T., and Jones, D. P. *Indicators of "Good Practice" in Undergraduate Education: A Handbook for Development and Implementation*. Boulder, Colo.: National Center for Higher Education Management Systems, 1996.

Ewell, P. T., and Ries, P. *Assessing Student Learning Outcomes: A Supplement to Measuring Up 2000*. San Jose, Calif.: National Center for Public Policy and Higher Education, 2000.

Ewell, P. T., Jones, D. P., and Kelly, P. J. *Conceptualizing and Researching the Educational Pipeline*. Boulder, Colo.: National Center for Higher Education Management Systems, Feb. 2003.

Ewell, P. T., Paulson, K., and Wellman, J. V. *Refashioning Accountability: Toward a "Coordinated' System of Quality Assurance for Higher Education*. Denver, Colo.: Education Commission of the States, 1997.

Ewell, P. T., Schild, P. R., and Paulson, K. *Tracking the Mobile Student: Can We Develop the Capacity for a Comprehensive Database to Assess Student Progression?* Indianapolis, Ind.: The Lumina Foundation for Education, 2003.

Feldt, L. S., and Brennan, R. L. "Reliability." In R. L. Linn (ed.), *Educational Measurement*. Phoenix, Ariz.: Oryx Press, 1993.

Fish, S. "Give Us Liberty or Give Us Revenue." *Chronicle of Higher Education*, Oct. 31, 2003, p. C4.

Fiske, E. B., and Logue, R. *The Fiske Guide to Colleges 2004*. Naperville, Ill.: Sourcebooks, 2003.

Geiger, R. L. *High Tuition, High Aid: A Road Paved with Good Intentions*. Paper presented at Association for the Study of Higher Education, Sacramento, Calif., 2002.

Geiger, R. L. *Knowledge and Money: Research Universities and the Paradox of the Marketplace*. Palo Alto, Calif.: Stanford University Press, 2004.

Geiger, R. L., and Feller, I. "The Dispersion of Academic Research in the 1980s." *Journal of Higher Education*, 1995, *66*(3), 336–360.

Gershuny, J., and Robinson, J. P. "Historical Changes in the Household Division of Labor." *Demography*, 1988, *25*, 537–552.

Gilland, M. "Organizational Change and Tenure." *Change*, 1997, *29*(3), 30.

Goldberger, M. L., Maher, B. A., and Flattau, P. E. (eds.). *Research-Doctorate Programs in the United States: Continuity and Change*. National Research Council. Washington, D.C.: National Academy Press, 1995.

Golden, A. J. "Project for Area Concentration Achievement Testing." *Assessment Update,* 1991, *3*(2), 10–11.

Graham, H. D., and Diamond, N. (eds.). *The Rise of American Research Universities.* Baltimore: Johns Hopkins University Press, 1997.

Graham, P., Lyman, R. W., and Trow, M. "Accountability of Colleges and Universities: An Essay." In *The Accountability Study.* New York: Trustees of Columbia University, 1995.

Grunig, S. D. "Research, Reputation, and Resources: The Effect of Research Activity on Perceptions of Undergraduate Education and Institutional Resource Acquisition." *Journal of Higher Education,* 1997, *68*(1), 17–52.

Guba, E. G., and Clark, D. L. "Levels of R&D Productivity in Schools of Education." *Educational Researcher,* 1978, *7*(5), 3–9.

Hagstrom, W. O. "Inputs, Outputs, and the Prestige of University Science Departments." *Sociology of Education,* 1971, *44,* 375–397.

Haladyna, T. M. *Writing Test Items to Evaluate Higher Order Thinking.* Boston: Allyn & Bacon, 1997.

Hansford, B. C., and Hattie, J. A. "The Relationship Between Self and Achievement/Performance Measures." *Review of Educational Research,* 1982, *52,* 123–142.

Harcleroad, F. F. "Accreditation on Trial: The Indictment." In K. E. Young, C. M. Chambers, and H. R. Kells (eds.), *Understanding Accreditation.* San Francisco: Jossey-Bass, 1983.

Hartman, L. M. *Graduate Education: Parameters for Public Policy.* Washington, D.C.: National Science Board, National Science Foundation, 1969.

Hebel, S. "Public Colleges Emphasize Research, but the Public Wants a Focus on Students." *Chronicle of Higher Education,* May 2, 2003a, p. A14.

Hebel, S. "Private Colleges Face Cuts in Public Dollars?" *Chronicle of Higher Education,* Aug. 1, 2003b, pp. A19–A20.

Hirsch, W. Z. "Initiatives for Improving Shared Governance." In L. E. Weber (ed.), *Governance in Higher Education: The University in a State of Flux.* London: Economica, 2001.

Hossler, D. "The Problem with College Rankings." *About Campus,* 2000, *5*(1), 20–24.

Hossler, D., and Foley, E. M. "Reducing the Noise in the College Choice Process: The Use of College Guidebooks and Ratings." In R. Dan Walleri and M. K. Moss (eds.), *Evaluating and Responding to College Guidebooks and Rankings.* New Directions for Institutional Research, no. 88. San Francisco: Jossey-Bass, 1995.

Hoxby, C. H. "The Return to Attending a More Selective College: 1960 to the Present." Cambridge, Mass.: Harvard University Economics Department, Working Paper, 1998.

Hutchings, P., and Marchese, T. W. "Watching Assessment: Questions, Stories, Prospects." *Change,* 1990, *22*(5), 12–38.

James Madison University, Center for Assessment and Research Studies. "Assessment Instruments." [http://www.jmu.edu/assessment/ainstr. shtml]. Aug. 2003a.

James Madison University, Center for Assessment and Research Studies. "Dictionary of Outcome Assessment." [http://people.jmu.edu/ yangsx/]. Aug. 2003b.

Joint Committee to Develop a Master Plan for Education. *The California Master Plan for Education.* Sacramento, Calif.: Joint Committee to Develop a Master Plan for Education, 2002. [http://www.sen.ca.gov/ ftp/SEN/COMMITTEE/JOINT/MASTER_PLAN/_home/ 020909THEMASTERPLANLINKS.HTML]. July 2003.

Jones, D. P. *Different Perspectives on Information About Educational Quality: Implications for the Role of Accreditation.* Washington, D.C.: Council on Higher Education Accreditation, 2002.

Jones, D. P., and Ewell, P. T. *Accountability in Higher Education: Meaning and Methods.* Boulder, Colo.: National Center for Higher Education Management Systems, 1987.

Kane, T. *The Price of Admission: Rethinking How Americans Pay for College.* Washington, D.C.: Brookings Institution Press, 1999.

Katz, S. "Defining Education Quality and Accountability." *Chronicle of Higher Education,* Nov. 16, 1994, p. A56.

King, A. "The Changing Face of Accountability: Monitoring and Assessing Institutional Performance in Higher Education." *Journal of Higher Education,* 2000, *71*(4), 414–431.

Kirp, D. "No Brainer. " *The Nation,* pp. 1–3. [http://www.thenation.com/ doc.mhtml?i=20031110ands=kirp]. Oct. 23, 2003a.

Kirp, D. *Shakespeare, Einstein, and the Bottom Line: The Marketing of Higher Education.* Cambridge, Mass.: Harvard University Press, 2003b.

Kirp, D. "Education for Profit." *The Public Interest,* 2003c, *152,* 100–112.

Klein, S. *The Search for Value-Added: Assessing and Validating Selected Higher Education Outcomes.* Paper presented at the American Educational Research Association, Chicago, 2003.

Knight Higher Education Collaborative. "The Third Imperative." *Policy Perspectives,* 1999, *9*(1), 1.

Knight Higher Education Collaborative. "Of Precept, Policy, and Practice." *Policy Perspectives,* 2002, *11*(1), 1.

Knudsen, D. D., and Vaughn, T. R. "Quality in Graduate Education: A Re-evaluation of the Rankings of Sociology Departments in the Carter Report." *American Sociologist,* 1969, *4,* 12–19.

Kuh, G. D. "Assessing What Really Matters to Student Learning: Inside the National Survey of Student Engagement." *Change,* 2001, *33*(3), 10–17, 66.

Kuh, G. D. *The National Survey of Student Engagement: Conceptual Framework and Overview of Psychometric Properties.* Bloomington, Ind.: Center for Postsecondary Research and Planning, Indiana University School of Education. July, 2002. [http://www.indiana.edu/~nsse/html/2002_NSSE_report/html/conceptual_1.htm]. July 2004.

Kuh, G. D. "What We're Learning About Student Engagement from NSSE: Benchmarks for Effective Educational Practices." *Change,* 2003, *35*(2), 24–32.

Kuh, G. D., and Banta, T. W. "Faculty-Student Affairs Collaboration on Assessment: Lessons from the Field." *About Campus,* 2000, *4*(6), 4–11.

Kuh, G. D., Hayek, J. C., Carini, R. M., Ouimet, J. A., Gonyea, R. M., and Kennedy, J. *NSSE Technical and Norms Report.* Bloomington: Indiana University Center for Postsecondary Research and Planning, 2001.

Laing, J., Swayer, R., and Noble, J. "Accuracy of Self-Reported Activities and Accomplishments of College-Bound Seniors." *Journal of College Student Development,* 1989, *29,* 362–368.

Landauer, T. K., Foltz, P. W., and Laham, D. "An Introduction to Latent Semantic Analysis." *Discourse Processes,* 1998, *25,* 259–284.

Langenberg, D. N. "Diplomas and Degrees Are Obsolescent." *Chronicle of Higher Education,* Sept. 12, 1997, p. A64.

The Learning Alliance. "The Landscape." *Change,* 2003, *35*(5), 55–58.

Levine, A. "Higher Education's New Status as a Mature Industry." *Chronicle of Higher Education,* Jan. 31, 1997, p. A48.

Liddell, D. L. *Measure of Moral Orientation.* Iowa City, Iowa: Liddell, 1990.

Lingenfelter, P. E. "Educational Accountability: Setting Standards Improving Performance." *Change,* 2003, *35*(2), 19–23.

Litten, L. H., and Hall, A. E. "In the Eyes of Our Beholders: Some Evidence on How High School Students and Their Parents View Quality in Colleges." *Journal of Higher Education,* 1989, *60*(3), 302–324.

Lively, K. "Campus 'Accountability' Is Hot Again." *Chronicle of Higher Education,* Sept. 23, 1992, p. A25.

Lowman, R. L., and Williams, R. E. "Validity of Self-Ratings of Abilities and Competencies." *Journal of Vocational Behavior,* 1987, *31,* 1–13.

Machung, A. "Playing the Rankings Game." *Change,* 1998, *30*(4), 12–16.

Marginson, S., and Considine, M. *The Enterprise University: Power, Governance and Reinvention in Australia.* Cambridge, England: Cambridge University Press, 2000.

Massy, W. F. *Energizing Quality Work: Higher Education Quality Evaluation in Sweden and Denmark.* Technical Report. National Center for Postsecondary Improvement, Stanford University, Palo Alto, Calif., 2000.

Massy, W. F. *Honoring the Trust: Quality and Cost Containment in Higher Education.* Boston: Anker, 2003a.

Massy, W. F. "Access to What? Putting 'Quality' into National QA Systems." Keynote address on Quality and Standards: The National Perspective. International Network of Quality Assurance Agencies in Higher Education (INQAAHE) Conference, Dublin, Ireland, Apr. 14–17, 2003b.

Massy, W. F. "Auditing Higher Education to Improve Quality." *Chronicle of Higher Education,* June 20, 2003c, pp. B16–B17.

Massy, W. F. *Markets in Higher Education: Do They Promote Internal Efficiency?* Paper presented at the Centre for Research in Higher Education Policies/Hedda Seminar Markets in Higher Education: Mature Economies. Douro, Portugal, Oct. 2–6, 2003d.

Massy, W. F., and French, N. J. "Teaching and Learning Quality Process Review: What the Program Has Achieved in Hong Kong." *Quality in Higher Education,* 2001, 7(1), 33–45.

McGuinness, A. C. "The Changing Structure of State Higher Education Leadership." In *State Postsecondary Education: Structures Handbook.* Denver, Colo.: Education Commission of the States, 1994.

McGuinness, A. C. "Essay: The Functions and Evolution of State Coordination and Governance in Postsecondary Education." In *1997 State Postsecondary Structures Sourcebook.* Denver, Colo.: Education Commission of the States, 1997.

McGuinness, A. C. "Reflections on Postsecondary Governance Changes." *ECS Policy Brief,* 2002. [http://www.ecs.org/clearinghouse/37/76/3776.htm]. July 2003.

McGuire, M. D. *Validity Issues for Reputational Studies.* New Directions for Institutional Research, no. 88. San Francisco: Jossey-Bass, 1995.

McKeon, H. "Controlling the Price of College." *Chronicle of Higher Education,* July 11, 2003, p. B20.

Mercer, J. "States' Practice of Grading Public Colleges Gets an F from Critics." *Chronicle of Higher Education,* Sept. 1, 1993, p. A37.

Merriam-Webster, *Dictionary,* Online. [http://www,n-w.com/cgi-bin/dictionary]. July 2003.

Messick, S. "Validity." In R. L. Linn (ed.), *Educational Measurement.* Phoenix, Ariz.: Oryx Press, 1993.

Middle States Association, Commission on Higher Education. *Student Learning Assessment: Options and Resources.* Philadelphia: Middle States Commission on Higher Education, 2003.

Miller, M. A. "Measuring Up and Student Learning." In *Measuring Up 2002.* San Jose, Calif.: National Center for Public Policy and Higher Education, 2002.

Mississippi Steering Committee. *Building Opportunity in Mississippi Through Education: A Report from the Steering Committee for the Mississippi Leadership Summit on Higher Education.* Washington, D.C.: Association of Governing Boards, 2002.

Moe, T. M. "The New Economics of Organization." *American Journal of Political Science,* 1984, *28*(4), 739–777.

Moll, R. *Playing the Selective College Admissions Game.* New York: Penguin Books, 1994.

Monks, J., and Ehrenberg, R. G. "*U.S. News & World Report*'s College Rankings: Why They Do Matter." *Change,* 1999, *31*(6), 42–51.

Montell, G. "The Fallout from Post-Tenure Review." *Chronicle of Higher Education,* Oct. 17, 2002. [http://chronicle.com/jobs/2002/10/2002101701c.htm]. May 2004.

Morgan, D. R., Kearney, R. C., and Regens, J. L. "Assessing Quality Among Graduate Institutions of Higher Education in the United States." *Social Science Quarterly,* 1976, *57,* 670–679.

Morse, R. J., Donohue, J., Sanoff, G., and Shapiro, D. "America's Best Graduate Schools." *U.S. News & World Report,* 1994, *116,* 65–97.

Mortenson, T. G. "Institutional Graduation Rates by Control, Academic Selectivity and Degree Level: 1983 to 2001." *Postsecondary Education OPPORTUNITY,* Mar. 2002a, *117,* 1–6.

Mortenson, T. G. "State Appropriations, Public Institutional Tuition Rates, and State Student Financial Aid Appropriations: FY 1975 to FY 2002." *Postsecondary Education OPPORTUNITY,* July 2002b, *121,* 1–16.

Mumper, M. *Removing College Price Barriers.* Albany: State University of New York Press, 1996.

National Association of Independent Colleges and Universities. *Task Force Report on Appropriate Accountability: Regulations, the Responsibilities of Independence: Appropriate Accountability Through Self-Regulation.* Washington, D.C.: National Association of Independent Colleges and Universities, 1994.

National Association of Independent Colleges and Universities. "Institutional Examples, Profiles in Accountability." [http://www.naicu.edu/Accountability/inst/]. July 10, 2003a.

National Association of Independent Colleges and Universities. *Twelve Facts That May Surprise You About America's Private Colleges and Universities.* Mar. 2003b. [http://www.naicu.edu/pubs/NAICU12FactsNew.pdf]. May 2004.

National Association of State Student Grant and Aid Programs. *33rd Annual Survey Report on State-Sponsored Student Financial Aid 2001–2002 Academic Year.* New York State Higher Education Services Corporation, Apr. 2003. [http://www.nassgap.org/researchsurveys/33%20Nassgap%20Survey%20Report%204.pdf]. May 2004.

National Association of State Universities and Land-Grant Colleges. "Appropriations of State Tax Funds for Operating Expenses of Higher Education, 1981–82." [http://www.coe.listu.edu/grapevine/50state.htm], Mar. 2002.

National Center for Education Statistics. *Digest of Education Statistics 2002.* [http://nces.ed.gov/pubs2003/digest02/]. Aug. 2003a.

National Center for Education Statistics. "National Assessment of Adult Literacy." [http://nces.ed.gov/naal/design/design.asp]. Aug. 2003b.

National Center for Education Statistics. "Education Directory, Colleges and Universities." *Digest of Education Statistics 2002,* Washington, D.C.: National Center for Education Statistics, 2003c.

National Center for Public Policy and Higher Education. *Measuring Up 2000: The State-by-State Report Card for Higher Education.* San Jose, Calif.: National Center for Public Policy and Higher Education, 2000.

National Center for Public Policy and Higher Education. *Measuring Up 2002: The State-by-State Report Card for Higher Education.* San Jose, Calif.: National Center for Public Policy and Higher Education, 2002.

National Center for Public Policy and Higher Education. "Data Updates for the *Losing Ground* Report." San Jose, Calif.: National Center for Public Policy and Higher Education, May 2003a.

National Center for Public Policy and Higher Education. *Purposes, Policies, and Performance: Higher Education and the Fulfillment of a State's Public Agenda.* San Jose, Calif.: National Center for Public Policy and Higher Education, 2003b.

National Commission on Excellence in Education. *A Nation at Risk: The Imperative for Educational Reform.* Washington, D.C.: Department of Education, 1983.

National Governors Association. *Closing the Gaps with Higher Productivity.* Paper presented at a meeting of the NGA Center for Best Practices, San Francisco, 2003.

National Institute of Education. Report of the Study Group on the Conditions of Excellence in American Higher Education. *Involvement in Learning: Realizing the Potential of American Higher Education.* Washington, D.C.: U.S. Government Printing Office, 1984.

National Survey of Student Engagement. *Improving the College Experience: National Benchmarks for Effective Educational Practice.* Bloomington: Indiana University Center for Postsecondary Research and Planning, 2001.

National Survey of Student Engagement. *From Promise to Progress: How Colleges and Universities Are Using Student Engagement Results to Improve Collegiate Quality.* Bloomington: Indiana University Center for Postsecondary Research and Planning, 2002.

Newman, F. "Creating an Effective Market." *Crosstalk,* Summer 2003, *11*(3), 11–12. [http: www/highereducation.org/crosstalk/ct303/voices0303-market.shtml]. Sept. 2003.

Nicholson, J. M. "A Guide to the Guides." *Change,* 1991, *23*(6), 22–29.

Nodine, T. "Media Coverage of Measuring Up 2000." Paper presented at the State Policy Leadership Panel of the National Center for Public Policy and Higher Education, San Jose, Calif., Mar. 8–9, 2001.

North, D. C. *Institutions, Institutional Change, and Economic Performance.* New York: Cambridge University Press, 1990.

North Dakota Roundtable. *A North Dakota University System for the 21st Century: The Report of the Roundtable for the North Dakota Legislative Council Interim Committee on Higher Education.* Bismarck, N.D., May 2000. [http://www.ndus.nodak.edu/Upload/allfile.asp?id=332andtbl=MultiUse]. July 2003.

North Dakota University System. *2nd Annual Accountability Measures Report.* Bismarck, N.D.: North Dakota University System, 2002. [http://www.ndus.edu/Upload/allfile.asp?id=463andtbl=MultiUse]. July 2003.

Organisation for Economic Co-operation and Development. *Education at a Glance: OECD Indicators.* Paris, 2003.

Osborne, D., and Gaebler, T. *Reinventing Government: How the Entrepreneurial Spirit Is Transforming the Public Sector.* Reading, Mass.: Addison-Wesley, 1992.

PACAT Inc. Area Concentration Achievement Tests. [http://www.collegeoutcomes.com]. May 2004.

Pace, C. R. *Measuring Outcomes of College: Fifty Years of Findings and Recommendations for the Future.* San Francisco: Jossey-Bass, 1979.

Pace, C. R. *The Credibility of Student Self-Reports.* Los Angeles: University of California, Center for the Study of Evaluation, Graduate School of Education, 1985.

Palmer, J. C., and Gillian. S. L. State Higher Education Tax Appropriations for Fiscal Years 2002–03. Center for the Study of Education Policy, Illinois State University, Jan. 2003.

Pascarella, E. T. "Using Student Self-Reported Gains to Estimate College Impact: A Cautionary Tale." *Journal of College Student Development,* 2001a, *42,* 488–492.

Pascarella, E. T. "Identifying Excellence in Undergraduate Education: Are We Even Close?" *Change,* 2001b, *33*(3), 18–23.

Pascarella, E. T., and Terenzini, P. T. *How College Affects Students: Findings and Insights from Twenty Years of Research.* San Francisco: Jossey-Bass, 1991.

Pellegrino, J., Chudowsky, N., and Glaser, R. *Knowing What Students Know: The Science and Design of Educational Assessment.* Washington, D.C.: National Academy Press, 2001.

Peters, B. G., and Pierre, J. "Governance Without Government? Rethinking Public Administration." *Journal of Public Administration Research and Theory,* 1998, *8*(2), 223–243.

*Peterson's Four-Year Colleges 2004.* Princeton, N.J.: Thomson-Peterson's, 2003.

Peterson, M. W., and Vaughan, D. S. "Promoting Academic Improvement: Organizational and Administrative Dynamics That Support Student Assessment." In T. Banta and Associates (eds.), *Building a Scholarship of Assessment.* San Francisco: Jossey-Bass, 2002.

Pike, G. R. "The Relationships Between Self-Reports of College Experiences and Achievement Test Scores." *Research in Higher Education,* 1995, *36,* 1–22.

Pike, G. R. "Limitations of Using Students' Self-Reports of Academic Development as Proxies for Traditional Achievement Measures." *Research in Higher Education,* 1996, *37,* 89–114.

Pike, G. R. "The Constant Error of the Halo in Educational Outcomes Research." *Research in Higher Education,* 1999a, *40,* 61–86.

Pike, G. R. "The Effects of Residential Learning Communities and Traditional Residential Living Arrangements on Educational Gains During the First Year of College." *Journal of College Student Development,* 1999b, *38,* 609–621.

Pike, G. R. "The Influence of Fraternity or Sorority Membership on Students' College Experiences and Cognitive Development." *Research in Higher Education,* 2000, *41,* 117–139.

Pike, G. R., and Banta, T. W. "Assessing Student Educational Outcomes: The Process Strengthens the Product." *Virginia Community College Association Journal,* 1987, *2*(2), 24–35.

Pohlman, J. T., and Beggs, D. L. "A Study of the Validity of Self-Reported Measures of Academic Growth." *Journal of Educational Measurement,* 1974, *11,* 115–119.

Porter, S., and Toutkoushian, R. K. "Institutional Research Productivity and the Connection to Average Student Quality and Overall Reputation." Paper presented at the 2002 annual meeting of the Western Economic Association, Seattle, 2002.

The Princeton Review. *Complete Book of Colleges, 2004 Edition.* New York: Random House, 2003.

Pulley, J. L. "Stanford and Duke Consider Job Cuts." *Chronicle of Higher Education,* Nov. 15, 2002, p. A33.

Ratcliff, J. L., Lubinescu, E. S., and Gaffney, M. *How Accreditation Influences Assessment.* New Directions for Higher Education, no. 113. San Francisco: Jossey-Bass, 2001.

Reisberg, L. "Are Students Actually Learning?" *Chronicle of Higher Education,* Nov. 17, 2000, *47*(12), A67.

Report of the Commission on the Future of Higher Education in Virginia. *Making Connections: Matching Virginia Higher Education's Strengths with the Commonwealth's Needs.* Richmond, Va.: State Council on Higher Education of Virginia, 1996.

Richardson, R. C., and Martinez, M. C. "New Jersey and New Mexico: Explaining Differences in Performance." [http://www.nyu.edu/iesp/aiheps/research.html]. 2002.

Richardson, R. C., Bracco, K. R., Callan, P. M., and Finney, J. E. *Designing State Higher Education Systems for a New Century.* Phoenix, Ariz.: Oryx Press, 1999.

Ross, J. "Colleges Should Stop Counting Their National News Clips." *Chronicle of Higher Education,* Feb. 21, 2003, p. B16.

Rowles, N. S. "Halfway in the Can: An Examination of Data Use in College and University Decision Making." Unpublished doctoral dissertation, University of Pennsylvania, 2003.

Roy, R. M. "An Historical Study of Doctoral Program Review, 1964–77: Significant Components of Change and Type of Policy Engendered by the New York State Board of Regents." Unpublished doctoral dissertation, College of Education, SUNY Albany, 1996.

Rugg, F. *Rugg's Recommendations on the Colleges.* Fallbrook, Calif.: Rugg's Recommendations, 2003.

Ruppert, S. S. *Charting Higher Education Accountability: A Sourcebook on State-Level Performance Indicators.* Denver, Colo.: Education Commission of the States, 1994.

Ruppert, S. S. "Roots and Realities of State Level Performance Indicator Systems." In G. Gaither (ed.), *Assessing Performance in an Age of Accountability: Case Studies.* New Directions for Higher Education, no. 91. San Francisco: Jossey-Bass, 1995.

Ruppert, S. S. *Where We Go from Here: State Legislative Views on Higher Edu-*

*cation in the New Millennium.* Washington, D.C.: National Education Association, 2001.

Ruppert, S. S. *Closing the College Participation Gap: A National Summary.* Denver, Colo.: Education Commission of the States, 2003.

Schedler, A. "Conceptualizing Accountability." In A. Schedler, L. Diamond, and M. Plattner (eds.), *The Self-Restraining State: Power and Accountability in New Democracies.* Boulder, Colo.: Lynne Rienner, 1999.

Schmidt, D. "Governor of South Carolina Offers to Let Some Public Colleges Go Private." *Chronicle of Higher Education,* Dec. 8, 2003. [http://chronicle.com/prm/daily/2003/12/2003120801n.htm]. Dec. 2003.

Schmitz, C. C. "Assessing the Validity of Higher Education Indicators." *Journal of Higher Education,* 1993, *64*(5), 503–521.

Scott, J. L. *Seeing Like a State: How Certain Schemes to Improve the Human Condition Have Failed.* New Haven, Conn.: Yale University Press, 2001a.

Scott, K. "Feds Try to Push Colleges for More Accountability." *Lansing State Journal,* June 5, 2003. [http://www.lsj.com/news/local/p_030605_college_1a-9a.html]. Sept. 2003.

Scott, P. "Universities as Organizations and Their Governance." In L. E. Weber (ed.), *Governance in Higher Education: The University in a State of Flux.* London: Economica, 2001b.

Selingo, J. "What Americans Think About Higher Education." *Chronicle of Higher Education,* May 2, 2003, p. A10.

Seppanen, L. J. "Linkages to the World of Employment." In P. T. Ewell (ed.), *Student Tracking: New Techniques, New Demands.* New Directions for Institutional Research, no. 87. San Francisco: Jossey-Bass, 1995.

Seymour, D. T. *On Q: Causing Quality in Higher Education.* New York: American Council on Education and Macmillan, 1992.

Shakespeare, W. "The Tragedy of Hamlet, Prince of Denmark." [http://the-tech.mit.edu/Shakespeare/hamlet/hamlet.3.1.html]. Nov. 2003.

Shakespeare, W. "The Tragedy of Macbeth." [http://the-tech.mit.edu/Shakespeare/macbeth/macbeth.4.1.html]. Nov. 2003.

Shaman, S., and Zemsky, R. "Perspectives on Pricing." In L. H. Litten (ed.), *Issues in Pricing Undergraduate Education.* New Directions for Institutional Research, no. 42. San Francisco: Jossey-Bass, 1984.

Shavelson, R. "Assessing Student Learning: The Quest to Hold Higher Education Accountable." Center for Advanced Study in the Behavioral Sciences Seminar, Dec. 13, 2000. [http://www.stanford.edu/dept/SUSE/SEAL/Presentation/Presentation%20PDF/Assessing%20student%20CASBS%20Seminar%202000.pdf]. May 2004.

Shavelson, R., and Huang, L. "Responding Responsibly." *Change,* Jan./Feb. 2003, *35*(1), 11–19.

Shaw, K. A. In T. J. MacTaggart and Associates (eds.), *Seeking Excellence Through Independence.* San Francisco: Jossey-Bass, 1998.

Shermis, M. D., Mzumara, H. R., Olson, J., and Harrington, S. "On-Line Grading of Student Essays: PEG Goes on the World Wide Web." *Assessment and Evaluation in Higher Education,* 2001, *26*(3), 247–259.

Shulock, N. "A Fundamentally New Approach to Accountability: Putting State Policy Issues First." Paper presented at the Association for the Study of Higher Education: Forum on Public Policy in Higher Education, Portland, Ore., Nov. 2003.

Singleton, Jr., R. A., Straits, B. C., and Straits, M. M. *Approaches to Social Research.* New York: Oxford University Press, 1993.

Sklaroff, S. (ed.). "America's Best Colleges, 2004." *U.S. News & World Report.* Washington, D.C.: U.S. News & World Report, 2004.

Sklaroff, S. (ed.). "America's Best Graduate Schools, 2004." *U.S. News & World Report.* Washington, D.C.: U.S. News & World Report, 2004.

Smith, B.L.R. *American Science Policy Since World War II.* Washington, D.C.: Brookings Institution, 1990.

Solomon, L.C., and Astin, A. W. "A New Study of Excellence in Undergraduate Education—Part One: Departments Without Distinguished Graduate Programs." *Change,* 1981, *13,* 22–28.

Steinberg, J., and Henriques, D. B. "When a Test Fails the Schools, Careers and Reputations Suffer." *New York Times,* May 21, 2001, p. A1.

Sundre, D. L., and Kitsantas, A. L. "An Exploration of the Psychology of the Examinee: Can Examinee Self-Regulation and Test-Taking Motivation Predict Consequential and Non-Consequential Test Performance?" *Contemporary Educational Psychology,* 2004, *29*(1), 6–26.

Taft, B. *The Governor's Charge to the Commission on Higher Education and the Economy.* Columbus, Ohio: Governor's Office, 2003.

Tan, D. L. "A Multivariate Approach to the Assessment of Quality." *Research in Higher Education,* 1992, *33*(2), 205–226.

Thompson, F., and Zumeta, W. "Effects of Key State Policies on Private Colleges and Universities: Sustaining Private-Sector Capacity in the Face of the Higher Education Access Challenge." *Economics of Education Review,* 2001, *20,* 517–531.

Thorndike, R. M. "The Washington State Assessment Experience." *Assessment Update,* 1990, *2*(2), 7–9.

Toutkoushian, R. K., Porter, S., Danielson, C., and Hollis, P. "Using Publications Counts to Measure an Institution's Research Productivity." *Research in Higher Education,* 2003, *44*(2), 121–148.

Trainer, J. F., and Sapp, M. "Identifying Measures of Quality in American Higher Education." *Case International Journal of Educational Advancement,* 2000, *1*(2), 165–181.

Trow, M. "Federalism in American Higher Education." In A. Levine (ed.), *Higher Learning in America*. Baltimore: Johns Hopkins University Press, 1993, pp. 39–66.

Trow, M. "Trust, Markets and Accountability in Higher Education: A Comparative Perspective." *Higher Education Policy,* 1996, *9*(4), 309–324.

Turner, C. F., and Martin, E. (eds.). *Surveying Subjective Phenomena* (Vol. 1). New York: Russell Sage Foundation, 1984.

University of Missouri-Columbia. "College BASE." [http://arc.missouri.edu/collegebase/]. Aug. 2003.

Upcraft, M. L., and Schuh, J. H. *Assessment in Student Affairs: A Guide for Practitioners.* San Francisco: Jossey-Bass, 1996.

U.S. Bureau of the Census. *Current Population Survey.* March 1947 and 1942 to 2002, March Current Population Survey (noninstitutional population, excluding members of the Armed Services living in barracks; 1940 and 1950 Census of Population (resident population). Washington, D.C.: U.S. Census Bureau, Education and Social Stratification Branch, 2003.

U.S. Department of Education. "No Child Left Behind." [http://www.ed.gov/nclb/accountability/ayp/testing-faq.html]. Aug. 2003.

Van Der Werf, M. "Slashing Prices Draws a Crowd." *Chronicle of Higher Education,* Aug. 1, 2003, p. A25.

Van Liere, K. D., and Lyons, W. "Measuring Perceived Program Quality." In T. Banta (ed.), *Performance Funding in Higher Education: A Critical Analysis of Tennessee's Experience.* Boulder, Colo.: National Center for Higher Education Management Systems, 1986.

van Vught, F. "The New Context for Academic Quality." Enschede, Netherlands: University of Twente, Center for Higher Education Policy Studies. Paper prepared for the symposium, University and Society, Vienna, Austria, June 9–10, 1994.

Vidovich, L., and Slee, R. "The Unsteady Ascendancy of Market Accountability in Australian and English Higher Education." Paper presented at the Australian Association for Research in Education Conference, Sydney University, Dec. 2000.

Volkwein, J. F. "Responding to Financial Retrenchment: Lessons from the Albany Experience." *Journal of Higher Education,* 1984, *55*(3), 389–401.

Volkwein, J. F. "Campus Autonomy and Its Relationship to Measures of University Quality." *Journal of Higher Education,* 1986, *57*(5), 510–528.

Volkwein, J. F. "Changes in Quality Among Public Universities." *Journal of Higher Education,* 1989, *60*(2), 136–151.

Volkwein, J. F. "Using and Enhancing Existing Data to Respond to Campus Challenges." In F. K. Stage and K. Manning (eds.), *Diverse Re-*

*search Approaches and Methods Applied to the College Environment.* New York: Brunner-Routledge, 2003.

Volkwein, J. F., and Malik, S. M. "State Regulation and Administrative Flexibility at Public Universities." *Research in Higher Education,* 1997, *38*(1), 17–42.

Volkwein, J. F., Shibley, L. R., Mockiene, B., and Volkwein, V. A. "Comparing the Costs and Benefits of Re-Accreditation Processes at Public and Private Universities." Research paper presented at the Association for Institutional Research Forum, Tampa, Fla., 2003.

Walleri, R. D., and Moss, M. K. *Evaluating and Responding to College Guidebooks and Rankings.* New Directions for Institutional Research, no. 88. San Francisco: Jossey-Bass, 1995.

Weber, E. "The Question of Accountability in Historical Perspective: From Jackson to Contemporary Grassroots Ecosystem Management." *Administration & Society,* 1999, *31*(4), 451–494.

Webster, D. S. "Reputational Rankings of Colleges, Universities, and Individual Disciplines and Fields of Study, from Their Beginnings to the Present." In J. C. Smart (ed.), *Higher Education: Handbook of Theory and Research* (Vol. 8). New York: Agathon Press, 1992.

Wellman, J. "State Accountability for Student Learning: Building Models to Connect Learning Assessments with Public Accountability Structures." Paper presented at the meeting of the National Governors Association State Accountability for Student Learning, Salt Lake City, Utah, June 2003.

Wentland, E. J., and Smith, K. W. *Survey Responses: An Evaluation of Their Validity.* New York: Academic Press, 1993.

Wergin, J. F. *Departments That Work: Building and Sustaining Cultures of Excellence in Academic Programs.* Bolton, Mass.: Anker, 2003.

Westerheijden, D. F., Brennan, J., and Maassen, P. *Changing Contexts of Quality Assessment: Recent Trends in West European Higher Education.* Utrecht, Netherlands: Lemma, 1994.

Western Association of Schools and Colleges. *Evidence Guide—A Guide to Using Evidence in the Accreditation Process: A Resource to Support Institutions and Evaluation Teams.* Alameda, Calif.: Accrediting Commission for Senior Colleges and Universities, Western Association of Schools and Colleges. Working draft, Jan. 2002.

Western Interstate Commission for Higher Education. "The Changing Nature of Accountability." *Western Policy Exchanges,* Mar. 2002. [http://www.wiche.edu/Policy/Exchanges/WPE-changing_nature.pdf]. Aug. 2003.

Williams, G. L. "The Marketization of Higher Education Reforms and Potential Reforms in Higher Education Finance." In D. D. Dill and B.

Sporn (eds.), *Emerging Patterns of Social Demand and University Reform: Through a Glass Darkly.* Tarrytown, N.Y.: Elsevier Science, 1995.

Winston, Jr., R. B., Miller, T. K., and Cooper, D. L. *Student Developmental Task and Lifestyle Assessment.* Athens, Ga.: Student Development Associates, 1999.

Wolff, R. A. "Restoring the Credibility of Accreditation." *Trusteeship,* Nov.-Dec. 1993, *1*(6), 20–21, 23–24.

Yale Daily News. *The Insider's Guide to the Colleges 2004.* (30th ed.) New York: St. Martin's Press, 2003.

Yudof, M. G. "Is the Public Research University Dead?" *Chronicle of Higher Education,* Jan. 11, 2002, p. B24.

Zemsky, R. "Have We Lost the 'Public' in Higher Education?" *Chronicle of Higher Education,* May 30, 2003, p. B7.

Zemsky, R., Shaman, S., and Shapiro, D. *Higher Education as Competitive Enterprise: When Markets Matter.* New Directions for Institutional Research, no. 111. San Francisco: Jossey-Bass, 2001.

Zumeta, W. *State Policies and Independent Higher Education: A Technical Report.* Report to the Education Commission of the States, Task Force on State Policy and Independent Higher Education. Denver, Colo.: Education Commission of the States, 1989.

Zumeta, W. "Meeting the Demand for Higher Education Without Breaking the Bank: A Framework for the Design of State Higher Education Policies for an Era of Increased Demand." *Journal of Higher Education,* 1996, *67*(4), 367–425.

Zumeta, W. *How Did They Do It? The Surprising Enrollment Success of Private, Nonprofit Higher Education from 1980 to 1995.* Paper presented at the Association for the Study of Higher Education annual conference, San Antonio, Nov. 1999.

Zumeta, W. "Accountability Challenges for Higher Education." *The NEA 2000 Almanac of Higher Education.* Washington, D.C.: National Education Association, 2001.

# Name Index

# Subject Index

## A

AACSB. *See* Association to Advance Collegiate Schools of Business (AACSB)

AAC&U. *See* American Association of Colleges and Universities (AAC&U)

AAHE. *See* American Association for Higher Education (AAHE)

ABET. *See* Accrediting Board for Engineering and Technology (ABET)

Academic audits. *See* Audits

Academic concerns, 22–23, 128–129

Academic culture, 238

Academic Profile (AP), 139

Academic programs: faculty governance in, 70; protection of, by private universities, 34

ACAT. *See* Area Concentration Achievement Tests (ACAT)

Access: government's support of, 15–16; in New Jersey, 68

Accountability: balancing autonomy with, 5; basis for, 124; characteristics of effective systems of, 320–323; conceptual treatment of, 104–105; confusion over, 1–2; definition of, 2, 104; demands of, 2; discharge of, 122–124; drivers of, 304; historical trends in, 6–9, 28–30, 199–204, 296–298; models of, 10–14; partners in, 19–20; problems with, 209–210, 319–320; purpose of, 4; questions regarding, 2–3; recent changes in, 216–217; types of, 3

Accountability reports, 76

Accountability Triangle: audits in, 195–196; and history of accountability, 296–298; overview of, 21–24; performance programs in, 239–241; program positions on, 307–315; ratings and rankings in, 272–273

Accreditation: Accountability Triangle position of, 307–309; challenges to, 80–81; cost-effectiveness of, 86–87; disclosure regarding, 99–101; and distance learning, 97–98; effects of, on long-term change, 89; focus of, 302–303; foundations of, 81–83; future challenges to, 95–101; higher education's view of, 86; importance of, 101–102; versus licensure, 83–84; and market forces, 79; new visit process for, 94–95; from 1995 to present, 113–117; overview of, 78–79; questions of efficacy regarding, 86–89; recent changes in, 79–80, 102–103, 115; reform efforts in, 89–95; role in combining programs, 315–316; self-reviews for, 91; state and federal government interests in, 83–84; student learning assessment for, 92–93, 96–97, 113–117; and transfer of credit, 98–99

Accreditation Quality Improvement Program (AQIP), 90, 91, 92, 94

Accrediting agencies: assessment of, 82, 91; changing role of, 95; dimensions of quality adopted by, 91–93; formation of, 81; quality processes responsibilities of, 180;

Southern Illinois University Edwardsville, 168

Specialized accreditation agencies, 82–83

SPREs. *See* State Postsecondary Review Entities (SPREs)

Sputnik space satellite, 30

Staff, nonacademic, 73

Standardization, 133–135

Standardized testing: academic concerns regarding, 128–129; Accountability Triangle position of, 314–315; and credit transfer, 132; emotional conflicts over, 143–144; faculty's response to, 129; and federal government, 128; and funding, 129; and market forces, 130–133; need for clarity regarding, 142–143; quality of, 136–138; recommendations for, 143–147; and state government, 126–128; topical areas of, 138–143; types of, 133–136; varying perspectives of, 125–133

Standards, of performance programs, 221

State government: challenges of, 215; fiscal policies of, 67–69, 76; and interface agencies, 64–67, 76; involvement of, in pricing, 279–280; jurisdiction of, 298–299; responsibilities regarding accreditation, 83–84; role in private institutions, 31–37; rules of the game for, 61–62; and standardized testing, 126–128; use of reputation ratings by, 265

State higher education executive officers (SHEEOs), 66, 220–221

State policies, 58–59, 60–61, 75

State Postsecondary Review Entities (SPREs), 85

State priorities, 22–23

State report cards, 209–215, 289–292, 313

State University of New York, 71, 261

Stock market, 11

Strategic investment model, 230–231, 247

Student affairs professionals, 167

Student aid: for distance learning, 97; effect of, on enrollment, 33; historical trends in, 46–47; in private institutions, 32–34; simplification of, 49

Student Descriptive Questionnaire, 150

Student development tests, 141

Student engagement, 162, 164, 261

Student Learning Assessment: Options and Resources (Middle States Association), 93

Student loan defaults: government pressures regarding, 30; historical trends in, 46–47

Student surveys: Accountability Triangle position of, 314; advantages of, 149–150; design of, 165–167; for entering students, 150–151; factors limiting use of, 157–162; focus of, 303; increased use of, 158–159; multiple sources of information and, 169; number of students responding to, 168; overview of, 148–149; public communication of results of, 159–160, 164, 169–170; purpose of, 159–160; for quality assurance, 162–163, 164–171; recommendation for interpreting results of, 167–168; reliability and validity of, 157–158; Tennessee's example of, 156–157; types of, 150–156; use of results from, 160–162

Students: choice process of, 278–279; competition among, 256; criticisms of, 217; higher education's sorting of, 285–286; requests for college information by, 130–131; satisfaction of, 154–155. *See also specific types*

Students Development Task and Lifestyle Assessment, 141